CHORA: Intervals in the Philosophy of Architecture
Managing Editor: Alberto Pérez-Gómez
Edited by Alberto Pérez-Gómez and Stephen Parcell

Volume 1 (1994)
Volume 2 (1996)
Volume 3 (1999)
Volume 4 (2004)
Volume 5 (2007)

Chora 5: Intervals in the Philosophy of Architecture

Intervals in the Philosophy of Architecture

CHORA

VOLUME FIVE

Edited by Alberto Pérez-Gómez and Stephen Parcell

McGill-Queen's University Press
Montreal & Kingston • London • Ithaca

CHORA is a publication of the History and Theory of Architecture graduate program at McGill University, Montreal, Canada.

For author information and submission of articles please contact www.mcgill.ca/arch/theory/index.htm

Legal deposit first quarter 2007
Bibliothèque nationale du Québec

Printed in Canada on acid-free paper

ISBN 978-0-7735-3260-1 (cloth)
ISBN 978-0-7735-3262-5 (paper)

Library and Archives Canada has catalogued this publication as follows:
Chora (Montréal, Québec) Chora.

Each issue also has distinct title.
Irregular.
Vol. 1 (1994)–
ISSN 1198-449X
ISBN 978-0-7735-3260-1 (volume 5) (bnd)
ISBN 978-0-7735-3262-5 (volume 5) (pbk)

1. Architecture—Philosophy—Periodicals. I. McGill University. History and Theory of Architecture Graduate Program II. Title.

NA1.C46 720'.1 C94-900762-5

This book was designed and typeset by studio oneonone in Sabon 10/13

This volume of *Chora* is dedicated to the memory of Barry Bell.

Contents

Foreword

Ricardo L. Castro

"CHORA" (χώρα) WAS THE ANCIENT GREEK word for "space." During the past two hundred years, space has become associated with the unbounded, homogeneous space of three mathematically quantifiable dimensions, but this modern notion did not exist in ancient Greece. Although we tend to oppose "space" and "place," this distinction also was not evident to the Greeks. "Place" (τόπος) was described as a bounded, limited domain by Archytas of Tarentum (428–347 B.C.) in a now-fragmentary treatise on place and later by Aristotle (384–322 B.C.) in *Physics*. Χώρα is related to χορός, a word with several meanings: a band of dancers such as the chorus of an Attic drama, the dance itself, and the place for dancing; eventually it would refer to the circular centre of a Greek theatre between the audience and the stage for actors. In *Timaeus*, Plato describes χώρα as a receptacle not unlike a mother's womb, as a primordial element from which the stuff of the world is formed, and as a set of nonmaterial qualities that are experienced as fire, earth, air, and water. Clearly, space in ancient Greece was neither homogeneous nor limitless.

The concept of space as an unbounded domain seems to have emerged during medieval times. In the sixth century A.D., Johannes Philoponus challenged many of Aristotle's ideas and developed a new concept of space as an empty void into which bodies could move; however, this was not yet an infinite space. Near the end of the medieval era, during the thirteenth century, St Thomas of Aquinas demonstrated the need for a concept of the infinite without endorsing it, arguing that it illustrated one of God's unique characteristics: infinity.

Starting in the Renaissance, new notions of space emerged to accompany scientific discoveries and cultural developments. The global territorial conquests at that time were driven by a hunger for something resembling the modern notion of unbounded space rather than for bounded place. Later, the vistas of the Baroque garden ambitiously projected space to infinity. In these situations, space became associated with the universal and was privileged over place, which had become associated with the particular and the intimate.

The notion of place, however, was not lost. A commonplace in the theory and practice of late-eighteenth- and early-nineteenth-century architecture and landscape architecture was the ruin. Located in particular places, ruins offered gateways to ancestral worlds. The fascination with the classical world, the emergence of travel journals and descriptions, and the consolidation of the novel during the eighteenth and particularly the nineteenth centuries engaged particular places in various ways. To express this expanded field of cultural meanings, the word "place" was joined by more modern terms, including "site" and "landscape" – an old word with a long history.

In architectural discourse and praxis during the past thirty years, there has been a concerted effort to recover and develop concepts of place and to challenge the relative importance of bounded and unbounded domains – place and space. Phenomenology, for instance, has guided both theoreticians and practitioners in studying the condition, characteristics, and prospects of particular places.

Today, as the processes of global homogenization continue to creep detrimentally into architecture and into rural and urban landscapes, there is an urgent need to reconceive architecture as a place-making practice rather than strictly as a spatial practice. Two chapters in this volume of *Chora* address the issue explicitly: philosopher Edward S. Casey's "Looking around the Edge of the World: Contending with the Continuist Principle and the Plenarist Passion"; and architectural historian Marco Frascari's "Horizons at the Drafting Table: Filarete and Steinberg." These chapters were first presented at the international colloquium "The Limits of Place in Architectural Discourse," which was organized by the Institut de recherche en histoire de l'architecture (IRHA) while I was its director and was hosted in collaboration with the Canadian Centre for Architecture during the spring of 2002. Both chapters focus on the role of boundaries in "place" – in particular, the horizon.

Casey's essay points out that edges are "something that we don't usually pause to consider ... [and] are found everywhere ... [a] virtual tyranny in our ongoing lives." To him, edges provide a complex mediation in our engagement with the phenomenal world. He begins with a discussion of ancient Greek naval exploration beyond the bounded basin of the Mediterranean and the Greeks' anxious encounter with the limitless ocean, which they found both alluring and terrifying. Following his analysis of edges in geography, Casey reflects on anxious arguments in philosophy for a dense, continuous world of being or appearance in response to fear of the utter void that we presume to be its alternative. With implications for architecture, he suggests that Merleau-Ponty's idea of the fold avoids this binary opposition and reminds us of the necessity of edges.

In a different mood, Frascari's chapter is an important call to everyone involved in making architecture. He introduces another type of edge, the horizon – not the ancient Greek horizon, where, according to Heidegger, things begin to appear, but the horizons that "architects trace … within the horizons of their drafting tables," showing how architecture emerges through the act of drawing. To pursue this thought, Frascari focuses on two "comic" characters whose personal horizons intersected in Milan, although they were separated by centuries: Antonio Averlino, a Renaissance architect and treatise writer, better known as Filarete; and Saul Steinberg, a twentieth-century architect who became famous for his work as a cartoonist for the *New Yorker* magazine.

Fugitives in Sight: Section and Horizon in Andreas Vesalius's *De Humani Corporis Fabrica*

Manuela Antoniu

Chora

ON THE AUTHORITY OF CELSUS, the medical arts began with the Greeks, so closely in the shadow of philosophy that "treating the sick [*morborum curatio*] and the study of nature [*rerum naturae contemplatio*] partook of the same origin."[1] The groundbreaker of ancient medicine, Hippocrates, had loosened the Homeric bonds of the humans' relations to the gods with a question, "Why?" (*dia ti*),[2] thus anticipating Aristotle. In his turn, positing that neither sickness nor health can exist in beings devoid of life,[3] Aristotle asked "Why movement?" and thus opened up the living body to philosophical scrutiny by wielding a literal scalpel. The radical epistemological change that the "second Hippocrates" (as the tradition later named him) introduced in Greek medical thinking rested on Aristotle's unprecedented dissections on animals. Anatomical knowledge, however, had to wait until Aristotle's near contemporary, Herophilus of Alexandria, penetrated the invisible world of the human body's interior. Yet Herophilus's theories on the states of the body in good health, a subject ignored by the Hippocratic tradition, were formulated in terms of a model of *techné* that equally applied to architecture.[4] Given that the humanist questions raised in the century of Pericles were reprised in the Renaissance, the *dia ti* of a model that allows architecture and human anatomy to share it seems worth asking.

SOLDIERING ON

Despite the vast range of aspects related to human health that the Hippocratic corpus encompassed, one other subject that it curiously overlooked is the treatment of battle wounds. This omission is all the more surprising given that armed conflict seems to have been a constant note throughout the din of antiquity. As attested to in the classical literature, there appears to have been no interval during which either the Greek or Roman army was not actively engaged in combat, and the treatment of battle wounds is the only kind of medical treatment mentioned in the *Iliad*.[5]

The Hippocratic omission was later redressed by Galen,[6] whose writings – at least in part – must have been influenced by his biographical details. He claims direct architectural filiation through his father, an architect who had him tutored by philosophers. Galen was employed as a physician not only to the gladiators in his home town of Pergamon, but also to soldiers on the battlefields during Marcus Aurelius's campaign of A.D. 167 against the Germanic tribes.[7] In his *Administrationes anatomicae* Galen mentions the importance of anatomical knowledge for surgery, no doubt having witnessed, in gladiators and soldiers alike, some of the deepest forays into human flesh inflicted by sharp objects.

Perhaps due to its sectioning capabilities, the apparatus of warfare has also interested architects throughout the centuries. Vitruvius, who apparently had a lucrative occupation as a weapon trader,[8] prescribes in *De architectura* the piercing of human flesh with a metallic instrument: "For if a man be placed flat on his back, with his hands and feet extended, and a pair of compasses centred at his navel, the fingers and toes of his two hands and feet will touch the circumference of a circle described therefrom."[9]

Whether the instrument is geometric, military, or surgical, its effect on the interiority of the body is the same. But what kind of body? The "well-shaped man" (*homo bene figuratus*) that Vitruvius recommends for the surgico-geometrical operation to establish the architectural ideal harks back to the Homeric epic in which the theme of wounding and the image of the hero are conceptually linked. The *Iliad* frequently mentions the importance of dying as a warrior, invariably as a young and beautiful warrior. In the world of the Greek epic, a heroic death was a mortal blow sustained in combat.[10] However, death from a fatal wound depended on the type of protective armour and the lethal potential of the weapon. An inventory of the sources shows that sword wounds were always lethal.[11]

MOVING IN CIRCLES

If we take the sword to be the closest military equivalent of the scalpel, the choice of General Alfonso d'Avalos, in *écorché*, for the second of the fourteen anatomical plates in book 2 of Andreas Vesalius's *De humani corporis fabrica libri septem* (On the fabric of the human body) – shown contiguous from left to right in fig. 1.1 – could be illuminating.[12] The military man cuts a singular figure among the others in that his image is the only one presented in profile (*in profilo*). He (or rather, his flayed alter ego) displays the logical implausibility of an animate cadaver and is shown in thirteen other hypostases that are drawn with decreasing body residue resulting from an implicit paring away through dissection. The series illustrates the human muscular system in the second of seven

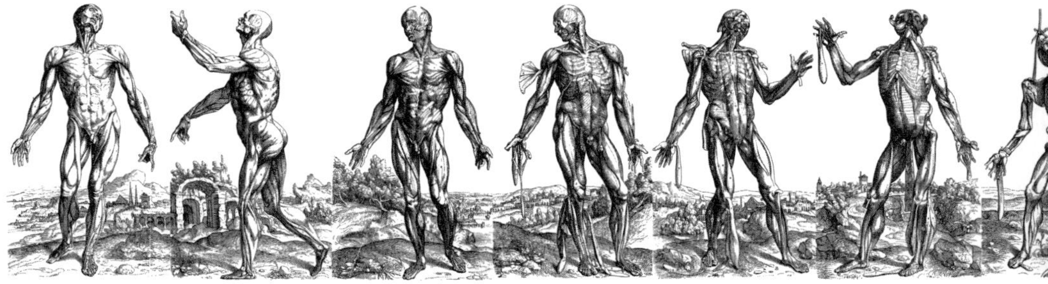

1.1 Andreas Vesalius, *De humani corporis fabrica* (Basel, 1543), plates illustrating book 2. Wellcome Institute Library, London. Concatenation of the plates, in the order in which they appear (first to fourteenth, from left to right).

books that comprise the best-known treatise in the history of Western medicine.[13]

Published at Basel in 1543, the same year that Copernicus published his own momentous *De revolutionibus orbium caelestium*, Vesalius's *Fabrica* represented a radical break from all previous approaches to human anatomy, which had unwaveringly followed the tradition established by Aristotle and Galen. As a young humanist, Vesalius was influenced by the revival of classical culture, but his vision for anatomical knowledge rested equally on direct observation of the human body through dissection. On assuming the chair of anatomy at the University of Padua, Vesalius taught in an academic environment that had considered dissection an integral part of medical training from at least the early fourteenth century.[14] Despite Vesalius's veneration for Galen's writings, it was inevitable that his work on the *Fabrica* would expose the fundamental shortcoming of the Galenic corpus: its exclusive reliance on animal, rather than human, dissection.

Apart from its critiques of Galen and its unprecedented detailed descriptions of all parts of the human body, the *Fabrica* is also imposing in

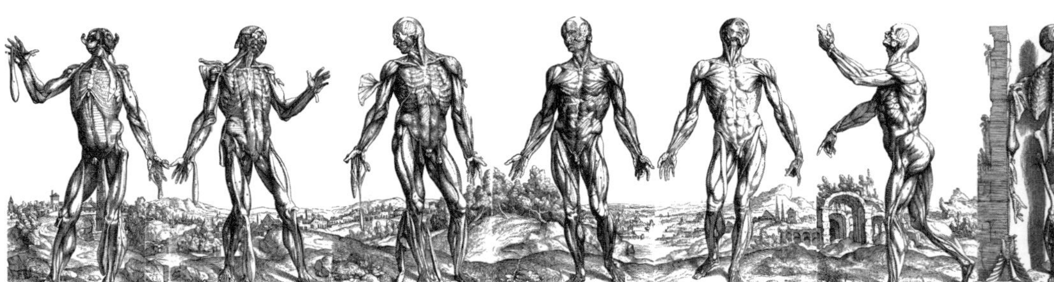

1.2 Andreas Vesalius, *De humani corporis fabrica* (Basel, 1543), plates illustrating book 2. Wellcome Institute Library, London. Proposed rearrangement of plates from fig. 1.1.

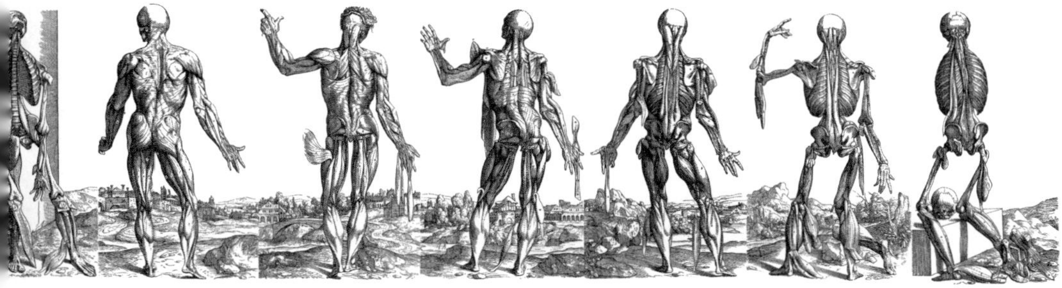

its imagery. Curiously, for a book of such stature, the treatise leaves its illustrator or illustrators uncredited. This has generated an art historical debate that remains unresolved, although Vasari had attributed the drawings, from which the woodblocks for the plates were cut, to his friend, the Flemish Jan Stephanszoon van Kalkar, and Vesalius himself intimated in the text that he was responsible for some of them.[15] The current consensus is that the illustrations emerged from the atelier of Titian, where all the contenders (i.e., Titian himself, Kalkar, and Titian's landscape draftsman, Domenico Campagnola, among others) had worked together.[16]

Notwithstanding the controversy over artistic attribution, publication of the *Fabrica* offered an exemplary fusion of the most advanced art and science of the time.[17] Although its anatomy has long been superseded, only at the beginning of the twentieth century was a discovery made in the illustrations to book 2, the series of so-called "musclemen": if the fourteen plates are rearranged and placed contiguously – although this disrupts the progressive sectioning from superficial to deeper layers of muscles – the background reveals a continuous landscape.[18] The site was

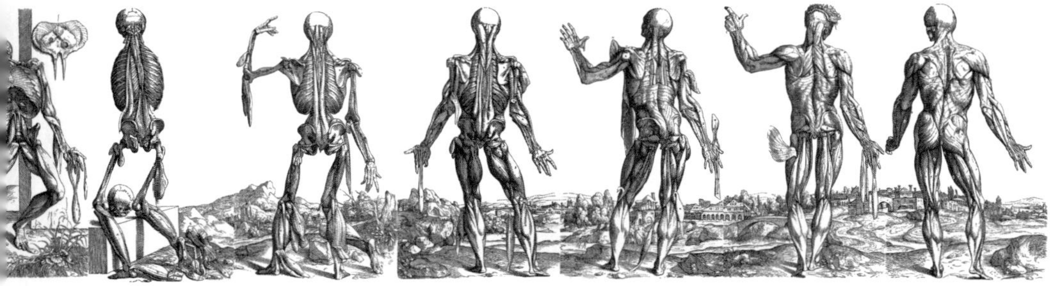

identified as the Colli Euganei region southwest of Padua, the countryside of Petrarch, and recognized *in situ* were the old Roman *thermae* (baths) of Abano, the Bacchiglione and Brenta Rivers, and the rugged trachytic rocks that form the pastoral element of the landscape.[19] Several such rearrangements were proposed by various authors, but each had its own deficiency.[20] Either new discontinuities in the background intervened, or eliminating them for the sake of graphic continuity meant dispensing with some of the plates altogether. However, while some of the proposals favoured the background and others favoured anatomical consistency, none addressed the extremities of their respective rearrangements, thus leaving the termini unproblematized.

The arrangement that I suggest here (fig. 1.2) uses one of the proposals, from Robert Herrlinger's *History of Medical Illustration*, but substitutes the two middle plates of the original sequence (in reversed order) for his unresolved median axis of discontinuity. Configured in this way, the landscape no longer begins and ends arbitrarily but seems to be contiguous across the terminal plates, thus closing a chthonic circle and endowing the series with a cyclical narrative (fig. 1.3).

However, a closer look reveals a few inconsistencies: some of the landscape details are not continuous across the two plates, while others blend seamlessly. The probability that this might have been an oversight by the artist is not entirely persuasive, given the images' high level of accomplishment. It is more engaging to hypothesize that, rather, it seems to be a skilfully subtle way of reflecting the complexity of the epistemic program embraced here. The graphic ambiguity simultaneously eschews circularity as well as noncircularity. Either linearity or panorama (notionally more than two centuries ahead of its time) would be too reductive as a definition of time through bodies, buildings, and their intersections.

CUTTING DEEPER

This panorama of human transience is enhanced by a concurrent program of architectural fragmentation, both within it and in the background. The quasi-circularity of the landscape that is achieved by joining the end plates is disrupted only by the caesura introduced by the two middle plates (fig. 1.4). With their original sequence reversed, these two plates now share a contiguous ground, forming a small, self-contained landscape within the larger landscape that they rupture. It is plausible that the

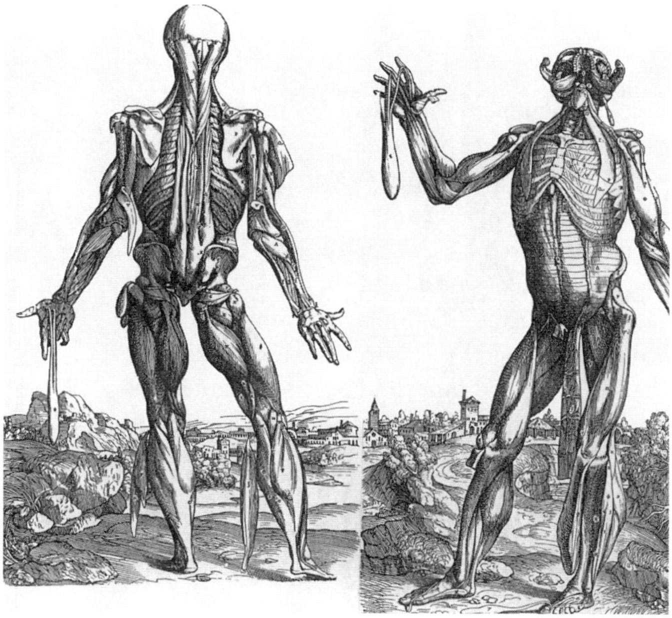

1.3 Andreas Vesalius, *De humani corporis fabrica* (Basel, 1543), plates illustrating book 2. Wellcome Institute Library, London. Adjacency of the terminal plates from fig. 1.2.

two ends of this invading landscape may also be joined to form a smaller panorama, with the two figures at opposite ends of the same partially ruined wall. In this way, the fracture in both the larger and smaller panoramas is produced by a sectioned architectural element. In addition, the middle plates are the only images in the series where architecture is foregrounded, and where architecture appears as a fragment. Inasmuch as the pair also separates the anterior and posterior presentations of the animated cadaver, the plates on each side of it are also of interest. To the right, as if exhausted at the end of a long journey, an armless skeleton leans into a plinth (an architectural beginning), on which lies a human skull (a corporeal end). The figure also marks the end of the dorsal sequence of dissection, when read from right to left. Meanwhile, to the left of the median pair, the figure of the general inaugurates the frontal dissection sequence when this is read also from right to left. His own architectural prop, however, is the most conspicuous analogue of the entire background. The identified *thermae* are not only the architectural structure that is closest to the viewer, but also present a clean-cut, full-height architectural section "in the flesh." Given that architectural sections are, for the most part, graphic speculations, only a violent cataclysm or deliberate demolition can produce a palpable full-height section. As the background for the only figure shown in profile, this architectural section

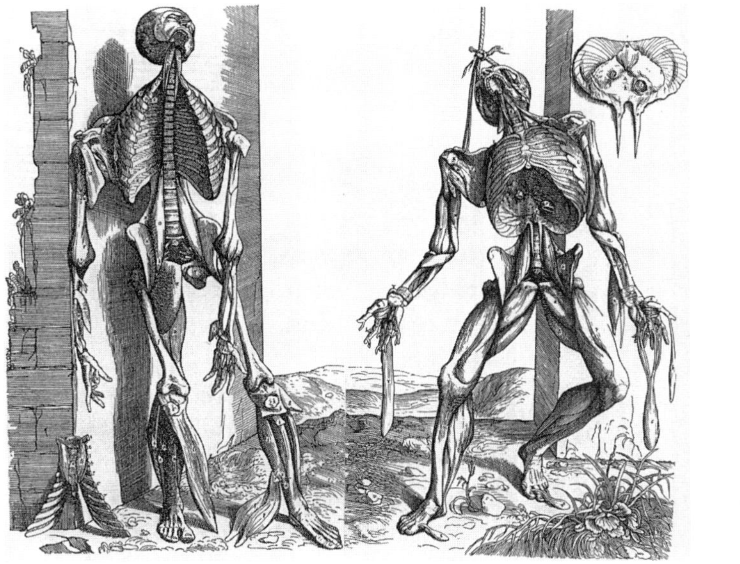

1.4 Andreas Vesalius, *De humani corporis fabrica* (Basel, 1543), plates illustrating book 2. Wellcome Institute Library, London. Adjacency of the 8th and 7th plates from fig. 1.1 (left to right).

resonates not only with the general's erstwhile occupation as a military man, but also with his singular bodily orientation.

Starting with Daniele Barbaro's 1567 translation of Vitruvius's *De architectura*, the term *profilo* came to denote "section" by translating the original triad of architectural representation – *ichnographia, orthographia, scaenographia*[21] – into the Italian *la pianta, lo in piè, il profilo*.[22] However, in his commentary, where a correspondence between *scaenographia* and *profilo* would be expected, Barbaro writes, as though recapitulating: "The third idea [drawing] is the profile, called *sciography*."[23] Thus, through the mediation of the Italian language, Barbaro effects a transmutation between two Latinized Greek terms: *skenographia* and *skiagraphia*. Why does he do this? Does it reflect the inevitable violence of every act of translation, summed up in the dictum *traduttore traditore* (translator traitor)? The careful manoeuvring with which he steers both the translation and the commentary through language seems to suggest, rather than a mistranslation,[24] a definite intention with arguably anatomical overtones.

The verb that Barbaro uses in translation is the key to a first anatomical understanding of *profilo*. By comparing Vitruvius's definition of the original term ("scaenographia est frontis et laterum abscedentium adumbratio") with Barbaro's rendition of it ("il profilo è adombratione della fronte, & dei lati che si scostano"), we immediately see how the transitive, passive "abscedo" of the Latin text is transformed into the reflexive, active "scostarsi" in Italian. The former is generally translated into English as "to recede," thus rendering the Vitruvian "laterum abscedentium" as "the [inert] sides in the background," whereas the latter is an active proposition of removal, "to move (away), to move aside, to move out of the way," all of which are understood in a nonfigurative sense.[25] Thus Barbaro seems to establish *profilo* as a cut feature in architecture, involving some form of physical removal and concomitant distancing.

A second surgical intimation of *profilo* arises when Barbaro extols its "grande utilità" (great usefulness), explaining that only with its help can we comprehend the depth of walls and the projection of every element, and that the architect, like a physician (or rather the architect as physician), can show all the interior and exterior parts of the works of architecture.[26] Later interpretations of *profilo* become more pointed and prosaic: it is the drawing that "lets one see the inside of a building."[27]

PERAS

Within the continuous Vesalian landscape, the figure *in profilo* can be understood not only as a multivalent embodiment of the notion of section, but also as a limit, given that it inaugurates the right-to-left sequence of the body's dissection in frontal presentation. At the same time, due to its proximity to the caesura in the landscape, it is also a limit in the left-to-right reading of the series. Similar graphic and narrative limits can be ascribed to its counterpart across the cut, the armless skeleton *a tergo* (from behind). The cut itself, the only clean break in the circularity of the landscape, is marked by the freestanding wall that foregrounds the middle two figures. The cutting potential of the wall is also visually inscribed by the sharp vertical edge at each end of the wall.

A panoramic reading of the landscape suggests multiple combinations for the relative positioning of viewer and *écorchés*. These readings increase in number when temporal splicing is also considered. However, what seems to persist, sustained by the near symmetry between the frontal and dorsal presentations of the figures, is the consequent allusion of concavity and convexity scalloped on either side of the cut. For instance (notwithstanding the pair in the caesura), assuming that the twelve characters (six frontal and six dorsal) animating the panorama are simultaneously present and enclose the viewer by the circle that they form, then both the frontal and the dorsal sequences share a resultant concavity in relation to the viewer. If, on the other hand, the frontal and dorsal presentations are simultaneous views from inside and outside the circle of only six characters, then each of the two sequences is convex and concave, by turns. A conceptual antecedent to a section which is also a double-sided limit precisely in the sense that it has interiority and exteriority is found in the cosmologic vision of the post-Aristotelians. Having previously been established as the constitutive element of the definition of the cosmos (*peras kosmou*), the limit of the world is for Epicurus quite clearly a sharp cut. In his *Letter to Pythocles* Epicurus writes:

> A world is an envelope of the sky, enclosing stars and earth and all other visible things with a cut which separates it from the illimited, and which terminates at a limit either lax or firm whose dissolution would entail the ruin of all that it contains within it.[28]

In all the modern languages that were consulted, translations of the Greek term *apotomé* refer unmistakably to a section.[29] A French commentary further elaborates on this section's nature:

> The *Kosmos* is an envelope of a certain thickness, such that on one side of it (towards the interior) it ends in a border whose vanishing entails the dissolution of all the things that came into being within this enclosure, because it represents their very last protection against the assaults of the illimited; ... on the other hand, this envelope is in contact with the illimited through a membrane which Epicurus gives us to understand is sufficiently resistant ... The envelope is a "cutting-off" of the infinite; *apotomèn echousa* must not be understood as a substitute of *apotmetheisa* (the envelope is not separated from the infinite, but separates from the infinite that which the universe encloses within it). The definition of the cosmos implies therefore *an interior limit*, characterized by the capacity to enclose and contain, and *an exterior limit* characterized by a difference: the severance from the illimited.[30]

This illuminates Aristotle's distinction, for bodies in general, between *to peperanthai* (the condition of being limited) and *to haptesthai* (contact).[31] Aristotle shows that the former denotes a folding of the body onto itself while the body retains its irreducibility, whereas contact keeps it in relativity and exteriority.[32] Thus, for both Aristotle and Epicurus, limit is understood not as a mere surface of the body but as the external projection of the body's interiority that reveals its identity.[33]

PEIRAR

The words used for limit are all derived from the root *per-*, giving the Homeric *peirar* and the post-Homeric *peiras* for *peras* (limit, end, extremity). A philological debate exists about whether *peirar* adds to the semantic field of *peras* by also denoting rope, cord, tie, knot.[34] On the basis of several passages in the *Iliad*, Richard Onians insists that the concreteness that the meaning of rope confers on the term (he uses the form *peirar* for the singular, rather than *peras*) is to be categorically preferred to the abstract understanding of it as a limit or end[35] in that it presents "a graphic image."[36] From this, we can derive that an architectural section is the concrete "graphic image" of an abstract "cutting" if we bring to bear on it the Epicurean meaning of limit. We can also return with it to the Vesalian series of musclemen, in which one of the two figures of the "cut" hangs listlessly by a rope. A related image is found in another series of *écorchés* from the mid-sixteenth century (fig. 1.5).[37]

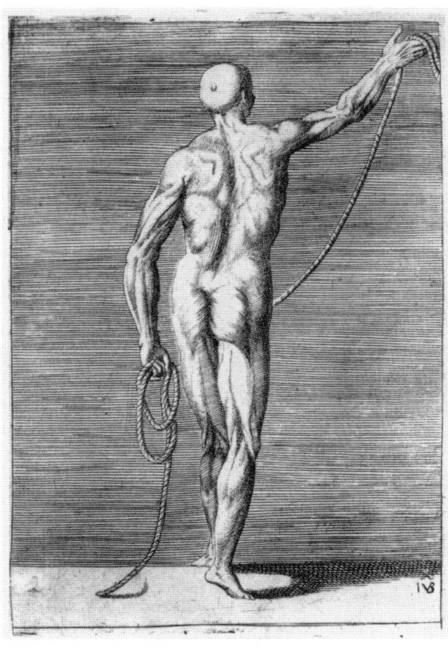

1.5 Giulio Bonasone, loose-sheet anatomical engraving, 9th in series of 14 (Bologna, mid-1500s). Warburg Institute Library, London.

At the time of Vesalius, human dissections were typically performed on the bodies of condemned criminals, most of whom had been executed by public hanging.[38] In Bonasone's image, the rope, the condemned man's *peirar*, is proffered from *terra firma* toward the nether space of the future, anticipating the execution that has already happened. Here, the man's limit is also the instrument of his discontinuity as well as a "drawing instrument." Like other figures in Bonasone's series (e.g., figs 1.6 and 1.7), he is set against the limit of the horizon line. They touch the horizon with their feet, implying that they are on the brink of overstepping the line. As condemned criminals, their lives came to their perata by having transgressed a limit. The rope brings their lives to an abrupt end, the precipitous Epicurean "cut." For Xenophanes, at the beginning of the fourth century B.C., the upper limit of the earth resulted from the meeting of the earth and "air," thus forming a horizon line "para possin horatai"

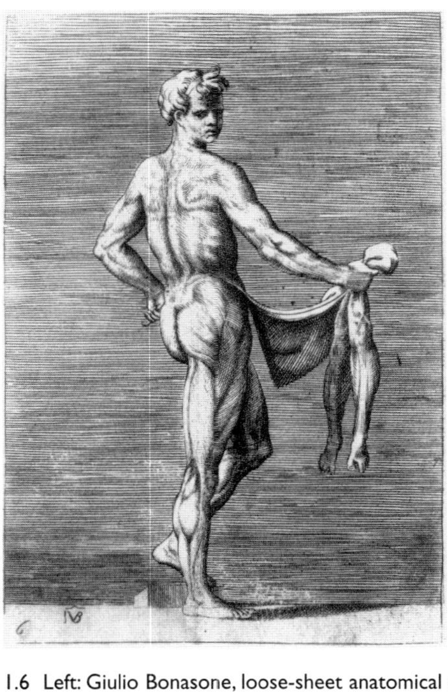

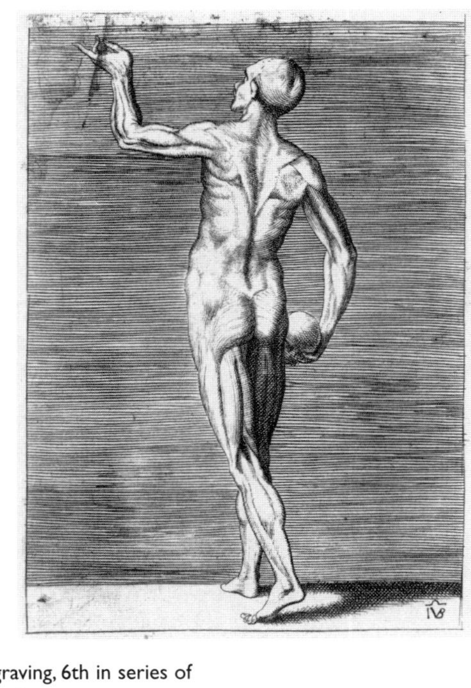

1.6 Left: Giulio Bonasone, loose-sheet anatomical engraving, 6th in series of 14 (Bologna, mid-1500s). Warburg Institute Library, London.

1.7 Right: Giulio Bonasone, loose-sheet anatomical engraving, 8th in series of 14 (Bologna, mid-1500s). Warburg Institute Library, London.

(visible at our feet).[39] Bonasone's precise meeting of earth and air and Vesalius's rugged and unpredictable one are both phenomenologically pertinent in pointing to the paradox of the horizon line: it is well defined, visually apprehensible, yet unattainable. The perception of distance while traversing a landscape therefore includes an intuition of the illimited. This is why a *topos* such as the one in the *Fabrica* is necessarily utopic, rendering art historical discussions about its exact location in the Veneto unimportant. Its presentation as a landscape of traversable distance is reinforced, albeit in different ways, both by the peripatetic posture of Alfonso d'Avalos and by the hanged cadaver.[40] Both suggest motion, which for the early Greeks was synonymous with life itself. This equation is nowhere as apt as on a battlefield.

TOYING IN CIRCLES

In Jean Bollack's commentary on the *Letter to Pythocles*, section is the ultimate shield against the assaults of the illimited. In the *Iliad*, the preeminent narrative of the battlefield, there are abundant descriptions of armour, "the man-made barrier between warrior and weapon,"[41] as a shield assembled from cut-out pieces.[42] Armour is probed visually in one of the plates from the anatomical treatise of Juan Valverde (fig. 1.8), which he published after Vesalius's *Fabrica*.[43] As a battle shield, the protective armour is incarnated into the wearer to the point of assuming his bodily identity but ironically is shown as being defenceless against the penetrating blade of the anatomist's scalpel.

A different thaumaturgy is invoked in the Homeric descriptions of armour that are associated with *daidala* (wondrous man-made objects, including the first moving statues, said to have been fashioned by Daedalus). As several detailed studies have shown,[44] inanimate *daidala* demonstrated spectacular self-generated movements. Again, in the Vesalian series, the only figure whose potential movement suggests an external mover is the one suspended by a rope. The figure's posture depends entirely on the manipulation of the rope, whose other end is, significantly, cut off from view. This is underscored by the absence of shadows cast on the architectural fragment, in contrast to the immediately adjacent figures. If this evokes a puppet on strings, the image comes directly from Aristotle. While pursuing the fundamental question of his *De motu animalium* (On the movement and progression of animals) – "Why

1.8 Juan Valverde de Hamusco, *Historia de la composicion del cuerpo humano* (Rome, 1556), bk 3, plate 2. British Library, London.

movement?" – Aristotle compares the movement of animals (and, by extension, humans) with "ta autòmata" (automatic puppets). He illustrates the comparison with two examples: a puppet on strings; and a toy cart, which, although pushed "straight forward … it moves in a circle because it has wheels of unequal size: for the smaller acts like a centre, as happens in the case of the cylinders."[45] Galen takes up both examples in his *De usu partium corporis humani* (On the usage of the parts of the human body), where he uses the puppet to illustrate the tendons of the arm and leg, and refers to the circular motion of the toy cart to contrast its shape with that of columns.[46] The *autòmaton* that moves by itself and does so in a circular motion brings Aristotelian and Galenic authority to the *Fabrica* in support of its daring enterprise.

The centrality assigned to the human body in sixteenth-century Western culture is poignantly implied in the central position of the observer in the Vesalian landscape. Commanding a panoramic view of concentric horizons – one corporeal, the farther tectonic – the viewer performs the Delphic exhortation *nosce teipsum* (know thyself).[47] Here, self-knowing occurs through nested reflections. First, the implied viewer watches his/her mortality being mirrored in the animated yet gradually disintegrating cadaver. This reflection is then mirrored in the fractured architectural fabric of the distant horizon, which mimetically spans the full tectonic range between integrity and ruin. However, both the human being and the architecture, represented as horizons, forever recede from the voyager's grasp: the *apeiron* of *peras* itself.

NOTES

1 Celsus, *De medicina*, bk 1, sec. 11, quoted in Mirko D. Grmek, ed., *Histoire de la pensée médicale en Occident* (Paris: Éditions du Seuil, 1995), vol. 1, 8.

2 Hippocrates, *De arte*, 6, quoted by Jacques Jouanna, "La naissance de l'art occidental," in Grmek, ed., *Histoire*, vol. 1, 25–66 at 48; Giorgio Agamben, *Potentialities: Collected Essays in Philosophy*, ed. and trans. Daniel Heller-Roazen (Stanford, CA: Stanford University Press, 1999), 230–2.

3 Aristotle, *De sensu*, quoted by Mario Vegetti, "Entre le savoir et la pratique: La médecine hellénistique," in Grmek, ed., *Histoire*, vol. 1, 67–94 at 70.

4 Vegetti, "Entre le savoir," in Grmek, ed., *Histoire*, vol. 1, 78.

5 Christine Salazar, "The Treatment of War Wounds in Graeco-Roman Antiquity" (PhD thesis, Cambridge University, June 1991), 1, microfilm.

6 Born in Asia Minor c. A.D. 129, during the reign of the Emperor Hadrian, Galen left behind the most extensive collection of Greek medical literature written by a single author (twenty-two volumes). Part of the Galenic corpus is a commentary on the Hippocratic treatises.

7 Salazar, "Treatment of War Wounds," 7; Grmek, ed., *Histoire*, 110.

8 Alberto Pérez-Gómez, *Architecture and the Crisis of Modern Science* (Cambridge, MA: MIT Press, 1984), 181, n25.

9 Vitruvius, *De architectura*, bk 3, 1.3, trans. Morris Hicky Morgan (Cambridge, MA: Harvard University Press, 1914), 73.

10 Nonfatal injuries were not addressed in the *Iliad*, except in Hector's threat to the Achaeans that, after their flight from Troy, some of them would still labour with – literally, *digest* (*péssi*) – a wound; See *Iliad*, bk 8, 513, quoted in Salazar, "Treatment of War Wounds," 129.

11 Salazar, "Treatment of War Wounds," 143.

12 The term *écorché* denotes in French a literally flayed body. It is used in painting and sculpture when human musculature needs to be emphasized. The art historical identification of the Vesalian *écorché* with an actual historical figure was made (by Erwin Panofsky) on the basis of the striking postural resemblance that the former bears to Titian's commissioned painting of the latter, in which the general is rendered fully fleshed and fully clothed; see Titian, *The Allocution of Alfonso d'Avalos, Marquis of Vasto, to his Troops*, Madrid, Museo Nacional del Prado, painted between 1540 and 1541. An "allocution" is a general's address to his army.

13 The six other books that comprise the *Fabrica* deal with the skeletal system (bk 1), the venous system (bk 3), the arterial system (bk 4), the organs of the abdomen (bk 5), the organs of the thorax (bk 6), and the organs of the head (bk 7).

14 Katharine Park, http://www.octavo.com/aboutthebooks/vlshum.

15 Vesalius had indeed authored three of the six eponymous illustrations in his earlier work, *Tabulae anatomicae sex* (Venice, 1538).

16 J.B. de C.M. Saunders and Charles D. O'Malley, *The Illustrations from the Works of Andreas Vesalius of Brussels* (New York: Dover, 1973), 22–9; Jonathan Sawday, *The Body Emblazoned: Dissection and the Human Body in Renaissance Culture* (London: Routledge, 1995), 289n63. However, Martin Kemp challenges this consensus in "A Drawing for the Fabrica and Some Thoughts upon the Vesalius Muscle-Men," *Medical History* 14 (1970): 277–88.

17 However, some have argued that if Leonardo had managed to publish the voluminous and profusely illustrated anatomical treatise that he had been devising since 1489 with the help of the anatomist Marcantonio della Torre, Vesalius would have easily been displaced, before the fact, as the father of modern anatomy, his *Fabrica* supplanted both scientifically and artistically.

18 E. Jackschath, "Zu den anatomischen Abbildung des Vesals," *Janus* 9 (1904): 238.

19 Harvey Cushing, *A Bio-Bibliography of Andreas Vesalius* (New York: Schuman's, 1943), 92, 108. However, G.S.T. Cavanagh, *The Panorama of*

Vesalius: A 'Lost' Design from Titian's Studio (Athens, GA: Sacrum, 1996), cites "failed attempts" in the twentieth century to identify the features of the scene *in situ.*

20 See Robert Herrlinger, *History of Medical Illustration: From Antiquity to AD 1600*, trans. G.F. Callenbach (Nijkerk, Netherlands: Pitman Medical and Scientific Publishing, 1970), 108–9; G.S.T. Cavanagh, "A New View of the Vesalian Landscape," *Medical History* 27, no. 1 (1983): 77–9.

21 Vitruvius, *De architectura*, bk 1, 2.2.

22 Daniele Barbaro, *I Dieci libri dell'architettura di M. Vitruvio* (Venice, 1567; facsimile reproduction, Milan: Edizioni Il Polifilo, 1987), 29.

23 Ibid., 30, emphasis added, my translation: "La terza idea è il profilo, detto *sciografia.*"

24 For this interpretation, see, for instance, Marco Frascari, "A Secret Semiotic Skiagraphy: The Corporal Theater of Meanings in Vincenzo Scamozzi's *Idea of Architecture*," *Via: The Architectural Journal of the Graduate School of Fine Arts, University of Pennsylvania* 11 (1990): 32–51 at 44; Jacques Guillerme and Hélène Vérin, "The Archaeology of Section," *Perspecta: The Yale Architectural Journal* 25 (1989): 226–57 at 230. Barbaro appears, on the contrary, to have been quite preoccupied with the notion of section, and in the translation's commentary, he concedes the term's "difficultà." But it is precisely in its complexity, according to him, that its "utilità" lies, and after a lengthy exposition he seems to consider his justification sufficiently argued to surprise the reader by declaring: "This usefulness of profilo prompts me to render it as sciografia, and not as scenografia" ("Questa utilità del profilo mi muove ad interpretare sciografia, & non scenografia"; *I Dieci libri*, 30, my translation), which, after a considerable delay and much ink, reveals that he had been fully aware of the Vitruvian appellation for the third kind of *dispositio* all along.

25 *Collins Sansoni Italian-English Dictionary* (Florence: Sansoni, 1988).

26 Barbaro, *I Dieci libri*, 30: "and here, the Architect as Physician shows all the internal and external parts of the work" ("& in questo l'Architetto come Medico dimostra tutte le parti interiori, & esteriori delle opere"; my translation).

27 Jacques Ozanam, *Dictionnaire de mathématique* (Paris: Jean Jombert, 1691), quoted in Guillerme and Vérin, "Archaeology of Section," 230.

28 The letter is found in book 10 (dedicated to Epicurus) of Diogenes Laertius, *De vita et moribus philosophorum libri X* [Lives and opinions of

eminent philosophers], emphasis added: "Kósmos estí perioché tis ouranou, astra te kai gen kai panta ta phainómena, *apotomèn echousa* apò tou apeirou." There, after listing some of Epicurus's best of about 300 works, Diogenes states that their epitome is to be found in three letters written by Epicurus to, respectively, Herodotus (on physics), Pythocles (on celestial phenomena), and Menoeceus (on human life); see R.D. Hicks, trans., *Diogenes Laertius: Lives of Eminent Philosophers*, The Loeb Classical Library (London: William Heinemann, 1925), 555–9, 613–77. The passage quoted in this chapter from the letter to Pythocles (sec. 88, lines 5–12) has been rendered in English as an amalgamation of translations from the Greek into the following languages: English, in Hicks, trans., *Diogenes*, 616–17; French, in Jean Bollack and André Laks, eds, "Épicure à Pythoclès: Sur la cosmologie et les phénomènes météorologiques," *Cahiers de Philologie*, vol. 3 (Lille: Publications de l'Université de Lille III and Éditions de la Maison des Sciences de l'Homme, 1978), 78–9; German, in Arthur Kochalsky, *Das Leben und die Lehre Epikurs: Diogenes Laertius*, bk 10 (Leipzig: B.G. Teubner, 1914), 33–4; and Romanian, in Gabriel Liiceanu, *Despre limita* (Bucharest: Humanitas, 1994), 155.

29 Henry George Liddell, Robert Scott, and Henry Stuart Jones, *A Greek-English Lexicon* (Oxford: Clarendon, 1966–68), 223–4, render it into English as a sheer, precipitous cutting-off, a division into sections. In the other translations consulted, this is rendered as *section, coupe vive* (French); *Ausschnitt* (German); and *sectiune, taietura* (Romanian).

30 Bollack and Laks, eds, "Épicure," 132–3, emphasis added, my translation.

31 Aristotle, *Physics*, bk 3, sec. 8, subsec. 208a, line 11, trans. Robin Waterfield (Oxford: Oxford University Press, 1996), 76: "being finite has to be distinguished from being in contact. Contact is relative and is contact *with* something ... contact may be a coincidental attribute of a finite object, but that does not make the finite object relative."

32 Liiceanu, *Despre limita*, 156.

33 Ibid.

34 Ibid., 151n1. Curiously, the listed proponents do not include Richard Onians.

35 Richard B. Onians, *The Origins of European Thought about the Body, the Mind, the Soul, the World, Time, and Fate*, 2nd ed. (1st ed. 1951; Cambridge, UK: Cambridge University Press, 1988), 310–14.

36 Ibid., 324.

37 This was one of fourteen *écorchés* designed and engraved by Giulio Bonasone circa 1555; see Stefania Massari, *Giulio Bonasone: Catalogo* (Rome: Edizioni Quasar, 1983); and Edith Wyss, *The Myth of Apollo and Marsyas in the Art of the Italian Renaissance* (Newark, NJ: University of Delaware Press, 1996).

38 This practice was to continue for centuries, having started in Bologna in 1315; see, among others, Zofia Ameisenowa, "The Problem of the Écorché and the Three Anatomical Models in the Jagiellonian Library," in A. Potocki, trans., *Monographs of the Committee of the History of Science and Technology*, vol. 20, 7–84 (Wroclaw: Polska Akademia Nauk, 1963), 18.

39 Xenophanes, quoted in Liiceanu, *Despre limita*, 153.

40 It is well known that, having already been hanged in life, cadavers were moved around artists' studios in suspension, by means of ropes.

41 Sarah P. Morris, *Daidalos and the Origins of Greek Art* (Princeton: Princeton University Press, 1992), 4.

42 Indra Kagis McEwen, *Socrates' Ancestor: An Essay on Architectural Beginnings* (Cambridge, MA: MIT Press, 1993), 48.

43 See Juan Valverde, *Historia de la composicion del cuerpo humano* (Rome: Antonio Salamanca and Antonio Lafrerij, 1556). The illustration is one of only a few in Valverde's tome that he did not copy from the *Fabrica*. In the introduction, he provides a disarming explanation of why he appropriated Vesalius's plates.

44 Apart from Morris, *Daidalos*, see also Françoise Frontisi-Ducroux, *Dédale: Mythologie de l'artisan en Grèce ancienne* (Paris: François Maspero, 1975); Jeannette Papadopoulos, *Xoana e sphyrelata: Testimonianza delle fonti scritte* (Rome: "L'Erma" di Bretschneider, 1980); and McEwen, *Socrates' Ancestor*, to which I am indebted for the first two bibliographic references in this note.

45 Aristotle, *De motu animalium*, 701b, in Martha Nussbaum, trans., *Aristotle's De Motu Animalium* (Princeton: Princeton University Press, 1978), 42. For a historical discussion of the examples, see Martha Nussbaum, "The Text of Aristotle's *De Motu Animalium*," in Albert Henrichs, ed., *Harvard Studies in Classical Philology*, vol. 80, 111–59 (London: Harvard University Press, 1976).

46 Nussbaum, trans., *Aristotle's De Motu Animalium*, 348.

47 The exhortation's meaning shifted from the realm of the mind to the realm of the body. The apophthegm of the oracle found resonance in the anatomical culture of the sixteenth century, which was founded on the act of seeing. Thus it appears "inserted in the prefaces of nearly all ... treatises on human anatomy, inscribed in frontispieces and illustrations, chiselled into the architecture of anatomy theatres"; see Andrea Carlino, *Paper Bodies: A Catalogue of Anatomical Fugitive Sheets, 1538–1687* (London: Wellcome Institute for the History of Medicine, 1999), 107. See also Sawday, *Body Emblazoned*, 110.

Roads and a Mountain, a Lake, and a Runway: Interpreting Infrastructure at Mae Hong Son, Thailand

Barry Bell

Chora

INFRASTRUCTURE OFTEN PREDATES ARCHITECTURE. Thus it provides architecture's support and creates its context. Conversely, infrastructural design may further or stand in contrast to the ideals of a setting that is already defined architecturally. Independent of any other ambitions, both architecture and infrastructure will also relate to a topography. Indeed, the three concerns of architecture, topography, and infrastructure interact in a complex relationship that controls the perception and experience of a building, town, or landscape.

Despite these links, architecture and infrastructure are normally treated differently and by different protagonists. Infrastructure presents the serious side of urban development, where administrative authority and major financial investment demand practical and accountable solutions. Controlled by parameters of economic expansion, large-scale infrastructural investment is closely tied to macroeconomic issues, especially in the developing world. Favoured by engineers and bureaucrats, these structures are intended to promote growth and predict the future with confidence. Success is recorded on a regional or even national, rather than local, scale. Thus infrastructure is conventionally separated from architectural design. It is too important to be left to the whims of artists; its scale is too broad. Oddly, this sensibility perseveres even though many major infrastructural works have resonated strongly with their public and have both benefited from and influenced architectural understanding. The aqueducts (and sewers) of Rome; Carcassonne's walls, communication towers, and dams; Angkor's baray: the examples are numerous and potent.

The corollary of this technical determinism is equally conventional. An architectural response to an infrastructure may be significant to a city and its quality of life but is usually regarded as a decorative embellishment. Architecture dresses infrastructure.[1] Whether inspired by an infrastructure or attempting to improve it, building makes infrastructure visible. Therefore, architecture is normally responsible for manifesting the culture of a place, perhaps adding symbolic intent to a primarily technical framework. Unfortunately, this implicitly accepts a subordinate role for building. Perhaps more significantly, it also undervalues the symbolic and communicative potential of infrastructure.

The challenge is to discover potential for urbanity in the interaction of infrastructure and architecture. Within the apparently technical nature of infrastructure is a latent power to extend – and perhaps even create – a city's symbolic sensibilities.[2] A city's infrastructure may provide a coherent image that transcends its individual buildings. A distinctive architecture may result from a creative response to these conditions.[3]

TECHNICAL OR COLONIAL?

The challenge of associating infrastructure with indigenous spatial, architectural, or symbolic sensibilities appears particularly difficult in the rapidly developing context of Southeast Asia. Its contemporary infrastructural practices tend to be associated with Westernization as well as modernization. Airports, subways, and expressways have no obvious affinity with vernacular traditions. While vested financial and political interests are often eager to import efficient foreign models, the insertion of these alien forms may impinge upon traditional patterns of land use and social activity.[4]

New practices may threaten phenomenal and cultural relationships to a landscape. Replacing most of Bangkok's canals with roads has radically transformed the city and its rhythms, arguably for the worse.[5] This shift away from an aquatic sensibility, argues Sumet Jumsai, has led to an existential void in Thai material and psychological culture.[6] Importing the notion of a fixed geography through Western maps, claims Thongchai Winichakul, has significantly changed the country's understanding of its own history and political coherence.[7]

Despite these risks, infrastructural change should not be rejected. The cities of the developing world have a right to the benefits of modernity like everyone else.[8] The aim is not to avoid new infrastructure but to consider its full potential impact within the cultural context.

Focusing on the simple contrasts between the traditional city and the modern city – or the assumed differences between East and West – obscures the more fundamental issues regarding infrastructure and its expression. Can certain infrastructural principles help to explain curiosities in the form or life of a town? Can thinking about infrastructure symbolically rather than just technically lead to provocative possibilities for urban development and its architecture? The rapidly developing cities of Southeast Asia – and Thailand, in particular – provide intriguing settings for exploring these questions.[9] With the evident friction between old and new or between different cultural sensibilities, the reactions to infrastructural change are much more visible than in Western Europe, for example, where modern large-scale infrastructure has become familiar.

This chapter investigates interactions among topography, architecture, and infrastructure through an analysis of Mae Hong Son, a small town in northern Thailand.

INFRASTRUCTURE: CAUSE OR EFFECT?

Mae Hong Son is situated in a deep valley, in a rugged mountainous landscape. The town functioned originally as a logging and trading centre for the region. The surrounding hills are home to a number of small villages, populated by culturally distinct peoples known as "hill tribes." A range of diverse ethnic and linguistic groups coexist in a tight geographical area centred on the town and have likely influenced the town's sensibilities.[10] However, the present significance of Mae Hong Son is primarily based on its status as a provincial capital and popular tourist destination. The region's hills, waterfalls, and rivers provide attractions, just as the occasionally fractious relationship with Myanmar, its neighbouring country only 30 kilometres away, requires a significant political and military presence. The closest major city, Chiang Mai, is about eight hours away by bus.

The town is interesting for a number of reasons. Its form is changing rapidly due to urban growth and the increasingly automotive nature of its society. Most of its large governmental buildings are located on the distant outskirts of the town. Still, its architectural and social structures are rooted in diverse local cultures that are rustic in the extreme. Although increasingly supplemented by the more official and politically important "Thai," Mae Hong Son's population is a social microcosm of various peoples in a little-known region.[11] This condition creates powerful dialectics between the traditional and the new, but also between diverse local traditions.

The indigenous urban sensibility is arguably distinct from the more centralized Thai. Its foundations, however, are obscure.[12] Neither Mae Hong Son's urban intentions nor its historical transformations are well known. More surprising, this condition also applies to the country as a whole. One of the intriguing challenges facing the study of architecture

2.1 The regional landscape of Mae Hong Son. Photograph by author.

2.2 A hill-tribe festival at the inauguration of Buddhist Lent. Photograph by author.

and infrastructure in Thailand is the relative absence of material on the symbolic foundations of its various urban traditions.

ACADEMIC CHALLENGES AND FRAGMENTARY FOUNDATION

A symbolic interpretation of infrastructure and form in Thailand faces many unique difficulties, especially when compared to architectural history in the West. The first concerns the nature of historical knowledge and historiographic traditions. Although early chronicles do exist, along with some contentious inscriptions, historical research is largely an early twentieth-century creation, paralleled by the educational and political reforms of the Fifth Reign.[13] Equally problematic, there are few primary sources.[14] Thai historiography is plagued by a lack of historic texts. It is claimed that the sack of the capital Ayutthaya in 1767 destroyed up to 90 per cent of the country's literary heritage, which was probably fragmentary to begin with.[15]

The material that might clarify urban ideals is by no means conclusive. The basic threads are Indianized political traditions, Buddhist foundations, and indigenous animistic beliefs that commingle in complex ways. This mixture of influences is further complicated by regional variation. Although Mae Hong Son was part of the Lanna kingdom centred on Chiang Mai, it was distant from this urbanizing influence and manifests a different culture. Both were distinct from the centralized kingdoms of Sukhothai and Ayutthaya to the south. This absence of firm historical foundations is compounded by a limited awareness of how urban and architectural ideals may have changed over time. In contrast, the separation of technological and experiential values in modern European architecture has been well documented.[16] Although the founding principles of European cities are rooted in a distant past, they are still partly accessible. Whether long obscured by subsequent practices or familiar in convention, these origins are preserved through their physical continuity, albeit with meaning transformed. For example, it has been demonstrated that seemingly technological systems such as grids and orthogonal planning were once strong cultural symbols.[17] The inherited texts of antiquity, although by no means complete, continue to provide a body of knowledge for consultation and reinterpretation.

In Thailand the contemporary city is certainly a focus of attention, in part because Bangkok occupies such a commanding position in the country's politics and economy. These discussions tend to focus on recognizable problems such as traffic, often in a technical way.[18] However, there is also a subtle but persistent sense of a loss of meaning, symbolic significance, and cultural integrity. With the rise of rampant commercialism, the sacrifice of "Thai values" and traditions and subsequent attempts to reconstruct them are recurring themes in the press, literature, and academic symposia.[19] This concern is expressed as nostalgia for lost values or for a distinct Thai culture that may be disappearing rapidly in the contemporary world. Although Thai authors convey a more nuanced understanding of the hard realities of village life than many Western writers, the city is still regarded as an alien creature.[20]

Contemporary archaeology is beginning to fill in some of these gaps, although obstacles remain. Thai culture was not archaeologically inclined until recently, especially at the lightly developed outer edges of the kingdom.[21] The status of archaeological knowledge is further complicated by historic construction practices. All domestic buildings, including palaces, and major portions of temples were made of wood that has now disintegrated. Masonry remains are fragmentary and offer only partial archaeological traces.

In contrast, historical settlements in Europe, and more recently the Americas, have provided dense physical "texts" for analysis. Despite occasional demolition, centuries of continuous inhabitation have left complex artefacts for study. Questions of continuity and transformation can be addressed by analyzing their current states, overlaid on barely hidden foundations. Seminal forms and perhaps remnants of cultural intent remain latent in the embodied experience of these dense urban compilations. The Piazza della Signoria in Florence, for example, does not necessarily celebrate the meeting of the Roman *cardo* and *decumanus* as the sacred centre of a cosmologically ordered settlement, but the piazza still sits on the Roman forum's foundations and remains the focus of political and social life in the city. Traces of the original values remain in the inherited patterns of inhabitation. Similar situations are very difficult to find in Thailand. Its capitals have frequently moved, and regions that were once densely populated may have been abandoned or depopulated.[22] Its cities appear to float rather than to put down fixed roots.

THE EXTREMES OF SCALE

The complexities facing urban study are well demonstrated by Bangkok, Thailand's central metropolis. The city is relatively young, founded in 1782 after its predecessor, Ayutthaya, was abandoned following its destruction by the Burmese in 1767.[23] The royal centre of palaces and major temples occupies a site that was formerly a small trading community, set on marshy terrain beside the Chao Phraya River. The Chronicles of the First Reign record the building activities carried out by Rama I, the founding monarch, but they do not relay any sense of symbolic intent.[24] Two significant temples adjacent to the Grand Palace, Wat Phra

Chetuphon and Wat Mahathat, occupy the sites of earlier religious institutions whose historic foundations were destroyed in the official rebuilding of the capital under the new dynasty. From the royal centre, Rattanakosin Island, the city extends out in a series of inflected concentric rings.[25] While the basic outlines of this centre have remained fixed, development has spread out over the agrarian plains.

Bangkok's rapid twentieth-century growth has imported alien elements in the name of modernization. Its canals were replaced by roads that radically changed life in the formerly aquatic city.[26] More recently, the flat terrain has acquired a more complex section due to the construction of a sky train, subway, and elevated walkways. The massive importation of foreign technology, building materials, and practices has challenged the city's original urban and cultural ideals.

These developments assisted Bangkok's mutation into a metropolis of over 10 million people but were overlaid onto a city that was already a cultural hybrid. A conscious urban program based on Western models had been carried out in the late nineteenth and early twentieth centuries. During the reign of King Chulalongkorn, Rama V, European roads and railways were emulated to modernize the city and demonstrate Thailand's progressive nature in the face of the colonial threat.[27] Bangkok has embraced novel infrastructures throughout its history, so the concept of "traditional" is problematic.

The historical layering and gradual transformation in cities such as Rome and Florence are not evident in Bangkok. There is little physical resemblance between the new urban forms and their predecessors. Bangkok's rapid growth, its acceptance of new models, and its great change in architectural scale have created a city that seems to have little in common with its origins. While its historical centre has remained fairly intact, recent growth has all but ignored it, preferring to spread out rather than adapt to or transform these earlier foundations. In Thailand's most significant historical cities, Sukhothai and Ayutthaya, development also occurred adjacent to the original centre, rather than being applied onto it. Although they respect the earlier structures, the contemporary cities appear alien and disconnected. They were not influenced by the power of strong foundations, unlike Piazza Navona in Rome and Piazza del Anfiteatro in Lucca.[28]

Bangkok, the capital and most significant city in the country, may be the culmination of Thai urbanism. It demonstrates the culture's desire for change as much as for historic form, yet local sensibilities seem to persist, even in Bangkok's new extreme state.[29] Forms are adapted and qualities are exaggerated. The sky train, for example, has spawned a new shaded pedestrian walkway slung beneath its principal structure. Shopping centres are gradually transformed into markets. Self-contained villages sprout up in the small streets (*soi*) perpendicular to the main avenues, immediately adjacent to major commercial developments. Office towers are animated by shrines dedicated to the indigenous spirits of the land. If urban continuity is present here, it exists through sensibilities rather than through form. Indeed, Bangkok's ideals are revealed more in its social practices than in archaeological excavation or historical forms. These behavioural traits appear in curious ways and are difficult to measure, but they provide useful insights into the cultural values of a city when physical evidence is absent.

Bangkok is large and complex, and its contemporary buildings are clearly international in approach. It may be possible to discern symbolic relations among architecture, infrastructure, and urban culture more clearly in a smaller, less developed setting where the frictions are sharper and the collisions more abrupt. Mae Hong Son provides a compelling example. Its landscape is dramatic, its temple architecture distinctive, and its recent growth rapid. While local traditions and values must be inferred through architectural fragments and social practices, the city has qualities that are different from the urban traditions of central Thailand. Mae Hong Son provides a poignant site for reflecting on the implicit values of the city and their possible transformation, extension, or destruction during rapid development.

For this purpose, three specific places in Mae Hong Son are investigated: roads and a mountain, a lake, and an airport runway.

ROADS AND A MOUNTAIN

Mae Hong Son's roads provide its primary infrastructure. Unlike the historic Thai cities of the central plains, such as Ayutthaya, it has no canals, nor is the city located beside a watercourse. A small stream encircles the town but does not interact with it. Mae Hong Son is not served by a railway, but it does have an airport, a relatively recent addition.

Unlike most older Thai settlements, Mae Hong Son has no fixed perimeter, nor any traces of an earlier geometric boundary. While the early

2.3 Mae Hong Son. Photcgraph by author.

cities of the Dvaravati period were conch-shaped, the later capitals of Sukhothai and Ayutthaya were basically square.[30] In each case, the external boundary was a fundamental concern, likely a cosmological analogy.[31] Chiang Mai, the historic Lanna capital to the east, is square in plan and bounded by major walls and a moat. This orthogonal foundation was carried into the city's interior through its principal roads and the orientation of its temples. Chiang Mai is organized around a major east-west axis that leads to its principal monastery, Wat Phra Sing Luang, located far west of the town's geometric centre.[32]

Mae Hong Son is not organized geometrically, and its edges are not marked in a physical way. Sited along a major highway running north-south, the city occupies a valley that opens to the east, with a small mountain defining its western edge. The town's central intersection is a T-junction with its perpendicular road leading into the valley. Most commercial development occurs along these two principal roads, with housing filling the interstitial areas. Clearly, the topography is a strongly determining factor in the town's form and location. Roads and settle-

2.4
Urban plan of Mae Hong Son. Drawing by author.

ment follow valleys, yet the town's location is not the most practical in developmental terms. The area just to the south, where large-scale building has been introduced recently, is both flatter and more open. The city could have spread more evenly across this terrain, but the more constricted area at the base of the mountain was chosen instead. In addition, certain deformations in the alignments of the highway and streets cannot be explained by the landscape alone. The variety of road orientations within the town is perplexing and cannot be attributed easily to a practical cause.

An analysis of the city's site plan begins to reveal some interesting aspects. The highway bends for no apparent reason as it approaches Mae Hong Son's central area and is redirected upon departure. This inflection posits a different sensibility within its notional border. It marks an edge and a symbolic town wall that is legible in the plan but, more significantly, in a series of reoriented views.

2.5 Wat Phra Non.
Photograph by author.

The canting of the highway follows a gentle and roughly symmetrical arc whose centre is located at the summit of the mountain to the west. As it approaches the city, the highway faces the mountain, providing a clear view of its summit; however, this relationship is not axial but tangential. More precisely, the highway from the south points toward the mountain's base, a zone occupied by a pair of temples, Wat Phra Non and Wat Muai Toi. Where it meets the town, the highway turns abruptly to the east, toward the commercial centre.

This inflection creates a space for significant inhabitation between the highway and the mountain. In this quiet zone are located the two temples.[33] This shift also keeps the main street of the town, lined with commercial buildings, away from the mountain. The secular city is both separated from and reconnected to the mountain by its religious institutions. The combination of temple and landscape defines the mountain more as a spatial region than as a point; it is approached and then avoided, flanked rather than intersected.

Where the highway veers away, visual connection from the town to the mountain is reinforced by the roughly perpendicular east-west streets on a loose orthogonal grid. Like the highway, they offer a tangential view of the mountain rather than an axial focus but are oriented generally toward Wat Hua Wiang, the only monastery in the city centre. Wat

2.6 Roads and mountain. Photograph by author.

Hua Wiang itself is roughly parallel to Wat Pra Non and Wat Muai Toi at the base of the mountain, although not aligned. The mountain summit, the apparent cause of the highway's reorientation, is addressed more directly by some of the smaller east-west streets that change direction to face the mountain, distorting the city's grid.

The mountain is a strong natural feature. Densely wooded, it hovers above the city, providing a vegetal and topographic backdrop to urban life. Its significance, however, is also architectural. Wat Phra That Doi Kong Mu, the most important Buddhist shrine in the area and perhaps one of the reasons for Mae Hong Son's existence, occupies the summit in a series of terraces. Housing a number of *chedi* and *viharn* (Buddhist assembly halls), a large standing Buddha, and supporting domestic structures, Wat Phra That Doi Kong Mu is a self-contained precinct, independent from the city below, yet it engages in a symbiotic conversation by facing the town from its elevated position. The temple is related visually to the life below, although distanced by the intervening landscape. Wat Doi Kong Mu is both a landmark and a founding principle, overlooking the town and defining its conscience.

It appears that the mountain, temple, and inhabited valley to the east govern Mae Hong Son's location, with the city looking up at a hilltop shrine to the west.[34] The landscape and its religious significance are

2.7 Wat Doi Kong Mu. Photograph by author.

emphasized by the inflected infrastructure. Symbolically, Wat Phra That Doi Kong Mu and its mountain are presented to the town below, which arranges its form accordingly. At a different scale, the same condition is evident at Chiang Mai, where the city is linked to a distant landscape. A mountain, Doi Suthep, is also inhabited by a major shrine, Wat Phra Boromathat Doi Suthep, which defines the western boundary of the city's plain. It forms a distant endpoint of the town's central axis, temporarily interrupted by Wat Phra Sing Luang.[35] In Mae Hong Son the condition is much more direct with neither the intervening distance nor the contrasting formalization of Chiang Mai's walls and moat. While functionally separate, the mountain "centres" the town both visually and symbolically.

The adjoining *wat* at the base of the mountain form a partial city wall, a buffer between the town and the landscape. Wat Phra Non and Wat Muai Toi provide a more immediate focus for views and direct access. The city's more secular aspects, its roads and commercial activities, are politely kept away from the mountain. Visually, the *wat* act as pointers, leading up and out to the landscape beyond. The superimposed roofs of the *viharn* and the stepped *chedi* create images of layered passage up the mountain. Wat Phra Non and Wat Muai Toi become the face of the landscape and perhaps even transform it into architecture. They are intermediaries, an architectural foreshadowing that defines a visual path to Wat Doi Kong Mu above.

The *wat* not only present an image of ascent, they also direct physical passage toward the mountain. These links are established in a variety of ways to accentuate the diverse routes to the summit.[36] Whether implied or actual, paths are outlined and celebrated architecturally. The symbolic value of these journeys is demonstrated by the sculpted *naga* figures that adorn the temples. *Naga* are serpent deities who inhabit the underworld, living in their own glorious shining palaces. Identified with rain and fertility, they are transformative figures who can change shape and inhabit different realms at will. Also associated with rainbows, the *naga* link worlds at different levels. They both protect the Buddha and mark his journey.[37] At the *wat* the *naga* images frame views and physical passages, enlivening staircases and the roof profiles of the *bot* and *viharn*, the temples' assembly halls. Wat Phra Non and Wat Muai Toi provide urban and visual links to the more distant Wat Doi Kong Mu and demonstrate the symbolic nature of the landscape through their representational forms.

The mountain and its *wat* present a symbolic ascent, or perhaps a descent, as the Buddha and Wat Doi Kong Mu are visually brought into the city that arranges itself to greet them. The landscape becomes significant

2.8 Wat Muai Toi. Photograph by author.

2.9 *Naga* at Wat Muai Toi. Photograph by author.

through this architectural and infrastructural celebration, yet the relationship remains somewhat ambiguous. The approach to the summit is not simply a formal procession but an intriguing game of distance and displacement. Although Wat Doi Kong Mu is clearly visible from a distance, it gradually disappears from view due to the slope of the mountain. The lower *wat* take precedence and engage us directly in their own architectural worlds, set against the dark forested landscape. As with the inflected highway, destinations are presented, then replaced, as alternate compositions take precedence. Direct access to the original destination is blocked.[38]

LAKE AND CENTRE

While the mountain is Mae Hong Son's symbolic focus, its scenographic heart is a small lake within the town. Lake Jongkam, however, is a curious centre. The town's commercial roads bypass it, as though they were keeping a safe distance. Aside from a rarely used fitness park, it has no literal function. The lake and its precinct are more symbolic than

2.10 Lake Jongkam. Photograph by author.

functional. Surrounded by a public park and a pair of temples, Lake Jongkam is Mae Hong Son's most striking image.

As with the mountain, this visual effect is created by a powerful combination of nature and religious architecture. The outer (southern) edge of the lake is inhabited by Wat Chong Klang and Wat Chong Kham. The pair of *wat*, located perpendicular to the line of sight and entry, establish the lake's boundary. Similar to Wat Phra Non and Wat Muai Toi at the base of the mountain, this composition constitutes a town wall. These sacred institutions define the perceptual edge of the city, juxtaposed against the landscape beyond.

Although the lake occupies the physical centre of the town, it is inflected experientially by the strong forms of the temples. As a result, the lake is perceived more as a threshold that separates the viewer from the landscape. The *wat* are built along the outer, natural edge of the lake. The urban edges of the lake are more domestic, with houses, small inns, and restaurants. The water creates a buffer between the commercial city and the religious precinct beyond, with the surface of the water serving as a forecourt to the *wat*. This accentuates their scenographic quality but also reinforces their separation. Although visual appreciation is heightened, physical access is necessarily indirect.

Viewed from across the lake, the roofs of the *wat* provide an impressive sight. The glistening white and gold figures reflected in the water are poised between the city and the landscape and between water and sky. With their parts arrayed along a line, Wat Chong Klang and Wat Chong

Kham are visually recessed by the water's surface, yet their reflections bring them forward and toward the viewer. Ethereal and even magical, the compressed reflection of *wat* and mountain appears close yet intangible, complementing the more precise yet distant figures. Especially with Mae Hong Son's frequently changing weather, this combination of building and landscape, sky and water, is constantly alive, simultaneously serene and dynamic.

The *wat*'s exterior appearance is characterized by their façades, best seen from across the lake and juxtaposed with the surrounding hills. Within the temples, the views become more localized, controlled by the architecture. Unlike Wat Phra Non and Wat Muai Toi at the base of the mountain, there are no paths or vistas to the landscape beyond. Axial paths lead to the assembly halls, where they transform visually into vertical journeys of layered roofs or extend physically into modest interiors. The earlier dramatic views of temples in the landscape seem to end modestly, almost as an architectural anticlimax. This visual path is consciously redirected, its temporary endpoints anticipating new destinations.

In an interesting twist, the axis of view and entry that ends at the *viharn* is reoriented transversely to present a framed view of Wat Doi Kong Mu and its mountain. The *wat*'s internal arrangement creates a subtle alternative to their more obvious frontal image. The perpendicular path that links the temples is even reoriented slightly to focus on Wat Doi Kong Mu. The earlier relationship among lake, *wat*, and landscape disappears, but the lateral view defined by the temples' internal layout reestablishes the mountain as its primary focus.

The slightly displaced street that follows this redirected path departs from the basic grid to face the mountain directly, yet this view also connects the lake to the mountain. In a related quirk, the redirected highway within the town is centred between Lake Jongkam and Wat Phra Non and Wat Muai Toi at the base of the mountain. These two natural figures – lake and mountain – frame this new urban element but keep their distance from it.

The lake and the mountain – void and figure – are natural polarities. It is interesting that the sculpted *naga*, the figures that direct passage up the mountain, represent chthonic deities. They are identified with the underworld, which in Thai cosmology is aquatic rather than earthly. Vertical travel within the *wat* is associated with the *naga*'s mysterious watery origins. The symbolic pairing of water and distant sky is fulfilled in the

2.11 The redirected view. Photograph by author.

2.12 Wat Chong Klang: distant juxtapositions. Photograph by author.

relationship between lake and mountain. A mythical duality is formed by the dialectical tension between the contrasting symbols.[39] The *wat*'s roofs and their directed passages make this link explicit.

The lake is a place to view from. It brings the mountain and temples to the observer and enhances their qualities with its flickering reflections. Except for an occasional young swimmer, people remain at the lake's edge. The lake sharpens one's perceptions of the surroundings by keeping one on the outside, at a distance. In this way, Lake Jongkam offers different perceptions of the landscape. At its simplest level, it is a forecourt to Wat Chong Klang and Wat Chong Kham that eliminates urban distractions to focus attention on the elaborate roof structures and the landscape. Once inside the temple precinct, however, the central path focuses attention on Wat Doi Kong Mu, although more subtly.

As an infrastructural element, the lake is interesting. It creates a symbolic image for the town by keeping the practical activities of urban life away from it. The principal commercial roads bypass it. Instead, a more sacred conversation between nature and religion holds sway, as though two cities, symbolic and secular, are independent yet adjacent. Domestic life fills in the spaces between the more significant figures of lake and mountain, without impinging on one's appreciation of their presence.

RUNWAY AND MARKET

This symbiotic relationship between urban infrastructure and nature is also demonstrated in a curious, more contemporary way. An airport runway, Mae Hong Son's most significant piece of modern infrastructure, is sited near the north end of the town.[40] The city's status as a provincial capital, together with its distance from Chiang Mai, justifies up to six flights per day and a runway that can handle mid-sized jets. The contrast between the airplanes and the adjacent small wooden buildings is provocative in itself, but even stranger is the runway's social function. Each evening, after the last plane has departed, the runway transforms into the city's primary social space.

Jogging, picnics, badminton, and soccer games animate the large asphalt field. The seemingly nonarchitectural infrastructure for air travel has developed an alter ego as a grand piazza. This is an intriguing example of a new social use for a place that was designed for something else. The functions seem contradictory: planes and social activities have different

2.13 Planes in the village.Photograph by author.

requirements. Indeed, the evening activities are rendered poignant by the juxtapositions of scale and expectation, yet the location and character of the space attract this unconventional use.

The runway flanks Mae Hong Son's principal market, which expands each evening to sell prepared foods. The market probably predated the runway but has also reacted to it. Stretched along the road adjacent to the runway, this linear market also leads to the modest entry. During the day, this entry is blocked when planes are taking off and landing. Otherwise, it remains open to allow pedestrians to reach the rest of the town to the north. After the last plane has departed, the runway becomes completely public to welcome its new inhabitants.

Although this recreational use is dependent on administrative generosity, it is an accidental byproduct of the infrastructure. Certainly, there are no signs that social occupation was a concern for the designers. The entry is a modest path cut through the surrounding shrubbery at the end of a small road. However, the social inhabitation of the space is clearly a response to the new infrastructure. The symbiotic relation between the runway and the market defines it as a social focus of the town, complementing the sacred spaces elsewhere.

This might imply that an infrastructure project can happily ignore the conventions and traditions of a place as long as its use remains flexible, expecting a city to adapt to this new intervention and express its personality. If this were the case, new infrastructure would provoke a contextual response, architecturally and socially. This assumption would relieve infrastructure of all cultural responsibility, freeing it to solve practical

2.14 The runway as an urban square. Photograph by author.

problems while expecting the city to take care of itself. In the case of the airport runway, it does this in a remarkable way.

Unfortunately, many infrastructural changes have had disastrous results. The highways that have carved up many Western cities should challenge complacency. Interestingly, other large interventions in Mae Hong Son have not had the same positive effect. A romantic park at the south end of the city lies empty and forlorn. Clearly designed for recreation, it stands as a monument to hopeful but unsuccessful planning. The park presents an image of recreational use rather than a real setting for it. Its form is didactic and functionally inflexible. A night market was designed and built along the main road in the centre of the city, but it also sits empty while the impromptu shelters thrive along the runway.

The runway's inhabitation cannot be explained by a lack of other options. Although its success was undoubtedly accidental, it points to the positive qualities of the runway. Paradoxically, the runway's provocative use is a result of its design. The runway is an exciting space in itself, but more important, it follows the principles of the other infrastructural conditions discussed above, enabling it to engage and clarify Mae Hong Son's urban character.

The space of the runway is large and open. It is raised above the level of the surrounding streets, creating a dramatic stage-like quality. Recreational and social activities are heightened by the natural backdrop. Although its plan form is defined by the rectangular asphalt surface, it remains spatially open. It is the only place in the town where one can experience the breadth of the surrounding landscape. It presents a striking visual forecourt to Wat Doi Kong Mu and more generally to the hills that encircle the city. Vast, open, and uncluttered, the dramatic panorama relates the social space of the city to its larger setting.

The runway flanks the market precinct and establishes a strong edge to which the small-scale commerce reacts. Their tight adjacency heightens the contrast between these activities. In the market, which is dark and densely populated, the town's different social and ethnic groups are united in trade. From the runway, this practical city effectively disappears because it is situated at a lower level. This visual separation of commerce and public space strengthens the more symbolic conversation between the viewer and the landscape. The broad exposure of the runway is an extreme contrast to the market's interior. In this sense, the runway is similar to the lake and the mountain discussed above. It is spatially dramatic, even beautiful. Its experience reinforces the special and even sacred quality of the landscape by keeping the practical city at bay. The visual masking of secular realities allows a more direct interaction between the viewer and the hills, across the abstract intervening space of the large asphalt surface. Here, social inhabitation has replaced the sacred, although in the Thai context this is a difficult distinction to make.

LATENT SENSIBILITIES

The most important Thai historic document, an engraved stone stele named Inscription One, describes the state of Sukhothai at the time of its consolidation into the capital of the first Thai kingdom. The virtues and piety of its ruler are extolled, the happiness of the people celebrated. It presents a golden age of the culture and has acted as a national reference point up until the present.[41]

2.15 View from the mountain to the runway: the linked figures. Photograph by author.

The king is a key supporter of Buddhism and is responsible for constructing an ordered capital, yet an intriguing passage in the inscription describes a ritual pilgrimage to the surrounding hills to pay homage to the city's guardian spirit. The city's foundations are rooted animistically in nature, although the hill is outside the city. Indeed, the formal city and its landscape are linked symbiotically, just as its animistic spirits coexist with more official Buddhist practice.

In the case of Mae Hong Son, the city has not inherited Sukhothai's formal structures, which would be alien to its indigenous population, yet the link between Buddhism and nature is clearly evident in the siting and design of its temples. The enduring power of the animistic landscape also remains palpable in the social inhabitation of the runway.

CAUSE OR EFFECT?

The inhabitation of the runway is a strange response, unrelated to its original intention. This social reaction to an alien infrastructure is provocative because it is a direct expression of a living culture, a realm in which architecture should operate. The runway's inhabitation points to the virtues of strong forms and a relaxed approach to their use. It does not dictate activity, but supports it. As a result, the runway is an interesting example of how contemporary infrastructure can become integrated into a city through social participation. As argued above, this use derives not from convenience but from the particular qualities and context of the runway. While these qualities are impressive in themselves, they reinforce cultural practices and infrastructure elsewhere in the city. The active use of the runway demonstrates the enduring value of this local relationship to the landscape.

The accidental success of the runway shows the importance of relating infrastructure to the spirit and symbolic practices of a place. Its value, and potentially the value of any new development, relies on the principles and practices of the city. It may be difficult to predict exactly how open-ended infrastructure will be used, but this set of examples suggests the integral and positive role of infrastructure and its capacity to direct architectural development in a meaningful way.

One cannot always rely on accidents. Rather than blindly waiting for such provocative moments, we should investigate the underlying values of the city in advance so that possible extrapolations in design can be tested. Thus the sterile debates between traditional and modern or between East and West can be replaced by provocative speculations that extend the fundamental character of a place without recourse to nostalgic form.

NOTES

1 A related concern exists in commercial architecture, where the architect is often an exterior skin consultant for a building form that is determined largely by financial criteria.

2 Rem Koolhaas, *Delirious New York* (New York: Oxford University Press, 1978), proposes a compelling relationship between the architecture of Manhattan and its powerful grid.

3 The Renaissance *palazzi* of Venice, for example, adapt terrestrial models to suit their canal settings with striking results, just as Bangkok's traditional river-based inhabitation was highly distinct.

4 An exception is the eager acceptance of large shopping malls in Bangkok, which provides an intriguing example of how seemingly alien forms can be domesticated and transformed.

5 Steve Van Beek, in his account of a major river trip through Thailand, describes how this changed relationship to water is not limited to the metropolis. The formerly river-based culture has become increasingly land-based due to its reliance on highways and roads for the practicalities of daily life; see Steve Van Beek, *Slithering South* (Hong Kong: Wind and Water, 2002). See also Steve Van Beek, *The Chao Phya: River in Transition* (Kuala Lumpur: Oxford University Press, 1995).

6 Sumet Jumsai, *Naga: Cultural Origins in Siam and the West Pacific* (Bangkok: Chalermnit Press, 1997).

7 Thongchai Winichakul, *Siam Mapped: A History of the Geo-Body of a Nation* (Honolulu: University of Hawaii Press, 1994).

8 A nostalgia for a (perhaps imaginary) golden past, especially when professed by outsiders, is not overly helpful in dealing with the real issues facing urban development; see, for example, William J. Klausner, *Reflections of Thai Culture* (Bangkok: The Siam Society, 1993), for a representative example. While the text offers many insights into Thai village life, it is pervaded by a general, but undemonstrated, assumption that the culture has suffered through its contact with modern life.

9 Thailand is distinct in this context because it avoided being colonized. While Western models were eagerly emulated in the Fifth Reign, which some have argued was a form of self-colonization, the earlier changes carried out by, for example, the French in Phnom Penh have no real parallel here. It is also interesting that the great Khmer irrigation and planning schemes carried out at Angkor were never copied in Thailand despite considerable architectural contact between the two societies.

10 Known as the Shan, Karen, and Hmong, these groups vary in size and degree of integration with the more mainstream society. Many inhabit the border regions with Burma (Myanmar), and indeed their traditional lands do not recognize the border distinction. Generally, these groups have been considered distinct from the more centralized Thai, culturally, socially, and politically; see Winichakul, *Siam Mapped*, for a discussion of this form of cultural exclusion.

11 In addition to referring to the citizens of contemporary Thailand, "Thai" or "Tai" is also an ethnic definition. As a result, writers such as Sumet Jumsai and Thongchai Winichakul prefer to use the earlier term "Siam" rather than Thailand when referring to the country, as it is less restrictive and does not exclude longstanding non-Tai residents from the country's definition.

12 Of course, there are many similarities throughout Southeast Asia. It is perhaps more accurate to regard these traditions as inflections of greater regional sensibilities, yet the local differences are compelling.

13 The reign of King Chulalongkorn, Rama V, was noted for its educational and cultural reforms, in many cases following Western models; see David Wyatt, *Thailand: A Short History* (New Haven: Yale University Press, 1982); and David Wyatt, *Studies in Thai History* (Chiang Mai: Silkworm Books, 1994).

14 Dhida Saraya, *(Sri) Dvaravati* (Bangkok: Muang Boran, 1999), is an example of the growing interest in these foundations.

15 The premodern Thai approach to historiography is both complex and significant; see, for example, Wyatt, *Thailand*; and Wyatt, *Studies*. The lecture by King Chulalongkorn on the role of history, presented to the Siam Society in 1907, makes the point clearly; see King Chulalongkorn, "The Antiquarian Society of Siam," *Journal of the Siam Society* 89, no. 1–2 (2001).

16 See Alberto Pérez-Gómez, *Architecture and the Crisis of Modern Science* (Cambridge, MA: MIT Press, 1983), for a classic treatment of this issue. The philosophical and cultural foundations for the transformation are well documented in the text.

17 See Joseph Rykwert, *The Idea of a Town* (London: Faber and Faber, 1976), for an investigation of the symbolic foundations of urban form in Rome.

18 See Marc Askew, *Bangkok: Place, Practice and Representation* (London: Routledge, 2002), for a survey of the major debates over recent urban issues.

19 See, for example, Srisurang Punyodyana, *Thai Customs and Social Values in the Ramakien* (Bangkok: Thammasat University, 1981). For more current popular discussions, both the *Bangkok Post* and *The Nation*, Bangkok's two English newspapers, often deal with urban concerns.

20 For a sense of the complex relationship between village and city, tradition and modernity, see, for example, Pira Sudham, *Monsoon Country* (Bangkok:

Rother, 1993); or Pira Sudham, *Pira Sudham's Best* (Bangkok: Shire Books, 1991), a collection of short stories.

21 The first published book on Thai archaeology, *Prehistory*, by Prince Damrong, a noted historian and cultural figure, was published in 1938. For a more recent survey of Thai archaeological knowledge, see Pisit Charoenwongsa and M.C. Subhadradis Diskul, *Thailand: Archaeologia Mundi* (Geneva: Nagel, 1978). For discoveries from more recent decades, see Saraya, *(Sri) Dvaravati.*

22 Thailand, like its neighbours, was historically underpopulated with respect to the land's optimum productivity. As a result, wars were often fought over people, with prisoners relocated to settle regions of the victors' territories.

23 An interim capital was situated at Thonburi, across the Chao Phraya River from Bangkok's current centre.

24 *The Dynastic Chronicles: The First Reign*, Chaophraya Thiphakorawong edition (Tokyo: The Center for East Asian Cultural Studies, 1978).

25 The rings are inflected due to the centre's location on the river bank, the city's formal expansion taking place only to the north, east, and south. Rattanakosin Island was formed by the excavation of a major canal along the eastern edge of the royal centre. Framed between the canal and the river, the city maintained an aquatic perimeter, following the example of Ayutthaya. The name Rattanakosin translates as the Emerald Island of Indra. In Thai Buddhist cosmology, Indra is the god/ruler of Tavatimsa heaven, set on Mount Meru; see Frank Reynolds and Mani B. Reynolds, trans, *Three Worlds According to King Ruang: A Thai Buddhist Cosmology* (Berkeley: University of California, 1982).

26 There were very few significant roads until the mid to late nineteenth century. New Road, for example, which links the historic centre to the more commercial and Western populated area to the south, was constructed to provide the growing Western community with a place to exercise and ride their carriages.

27 See, for example, David Wyatt, "Education and Chulalongkorn," in *Siam in Mind*, 87–92 (Chiang Mai: Silkworm Books, 2002), for a brief introduction to this situation.

28 In both cases, earlier Roman stadia were occupied by medieval domestic constructions, replicating the plan forms in a very different architectural guise.

29 An attempt was made to decipher these sensibilities in Barry Bell, *Bangkok: Angelic Allusions* (London: Reaktion Press, 2003).

30 The Dvaravati period took place from the sixth to twelfth centuries. Little is known of its political or social structure. Its lineaments are structured primarily around its artefacts. It is interesting that Bangkok, whether by expediency or design, returned to a more elongated oval form in its plan, more like the earlier Dvaravati cities. Despite oft-described intentions to recreate Ayutthaya, the superimposition of a formal geometry as seen in the previous capital was rejected.

31 The idea of the Thai city as a cosmological construction, centred on the royal palace as a replication of Mount Meru, is discussed in, among other places, S.J. Tambiah, *World Conqueror and World Renouncer: A Study of Buddhism and Polity against a Historical Background* (Cambridge, UK: Cambridge University Press, 1976). See also H.Q. Quaritich Wales, *The Universe around Them: Cosmology and Cosmic Renewal in Indianized Southeast Asia* (London: Arthur Probsthaim, 1977).

32 On the same axis, although well outside the city to the west, is the shrine of Wat Phra Boromathat Doi Suthep, situated on the summit of a significant hill. A related condition may be seen at Mae Hong Son, discussed below.

33 South of the temples is a sports field and a school, continuing the institutional aspect, albeit in a transformed way.

34 The entrance to Thai temples (*wat*) is conventionally, although not exclusively, from the east. It is also notable that the *chedi*, the *stupa*-like reliquary monuments that are central to most temples and can be seen to represent symbolic mountains, are usually placed to the west of the main assembly hall (*bot*), although again not exclusively.

35 The Ping River is located just east of the city. It appears that Chiang Mai was sited in relation to both mountain and river and may be seen as a link between them. The possibly related role of the lake in Mae Hong Son is discussed below.

36 It is notable in this context that the vertical has a special meaning in Thai culture, and the idea of the sacred mountain is key to its founding literature. Mount Meru, the home of the gods and centre of cosmological order, is a mountain; see Tambiah, *World Conqueror*. See also Quaritich Wales, *The Universe around Them*.

37 The *naga* king, Muchalinda, protected the Buddha during his meditations

by forming a great canopy over his body. For the significance of the *naga* in architectural culture, see Sumet Jumsai, *Naga: Cultural Origins in Siam and the West Pacific* (Bangkok: Chalermnit Press, 1997).

38 The original access to Wat Doi Kong Mu was via a lengthy road that wrapped behind the mountain. More recently, a frontal pedestrian approach has been constructed just north of Wat Muai Toi. Laid out as a series of switch-backed paths, this route brings the upper temple into an even more tangible relation with the city.

39 Dialectical structures appear consistently within Thai sacred architecture. *Bot* and *viharn*, the wooden assembly halls, are paired with *chedi*, the solid masonry relic monuments. The *naga* are seen in conflict with the *garuda*, the great birds representative of the sky. There is a consistent sense of oscillation, even tension, between the different figures that animate the whole.

40 According to local sources, the runway was built by Japanese forces during the Second World War.

41 Conventionally dated to 1238, Inscription One is also understood as the first example of Thai writing, invented by King Ramkhamheng for the good of his people; see George Coédes, trans, "L'Inscription Du Roi Rama Gamhen de Sukhodaya," and H.R.H. Prince Wan Waithayakon, trans, "Stone Inscriptions of Sukhothai," both presented in a single pamphlet (Bangkok: The Siam Society, 1965); and Phraya Anuman Rajadhon, *The Nature and Development of the Thai Language* (Bangkok: Fine Arts Department, Government of Thailand, 1989). The veracity of Inscription One has been challenged by recent scholars, some of whom claim that it is a nineteenth-century forgery. Although highly acrimonious, the debate does not appear to be conclusive. For an example of the discussions, see Mukhom Wongthes, *Intellectual Might and National Myth: A Forensic Investigation of the Ram Khamhaeng Controversy in Thai Society* (Bangkok: Matichon, 2003).

Erudite Laughter: The Persiflage of Viel de Saint-Maux

Ramla Benaissa

Chora

> Malicious laughter, *perfidium ridens*, is something else: it is the joy of humiliating others. With mocking bursts of laughter, with *cachinnum* (a term we lack), we hound those who promised us wonders but did only silly things. It is a booing rather than a laughing.[1]

VOLTAIRE WAS REPUTED TO BE the greatest *persifleur* of the Enlightenment. It is even believed that the word was coined to describe his works. Persiflage was a characteristic trait of the French Enlightenment style, so much so that the word was judged untranslatable and was adopted by other European languages, as though the Germans, Spanish, and English didn't know such a thing. Some even characterized the France of Voltaire as the nation of persiflage.[2] The 1980 Robert dictionary defines the verb "persifler" as "to ridicule someone by using mockery or an ironic tone," but in the eighteenth century the meaning was more complex. The word appeared first in 1734 in the writings of Voltaire and was followed by its derivatives: "persiflage" appeared in 1735 and "persifleur" in 1744.[3] The various dictionary definitions in the 1750s include:

> To indulge in a banter of ideas and expressions that leaves doubt or confusion in their real meaning.[4]

> Say amusingly serious things, and seriously frivolous things.[5]

> To speak ironically in a mocking tone.[6]

The two last definitions correspond to the notion of "philosophical persiflage." In 1767 Voltaire denounced the craze of his contemporaries for this fashionable vicious neologism: "As soon as a vicious expression is introduced, the crowd picks it up. Tell me, did Racine mock Boileau? Did Bossuet mock Pascal? And did both mystify La Fontaine, sometimes taking advantage of his simple-mindedness?"[8]

In the 1760s the use of persiflage was part of the philosopher's effort to interest the public in philosophy. Voltaire understood that witticism was the best way to hold public attention, but his use of persiflage went far beyond an effort to seduce salon culture.[8] In Voltaire's writings, as in the writings of other philosophers of his time, it took on a truly philosophical meaning. Voltaire's *Traité sur la tolérance* was published in 1763, and the following review of it appeared in the *Correspondance littéraire*: "We have here some copies of the *Traité sur la tolérance* of this famous writer. I have read it, and I was not satisfied by it. There are some beautiful things; but too much persiflage, and jokes are nowhere more uncalled for than in humankind's plea against the cruelty of fanaticism and hypocrisy."[9]

On his fight for religious tolerance, Voltaire wrote to a friend, "Spread some handfuls of salt and spices in the stew you are presenting to your readers, mix mockery to reason, try to engender indifference. Only then will you obtain tolerance."[10]

Philosophers tried to develop a philosophical gaiety different from *persiflage mondain*. In book 7 of *Les Confessions*, Rousseau mentions a journal on which he planned to collaborate with Diderot: "There, I conceived the project of a periodical publication entitled *Le Persifleur* that Diderot and I were to produce alternately."[11] According to Rousseau *Le Persifleur* was meant "to analyze the new works being published, express his opinion and communicate both to the public."[12] In fact, beyond the search for "l'esprit pour l'esprit," Rousseau intended to scrutinize the so-called knowledge of his contemporaries. In *Le Persifleur* Rousseau's superiority of mind justified his wickedness, and his wit[13] was supposed to make his personal critique appeal to the public. Rousseau tried to entertain his contemporaries by writing on a variety of subjects in a tone that was both serious and ironic. In *Le Persifleur* Rousseau displayed a blatant self-complacency and impertinence, mellowed by a careful distance and self-consciousness.[14] "Having begun by mocking myself, I will have plenty of time to mock others."[15]

Salon culture might have developed a taste for persiflage, but for Diderot, Voltaire, and Rousseau, it was a major philosophical weapon. Philosophical persiflage was a school of skepticism and also had a pedagogical role. To philosophers, persiflage was a way to protect readers from enthusiasm, the most dangerous pitfall for the man of the Enlightenment.

Jean-Louis Viel de Saint-Maux was a member of the Académie de Marseille as an architect and a painter. In 1762 he wrote *Considérations sur l'origine de la peinture et du language*.[16] On 11 August 1786 the Académie de Marseille received two anonymous works, later attributed to Viel de Saint-Maux.[17] The first, a novel, was entitled *Clomella et Noceis*. The second, described in the author's words as a more "singular" work "destined to amuse my colleagues of Marseilles," was entitled *Antidote contre les cocus, ou Dissertation sur les cornes*[18] *antiques et modernes, ouvrage philosophique dédié à MM. Les savants, antiquaires, gens de lettres, poètes, avocats, censeurs …*[19] The witticism of the title

LETTRES
SUR
L'ARCHITECTURE
DES ANCIENS,
ET CELLE DES MODERNES,
DANS lesquelles se trouve développé le génie symbolique qui présida aux Monumens de l'Antiquité.
Par M. VIEL DE SAINT-MAUX,
Architecte civil & militaire, Associé de l'Académie Royale des Beaux-Arts & Architecture navale de Marseille, & Correspondant de plusieurs Académies.
A PARIS.
1787.

3.1 Frontispiece from Jean-Louis Viel de Saint-Maux, *Lettres sur l'architecture des anciens, et celle des modernes* (Paris, 1737; reprint, Geneva: Minkoff, 1974).

and its deliberate ambiguity do not say much about the scope of the work, but they do reveal the author's frame of mind.

Lettres sur l'architecture des anciens, et celle des modernes, dans lesquelles se trouve développé le génie symbolique qui présida aux Monuments de l'Antiquité was published one year later, in 1787. When the first copy of *Lettres* was sent to the Académie de Marseille in 1779, the academy refused even to discuss the work but issued an ironic account explaining the pointlessness of this kind of research for the arts. Viel gathered ideas on architecture, philosophy, history, and cultural and religious systems that had never been assembled before. Compiling architectural treatises, sacred texts, myths, travel accounts, and historical works, Viel crossed cultures and fields. In 1786, commenting on the *Antidote contre les cocus*, the secretary of the academy complimented Viel on his studies of antiquity and compared his style to that of Montesquieu. In *Lettres* Viel developed his ideas by constantly scorning theories and authors, using preposterous comparisons in the tradition of works such as *Persian Letters*.[20] The irony derided not only the language, but also the ideas. One might say that Viel learned from the philosophers the power of irony against the certitude and the dangers of "serious minds."[21] Many of the definitions of persiflage can be found in his rhetoric. This chapter is concerned with how Viel used persiflage and mystification to shatter certitude about ancient authors, contemporary architectural theory, and the edifice of architectural erudition.

THE LANGUAGE OF DERISION

> Irony: Latin, *ironia*, from the Greek, *eironeia*, interrogation.

> A historian has many duties. Allow me to remind you here of two that are of some importance. The first is not to slander; the second is not to bore. I can excuse you for neglect of the first because few will read your work; I cannot, however, forgive you for neglecting the second, for I was forced to read you.[22]

Montesquieu wrote that "one should not put vinegar but salt in one's writings."[23] He distinguished between authors who use irony to make a truth more striking and those who just want to make a witticism. Correct proportioning is very important, and he stressed that "irony must not be constant; otherwise it does not surprise anymore."[24] In *Lettres* Viel's use of irony as a literary device was an original way to build his argument about the origins of architecture and against contemporary works. He made no pretense of objectivity but instead provided subverted accounts from other works, or at least very personal interpretations. Viel mocked contemporary treatises for being mere compilations, yet his own work is an assembly of travel accounts, philosophical works, and historical studies. Viel's treatise is composed of seven letters, with extensive footnotes. The text is not long but is rather inarticulate, with much repetition from letter to letter. Irony maintained the reader's attention and distracted him from all the shortcomings and inaccuracies in the historical presentation. The ethnological and linguistic analyses are less than rigorous. Viel used contemporary references in an imprecise and creative way and sometimes used pure fiction to hide his ignorance of a subject.

Viel wanted to elaborate a theory on the origins of architecture, and to do so he reviewed the accounts of origins developed in the major treatises. He thought that their authors had overlooked what were for him the most important elements: the temple and the cult. Architects considered only the material features of buildings and were never able to rise up to the "mind" that conceived them. In monuments, architects saw mere stones, mortar, and arbitrary decorations. Buildings were praised for the ratio of their measurements or for their unverified attribution to a famous architect. Viel's major criticism was that authors fragmented buildings into parts, reducing them to an assembly of moldings, columns, and capitals, each part having a separate origin. He criticized the contradictory origins attributed to the various parts of a building and its ornaments.[25] To Viel, the moderns did not have the slightest idea of the "first monuments" and repeated opinions without really knowing their subject.[26]

Viel believed that all architectural writings were rebuses.[27] He regarded Vitruvius's *Ten Books*, above all, as an unintelligible text and believed that all attempts to interpret it had been a waste of time. One passage in the *Ten Books* had prompted a dispute about the orders and had led to many architectural writings and abuses.[28] To him, it seemed pointless to debate whether there are only three Greek orders or as many as five. Viel noted that some architects even conceived an upside-down order. He also did not miss the irony that some designs proposed a sixth order with a capital – a part that is supposed to support the huge weight of an entablature – decorated with ostrich feathers.[29] Although his contemporaries attempted to revive antiquity in their writings, Viel claimed that their architectural practices were motivated by taste and fashion.

Inspired by the persiflage and mystification[30] practised in salon culture, Viel also ridiculed the language of architectural erudition. He suggested that contemporary architects tried to sanctify their "absurd" writings by adding quotations that are more relevant in pious works, and he compared architects to priests who invoke Christ whenever their memories fail and they are short of words.[31] Viel took ideas from treatises out of context to make them seem absurd. He criticized their interpretations of building elements, such as comparisons between moldings and "blood sausages" and claims that moldings originated in the "mattresses and blankets that wrapped columns during transportation."[32] He ridiculed authors who see petticoats in flat moldings, slippers in stylobates, and even a "set of false teeth"[33] in part of a cornice. Viel noted that some treatises compare the architectural act to "curdling milk" and advise architects to "go to confession before starting a building." They also advise architects to "urinate in the mortar for the well-being of the edifice" and make obvious observations: for example, "a one floor house is less expensive than a two floor one" and "to dig a well you have to keep digging until you find water."[34]

When a conventional discourse is confronted with irony, its original meaning becomes displaced. Viel's persiflage attempted to transform architectural discourse and distort its message by opening up a space of derision between the original text and its interpretation. His irony criticized ideas in a way that prevented serious interpretation and offered no thoughtful discussion. He also created derision by juxtaposing words from different authors. Viel emphasized words more than ideas, the container more than the content, the particular more than the general. The language of architectural scholarship was supposed to follow certain rules, and the reader was expected to find in it all the conventional elements of the genre. Instead, Viel transgressed conventions by creating a comical parody involving himself, the reader, and the texts. In doing so, he underlined the precariousness of language.

VITRUVIUS, ALBERTI, AND LAUGIER

> You did humankind a service by wisely attacking the works meant to pervert it.[35]

Viel resented that Vitruvius's account of the origins of architecture was never really questioned, and he saved his most bitter criticism for Vitruvius. He noted that other ancient architects had formulated architectural theories but that their ideas had not reached modernity because only the *Ten Books* had survived. Consequently, it became a mandatory reference for everyone entering the field of architecture. Viel wondered how a book full of contradictions, which "affirmed that the earth followed the moon's revolutions, spoke of islands that never existed and presented other puerile tales of the origins of sciences and arts," could be adopted unanimously by architects. To him, the only explanation was that Vitruvius had relied on man's perpetual stupidity.[36] He noted that the *Ten Books* prescribed that an architect should know the sciences, arts, physics, poetry, and music, but this "famous, supposedly ancient author" considered the monuments only through the ratios of their dimensions.[37] Viel attacked Vitruvius mainly for describing antique temples only in terms of modules, proportions, and measurements.[38] Modern architects followed him by producing books with elaborate systems of measures and proportions that repeated the tale of the primitive hut under the guise of theory.

Viel suggested that "the *Ten Books* could be useful only on the island of Robinson" because no one really needed it to understand the taste and principles that governed the construction of ancient edifices. Because architects were obsessed with the *Ten Books*, they neglected nature, reason, and the monuments themselves. Viel scorned what he considered puerile explanations such as "Dorus invented the Doric" and noted that such silly tales were repeated in all the treatises. To Viel, it seemed ludicrous that subsequent writers placed so much importance on the allegorical names and vocabulary used in the *Ten Books*. He thought that Vitruvius – had he in fact existed in the ancient world – would have "made the Romans laugh."[39] To Viel, Vitruvius had pretended to establish principles of architecture by making up "puerile" accounts of its origins, teaching the art of building to a nation that had already been building throughout the Western world. Forcefully announcing the end

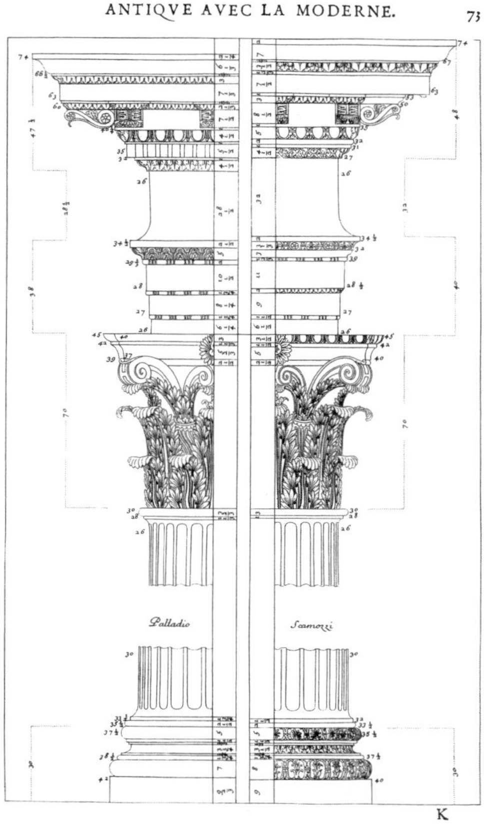

3.2 A comparison of Corinthian orders by Palladio and Scamozzi, in Roland Fréart de Chambray, *Parallèle de l'architecture antique et de la moderne* (1650).

3.3 Corinthian capital after Vitruvius, in Claude Perrault, *Les dix livres d'architecture de Vitruve* (1673).

of Vitruvianism, Viel thought that his own ideas were supported by Claude Perrault,[40] who had translated the *Ten Books*,[41] and concluded that Vitruvius was just a "simple-minded man."[42] Viel's questioning of Vitruvius's interpretation of antiquity was based on eighteenth-century discoveries of the Greek Ionic and Doric, which he thought were sanctioning the theory of Claude Perrault[43] a posteriori.

Viel condemned the Italian theoreticians of the Renaissance for establishing Vitruvius as the exclusive authority on architectural origins.[44] He believed that Vitruvius's Greek model froze the progress of architecture by erroneously presenting the orders as the foundation of architectural theory.

Alberti was not spared. Viel described Alberti as the most "entertaining" of all architects.[45] To Viel, *De re aedificatoria* consisted of several works bound together, and this assembly obscured its real origin. Although it was considered the keystone of architectural theory, it actually distorted architectural theory. He perfunctorily summarized *De re aedificatoria* as a treatise that dealt with "etymologies, secret remedies to cure fevers, how to kill bugs and rats, recovering sleep, poisoning forests, how to salute in a corridor, when a commode is needed,[46] and how to calculate the number of dogs and flies that can enter a palace."[47] Viel ridiculed Alberti by suggesting that he could not distinguish a temple from a court of justice but could discuss arcane topics such as "the con-

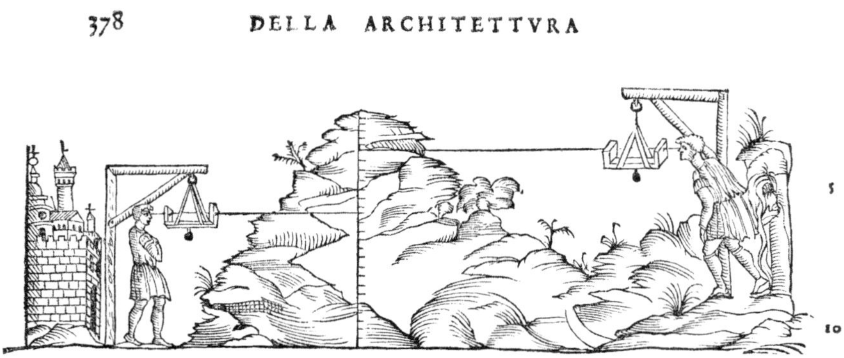

3.4 Illustration from Leon Battista Alberti, *L'architettura*, Bartoli edition (1565).

3.5 Frontispiece from Marc-Antoine Laugier, *Essai sur l'architecture* (1755).

formity of the womb, and what kind of hair women had to give to Sesostris when their husbands were vanquished."[48] Viel concluded that *De re aedificatoria* was a "carnival piece" more than an architectural treatise and wondered what the ancients, whose real concern was architecture, would have thought of such writings.[49] Viel argued that if the writings of the ancients (other than Vitruvius) had survived, they would have sanctioned his theories.

Viel also showed contempt for Laugier by refusing to name him or his work, *Essai sur l'architecture.*[50] Nevertheless, Laugier's ideas were fiercely attacked for what Viel considered to be an "old wives' tale" about the origins of architecture. To Viel, the primitive hut of the first man was neither sublime nor monumental, and by identifying traces of

3.6 The invention of fire from Vitruvius, *De Architectura*, Cesariano edition (1521).

the primitive hut in the most superb monuments, Laugier had made the origins of architecture more barbaric. Viel asked, "How could men rise to what is most distinguished in the Arts only by chance, without following a sure path, and without principle or vision?"[51]

Viel suggested that architectural tradition provided only one model for the origins of architecture since he considered Laugier's theory of the primitive hut to be a derivative of Vitruvius. The most serious fault of both Vitruvius and Laugier was that they attributed the invention of architecture to chance, as an arbitrary response to need and shelter.

Viel's criticism of Vitruvius, Alberti, and Laugier was based mainly on his rejection of eighteenth-century aesthetic categories such as nature, taste,[52] and *convenance* in favour of concurrent archaeological discoveries, travel accounts, and speculations on mythology, grammar, and universal history. He believed that only a real understanding of the origins of architecture could enable artists to go beyond the *manière* of academicism. By recovering the spirit of primitive times, artists of the eighteenth century could reach the sublime.[53] Declaring trees to be the origin of the column stripped antiquity of all merit and attributed artistic creation to chance. If this theory had been true, the ancients never would have succeeded in forming a complete body of knowledge. To Viel, thousands of treatises perpetuated a ludicrous theory about the origins of the orders. He insisted on the importance of the "stone book" rather than relying exclusively on written sources. Although he often referred to texts, he urged architects to look for origins in the built monuments.

Viel castigated the architectural theoretical debate and its fundamental texts. His vitriolic attacks on Vitruvius, Alberti, and Laugier are quite unscrupulous, but rather than using explicit criticism, Viel indulged in a game in which every comment is a pastiche of content and style, a caricature of words and ideas.

EXPERTS, MASONS, *TOISEURS*, AND OTHER IMPOSTERS[54]

> All the possible ways with which we abuse the trust or idiocy of men are as many impostures.[55]

Viel questioned the identity of Vitruvius and considered the *Ten Books* the most remarkable apocrypha of architectural tradition. He believed that this treatise could have been written in fourteenth-century Italy, so

Vitruvius may have been a phoney and his book may not have been a precedent: "this book, supposedly dedicated by Vitruvius to the Emperor Augustus, [is] a book well beneath its reputation."[56] Using skepticism, Viel tried to make the entire architectural tradition apocryphal.

Today, the identity of Viel is still an enigma. No birth or baptismal certificate has ever been found. He was a member of the lodges La Minerve (1777) and Les Neufs Soeurs (1779), which record his date of birth as 1736.[57] From 1763 to 1764 Viel worked in Lyons as a portrait painter and later specialized in miniatures. In 1762 he was accepted by the Académie de peinture et de sculpture de Marseille as a painter but failed to send his acceptance work and was officially nominated only in 1786.[58] What helped to define Viel's identity despite the successive name changes was his correspondence (or at least correspondence attributed to him) with the Académie de Marseille, retained in its archives and published by Etienne Parrocel.[59] The first two letters signed Viel are dated 30 May 1763 and 4 May 1764. In a letter dated 4 January 1770 and signed Viel, he announced his nomination in December 1769 to the Académie de Saint-Luc as an amateur and affirmed that "painting was no longer his main concern." The marquis de Paulmy, his protector, had already introduced him as an equerry and lawyer to the parliament. Pérouse de Montclos[60] has suggested that the title of equerry might be the basis for the name "de Saint-Maux" that Viel adopted between 1780 and 1785 and used when signing all subsequent correspondence. This confused Parrocel, who believed there were two Viels at the Académie de Marseille: one who signed Viel from 1763 to 1770 and another who signed Viel de Saint-Maux after 1785, whom he mistook for Charles-François Viel. The *Antidote contre les cocus* was published as an anonymous work but later was wrongfully attributed to Charles-François Viel by the *Bibliographie de la France*. *Lettres* was not published all at once. The first two letters were sent separately in 1779 and 1780 to the academy, under the name Jean Viel, "lawyer at the parliament, painter and architect."[61] On 16 April 1785 Viel addressed a copy of *Lettres sur l'architecture* to the Académie de Marseille. The dedication of the letters pretended that he had important relations, yet the identity of his correspondents was a mystery. In September 1785 Viel was asked by the secretary of the academy if he wanted to be received as a painter or an architect. He sent a painting but wrote that he could also send some architectural drawings and, "having retraced in other works the origins of painting and language," was also working on an "essay on the French school." *Considérations sur l'origine de la peinture et du language* is mentioned in note 4 of the seventh letter but never in any bibliography. In the same year, Viel published *Observations philosophiques sur l'usage d'exposer les ouvrages de peinture et de sculpture à Mme la baronne de Vassé.*[62] He also mentioned a small piece that had been on his mind for a long time, which he planned to call *Essai sur les artistes.*[63] Finally, on 7 April 1786 the Académie de Marseille received his miniature, confirmed his qualification as an architect, and announced his nomination. In 1787 *Lettres* was published as a whole book under the name Viel de Saint-Maux, who then described himself as a "civil and military architect, associate of the Royal Academy of Fine Arts and Naval Architecture of Marseilles, and correspondent of several academies."[64] The first name of the author is not indicated. For a long time, Viel de Saint-Maux was mistaken for Charles-François Viel.[65] The epistle of the reedition of Charles-François Viel's complete works is addressed to an architect brother whose identity has never been established but might be Viel de Saint-Maux. Although the confusion about Viel's identity was clarified in 1966 by Pérouse de Montclos,[66] we still do not know much about him.

In the sixth letter, Viel says that he conducted archaeological excavations on the Mediterranean coast, following in the footsteps of his father, who was inspector of the fortifications in Languedoc. He also says that he prepared a reform of building practices by simulating apprenticeship in various trade guilds under a false identity.[67] Like an undercover agent, he followed the *toiseurs* for six months, secretly made copies of their measurements of several edifices, and concluded that they used not mathematics but "barbaric rules." At some point, Viel bought a Charge de Grand-Juge de la Maçonnerie, appellé Maitre Général des Bâtimens du Rois, Ponts et Chaussées de France that would enable him to control the construction of buildings, but it was revoked and granted to a wine merchant. Viel pleaded his case with the Académie, arguing that control should be exercised solely by architects, but his case was dismissed.[68]

In the sixth letter, Viel explained what are an "expert," a mason, and a *toiseur*, and he described the ruses that they use to usurp the role of the architect and to cheat those who employ them. Although there is no record of Viel studying architecture or training with an architect, he claimed that it took him a long time to master "the science of architecture." He criticized authors who pretended to have a sufficient command of the field to write an architectural treatise. What Viel questioned was not really the competence, but the quality, of some of his contemporaries. He complained that the most lowly construction worker could reach the standard of an architect by learning some basic precepts or simply by "buying the science for only 12000 pounds and the price of a meal." By taking a basic geometry test and memorizing some "barbaric" terms adapted to architecture, they could become both contractors and architects: two antagonistic categories. Even the *toiseurs*, who merely measured buildings under construction, pretended to be architects. Masons usurped the role of the architect by offering plans that they pretended to have designed.[69] "But while the private person is unaware that the learned architect can help him out of the hands of cupidity, the mason builds as he pleases, and proposes new streets."[70]

Although Viel's letters indicate his intention to send some architectural drawings to the academy, no drawing ever surfaced. He noted that his work did not fit easily into the world of ideas and that it was more interesting to antiquarians than to artists.[71] Although his work cannot be circumscribed by any genre or category, Viel's identity was never entirely clear and his activity in the architectural field has never been established. Due to his elaborate literary disguises and the diversity of his activities, we are still not sure whether Viel was really an architect. In his first two letters, he describes himself as a "lawyer at the parliament."

An important element in Viel's work is his character impersonation. In the introduction, Viel says that he chose the epistolary form because it allowed him to respond easily to any detractors; however, it also enabled him to adopt different identities or personas.[72] Each letter is addressed to a different correspondent whose identity or relationship to Viel was never verified and might have been fabricated.[73] These correspondents helped Viel to build his own mystification. Viel's compulsive role-playing includes an element of parody that parallels his ironic interpretation of the texts. At the end of the first letter, Viel addresses the Comte de Wannestin as though he were answering questions raised in an earlier letter, but there is no evidence of this previous correspondence from the comte.[74] Parody and character impersonation enabled readers to be drawn in as active participants rather than as passive listeners.

The secrets surrounding the identities of Viel and his correspondents are typical libertine strategies. Viel's mystification places him in the lineage of Enlightenment philosophers and their precursors, the *érudits libertins* of the seventeenth century.[75] Secrecy was a strategy dictated by prudence but was also a conscious philosophical position. It was only in their private meetings that the libertines could dispense with irony and persiflage as they developed audacious ideas. In the seventeenth century, skeptics could not afford to present their position openly. To live, they had to hide, and writing was the best disguise. The *érudits libertins* were hidden unbelievers who carried out a silent revolt using satirical wit and philosophical freedom. Irony was the core of erudite conversations, and mystery was its natural companion.[76] This seventeenth-century tradition continued in the late eighteenth century, when the philosophers of the late Enlightenment also had to protect themselves from censorship. Montesquieu published *Persian Letters* anonymously, and both Diderot and Voltaire used mystification to escape censors. The successive changes in Viel's identity, the altered names that he gave to architects whom he criticized, and his obsession with secrets illustrate the context of persecution surrounding the old libertine circles. Viel used mystification to strengthen his relationship with his readers. Those who could decipher his language would feel that they belonged to a circle of initiates and were implicitly urged to support his ideas.

PLAGIARISM: THE LIBRARY OF ARCHITECTURE

> What exactly is a plagiarist? It is man who is willing to set himself up as an author at any price, but having neither the genius nor the necessary talent for that, not only copies sentences, but pages and entire excerpts from other authors and is dishonest enough not to quote them; ... nothing is more common in the *République des lettres*.[77]

Montesquieu wrote that an original work was almost always destined to generate five or six hundred others because authors would use the originals like mathematicians use their formulas.[78] Viel wanted his work to be a critical assessment of late-eighteenth-century scholarship and erudition. *Lettres* is a revolt against the power of the book and the flourishing of erudite works in the 1780s. Viel characterized architectural scholarship as thousands of authors endlessly plagiarizing one another. It seemed to him that architects did not write but instead copied from other sources. It is true that eighteenth-century authors did not quote or credit their sources, even when using them extensively. Viel suggested that architectural theory in the 1780s had generated as many as twelve hundred books written on architecture. To him, this architectural debate was profitable only for the business of printing. Nonetheless, as a writer, Viel had to rely on existing works. *Lettres* is a self-conscious compilation – albeit an ironic one – of the erudite library.

Viel wanted to provide an authentic historical vision of architecture, but he surveyed fields that he did not know first-hand and reiterated ideas from other authors, including their use of allegory and other literary techniques. For his theory of the origins of architecture, he developed ideas that had not yet appeared in architectural treatises but that had already been presented by Montfaucon,[79] Court de Gébelin,[80] and Pluche.[81] His ideas were not as personal as he wanted them to be, and he never fully acknowledged the extent of his debt to the works from which he drew. Viel noted that architects did not consult what he called the "stone book"; although ancient monuments had been partially exhumed and published by antiquarians and archaeologists, they were still buried under what he called the "other book," the multitude of scholarly publications. He firmly believed that texts are credible only if they rely on physical evidence, and he advocated the absolute value of the monuments by scrutinizing antiquarian scholarship as well as Vitruvian academicism. His theory of the origins of architecture, based on the free-standing stone, was not completely original. Fischer von Erlach[82] and Inigo Jones[83] had already reflected on the site of Stonehenge, but the *Recueil d'antiquités* by Caylus[84] was probably Viel's greatest source of inspiration. "Everything proves that, for the ancients, the monument was the book they presented to posterity."[85]

Although he mentioned other authors in the footnotes, Viel never really discussed his textual sources. Instead, he gathered scattered material from historical, antiquarian, and philosophical works. The conceptual frame of the *Lettres* is based on linguistic, archaeological, and historical sources.

At a time when many philosophers were trying to establish a link between language and architecture, Viel worked like an eighteenth-century scholar to reconstruct a complete account of the origins of architecture. Underlying Viel's concept of origins was a belief in a universal language from which all subsequent languages had developed. Like all of Viel's ideas on the agricultural and symbolic genius, this idea was drawn from *Le Monde primitif*.[86] Court de Gébelin also provided him with the idea that architecture originated in a coherent agricultural civilization. With the development of genealogy in the late eighteenth century, ancient civilization was no longer conceived of as an autonomous era but as a milestone from which the premises of the modern world could be traced. Viel tried to understand why the ancient world privileged the symbol without explaining it. He thought that the ancient world was without history because it was eternal. Rooted in nature, the first symbols were part of a primitive language whose iconography was still evident in buildings.

Although most eighteenth-century architects were concerned with the origins of architecture, *Lettres* occupied a special place in eighteenth-century discourse. Viel perverted the sources, both ancient and modern, and his work did not belong to any recognized genre or aesthetic category. A review published in the *Mercure de France* in September 1785 shows how *Lettres* was received:[87] "The ideas that Mr. Viel de Saint-Maux has developed in this work are too peculiar for him to pretend they will be generally adopted, but too remarkable to be kept silent."[88]

TRAVELLERS

> Persons may come and go, but it seems that philosophy does not travel; thus the philosophy of one people is not suitable for another. The reason is obvious, at least for faraway countries: there are only four kinds of men who travel the oceans: sailors, merchants, soldiers and missionaries.[89]

In the late eighteenth century travellers reached faraway worlds where they thought history was still alive. Foreign lands seemed like ideal conjunctions of past and present, where memories of an unfinished past could be revived. Travel accounts helped historians to reconstruct the evolution of human societies. When travellers encountered primitive societies, they thought that they were witnessing early human civilizations.

This prompted them to become historians and anthropologists for the societies that they visited.[90]

Viel used travel accounts to try to establish a linguistic kinship between the Orient and the Occident. He believed in a primitive universal civilization with a unique allegorical language. Human memory of primitive time had faded when the invention of the alphabet led to the loss of allegorical writing. When allegory was misinterpreted, it became history and mythology. With the advent of the alphabet, reason triumphed over imagination, yet imagination was the only means by which to understand mythology. Viel looked for the origin of customs common to all nations in similarities between practices of people who believe in God and practices of idolatrous nations. He drew most of his ideas from the travel accounts of Richard Pococke,[91] Engelbert Kaempfer, Caylus, Frederick Norden,[92] and Corneille de Bruine. Abbé Pluche provided Viel with the theory of an agricultural and astrological origin of the cults and religions of ancient people.[93] Pluche questioned the objectivity of historians and stated that all narratives are not equally credible.[94] Viel relied on Pluche extensively and quarrelled with historians and travellers about their descriptions as well as their interpretations.

Viel noted that Corneille de Bruine possessed only some drawing skills but still attempted to reconstruct a genesis of the world and to develop complex theories. He criticized Corneille de Bruine's travel accounts for what he considered a disregard for monuments. Viel also castigated his method: instead of presenting architectural vestiges, he made only useless drawings; when he found an interesting capital, he made "a drawing of a duck he ate." Viel scorned Corneille de Bruine for recording "the number of birds he killed, the flies he caught, and the stork nest he found in a column in Persepolis, and for describing the stem of the rhubarb as being a delicious food."[95] Norden was not spared. To Viel, he was no more learned, and he travelled through Egypt without learning anything from the monuments. Unable to understand their meaning, he recorded impressions of useless things such as water markings that floods left on rocks.

Relativism was inherent in eighteenth-century epistemology. At the heart of Locke's empiricism was the idea that knowledge and moral ideas are bound by experience, so values and beliefs are related to time and place. In *Persian Letters* Montesquieu used the satiric possibilities of relativism because he realized that laughter could change people's attitudes. By subverting the language of authority (the pope and the king), Montesquieu made the reader laugh at a whole system of belief. Looking at Christianity and European values through the eyes of the Persian, the reader realizes that his self-image and the world that he knows are relative to his human experience.[96] In the *Supplément au voyage de Bougainville* Diderot gave a full philosophical account of persiflage. A confrontation between the savage inhabitants of an island and a priest visiting them resulted in a burlesque reversal when the behaviour of the savages turned out to be more moral than that of the priest.[97] Relativism was an important idea for Viel. He thought that the primary mistake of modern artists was tracing the origins of architecture, science, and arts only through Italy.[98] He noted that when Pococke measured the vestiges of Egypt, he felt compelled to compare their dimensions to modern prescriptions for the orders. To Viel, Pococke was totally impervious to the genius of ancient peoples and failed to realize that a completely different mind was responsible for the design of these monuments.[99] Similarly, Pococke described his encounter with people who "worship evil" without indicating that the word has a different meaning in those countries. Viel did not trust translations either. To him, the French translation made Pococke "sound at the same time both learned and plain stupid,"[100] and the translations of the accounts of Kempfer's travels to Japan were ludicrous.[101] Viel suggested that most authors travel to avoid boredom.[102] Although he ridiculed those who have not travelled but claim to be able to instruct the reader about the world, Viel's only journeys were through France, as a phoney apprentice. He relied on travel accounts from the 1750s to develop his theory of the origins of civilization and architecture.

Some travellers developed an understanding of history by studying Greek and Latin sources during their travels. Ancient authors, especially Herodotus, often served as eighteenth-century guides.[103] In the late Enlightenment, historians tried to establish the linearity of knowledge and progress. Western civilization looked for its roots and the lineaments of its development in the historicity of newly discovered places. The ancient texts were still their primary means of knowledge and a testimony to the initial experience of humanity.[104]

Although travellers experienced the sensible world directly, previous scholarly knowledge still constituted the core around which interpretations were built. Travellers approached new places with earlier texts in mind, and their journeys were described in literary reminiscences. Their accounts were characteristic of a period that was anxious to record the content of the universe. At the end of the eighteenth century the representation of knowledge was still driven by the encyclopaedic spirit, especially among travellers whose cultural heritage and vocation embraced several disciplines. Although travellers were supposed to be objective witnesses, learned men were expected to establish linguistic and religious filiations among peoples, using symbolism and allegory. Viel wanted to escape banality by recovering an art free of rules. Finding a universal origin would liberate architecture from academic tradition. "Yes, sir, in Africa, Arabia, Persia and the Great India we see people and even empires that are still agricultural and live like the first inhabitants of the earth."[105] To Viel, a theory of architectural origins based on a history of built forms would not be viable; instead, he advocated a religious and spiritual history. Viel felt that only primitive customs and monuments could reveal true origins. Urbain Chevreau had discussed the advantages of history as well as the qualities necessary to write history properly.[106] He indicated who should become a historian, defined the historian's duties, and warned of mistakes to avoid. Viel borrowed from Chevreau yet entertained a different historical attitude based on a strong belief in the value and meaning of monuments and the need to reconstruct the foundations of knowledge. Although Viel questioned the accuracy of travellers' accounts and the relevance of their interpretations, he never demonstrated the sensibilities of a true historian. In the seventeenth century the word *libertin* designated those who free themselves from moral rules, dogmas, and religious beliefs to yield to their most excessive fantasies. The meaning of the expression *libertinage érudit* was different from *libertinage tout-court*; the former was a philosophical attitude that refused dogmas and preconceived ideas. An *érudit libertin* was a learned man whose reflections were essentially philosophical but were situated within an order that he contested. They were considered erudite because of their extensive polemical and strategic use of ancient literature. By endorsing selected ideas from the ancients, erudite authors could present theses that otherwise would be considered dangerous.[107]

In the *Discours préliminaire* of the *Encyclopédie* d'Alembert divided the literary world into three parts: the erudite, the philosophers, and the *beaux-esprits*. He associated memory with the first, wisdom with the second, and attractiveness with the third. The three "republics" into which d'Alembert divided the *gens de lettres* had little in common: "The country of erudition and facts is inexhaustible; we see, so to speak, effortless acquisitions increase its substance every day. On the contrary, the country of reason and discoveries has a rather small area, and often, instead of learning there what we ignored, by dint of studying we only unlearn what we thought we knew."[108]

To d'Alembert, memory was only the beginning of reflection. The poet and the philosopher regarded the erudite as a miser who accumulated ideas without enjoying them and who piled up the vilest metals with the most precious ones in an undiscerning way. The erudite could see the words but could not recognize the facts.

In *Lettres sur l'architecture* Viel warned of the pitfalls of erudition and the scholarly methods of the late Enlightenment. He resented the endless debates on theoretical questions that revolved around texts of dubious authority. For architects, the erudite attitude of accumulation without discernment was even more dangerous at a time of unprecedented writing in all fields, especially in architecture. The last letter ends with a provocation: "We would not be unhappy if so-called learned men with hackneyed notions did not think they are experts on the architecture of ancient people. This discussion could become the most biting of any that has been raised since antiquity, considering the intimate relation between the ancient monuments and human knowledge."[109]

NOTES

1 "Rire," in Denis Diderot and Jean le Rond d'Alembert, eds, *Encyclopédie, ou Dictionnaire raisonné des sciences, des arts et des métiers, par une société de gens de lettres* (Paris: Briasson, 1751–65), vol. 14, 298: "Le ris malin, le *perfidium ridens*, est autre chose; c'est la joie de l'humiliation d'autrui: on poursuit par des éclats moqueurs, par le *cachinnum* (terme qui nous manque), celui qui nous a promis des merveilles et qui ne fait que des sottises: c'est huer plutôt que rire." All translations are mine.

2 Elisabeth Bourguinat, *Le siècle du persiflage, 1734–1789* (Paris: Presses universitaires de France, 1998), 5.

3 *Dictionnaire historique de la langue française* (Paris: Dictionnaires Le Robert, 1994): "Persifler: le mot, littéraire ou soutenu désigne l'action de se moquer de quelqu'un, et aussi de quelque chose (1776) par des paroles ironiques; ... Tous ses dérivés remontent au XVIIIe siècle: persiflage (1735), persifleur (1744)."

4 *Dictionnaire de Laveaux* (1820) and *Dictionnaire de Raymond* (1832), quoted in Bourguinat, *Le siècle du persiflage*, 7: "Se livrer à un badinage d'idées et d'expressions, qui laisse du doute ou de l'embarras sur leur véritable sens."

5 Bourguinat, *Le siècle du persiflage*, 147: "Dire plaisamment des chose sérieuses, et sérieusement des choses frivoles."

6 Ibid., 7: "Parler ironiquement, d'un ton moqueur."

7 Letter to Pierre-Joseph Thoulier d'Olivet, 5 January 1767, in Voltaire, *Correspondance de Voltaire*, ed. T. Besterman, quoted in Bourguinat, *Le siècle du persiflage*, 2: "Dès qu'une expression vicieuse s'introduit, la foule s'en empare. Dites-moi si Racine a persiflé Boileau? Si Bossuet a persiflé Pascal? Et si l'un et l'autre ont mystifié La Fontaine en abusant quelquefois de sa simplicité?"

8 Bourguinat, *Le siècle du persiflage*, 159–64.

9 *Correspondance littéraire, philosophique et critique* ..., ed. Maurice Tourneux (Paris: Garnier, 1877–82; reprint, Geneva: Slatkine, 1968), December 1763, vol. 5, 422–3.

10 Voltaire, *Lettre à Moultou*, 9 January 1763, quoted in Bourguinat, *Le siècle du persiflage*, 162–3: "répand quelques poignées de sel et d'épices dans le ragout que tu presentes [à tes lecteurs], mêle le ridicule aux raisons, tache de faire naitre l'indifférence, alors tu obtiendras surement la tolérance."

11 Jean-Jacques Rousseau, *Confessions*, bk 7, in *Oeuvres complètes* (Paris: Gallimard, 1959–95), vol. 1, 347: "Je formais la le projet d'une feuille périodique intitulée *Le Persifleur*, que nous devions faire alternativement Diderot et moi."

12 Elisabeth Bourguinat, "Rousseau persifleur?" *Dix-huitième siècle* 26 (1994): 453–63 at 456: "faire l'analyse des ouvrages nouveaux qui paraitront, d'y joindre son sentiment et de communiquer l'un et l'autre au public."

13 "trait d'esprit."

14 Bourguinat, "Rousseau persifleur?" 460.

15 Rousseau, *Oeuvres complètes*, vol. 11, 34: "Après avoir commencé par me persifler moi-même, j'aurai tout le temps de persifler les autres."

16 Letter 7, n4. Letter numbers and pages refer to Jean-Louis Viel de Saint-Maux, *Lettres sur l'architecture des anciens, et celle des modernes* (Paris, 1787; reprint, Geneva: Minkoff, 1974). Viel's *Considérations sur l'origine de la peinture et du language* was never mentioned in any bibliography.

17 Jean-Marie Pérouse de Montclos, "Charles-François Viel, architecte de

l'Hopital Général, et Jean-Louis Viel de Saint-Maux, architecte, peintre et avocat au Parlement de Paris," *Bulletin de la Société de l'Histoire de l'Art Français* (1966): 257–69.

18 In French, the cuckold is called *cocu*, but also *cornard*, the one who bears horns. To be a cuckold is also "to wear horns."

19 Viel's *Antidote contre les cocus* was published as an anonymous work (Paris: Mme Veaufleury, 1785) and first attributed to Charles-François Viel by the *Bibliographie de la France* (1820).

20 Charles-Louis Montesquieu, *Lettres persanes* (1721; reprint, Paris: Flammarion, 1979). Written during the reign of Louis XIV, *Lettres* was published anonymously during the Regency to avoid censorship.

21 Bourguinat, *Le siècle du persiflage*, 178: "esprit sérieux."

22 Voltaire, "Lettre à Mr. Nordberg," in preface to new edition of *Histoire de Charles XII* (1744), quoted in Ernst Cassirer, *The Philosophy of the Enlightenment* (Princeton: Princeton University Press, 1951), 222–3.

23 Charles-Louis Montesquieu, *Cahiers: 1716–1755*, ed. Bernard Grasset (Paris: Grasset, 1941), 8–9.

24 Ibid.

25 Letter 1, 9–10.

26 Letter 6, 8.

27 Letter 1, 13; and Letter 2, 22.

28 Letter 6, 10.

29 Ibid. Viel refers to the French order. Designs by C.-A. d'Aviler and Roland le Virloys included ostrich feathers. Viel thought that to create a French order architects should work not with a pen but with a pick, excavating around the Mediterranean coast to retrieve the altars and the columns on which the ancients performed sacrifices; see Letter 6, n9.

30 "Mystification" is another eighteenth-century neologism that first appeared in 1768; see *Dictionnaire historique de la langue française*.

31 Letter 6, 15. Viel aims at Serlio, who "preaches," and at Delorme, who writes "sermons."

32 Letter 1, 11. In Viel's words, such descriptions were worthy of Rabelais.

33 "ratelier de dents."

34 Letter 6, 16.

35 Voltaire, *Facéties* (Paris: Presses universitaires de France, 1973), 33: "Vous avez rendu service au genre humain en vous déchaînant sagement contre les ouvrages faits pour le pervertir." Commenting on *Lettres persanes*,

Voltaire replied to Montesquieu in *Remerciement sincère à un homme charitable* (Amsterdam: Lausanne, 1761).

36 Letter 1, 13.

37 Letter 6, 8–9.

38 Letter 6.

39 Letter 7, 15.

40 In the Introduction to *Lettres*, speaking of Claude Perrault as "the illustrious Perrault, the first architect of France," Viel affirmed that the proceeds from his book would be devoted to building a monument dedicated to Perrault. Also, a sequel of *Lettres* that he planned to write, addressing the Peruvian and Brahman monuments, would be a tribute to Perrault. Viel praised Perrault for the colonnade of the Louvre, stating that it was the only instance of modern architecture where the parts could not be separated from the whole. Ironically, Perrault was not really the author of the colonnade.

41 Viel refers to Claude Perrault, *Les dix livres d'architecture de Vitruve, corrigés et traduits nouvellement en Français, avec des notes et des figures* (Paris: Coignard, 1673).

42 Letter 1, 15: "bon-homme."

43 Letter 6, 10. To Viel, Fréart de Chambray's *Parallèle de l'architecture antique avec la moderne* and the theory developed by Claude Perrault in *Ordonnance des cinq espèces de colonnes* should have put an end to the debate on the orders.

44 Letter 6, 12.

45 In Letter 2, 22, he uses the word "réjouissant." In Letter 7, 18, he uses "récreatif."

46 "chaise percée."

47 Letter 6, 13.

48 Letter 6, 18.

49 Viel opposes ancients and moderns. By "modern" he means the period beginning with the Italian Renaissance; by "ancient" he means ancient Greece and Rome. In "ancient people" he includes Gauls and Etruscans but also a chain of people linking Europe to Asia, Africa, and the New World.

50 Marc-Antoine Laugier, *Essai sur l'architecture* (Paris: Duchesne, 1753, 1755).

51 Letter 1, 11: "Que seraient des hommes qui ne s'élèveraient à ce qu'il y a de plus distingué dans les Arts, que par l'effet du hasard, et sans tenir aucune route sure, sans principe et sans vue?"

52 Germain Boffrand, author of the *Livre d'architecture* (Paris: G. Cavelier, 1745), is criticized for his ideas on taste, for writing in Latin, and for using Horace's *Ars poetica*; see Letter 7, 28.

53 Letter 3, 26.

54 "Toiseur," in Diderot and d'Alembert, eds, *Encyclopédie*, vol. 16, 385: "The functions of the *toiseur* are to measure the works every week so the workers are paid what is owed to them; he gives a copy of the measurements (*toisé*) to the contractor and one to the engineer."

55 "Imposture," in ibid., vol. 8, 600–1.

56 Letter 1, 13.

57 Alain Le Bihan, *Francs-maçons parisiens du Grand Orient de France* (Paris: Bibliothèque nationale, 1966), 478. See also Anthony Vidler, *The Writing of the Walls* (Princeton: Princeton Architectural Press, 1987), 139–46, n18.

58 Pérouse de Montclos, "Charles-François Viel."

59 Etienne Parrocel, *Histoire documentaire de l'Académie de peinture et de sculpture de Marseille* (Paris: Impr. Nationale, 1889–90).

60 Pérouse de Montclos, "Charles-François Viel."

61 "Avocat au parlement, peintre et architecte."

62 Jean-Louis Viel de Saint-Maux, *Observations philosophiques sur l'usage d'exposer les ouvrages de peinture et de sculpture à Mme la baronne de Vassé* (The Hague and Paris: Bleuet, 1785). Attributed to Charles-François Viel by the *Bibliographie de la France* (1820).

63 Pérouse de Montclos, "Charles-François Viel."

64 "Architecte civil et militaire, Associé de l'Académie royale des Beaux-Arts et Architecture navale de Marseille, et Correspondant de plusieurs Académies."

65 Charles-François Viel (1745–1818) studied with Chalgrin and was the architect of the Hopital général. He designed mostly hospitals, and his practice is well documented: he engraved all his designs and published them with essays as his *Oeuvres complètes* in five volumes. He also published *De la construction des édifices publics sans l'emploi du fer …* (Paris: J.-J. Fuchs, 1803). He is known mainly for his polemical work *Décadence de l'architecture à la fin du XVIIIème siècle* (Paris: Chez l'auteur et Perronneau, 1800), where he condemns Rococo and what he called the last generation of architects, Soufflot, Ledoux, and Boullée. His theoretical position and literary style are completely different from those of Viel de Saint-Maux.

66 For a detailed account, see Pérouse de Montclos, "Charles-François Viel."

67 Letter 6, n21.
68 Letter 7, n23.
69 Letter 6, 20, 22, 23.
70 Letter 6, 23: "Mais tandis que le particulier ignore que l'Architecte instruit peut le tirer des mains de la cupidité, le Maçon fait des constructions à sa guise, et propose des rues nouvelles."
71 Letter 7, 7.
72 "Introduction," in *Lettres*, viii.
73 Viel's correspondents are Monsieur le Comte de Wannestin; Monsieur le Duc de Luxembourg; Monsieur le Comte de Buffon; Messieurs des Academies Imperiales des sciences, Belles-Lettres, et Arts de Saint-Petersbourg; Messieurs de l'Academie Royale des Sciences et Belles-Lettres de Berlin; Monsieur le baron de Marivetz; and Monsieur le Comte de Vaudreuil.
74 Letter 1, 28.
75 René Pintard, *Le libertinage érudit dans la première moitié du XVIIème siècle* (Geneva and Paris: Slatkine, 1983), 121.
76 Ibid., 371–7.
77 "Plagiat," in Diderot and d'Alembert, eds, *Encyclopédie*, vol. 12, 679.
78 Montesquieu, *Cahiers*, 8–9: "Un ouvrage original en fait presque toujours construire cinq ou six cents autres; ces derniers se servant du premier à peu pres comme les géomètres se servent de leurs formules."
79 R.P. Dom Bernard de Montfaucon (1655–1741), *L'antiquité expliquée, et representée en figures* (Paris: F. Delaulne, 1719).
80 Antoine Court de Gébelin, *Le monde primitif* (Paris: Chez l'auteur, 1775).
81 Noël-Antoine Pluche (1688–1761), *Histoire du ciel: Où l'on recherche l'origine de l'idolatrie, et les méprises de la philosophie, sur la formation des corps célestes, & de toute la nature* (Paris: Estienne, 1748).
82 Johann Bernhard Fischer von Erlach, *Entwurff einer historischen Architectur* (Leipzig, 1725; reprint, Farnborough, UK: Gregg, 1964), bk 2, 14: "Surprenante structure de rochers en Angleterre dite Stonehengs, chorea gigantum, ou la danse des géants." Fischer considered this structure to be a monument: "Cette structure est moins surprenante par la grandeur des pièces, que par l'entreprise de les ranger. L'on voit d'abord, que ce sont des monuments d'un age, qui ne nous laisse plus de mémoire de leur fondation."
83 Inigo Jones, *Description of Stonehenge …* (London: n.p., 1725), 38.
84 Anne-Claude-Philippe, Comte de Caylus (1692–1765), was an engraver, academician, and patron of the arts. The Académie royale de peinture et

de sculpture accepted him in 1731 with the title of Amateur. From 1750 to 1753, he published many articles on the salons in the *Mercure de France* and on painting for the academy. In 1714 he travelled to Italy, Greece, and Turkey. In 1761–64 he published the *Recueil d'antiquités*, where he discussed the signification of the "raised stones." Caylus elaborated a myth of the origins of architecture radically opposed to that of Laugier since to the primitive hut he opposed the nonfunctional and grandiose "megalith" raised by an unknown people. His argument is based on the discovery, in the vicinity of Poitiers, of the monument that he calls "Pierre levée," anterior to the Roman monuments and which he attributes to the early Gauls. In a way more rational than Viel, Caylus had a conception of classical antiquity that not only included the canonical Greek and Roman monuments, but also extended to a larger field, including Oriental.

85 "Introduction," in *Lettres*, 10: "Tout prouve que le monument parmi les Anciens était le livre qu'ils offraient à la postérité."

86 Court de Gébelin, *Le Monde primitif*.

87 Quoted in Pérouse de Montclos, "Charles-François Viel."

88 "Les idées que M. Viel de Saint-Maux a développées dans cet Ouvrage, sont trop singulières, pour que l'Auteur puisse prétendre à les voir adopter généralement, mais elles sont trop remarquables aussi pour devoir être passées sous silence."

89 Jean-Jacques Rousseau, *Discours sur l'origine, et les fondements de l'inégalité parmi les hommes* (Paris, 1755; reprint, Paris: Flammarion, 1971), part 1, 193n1.

90 Nicole Hafid-Martin, *Voyage et connaissance au tournant des lumières, 1780–1820* (Oxford: Voltaire Foundation, 1995), 123–30.

91 A British traveller and clergyman, Richard Pococke (1704–65) travelled through the East from 1737 to 1742, collecting many ancient inscriptions. He published the first volume of *Description of the East and Some Other Countries* in 1743, the second volume in 1745, later enriched with a collection of Greek and Latin inscriptions. They were translated into French in 1771.

92 Frederic-Louis Norden (1708–42) was a Danish traveller and captain of the Royal Danish Navy. A draftsman and an engraver, he went to Egypt in 1737 with a mission to describe and draw antique monuments. His work *Voyage d'Egypte et de Nubie*, with 159 plates and maps, was published after his death (Copenhagen, 1752, 1755). The work was praised for the

ingenuity of the techniques of architectural representation and its documentary interest, and it was published again with notes and additions in 1795 and 1798.

93 Pluche, *Histoire du ciel*, bk 1, 17–26; bk 2, 372.

94 "Plan de cet ouvrage," in ibid., bk 1, iii–xxxvii.

95 Letter 3, 22.

96 Uzbek, the Persian visiting Paris, sees despotism in Europe but does not see it in his own society's harems, slaves, eunuchs, and so forth.

97 Diderot, *Supplément au voyage de Bougainville* (c. 1772; reprint, Paris: Flammarion, 1972), 176: "Oh the naughty country! If everything is ordered there as you are telling me, you are more barbaric than us" (spoken by the character Orou).

98 Letter 8, 15.

99 Letter 2, 17.

100 Letter 3, 23.

101 Ibid., 24.

102 Ibid., 21.

103 On Jean Potocki's use of Herodotus, see Hafid-Martin, *Voyage et connaissance*, 123–31.

104 Ibid., 175–7.

105 Letter 3, 5.

106 Urbain Chevreau, *Chevranea, ou Diverses pensées d'histoire, de critique, d'érudition et de morale* (Paris: Chez Florentin et Pierre Delaulne, 1700), vol. 2, 277.

107 Charles Daubert, "Le 'libertinage érudit': Problèmes de définition," in Antony McKenna and Pierre-François Moreau, eds, *Libertinage philosophique au XVIIème siècle*, 11–25 (Saint-Etienne: Publications de l'Université de Saint-Etienne, 1996).

108 Jean le Rond d'Alembert, "Discours préliminaire," in Diderot and d'Alembert, eds, *Encyclopédie*, vol. 1, xx.

109 Letter 7, 38.

The Hybrid: Labrouste's Paestum[1]

Martin Bressani

Chora

NINETEENTH-CENTURY ARCHITECTURE has always suffered from bad press within the discipline. Troubled by its recycling of historical forms and stylistic eclecticism, architects, critics, and historians have generally viewed it as a period of transition, a rather curious and shameful moment of inertia in Western architecture. In particular, early modernists vehemently stigmatized the period, viewing it as an era of revivalism and pastiche. In 1905 Dutch architect Hendrik Petrus Berlage called it a "*religious interregnum* between two cultural eras," going further to say that all "neo-historical styles" are (of necessity) "temporary episodes."[2] At the same time, Werkbund-master Hermann Muthesius bluntly labelled the era "inartistic." He characterized the nineteenth century as having "reshaped" every field but the "plastic arts," where it "played no role."[3] Even before such modernist polemics had been voiced, as early as the 1830s, the influential collector Thomas Hope ended his *Historical Essay on Architecture* with a call for an architecture that could properly express the dynamics of the nineteenth century.[4] Despite Hope's invectives, not to mention the stigma associated with historicist architecture, it flourished unabated well into the next century.

The shadow of nostalgia indeed lurks around architecture produced during the nineteenth century, that obscure transitional era when preindustrial ways of living and modes of production mixed with new technological inventions that transformed social life and human values, work and production, building, transportation, and communication. Shocked by the revolutionary violence that plagued the century, challenged by rapid changes in the domain of technology, architects seemingly had no choice but to seek refuge in the past. Increasingly fascinated by history, many refused to confront the widening gap between their architectural figments and the new world of production and satisfied themselves with the illusion of rootedness and continuity that a thick historicist mantel could confer on the architectural object.

However, burdens can sometimes be transformed into insights. The heavy mask of the architecture of the bourgeois city – so well exemplified by Garnier's monstrous opera in Paris (fig. 4.1) – wields a power all its own. A Baroque masquerade, it verges on kitsch but at the same time introduces a theatrical aspect into urban life.[5] The pompous boulevards of nineteenth-century Paris express frivolity and a certain hypocrisy, but also a joyfulness that invokes a carnivalesque atmosphere. From this sprang the "banquet years"[6] of early modernism, when living itself be-

4.1 Charles Garnier, sculptural detail in ceiling of the coach drop-off, Opera, Paris, 1863–75. Photograph by author.

came a special form of performance. Part of the secret of this rich moment in the history of the arts, according to Roger Shattuck, "lies no deeper than this surface aspect."[7] The revival of the grotesque at the end of the century – the cabaret scenes, the plays of Alfred Jarry – is couched in the theatricality inherent in the life of the *boulevardier*. We commonly associate the florid allegories of Art Nouveau with these unbridled years. But is that style so different from the strange hybrids produced earlier by Garnier, Ballu, Lefuel, Manguin, Esperandieu, Abadie, and other proponents of an architectural teratology long condemned at the modernist altar of authenticity?

The modernists' claim to "truthfulness" eventually would turn them against the seductions of the theatre.[8] Grain silos stood against Garnier's opera. There may well be an oedipal configuration in modernism's effort to divest itself of nineteenth-century affectation, liquidating the place of its birth. Its quest for autonomy – best illustrated in our context by Le Corbusier's desire to destroy Paris altogether – takes the form of a man struggling to deny his origins in order to become, in a sense, his own father.

Of course, it has been integral to the modern idea since Descartes to affirm identity by seeking to overcome the immediate past. As Octavio Paz succinctly expressed in a famous lecture, to be "modern" involves "a continual breaking away, a ceaseless splitting apart."[9] For Paz, it was not the twentieth-century avant-garde but nineteenth-century Romanticism that first put irony at the centre of artistic experimentation. The Romantics developed a taste for the transgressive, the strange, and the grotesque. Their poetry pioneered the exploration of "the underground regions of dream, unconscious thought and eroticism."[10] Can we thus see the "historical-mindedness" of nineteenth-century eclectic architects, their shameful "nostalgia," as a paradoxical act of "breaking away"? Isn't their technique of "masking" the most conspicuous form of scenography, their eclecticism, an overt espousal of heterogeneity? The very shame of the nineteenth-century historicist architect betrays the burden of irony. After the rupture of the French Revolution, historical monuments indeed appeared as sacred fragments to be preserved, remnants of an alien and fractured cosmos from which architects sought to reconstruct the bourgeois city. Romantics longed for a "restoration" of the past, but they themselves lived in transitional time. If the past could ever be relived, it could be only in the form of a dream.

Curiously, it is in the work of a rationalist who rebelled against his own century that we find the most succinct expression of the nineteenth-century eclectic method. In a significant passage of his *Entretiens sur l'architecture*, French architect and theoretician Viollet-le-Duc explains the creative process as an operation of memory that *must* integrate a measure of forgetfulness. After asserting that architecture cannot be based on pure invention, he describes the principle of formation of a new architecture by telling the story of a hypothetical barbarian who visits ancient Rome and, stunned by the magnificence of its monuments, returns home with the firm intention of recreating it:

The objects seen by him assume in his memory strange forms, like those which pass in dreams. What is great leaves on his mind the remembrance of something gigantic: if he has seen large masses lifted by powerful machines, these machines are transformed into monstrous beings; the sculptures are animated; the paintings look and speak. On returning to his native country, he desires to assemble his recollections. His passive imagination is feverishly excited, he too would build; but his active imagination sleeps, and can scarcely help him to produce from so many lively and poetical impressions some crude buildings.[11]

Yet it is from such "crude" hybrids that a new architecture is born, an architecture that emerges from memories animated and deformed. Thanks to the poetic distortions of a fevered imagination, the past is recreated as something supernatural and monstrous. What is most crucial to Viollet-le-Duc is the dynamic deformation generated by memory. Only from distorted remembrances can new significations arise. Unfortunately, he laments, "civilized man's" memory, unlike that of the "primitive barbarian," is "a dry catalogue"; in the presence of any phenomenon, "his passive imagination presents to him nothing more than the fact – he does not attribute this phenomenon to any supernatural influence."[12] So he concludes that "man needs some barbarian element, just as the soil needs manure; for production requires a process of mental fermentation, resulting from contrasts, from dissimilarities."[13] In his famous lectures at the École des Beaux-Arts in 1863, Viollet-le-Duc advised moderns to plunge back in time to the world that fits least easily in the "dry catalogue" of our minds: the animated and primitive universe of myth.

Architectural theory, of course, has always harked back to the primitive. In the Enlightenment this meant a return to an archaic simplicity, free of the conventions of civilization, but by the late eighteenth century the historical plot had thickened considerably. As antiquarians and early ethnologists encountered a primitive world increasingly more diverse and complex in its manifestations, the image of the "noble savage" was slowly eroded by new knowledge about rituals involving strange, even alien symbolism – particularly concerning religious cults of the Orient. The impact of this new knowledge on architectural thought is diffuse and difficult to track. However, the first stirrings of a reassessment of classical orthodoxy in mainstream debates in France are generally associated with the controversial issue of polychrome decoration of ancient Greek buildings. Architects and antiquarians of the first decades of the nineteenth century speculated that decorative schemes of a symbolic or ritualistic nature were rendered in variegated colour to enliven the sober language of the classical orders. It was the architect Henri Labrouste (1801–75) and his Romantic circle who would exploit this new vision of the ancient world to its fullest implications. It is thanks to Labrouste's generation that the discipline of architecture developed a new historical imagination.

Labrouste's famous restoration project of the ancient Greek temples at Paestum in southern Italy is widely recognized as a key document that *defined* the new attitude. The story of the project is well known.[14] Drawn in 1828–29 while the young Labrouste was a *pensionnaire* at the French Academy in Rome after having won the Grand Prix, the reconstruction project prompted a major academic controversy and was quickly hailed as the first Romantic manifesto in architecture. With the support of his friends Félix Duban, Louis Duc, and Léon Vaudoyer, Labrouste initiated his revolt against the eternal truths of academic classicism through a philosophical interpretation of the past that sought to understand the very nature of historical development.[15] The projects of Labrouste's circle manipulated and mixed historical types in search of a new synthesis. Some of their most remarkable buildings were partial restorations that combined new work with ancient architectural fragments, betraying obvious delight in the heterogeneity of forms. In these complex works, history was transformed into spatial and tectonic narratives and the experience of buildings into promenades through time.[16]

The three Doric temples at Paestum stand enigmatically in a row on a level plain on the Bay of Salerno, south of Naples (fig. 4.2). Built of a golden stone that marvelously catches the changing Mediterranean light, and sited between sea and mountain, these imposing structures were ideal monuments to stir a Romantic imagination. This unique set of temples, built between 550 and 460 B.C., had attracted the attention of architects and antiquarians long before Labrouste arrived in Italy. In the second half of the eighteenth century, Paestum indeed had emerged as the privileged site for investigations of the question of architectural beginnings. The temple complex at Paestum was a rare example of Greek architecture in Italy, more readily accessible to European architects and antiquarians than sites in Greece. Further, and perhaps more important, the monuments at Paestum were believed to hark back to the rise of the Doric tradition itself. Their presence on Italian soil heightened their

4.2 View of Paestum from the Eastern Gate, in Claude-Mathieu Delagardette, *Les ruines de Paestum ou Posidonia* (Paris: Barbou, an VII [1799]), plate 2. Private collection.

enigmatic character and stimulated much speculation about their origin. The French, under the impulse of Jacques-Germain Soufflot (1713–80), were the first to "rediscover" the site: the robustly primitive form of the Paestum temple was ideally suited to the neoclassical exaltation of rational values associated with structural elementarity and a return to natural simplicity. To find in Italy such a splendid example of primitive Doric architecture lent credence to the notion of a continuous classical tradition from Greece to Italy, leading to France of the modern age. Italian antiquarians and architects were obviously less inclined to regard the Italian peninsula as merely a transition point between Greece and France. Mario Guarnacci, Giovanni Piranesi, and Paulantonio Paoli argued that the Paestum temples represented a kind of *Ur*-architecture for an Italian tradition independent of the Greek, built by Etruscans who followed the true way of building in stone derived from Egypt and Asia Minor.[17]

These controversies had somewhat died down by the time Labrouste first arrived at Paestum in 1826, the Greek character of the Temple of Neptune – the biggest and most prominent of the three structures – having been firmly established in 1799 by the rigorous archaeological work of a French architect, Claude Mathieu Delagardette (1762–1805).[18] The two other temples, however, remained ambivalent in Delagardette's work: originally built before the Temple of Neptune, they had been, according to him, subjected to a later restoration by the Romans following their conquest of Magna Graecia. The indecisive character of these "minor" structures left the door open to further speculation, an opportunity that was not lost on Labrouste. In his own roundabout way, Labrouste would revive the old polemic of universal continuity versus national specificity. At Paestum, Labrouste documented how Greek architecture was altered when it was introduced to the foreign soil of Italy. What he sought to understand was the principle of architectural invention from its beginning. What he documented, however, was a process of architectural hybridization of Greek and Etruscan architecture. Studying in detail the transformation of an architecture, Labrouste confronted a striking example of the phenomenon for which Cuban historian and anthropologist Fernando Ortiz coined the term "transculturation" – not merely the transformation of one culture by contact with another, but a dynamic process that involves the uprooting and transplantation of an established culture to a new geographic and cultural context, resulting in a completely new third phenomenon.[19] Like his compatriots in the eighteenth century, Labrouste was arguing for a transnational continuity of the classical tradition, but instead of being understood through the stability of a set of universal canonic forms, it was conceived through a process of metamorphic transformation. This merging and mutation of previously distinct traditions into a new third cultural phenomenon was not far from Viollet-le-Duc's concept of mnemonic fermentation.

The great scandal generated by Labrouste's submission of his restoration of the temples at Paestum to the French Académie des Beaux-Arts in 1829 has long puzzled historians.[20] Indeed, little seems to distinguish it from traditional restorations produced at the same time in the French Academy at Rome.[21] Labrouste won the Grand Prix in 1824 and proposed the Paestum project as his fourth-year *envoi*, customarily the most ambitious restoration project carried out during a *pensionnaire*'s sojourn in Rome.[21] Typically, fourth-year *envois* comprised meticulously measured drawings of ancient (preferably Roman) classical monuments in their existing state, juxtaposed with careful reconstruction drawings of the monuments in what was imagined to be their original state. Although fourth-year *envois* often included historical information about the building, the aim of the investigation was not to elucidate a monument's historical meaning but to present it as a canonic example or model within a universal classical tradition. The kind of archaeology carried out at the French Academy was not scientific.[22] Although their work began with the focused – and often rigorous – collection of physical (archaeological) data, it was nourished by the prevailing tradition of the Ecole des Beaux-Arts in Paris, where "academic archaeology" was a speculative science directed toward contemporary practice. Labrouste's *envoi* was no exception. As a work of architectural theory, it was prone, as we will see, to imaginative reconstruction. However, Labrouste was not seeking canonic models at Paestum but reflecting on the nature of architectural development. Paestum, with its three distinct structures spanning roughly 120 years, enabled him to study historicity, unlike the customary single monument. Paestum was also a colony far from the cultural centres of Greece and Rome and thus was susceptible to architectural transformations caused by a combination of influences.

Labrouste could take as his starting point the relative dating for the three temples at Paestum established since the first scholarly account published by Thomas Major in 1768,[23] which was sustained by David Leroy and later by Quatremère de Quincy, a dating still considered valid today.[24] The Basilica, an odd structure with cigar-shaped Doric columns, was thought to be the earliest or most "primitive" (fig. 4.3). The Temple of Ceres, nearer in form to the canonic Doric temples of Greece, but with squat proportions and an unorthodox plan, was positioned second in the chronology (fig. 4.4). The Temple of Neptune, the largest and nearest to the Attic Doric temple type, was considered the most recent (fig. 4.5). The evolution of the profile of the *echinus* of the Doric capital was the standard key to this dating schema: the more convex and bulbous, the more primitive; the flatter, the more evolved.

The most obviously heretical aspect of Labrouste's restoration project was his challenge to the conventional chronology. Labrouste did not assign specific dates to each of the three temples but ranked the more classic Temple of Neptune as the earliest. He reasoned that the temple closest to the Greek canonic form was built first since the Greek settlers at Paestum would have observed their traditions most faithfully in the early years of the colony, when their memories of the motherland were still fresh. After several generations, new constructions would have lost the "primitive purity" of the Greek models as builders and architects gradually adapted their methods and technologies to local influences and conditions. Labrouste argued that the intelligent use of two different kinds of stone to build the Temple of Ceres and the Basilica – in contrast

4.3 The Basilica, Paestum, c. 550 B.C. Photograph McGill University, School of Architecture.

4.4 Top: Temple of Ceres, façade restored, in Henri Labrouste, *Les temples de Paestum* (Paris: Firmin-Didot et cie., 1877), plate 13. Private collection.

4.5 Bottom: Temple of Neptune, façade restored, in Henri Labrouste, *Les temples de Paestum* (Paris: Firmin-Didot et cie., 1877), plate 3. Private collection.

to the homogeneous composition of the Temple of Neptune – demonstrates that the builders had developed a greater knowledge of local materials. He therefore concluded that these two "hybrid" structures were built at a later date.

The basic premise of Labrouste's Paestum restoration is well known. Historian Neil Levine, the first to have studied it in detail in his groundbreaking dissertation of 1975,[25] clearly established the general intention behind Labrouste's revisionist history: the progressive modification of the Doric temple represents the formation of a new architecture that is no longer Greek but specifically "of Paestum," as Labrouste himself emphatically stated in his historical explanation.[26] The subtext, Levine argues convincingly, is that since the Greek forms changed substantially after being transplanted to the ancient Italian peninsula, they would have to be modified to a far greater extent if transplanted to nineteenth-century France. Levine concludes that "Labrouste made no attempt to set Greek forms in the context of the cross-cultural, ahistorical framework of the classical ideal. By this specificity, Labrouste offered a radical reinterpretation of Greek architecture as Greek and thus called into question the fundamental quality of classicism – that eternal reappearance of supposedly similar forms in certain chosen civilizations."[27]

Levine understood Labrouste's Paestum restoration as a polemical manifesto for a new architecture, the question of historical truth being less important. He believed that Labrouste's revision of the accepted chronology was a "willful act of distortion,"[28] a tactic to make noise and get his point across. On this point, I will depart slightly from Levine's interpretation. Labrouste's revision of the traditional chronology called for a reformulation of contemporary architectural practice, and it demanded from the reader a certain suspension of disbelief. But it did so to establish the conditions in which a new historical truth could be disclosed. Historical monuments were sacred relics for the Romantics. Although often inclined toward generalizations, they would not consciously manipulate data for mere polemical purpose. Historical monuments held the key to understanding cultural evolution and the creative process itself.

We should not dismiss Levine's skepticism too quickly, however, because it does point to a troubling aspect of the restoration. How could Labrouste seriously believe that the primitive-looking Doric capital of the Basilica had been sculpted after the graceful capitals of the Temple of Neptune (figs 4.6 and 4.7)? Labrouste emphasized this paradox by

4.6 Portico (Basilica), detail of Doric capital, restored, in Henri Labrouste, *Les temples de Paestum* (Paris: Firmin-Didot et cie., 1877), plate 19. Private collection.

claiming that the Temple of Neptune was the earliest because it was the purest of the three: "It reveals not art in its infancy but art arrived at its perfection."[29] The only way to resolve such anachronism is to interpret Labrouste's account not only as the documentation of architectural transformations caused by the displacement of Greek architects to the new context of southern Italy, but also as a more engrossing story of an architecture returning to the primitive: Greek architecture travelling back in time toward its own origin.

The most telling sign that Labrouste's Paestum is not merely about the adaptation of an architecture to a new environmental context is that the "degradations" of the canonic Greek architectural forms seen in the Temple of Ceres and the Basilica came not simply from new "material" conditions, but primarily from contact between Greek and Etruscan cultures. Levine noted the Etruscan character of the Temple of Ceres: the exaggerated overhang of the raking cornice and the non-Greek proportion of the height of its crowning *sima* invoke Etruscan forms (compare figs 4.4 and 4.5). Another Etruscan influence in Labrouste's restoration of this temple is the absence of a hung ceiling in the interior (fig. 4.8). Similar elements in the Basilica are consistent with other Etruscan features discussed below. These drawn elements were certainly enough to alert his audience at the Ecole des Beaux-Arts, but Labrouste also added an explicit historical note that the interior decoration of the Temple of Ceres was inspired by frescoes he had seen in Etruscan tombs at Corneto.

4.7 Temple of Neptune, detail of Doric capital, restored, in Henri Labrouste, *Les temples de Paestum* (Paris: Firmin-Didot et cie., 1877), plate 9. Private collection.

4.8 Temple of Ceres, lateral section, restored, in Henri Labrouste, *Les temples de Paestum* (Paris: Firmin-Didot et cie., 1877), plate 11. Private collection.

The Etruscan elements in Labrouste's restoration have been somewhat neglected by historians. One possible reason is that Labrouste himself, in the very first pages of his accompanying explanation, flatly dismisses the idea that the monuments of Paestum are Etruscan. He wants to ensure that his restoration does not revive the chauvinistic debates over attribution that had been launched by Italian archaeologists in the eighteenth century. But why bring up a controversy that had been resolved, if not because his restoration was susceptible to the old issues? Labrouste obviously did not subscribe to the extravagant claims by Piranesi and Paoli that the temples of Paestum were built by Etruscans. What he does consider, however, is the Etruscan influence at Paestum – a city located at the southernmost frontier of Etruscan territory – at the moment of its Greek colonization.[30] It is the contact between Greek and Etruscan architecture that interests Labrouste, not the question of authorship.

The importance of the Etruscans for Labrouste is undeniable. Etruscan decorative elements became a leitmotif in his own work,[31] including the famous Sainte-Geneviève library. It is also well known that Labrouste and his friends at the French Academy in Rome were called "Etruscans" by sympathizers and detractors alike, a most telling sign that these primitive Italians provided a touchstone for their practice. Indeed, in 1829 Etruscan civilization conjured up a universe of meaning shared not only by Labrouste, Duban, Duc, and Vaudoyer, but also by many Romantic archaeologists, historians, philosophers, and mythographers in Italy, France, England, and Germany. The Etruscan movement belonged to Romantic Orientalism and reacted against the hegemony of Greek classicism in Western culture and thought.

In Romantic historiography – in the work of Carl Niebuhr, Karl Ottfried Muller, Georg Friedrich Creuzer, and Jules Michelet, among others – the Etruscans and the Greeks were believed to have common ancestors in the Pelasgic tribes, the proto-inhabitants of Greece, who, according to Herodotus, originally roamed the primitive Mediterranean world. According to this circle of historians and mythographers, the Etruscans alone had preserved the foundational Pelasgic myths. In contrast, the Greeks had transformed and distorted these myths, thanks to their relentless imagination. For instance, the very influential German scholar of ancient Oriental and Greek myths Georg Friedrich Creuzer (1771–1858) wrote in his *Symbolik und Mythologie der alten Völker* (1819–28) that "primitive Pelasgic Greece reveals itself in its entirety, and with its true character, only in the Antique Italy of the Etruscans."[32] Because of their alleged common ancestry, the distinction between Greeks and Etruscans is often unclear in Romantic archaeology.[33] In his study of Paestum, Labrouste himself mentions in passing that the Etruscan tombs at Corneto were built by Greeks.[34] It is unclear whether he means that Etruscans were themselves Greeks or that they had brought in Greek artists. However, it does underscore his belief in the existence of cultural exchange between the two groups.

The presence of primitive Pelasgic tribes was supported by striking architectural evidence following the discovery of cyclopean structures in Italy and Greece: gigantic city walls made of enormous polygonal blocks of stone laid without mortar. This primitive architectural form had appeared throughout the entire Mediterranean basin, even suggesting links to the monolithic Celtic monuments of Western Europe. Pelasgic monuments offered concrete evidence of a unified early Western culture. To the Romantics, who were prone to panoramic historical sweeps, it suggested the existence of a heroic monumentality that would have preceded Babel.

The French archaeologist Louis-Charles-François Petit-Radel (1756–1836) – all but forgotten today but important for the development of Romantic archaeology – was the first to recognize the distinct character of these constructions. He regarded the Pelasgic monuments as the keystone of a vast historical scheme to prove the continuity of Western civilization from the biblical Genesis to classical antiquity and medieval Europe.[35] Petit-Radel described his method as a "historical lithology."[36] For him, stone, in the form of these gigantic cyclopean walls and the chronicles carved into the walls of temples, carried the primordial and palpable memory of this heroic period.[37] More than a text, stone was symbolic in and of itself. The frontispiece of his *Recherches sur les monuments cyclopéens ou pélasgiques*[38] makes it clear (fig. 4.9): two constructional systems show two different modes of thinking. On the right, the naked and Herculean figure of the Cyclops holds a flexible and polygonal rule; on the left, a classical Apollonian figure holds in his left hand the orthogonal rule. The orthogonal system bears upon the polygonal one, as the Greek inscription spells out.

According to Petit-Radel's genealogy, the Pelasgic peoples who built using polygonal masonry were descendants of the Caananites, and in turn of Cham, the fallen son of Noah from the land of ancient Phoenicia.[39] Petit-Radel meticulously reproduced the sculpted phalluses seen on cyclopean walls in the models for the Pelasgic architectural museum that he set in the Mazarine library in Paris. He associated the cyclopean temples with Bacchic cults, the basis not only of antique mysteries,[40] but also of Western civilization as a whole: "The cultivation of wheat and the foundation of walled cities are the simultaneous basis of European

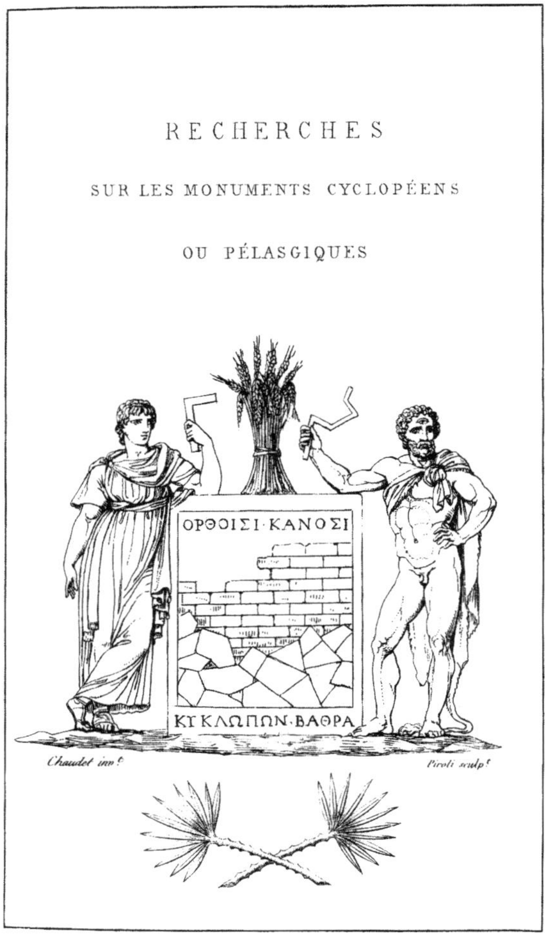

4.9 Frontispiece of Louis Petit-Radel, *Recherches sur les monuments cyclopéens ou pélasgiques* (Paris: Firmin-Didot et cie., 1841). Private collection.

civilization."[41] He traced the Pelasgic stone-god to the cult of the Cabeiri practised on the island of Samothrace, whose religious figure was itself a corruption of the sacred stone of Jacob. These historical speculations on the development of cultures, the nature of myths, and the origins of architecture were well suited to stir the Romantic imagination. In Germany, the philologist and critic Friedrich Schlegel, the great historian of Rome Carl Niebuhr, and the architect Leo von Klenze, to name only the most famous, debated Petit-Radel's theories and eventually integrated them into their historical concepts. In France, René de Châteaubriand, the great naturalist George Cuvier, the Saint-Simonians, Pierre-Simon Ballanche, and many antiquarians came to accept Petit-Radel's Pelasgic theory.[42]

Architecturally, the most significant aspect of Pelasgic construction was that it contained, in embryonic form, the structural principle of the arch. Petit-Radel had conducted full-sized structural experiments in Paris, demonstrating that the imbricated polygonal elements of cyclopean construction possessed properties akin to the *voussoirs* that form arches and vaults. Later, a series of archaeological discoveries in Asia Minor, Greece, and Italy established the persistence of the conical form and the pointed arch in Pelasgic structures, a shape that many antiquarians, including Petit-Radel, believed to have symbolic meaning as an expression of primitive phallic cults and as the source of the Gothic vault.[43]

The transition from the symbolic conical shape into an arcuated structural system was thought to have taken place in Etruscan Italy.[44] Working in tandem with Petit-Radel, Labrouste and his friends at the French Academy in Rome measured and drew a series of cyclopean wall structures and Etruscan arched city gates and interpreted them as an evolutionary series that led to the development of early Christian architecture.[45] In contrast to Greek architecture, this architectural transformation was driven by the nature of stone construction. The year that Labrouste was elaborating his restoration, his friend and fellow *pensionnaire* Léon Vaudoyer sent a letter to his father, praising Etruscan architecture and claiming that their buildings "in a primitive stone architectural style" were often "much more original than the (Greek) architecture of marble monuments."[46] The refined Greek civilization, enamoured of beauty, developed a knowledge of marble and created an extremely purified but abstract architecture. In contrast, the Etruscans maintained the lithic character of primitive cyclopean structures and were the first to understand the principle of the arch.[47] The invention of the arch negated the massiveness of cyclopean construction: huge blocks of stone could be suspended in the air as though they were weightless, invoking a mythic strength of promethean character.

The Labrouste archives in Paris hold a striking series of speculative reconstructions of Etruscan towns, carried out at the same time as Labrouste was elaborating his Paestum restoration (figs 4.10 and 4.11). Labrouste's reconstructions incorporated all of the key elements of primitive Italy as described by Petit-Radel: conical tombs, city walls built on primitive cyclopean foundations, and Etruscan arched gates. These sketches and drawings by Labrouste sought to resurrect the form of the ancient citadel. French Romantic philosopher of history Pierre-Simon Ballanche (1776–1847) described Etruscan cities in his *Essai de palingénésie sociale* (1827–29) as "a hieroglyph, a kind of plastic myth of

4.10 Henri Labrouste, sketch of Etruscan town, pencil (c. 1829), Sketchbook 327. Académie d'architecture, Paris.

the social institution."[48] Its form had a symbolic significance pregnant with the original motive of its formation. The French archaeologist Charles Lenormant (1802–59), active in Ballanche's circle, thought that ancient Etruscan and Roman cities embodied the Phrygian and Cabeiric goddess Cybèle. He described the latter as "the turreted goddess, symbolized by the brute rock, whose more profound meaning is that of union, cohesion, and expresses simultaneously the idea of mother, city, and people."[49]

Labrouste was particularly interested in the foundation rites of ancient cities. In his Paestum sketchbook, a mythological allegory reappears in several places (fig. 4.12) and is the only overtly symbolic figure apart from a sketch of Janus. In the foreground of the upper drawing is a pair of entwined olive trees festooned with a garland. In the background (and also in the lower drawing) two bovines are harnessed side by side, their horns also festooned with a garland, while the plough cuts a furrow into the land. A rock is laid at the foot of the olive tree.

4.11 Henri Labrouste, sketch of Etruscan town, pencil (c. 1829), Sketchbook 327. Académie d'architecture, Paris.

4.12 Henri Labrouste, Etruscan town foundation ritual, pencil (c. 1829), Sketchbook 330. Académie d'architecture, Paris.

This drawing depicts the ritual foundation of a city. Tracing boundaries with a plough was a widespread practice in the Roman world, following Etruscan customs. In his *Palingénésie sociale*, Ballanche had discussed at great length the meaning of this primitive gesture, "tracing the sacred furrow of the city."[50] It was thought to have been performed by the founder himself, using a curved bronze blade with a white cow and a bull harnessed to it. The cow was kept on the inside of the future city walls, the bull on the outside. The clods of earth lifted by the plough would fall to the inside and indicate where the city wall would be built, and the furrow would become the future city moat. Fertility was plainly one aim of the rite. As Joseph Rykwert has noted,[51] we shouldn't be too surprised to find an agricultural rite adapted to the foundation of an urban settlement: the Etruscans who "urbanized" northern Italy were largely an agricultural people. Furthermore, the act of ploughing was a mythological symbol of the highest order: a holy marriage of earth and sky. The entwined olive trees obviously refer to the caduceus, the age-old symbol of the tree of life, the coupling of male and female, and the divine principle of creation and regeneration. Pausanias, in a passage known to Labrouste, had associated it with the creation of territorial boundaries.[52]

Labrouste's little sketches of Etruscan foundation rites underscored the theme of natality, the creation of something new by delimiting previously undifferentiated space. The birth proceeded not from a single, divine-like act of will but from duality: two bovines, two twisted olive trees. The new unity consecrated by the ritual comes from the fusion of two separate, opposed beings, illustrating the principle of antagonism so dominant in Romantic thought. The act of founding the city was related symbolically to the fundamental structural principle of the arch, which delimits a space of passage in the mass of a stone wall by the mutual opposition of *voussoirs* pushing against each other.

For Labrouste, however, duality and antagonism were not merely manifestations of the natural principle of fertility, but also, I suggest, elements of a political principle. All of his imaginary reconstructions of Etruscan towns include a double-walled enclave, with one part of the city situated on lower ground than the other (fig. 4.11). Nineteenth-century historiography had established that the Etruscan state was founded on the principle of conquest and that its society was divided into a warlike sacerdotal, or patrician, caste and a plebeian class that enjoyed relative freedom despite being tied to the patrician class by a hierarchic feudal system.[53] The two-tier cities drawn by Labrouste thus reflected the two-tier class structure of Etruscan society. The dual character of ancient societies had been assigned considerable importance by many historians of the period who applied nature's genetic principle to the political world. Historical development was fuelled by the dynamism of two competing classes. Carl Niebuhr, who initiated the idea, used Roman history as the model for this political opposition.[54] French historian Augustin Thierry adapted the myth to France in his celebrated history of the medieval period.[55] Ballanche and Michelet made it universal in their own concept of world history.[56] The opposition envisioned by the Romantics was not based on a ruling class oppressing a working proletariat, as Marx would theorize, but was the outcome of inherent quasi-physiological antagonism between two races. Following Schelling, the Romantics regarded opposition as the foundation of all things finite. Creuzer, referring to Heraclitus, wrote that "battle fathers all things ...; it is the primitive opposition in diverse forms: the rising and laying, the night and the day. It is the discord of the universe which produces a concord like the harmony of the arc and that of the Lyre."[57]

The foregoing discussion affords us a better vantage point from which to consider the meaning of the Etruscan elements that infiltrated Labrouste's restoration of the Basilica and the Temple of Ceres at Paestum. Through these infiltrations, Labrouste signalled that colonial Greek society at Paestum was neither homogeneous nor contained but had sustained enough contact with Etruscan culture over the years to produce a hybrid culture. In his *Palingénésie sociale*, Ballanche had made such hybridization a specific stage within world history: following the primordial era of cyclopean constructions, wrote Ballanche, came the age of colonization and conquests, resulting in a mixture of races and the transformation of original traditions and institutions.[58] Many Romantic historians, such as François Guizot and Augustin Thierry, emphasized periods of transition in their genealogies of nation-states. Aside from philosophers and historians, the architect Jean-Nicolas Huyot, Labrouste's influential architectural history teacher at the Beaux-Arts,[59] had paid considerable attention to history's transitional moments, focusing on "the relationship between periods of conquests or emigrations of ancient people compared with the monuments."[60] In 1817–21 Huyot had undertaken a long journey from Italy to Greece, Asia Minor, and Egypt in order to unravel the thread of historical development, focusing on cities and monuments with mixed architectural traditions, such as Smyrne and Assos in Asia Minor and Nubia in Egypt.[61] These hybrid monuments provided, according to him, the key to understanding the development of classical architecture. The phenomenon of architectural blending was a means only to track formal sources and was not in itself a challenge to the idea of a universalizing classicism. Labrouste, in contrast, would make it a paradigmatic site for reflections on the nature of architectural change: hybridization was to become the fundamental method of architectural creation.

Poseidonia, as Paestum was called in its Greek period, was ideally located at the frontier between two dominant centres of culture. Situated at the northwestern boundary of Magna Graecia, it also coincided with the southern boundary of Etruscan territory that extended deep into the modern region of Campania. Around 500 B.C., Etruscans entered into open conflict with the Greeks who had colonized Paestum a century earlier, battling over cities such as Cumae and Aricia. Labrouste makes no mention of these historical events, but traces of Etruscan presence around Paestum provide a background for his restoration project. He even illustrates tombs found at the northern periphery of the city wall, whose form he observed as being "similar to that of the tomb of Tarquinium."[62]

In the first pages of his accompanying explanation, Labrouste mentions repeatedly that the Greek founders of Poseidonia were not the first inhabitants of the site; they ousted "Picentines and Samnites" when they colonized it. Labrouste does not suggest that these tribes had special meaning for the Greek colony, although they provide another layer of racial and cultural complexity during the Greeks' adaptation to foreign soil. What Labrouste did underscore, however, is the Pelasgic origin of the primitive city walls. The first plate discussed in the original version of Labrouste's explanation illustrates the ramparts of Paestum (fig. 4.13); significantly, this same passage was relegated to the end in the published version of 1877.[63] These walls, according to Labrouste, were built of "stones imbricated so as to support each other. This way of building, which seems to have evolved directly from Pelasgic or cyclopean construction, *of which these walls kept a few traces*, may indicate that they are of a great antiquity."[64] Resorting to wilful speculation – there are absolutely no traces of cyclopean construction at Paestum according to current archaeological reports[65] – Labrouste claimed that the founders

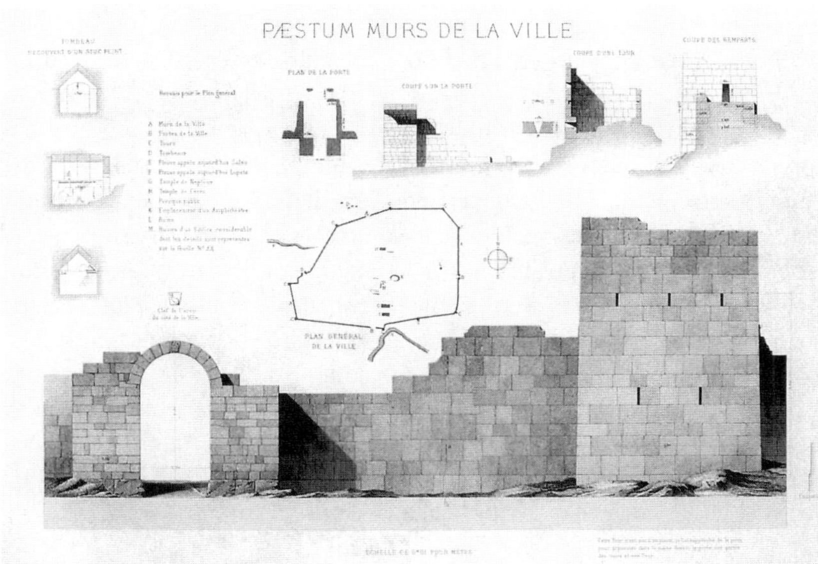

4.13 Paestum city walls, in Henri Labrouste, *Les temples de Paestum* (Paris: Firmin-Didot et cie., 1877), plate 21. Private collection.

of Poseidonia had not settled on virgin land but occupied a primitive Pelasgic city.[66] The claim was elaborated by Petit-Radel a few years later. His article of 1834, in which he refers directly to Labrouste, ends with a thought that the great Temple of Neptune might have been built on older foundations.[67] Speculations about historical stratigraphy supported Petit-Radel's attempt to fabricate a historical continuity around the Mediterranean Basin. For Labrouste, the alleged remnants of old walls also emphasized *discontinuities*, shedding light on the enigma of transitional historical periods, during which, as Ballanche claimed, mixtures of races and cultures initiated new departures. The Etruscan elements in the later buildings at Paestum thus could be conceived as signs of colonial contact with a foreign culture as well as a reacquaintance with the mythological and architectural origins of the Greek world itself.

Could Labrouste have conceived an opposition between the Temple of Neptune for the official god of the Greek colony and the Temple of Ceres for the precinct of a primitive fertility cult that harks back to the most ancient mysteries of Greece? The temples were sited at opposite ends of the Paestum precinct, perhaps suggesting a two-tier urban structure as in the imaginary Etruscan cities drawn by Labrouste in his notebooks. In his

Symbolik, Creuzer had explained how the cult of Ceres was related directly to archaic Cabeiric and Pelasgic rites, "the most important and most characteristic in ancient Italy,"[68] ensuring her appeal to an Etruscan population. Labrouste's restoration of the Temple of Ceres reflects the archaic nature of the rituals associated with the Greek goddess. Without support from direct archaeological evidence, he includes a treasury at the far end of the *cella* opposite the entry to suggest a ritualistic progression through space (fig. 4.14). Like a holy of holies, the tightly enclosed space is entered through a small passage under the statue of the cult figure. The directionality is emphasized by the unbalanced proportions of the front and back porches: the space between the front columns and the entry to the *cella* is twice the depth of the corresponding space at the rear. This contrast between front and back porches had been either corrected or lessened in Thomas Major's and Delagardette's restorations.

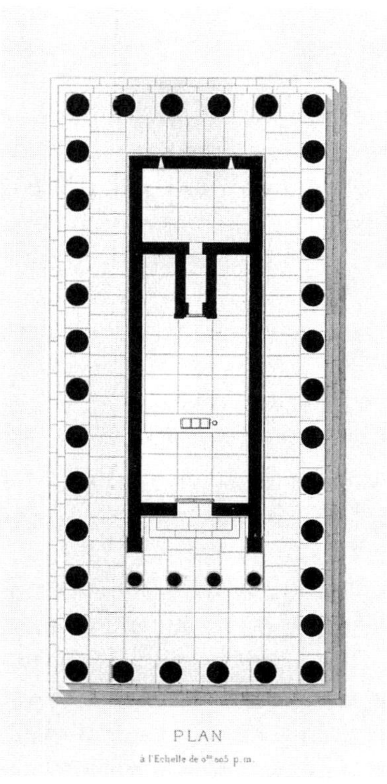

4.14 Temple of Ceres, plan, restored, in Henri Labrouste, *Les temples de Paestum* (Paris: Firmin-Didot et cie., 1877), plate 13. Private collection.

4.15 Temple of Ceres, detail of longitudinal section, restored, in Henri Labrouste, *Les temples de Paestum* (Paris: Firmin-Didot et cie., 1877), plate 13. Private collection.

Labrouste noted two significant hybrid elements in the Doric Temple of Ceres. First, the four Ionic columns at the entry to the *cella*, a quite uniquely configured combination of two orders in a single structure (significantly neglected by Delagardette), could be construed as another sign of Etruscan infiltrations (fig. 4.15). The smaller Ionic columns do not line up with the perimeter Doric colonnade, suggesting that the interior room of the temple is "floating freely" within its surroundings, as though one autonomous temple had been fitted into another.[69]

Second, and even more crucial for Labrouste, the temple combined two different types of stone: a solid masonry that actively bore the weight of the temple and a softer stone that passively received the sculpted ornaments. To Labrouste, the presence of two types of stone indicated a better knowledge of the materials available in the region and thus a greater involvement with local conditions. He interpreted this duality in both the Temple of Ceres and the Basilica as a decisive sign of the loss of "the primitive purity of the Temple of Neptune."[70] It led him to conclude that these two structures were *d'une architecture autre*, the "type" for an architecture that was neither Greek nor Etruscan *per se* but of Poseidonia itself.[71]

I would suggest that Labrouste regarded these dualities (two orders, two types of stone) as architectural metaphors for competing groups within Paestum society. The Ionic order, originating in Asia Minor, was widely used by Etruscans. Greater sophistication and cunning in the use of stone also exemplified a level of knowledge attributed to the Etruscans, the inventors of the arch. But beyond the question of attribution, it is the dual nature of these hybrid elements that seems most telling. The Ionic order is more graceful and feminine than the Doric, just as the harder stone contrasts with the softer one. Could they be architectural expressions of the difference between conqueror and conquered? Ballanche had described the period of colonization and conquests in this way: racial opposition was conceived as an active force colliding with a passive element, its archetype being the contrast between the Ionians (passive) and the Dorians (active): the one female, the other male.[72] For Ballanche, this association of gender and race was not immutable but changed according to historical context,[73] acknowledging both the contingencies and the give-and-take in the process of "transculturation."

The various dualities in the Temple of Ceres at Paestum are made even more manifest in the Basilica through a dramatic spatial gesture that splits the whole space into two halves (fig. 4.16). Labrouste, like many archaeologists before him, denied that the Basilica functioned as either temple or place of justice; he called it a portico instead of a basilica and described it as a civic meeting hall for debating municipal affairs. Curiously, this meeting hall has no centre, as it is bisected by a single row of Doric columns running through the middle. In his usual laconic fashion, Labrouste noted that the central row of columns generates a good ambulatory space and is more economical because it reduces the spanning distance for the roof. These comments seem rather understated given how obsessive this spatial arrangement would become for French Romantic architects.[74] It became literally an *idée fixe* for a whole generation. Even nonarchitects were attracted to the dynamic nature of such spaces; witness Victor Hugo's *Notre Dame de Paris*, which opens with a vivid description of a medieval festive contest in a double-nave hall with a central spine of columns, the *grand'salle* of the old Palais on the Île de la Cité.

A close reading of the accompanying explanation reveals a clue about the "Portico's" extended meaning within Labrouste's restoration. Explaining the importance of porticos in the ancient world, Labrouste mentions a story reported by Cicero about the new inhabitants of a colony in southern Italy quarrelling with the natives over the use of a portico. The latter is thus associated with the opposition of social groups. A few lines farther on, Labrouste adds that the Portico in Paestum could have been erected only after the Greek settlers had established their own power and reached relative political stability. At this time, struggles with indigenous groups would have ceased and a *modus vivendi* would have been established. The divided space thus may convey political meaning, representing dynamic exchanges between two groups that are distinct and opposed – but politically united. The historian Carl Niebuhr had described ancient Rome as a city of two distinct social groups whose unification had led to the construction of the Janus portal. This portal-building, explains Niebuhr, either "prevented unrestricted intercourse, out of which quarrel might arise," or served "as a token" symbolizing "that, though united, the two groups were distinct."[75] The Portico at Paestum could have had a similar mediating function, although this was not mentioned explicitly by Labrouste.

I also suggest that the walls with inscriptions in Labrouste's Portico may have been ceremonial rather than merely an "anecdotal dress"[76] serving as a signpost. According to a drawn-out argument in Petit-Radel's *Histoire des temps héroïques* (1827),[77] these writings on the walls served as the essential and permanent record of the historical annals of a city

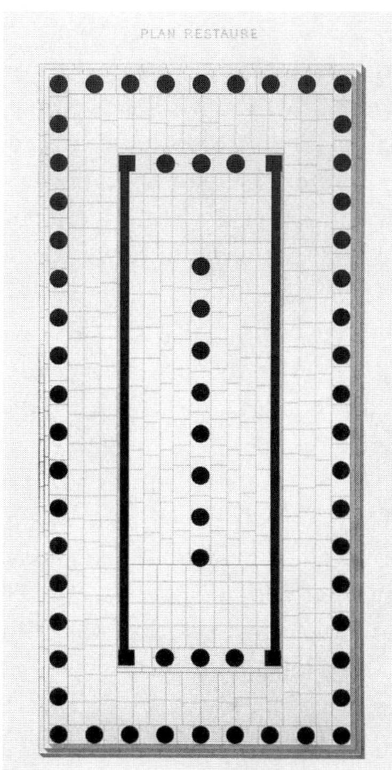

4.16 Portico (Basilica), plan, restored, in Henri Labrouste, *Les temples de Paestum* (Paris: Firmin-Didot et cie., 1877), plate 15. Private collection.

and the genealogy of its founders, thus establishing the authority of a particular social group. However, Labrouste is not so explicit, and the stucco veneer that covers his walls may suggest *impermanence* rather than permanence. Yet the manuscript version of his explanation does describe the writings on the Portico walls as "inscriptions in memory of the most important events."[78] The military shields that decorate the upper portion of the interior space certainly glorify the authority of a group. In his restored section of the Portico, the inscriptions are organized informally but seem to depict tales of travel and lists of names.

The Portico's central spine of columns was not only spatially meaningful, but also structurally significant for Labrouste. Neil Levine has already noted that, for many French classical theorists of previous generations, this structural arrangement had a primordial character.[79] The eighteenth-century archaeologist/architect David Leroy (1724–1803) had declared that a small rectangular cabin with a central spine of columns constituted the "primitive idea" of the Greek temple, as illustrated in his famous comparative plate on the history of temple form.[80] Apart from the Basilica in Paestum, little archaeological evidence supported Leroy's claim, but in one manuscript version of *De architectura* (a version used by French translators Jean Martin and Claude Perrault, considered inaccurate today), Vitruvius associated the origin of the column with the *culmen*, or king post, the vertical member at the centre of a simple roof truss that extends from the ridge to the middle of the tie-beam.[81] Unlike in modern roof trusses, king posts in ancient Greece were compressive members that supported the weight of opposing rafters rather than serving as a tensile tie in a triangulated system. Auguste Choisy's *Histoire de l'architecture* – a compendium of French rationalist knowledge published at the end of the nineteenth century – greatly emphasized these characteristics of ancient carpentry and pointed to the crucial importance of both the king post and central-spine temples in primitive Greek and Etruscan architecture (fig. 4.17).[82] Given the structural characteristics of ancient roof trusses, the central ridge of a pitched roof was indeed the most rational point of relief for large spans. Levine has already identified many drawings by Labrouste that demonstrate his fascination with ancient roof carpentry, particularly the central vertical post. One page of his sketchbook from 1829 depicts an imaginary "Etruscan" temple with a king post evident in the exterior pediment, a motif that Labrouste would reuse in his later work.[83] Similarly, Labrouste's brother Théodore

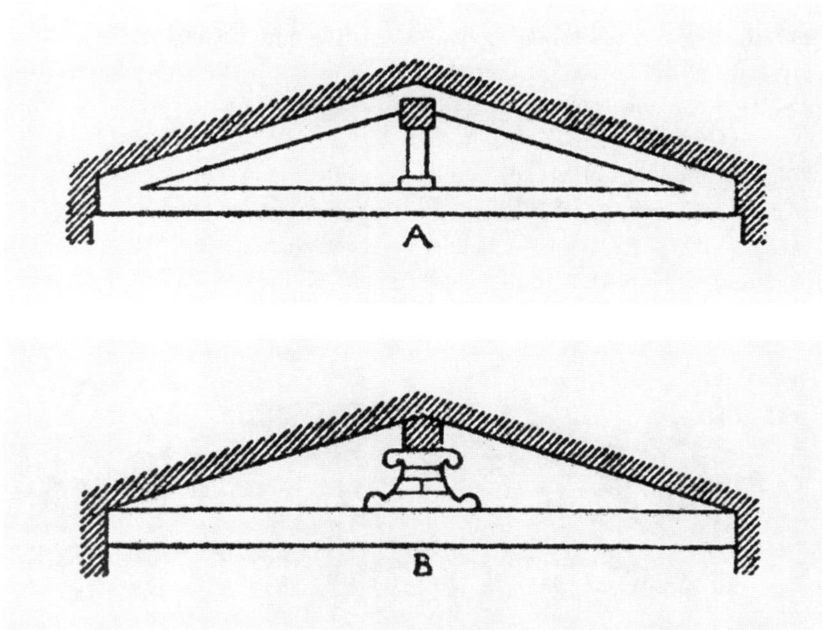

4.17 Etruscan carpentry detail, in Auguste Choisy, *Histoire de l'architecture* (1899; reprint, Paris: Serg, 1976), 205. Private collection.

would include such an element: a stubby, painted Ionic column in the roof space of his restored Temple of Hercules at Cora.

In his Paestum restoration, Labrouste refers neither to Vitruvius's discussion of the *culmen* nor to Leroy's "primitive idea," although both were obviously known to him. But in his justly famous section drawing of the Portico (fig. 4.18), he had emphasized the order of stubby piers running continuously below the ridge beam, an attic order that became a recurring motif in the architecture of Labrouste and his friends. Its extended meaning remains to be established, but we can assume that it represented an archetypal structural form. In both the Paestum restoration and Labrouste's later projects, this order of small piers was coupled with a shield motif, a war trophy that suggested an archetypal genre. Could there be a metaphoric link between the king post supporting the weight of opposing rafters and the Portico resolving social antagonism within Paestum society? There is no evidence that Labrouste drew such an association from the literature, yet a passage from book 23 of Homer's

Iliad makes a similar analogy; a wrestling match between Ajax and Odysseus is interpreted architecturally and is all the more interesting given that the contest ends in a tie:

> Both champions, belted tight, stepped into the ring
> And grappling each other hard with big burly arms,
> Locked like rafters a master builder bolts together,
> Slanting into a pitched roof to fight ripping winds.[84]

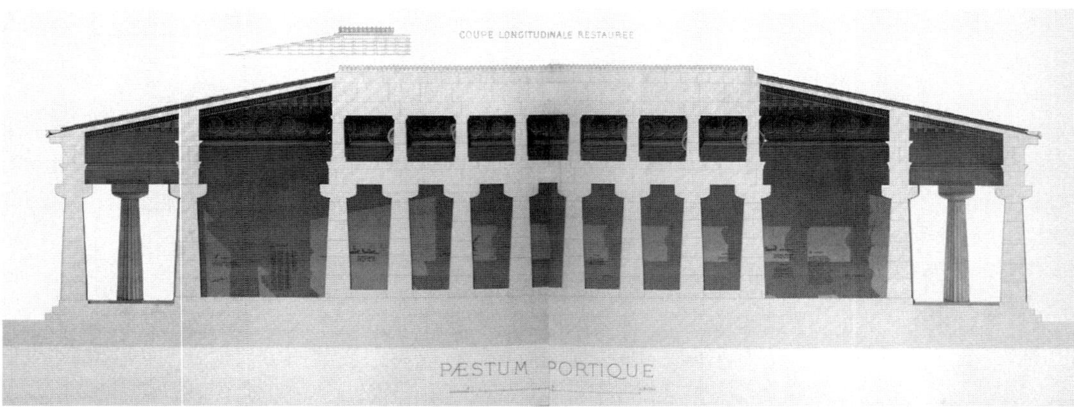

4.18 Portico (Basilica), longitudinal section, restored, ink and wash, drawing 20 by Henri Labrouste, fourth-year *envoi*, 1828, École nationale supérieure des Beaux-Arts, Paris.

What historical lessons can be drawn from Labrouste's Paestum restoration? What light does it shed on architectural evolution? Again, Neil Levine was the first to open the investigation. He speculated that the three buildings at Paestum corresponded in Labrouste's mind to the three phases of the historical progress of humanity as laid out in Auguste Comte's *Cours de philosophie positive*. Comte's well-known historical law specified that each branch of human knowledge must pass through three successive phases: the theological, the metaphysical, and the positive. Transposing the scheme to Labrouste's restoration of Paestum, Levine explains that the Temple of Neptune represented "the magico-religious embodiment of the tutelary deity," that the Temple of Ceres invoked "the metaphysical representation of human gratitude," and that the Portico expressed "the positive creation of a structure for human creation."[85]

This philosophical interpretation certainly rings true to Romantic archaeology, in which historical monuments were blithely appropriated for larger speculations on universal history. Petit-Radel's archaeological work on cyclopean construction is an early example of such ambitious conclusions, while Hugo's "This will kill that" is its literary expansion. Auguste Comte, however, is not an obvious model. Never much inspired by art and archaeology, Comte, to my knowledge, did not have great influence in architectural circles in the first half of the nineteenth century. Besides, Levine's specific reading runs into certain difficulties. First, it relies too much on the rigid three-stage evolutionary model. Although this tripartite historical schema – a Romantic commonplace – seems ideally suited to Paestum and its three monuments, Labrouste's restoration is not staged so clearly. To be sure, he describes the Temple of Neptune as the oldest structure, but he never indicates which building came next: the Temple of Ceres or the Portico.[86] Instead, he speaks of these two later monuments as representing a common architectural expression. In the manuscript version of Labrouste's explanation, the description of the Portico came *before* the description of the Temple of Ceres, an order that was reversed in the posthumous publication. But the order may well be interchangeable since it does not seem to correspond to any definite chronology.

It is also difficult to understand why the program of the Temple of Ceres would deserve the label "metaphysical." In Comte's evolution this was the stage of a more abstract relationship to the natural world. Yet the cult of Ceres was tied to the most vivid fertility rites in ancient mysteries and was discussed at great length in those terms by Romantic archaeologists and mythographers. To underscore this primordial character, Labrouste speaks of the settlers' "gratitude towards the fertility of their fields" and emphasizes the processional nature of the spatial sequence of the Temple of Ceres in his restoration.

Finally, to be valid, Comte's tripartite scheme would need some kind of architectural embodiment. In strictly architectural terms, what makes the Temple of Neptune "theological," the Temple of Ceres "metaphysical," or the Portico "positive"? The Portico most closely fits the bill because it is more economical and more utilitarian than the others, yet

Labrouste describes all three buildings in equally rational terms. He admired the double order of the *cella* in the Temple of Neptune for its unity, rational coherence, and utility. In contrast, he criticized the placement of the corner triglyphs in the Temple of Ceres. An evolutionary thread from the theological to the positive is thus not so easy to follow.

To comprehend the underlying plot of Labrouste's story about Paestum, it is safest to start from the elements that are most obvious. Certainly, the strongest undercurrent of the restoration – and its most scandalous affront to Beaux-Arts academic tradition – is the contamination of a "pure" Greek model by "foreign" elements. The first plate discussed in the original explanation illustrates the Pelasgic foundation of the city walls and the archaic, Etruscan-style tombs. The last plate describes the remains of an odd temple built during the Roman period, a building that Pierre Morey would later characterize as Etruscan.[87] Between the first and last plates – between the Pelasgic beginnings and the Roman conquest – we follow a process of degradation from the Temple of Neptune into the hybrid forms of the Temple of Ceres and the Portico. Instead of an evolution toward the pure form of the Temple of Neptune, Labrouste documents a devolution toward the eclectic.

This hybridization must have infuriated the classicist Quatremère de Quincy, particularly as he would have associated it with a leading theme of the Romantic rebellion. The year before Labrouste began his work at Paestum, Victor Hugo's preface to *Cromwell* had celebrated the creative energy gained from hybrid literary form, representing a forceful attack on the "entire system of classical dramatic art" with its "arbitrary distinction of genres" and its Aristotelian dramatic unities. Modern drama, claimed Hugo, embraces the heterogeneous, achieving "l'harmonie des contraires."[88] He had been particularly eloquent in describing the distinctive nature of modern poetry as the infusion of the grotesque within the ideal beauty of classical forms: the kiss of the beast endowed monotonous classical perfection with a new power that expressed the complexities of life. For Hugo, the grotesque was an element specific to modern poetry, yet its roots were within the primitive and archaic. The Cyclops already exemplified the grotesque for the ancients.

In his Paestum restoration, Labrouste does not resort to the use of the grotesque, although it would be exploited later by his brother Théodore in his restoration of the Temple of Hercules at Cora. Nonetheless, the two "late" buildings at Paestum evince an increased sense of freedom and a new force of expression. The nearly identical stocky Doric columns of the Temple of Ceres and the Portico, with their pronounced cigar-like shape and bulbous capitals, point back to the primitive beginnings of architecture and the brute strength of uncut rock. Creuzer had underscored the primitivism of Etruscan artists, for whom, he wrote, "beauty was not the first goal ... Like the old Pélasges and the first Greeks, they sought above all an expressive language."[89] That power of expression at Paestum came not from an undisturbed unity, but from its breakdown. The Portico's imaginative plan, with its central spine of columns, generated a divided space with a very dynamic ambulatory character. The combination of two different and nonaligned orders in the Temple of Ceres destabilizes a unified reading, producing an incoherence that is overcome through a stronger spatial directionality that ritualized the procession through the building. The use of two types of stone in these temples also generated a dynamic ritual of its own, according to Labrouste, by requiring the builders to renew the walls periodically with a stucco veneer. These dualities thus unleash various dynamic processes that augment their expressive power in society.

In the end, the concept of historical development in Labrouste's Paestum restoration is perhaps closest to the classic Saint-Simonian formulation, a model that Barry Bergdoll argues was central to the Romantic architects in Labrouste's circle:[90] history evolves through a cyclical alternation between short organic periods when all elements of culture are unified and long transitional periods when the various constituent elements of a society are no longer in harmony.[91] From the unified Temple of Neptune to the hybrid Temple of Ceres and the Portico, we move from the organic to the transitional. According to Labrouste, these last two structures show that the Poseidonians "voulurent se créer une architecture nouvelle."[92] They may well have striven for a new totality, but they succeeded in achieving the heterogeneous. This hybrid form is "the type of the architecture of Poseidonia," just as it is the type for the nineteenth century.

What sharply distinguishes Labrouste from the Saint-Simonians, however, is that the latter resented periods of transition, longing for the coherent organic moment that their utopian schemes sought to institute. Labrouste, in contrast, valued transitional periods for their potential renewal. He thus remained closer to Ballanche, whose historical system had been an influential source for the Saint-Simonians. In Ballanche's cyclical vision of history, the transitional had been poeticized as a rich period of rebirth, a *période palingénésique* for which ancient Italy provided the most potent model. Ancient Latium was a turning point, a monumental gateway between East and West.[93] Similarly, for Labrouste, the Etruscan element at Paestum signified a transition, a moment of natality leading to unforeseen new beginnings. During these moments, primitive creative energies could be unleashed. Thus his Paestum restoration traced a rite of passage from the universal architectural forms on Greek soil to the hybrid architectural forms in the colonial context that symbolized a ruptured polity: two antagonistic halves held in check by the double nave of the Portico.

There is perhaps no better way to conclude a discussion of Labrouste's Paestum restoration than to consider the project that he made in Rome one year later. In the last year of their tenure at the French Academy, *pensionnaires* had to produce a final *envoi*: an original design, based on a program of their choice, that summarized what they had learned during their twelve to fifteen years of education. Labrouste's final *envoi* has baffled everyone, including recent historians (fig. 4.19). This very modest bridge, reuniting France and Italy at a provincial location in the Savoie, has often been described as an essay in local colour, but also as a further act of provocation: a witty autobiographical memento celebrating Labrouste's imminent return to France. In my opinion, this small but powerful monument is above all a poetic expression of the importance of transitional moments in the process of creation.

As Levine has already noted, everything is Etruscan in this project: the arch inspired by the city gate at Perugia, the proportions of the attic, the diminutive engaged Ionic order, and the conical *cippi* that mark the frontier between the two countries.[94] Labrouste's bridge thus combined iconic elements from Oriental mythology, brought to Italy by the primitive Pelasgic people (particularly the cone and the Ionic order), and the arch, the more "advanced" architectural element developed in Etruria. He thereby reaffirms the importance of Etruscan culture as a link between East and West and as the crucible from which Roman civil society was forged. Even more important than the Etruscan motives was his choice

4.19 Henri Labrouste, Project for a monument … at the frontier between France and Italy, fifth-year *envoi*, ink wash (1829), original drawing lost. Photograph courtesy of Professor Neil Levine, Harvard University

of a *frontier monument*. Most interpretive essays on Etruscan myths published during the early nineteenth century focused on Janus, a divine figure with no equivalent in Greek mythology. He was an ambiguous character who controlled passages, Iani being a common appellation for arcuated gates in ancient Roman society. As we have seen, Niebuhr had described the primitive temple of Janus as a double-gated passage linking the two sides of the split society at the origin of Rome. In Labrouste's Paestum notebook, next to his many sketches of Etruscan cities, there is the figure of Janus, the herm that stands in the middle of the ancient Fabricius bridge in Rome (fig. 4.20). Recent mythological studies have shown that the double-gated bridge was probably the most primitive form for the Temple of Janus.[95] Romantic mythographers were already very sensitive to the multiple attributes of this Etruscan god. There are ample citations. This is what Creuzer wrote about Janus:

As god of nature, the Etruscan Janus is the bearer of the key; he is also the key holder as the god of doors ... the door of the orient and the door of the setting sun are both under his guard ... Janus, the first monarch, founds cities, raises ramparts, and their gates; becoming hero, he institutes sanctuaries ... and regulates civil order. He is called the inspector of time, then Time itself; cosmogonically, he is associated with chaos ... The very name of Janus expresses simultaneously a mountain and a river. Janus, the one who passes or flows ... We have now arrived at the fundamental point which is present in all religions of antiquity: the union of spirit and matter assembled as if by a magical tie; this mysterious alliance of an active principle with a passive one.[96]

4.20 Henri Labrouste, sketch of Janus herm on Fabricius Bridge in Rome, pencil (c. 1829), Sketchbook 330. Académie d'architecture, Paris.

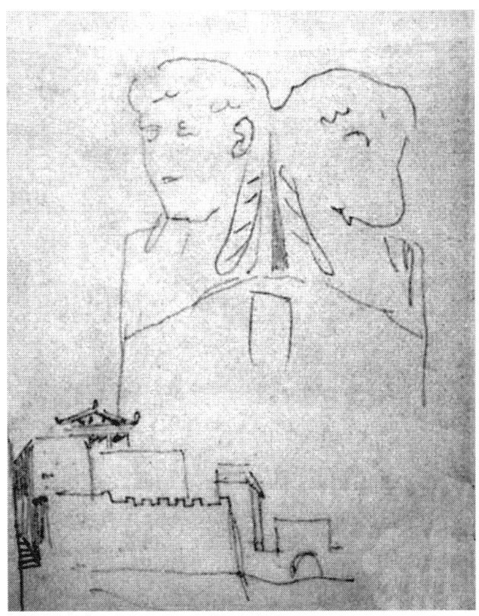

Janus is associated with passage, but is also the god of initiations: he presides over beginnings with an obstetric power that links earth and sky. With its two simple walls and corresponding gates set in a deserted and mountainous wilderness, Labrouste's bridge uses the simplest means to create a frontier space separated from the common world. Like Theseus, the legendary Greek creator of the first democratic institutions, who, in lapidary fashion, linked East and West by inscribing on a stone marker "Peloponnesia here, Ionia there," Labrouste inscribes the simple names France and Italia on the internal faces of his two frontier gates. In naming the two banks, he creates an odd void in the middle of the bridge, a transitional space that is neither France nor Italy but a domain where Janus rules in the powerful curve of a *cippe*. This sacred liminal space is simultaneously the site of transgression and continuity. It offers the possibility of tying together dispersed elements, linking opposites, and creating synthesis from chaos, but it also institutes a certain anarchic disorder since it is a nonplace, an unnamed and untamed zone of transition.

Labrouste's modest project clearly is not aligned with Saint-Simonian optimism nor with Comte's categorical divisions. Inhabiting a century condemned to await a new future, Labrouste was caught up in the fascination with origins and the pathos of loss. It is perhaps in such anxieties that his fragile poetry of transition found its source. It is the historicist anxiety, the trauma, described by Alan Spitzer, of a "pale, ardent, and neurotic"[97] generation born to the sound of martial music but ending up having to live with hybrid forms of government such as that of France's Louis-Philippe, split between democracy and monarchy. In an often quoted passage from *Confessions of a Child of the Century*, Alfred de Musset captured remarkably well the sentiment of anxiety that characterized Labrouste's era. It evokes the latent melancholy in Labrouste's bridge project, the hollowness that is both nostalgia for the past and anticipation of the future:

> Three elements entered into the life which offered itself to these children: behind them a past destroyed forever, still quivering on its ruins with all the fossils of centuries of absolutism; before them the aurora of an immense horizon, the first gleam of the future, and between these two worlds … something similar to the ocean that separates the old continent from the young America, something vague and floating, a rough sea filled with wreckage, traversed from time to time by a white sail or by some ship trailing thick clouds of smoke; the present century, in a word, which separates past from future, which is neither the one nor the other, and which resembles both, where one cannot know whether at each step he treads on a seedbed or a heap of refuse.[98]

NOTES

1 This chapter, first written as a public conference in 1998, was slowly transformed into its final shape thanks to the very precious editing help of Denise Bratton and Stephen Parcell.

2 Hendrik Petrus Berlage, "On the Likely Development of Architecture," in *Thoughts on Style, 1886–1909*, intro. Iain Boyd Whyte, trans. Iain Boyd Whyte and Wim de Wit, 156–64 (Santa Monica, CA: Getty Center for the History of Art and the Humanities, 1996), 157, original emphasis.

3 Hermann Muthesius, *Style-Architecture and Building-Art: Transformations of Architecture in the Nineteenth Century and Its Present Condition* (1902), intro. and trans. by Stanford Anderson (Santa Monica, CA: Getty Center for the History of Art and Humanities, 1994), 50.

4 Thomas Hope, *Historical Essay on Architecture* (London: John Murray, 1835), 560.

5 On this topic, see the suggestive article by Karsten Harries, "Theatricality and Re-presentation," *Perspecta* 26 (1990): 21–40.

6 Roger Shattuck, *The Banquet Years: The Origins of the Avant-Garde in France* (New York: Vintage, 1968), 3–6.

7 Ibid., 3.

8 Harries, "Theatricality," 25.

9 Octavio Paz, *The Children of the Mire* (Cambridge, MA: Harvard University Press, 1991), 27.

10 Ibid., 40.

11 Eugène-Emmanuel Viollet-le-Duc, *Entretiens sur l'architecture* (Paris: Morel, 1863), vol. 1, 177. I have used Benjamin Bucknall's 1877 English translation, *Lectures on Architecture* (New York: Dover, 1987), vol. 1, 175, except for minor modifications made to remain closer to the original text. All future references are to this translation.

12 Ibid., 174.

13 Ibid., 176.

14 See Neil Levine, "Architectural Reasoning in the Age of Positivism: The Neo-Grec Idea of Henri Labrouste's Bibliothèque Sainte-Geneviève" (PhD thesis, Yale University, 1975); and Neil Levine, "The Romantic Idea of Architectural Legibility: Henri Labrouste and the Neo-Grec," in Arthur Drexler, ed., *The Architecture of the Ecole des Beaux-Arts*, 324–416 (Cambridge, MA: MIT Press, 1977).

15 The most exhaustive account of their ideas is contained in Barry Bergdoll, *Léon Vaudoyer: Architecture in the Age of Industry* (Cambridge, MA: MIT Press, 1994). See also the excellent monograph on the "gang of four" by David Van Zanten, *Designing Paris: The Architecture of Duban, Labrouste, Duc, and Vaudoyer* (Cambridge, MA: MIT Press, 1987).

16 The most precise description of such architectural narrative is Richard Witman, "Felix Duban's Didactic Restoration of the Château de Blois: A History of France in Stone," *Journal of the Society of Architectural Historians* 55 (1996): 412–34.

17 For a systematic survey of early speculations about Paestum, see Joselita Raspi Serra, ed., *La fortuna critica di Paestum e la memoria moderna del dorico* (Florence: Centro Di della Edifimi, 1986), esp. Dieter Mertens, "I templi di Paestum nella prima storiographia dell'architettura antica," vol. 1, 160–98.

18 Claude-Mathieu Delagardette, *Les ruines de Paestum ou Posidonia, ancienne ville de la Grande Grèce …: Levées, mesurées et dessinées sur les lieux en l'an II* (Paris: Chez l'auteur et H. Barbou, an VII [1799]).

19 I borrow the concept of transculturation from Fernando Ortiz, developed in his classic *Cuban Counterpoint: Tobacco and Sugar* (New York: Knopf, 1947), 97–103. Thanks to Denise Bratton for pointing me to this source.

20 Today, some still claim that the project held no real controversial value, the conflict between Quatremère de Quincy and Horace Vernet being of a personal nature; see Pierre Pinon and François-Xavier Amprimoz, *Les envois de Rome (1778–1968): Architecture et archéologie* (Rome: École française de Rome, 1988), 321–4.

21 The text and drawings of Labrouste's restoration of 1829 were published by the French government in 1877 as *Les temples de Paestum: restauration exécutée en 1829 par Henri Labrouste* (Paris: Firmin-Didot et Cie, 1877). There are minor differences between the original manuscript of 1829 and its published version of 1877, most notably that the drawings became available in the form of engraving. Other minor variations are noted in the course of this article.

22 See Pinon and Amprimoz, *Les envois de Rome*, 73–197.

23 Thomas Major, *The Ruins of Paestum* (London: T. Major, 1768). The book was published simultaneously in French as *Les ruines de Paestum*.

24 For a summary of recent findings, see John Griffiths Pedley, *Paestum: Greeks and Romans in Southern Italy* (London: Thames and Hudson, 1990).

25 Levine, "Architectural Reasoning."
26 Labrouste, *Temples de Paestum*, 13.
27 Levine, "Architectural Reasoning," 792.
28 Levine, "Romantic Idea," 385–6.
29 Labrouste, *Les temples de Paestum*, 5.
30 That Paestum abutted on Etruscan territory at the time of the Greek settlement was an established fact in the early nineteenth century. Paoli had given clear evidence of this proximity, and Quatremère de Quincy, who otherwise denied Paoli's Etruscan thesis about the temples at Paestum, accepted the fact; see Quatremère de Quincy, *Encyclopédie méthodique*, vol. 2, *Architecture* (Paris: Agasse, 1801–20), 238.
31 For a clear instance of Etruscan elements in Labrouste's work, see Martin Bressani, "Projet de Labrouste pour le tombeau de Napoléon," *Revue de l'art* 125 (1999): 54–63.
32 For quotations from this magisterial work by Friedrich Creuzer, I have used the French translation (and augmentation) by Joseph Guigniaut, *Les religions de l'antiquité considérées principalement dans leurs formes symboliques et mythologiques* (Paris: Treuttel et Würtz, 1825–51), first part of vol. 2 (1829), 389. The French translation of Creuzer's *Symbolik* had just begun when Labrouste was in Italy (with two volumes published by 1829), but the influence of that study was already pervasive in French archaeological circles, particularly among the members of the Institut de correspondance archéologique de Rome. Unfortunately, no detailed study exists of the early phase of this important archaeological institute, which would later become the German Archeological Institute. However, the widespread influence of Creuzer is easily detected by simply perusing the early volumes of the *Annales de l'Institut de correspondance archéologique de Rome*, published in Italian and French from 1827 on.
33 See, for instance, the first volume of François Mazois, *Les ruines de Pompei* (Paris: Firmin Didot, 1812).
34 Labrouste, *Temples de Paestum*, 11.
35 L.C.F. Petit-Radel, *Examen analytique et tableau comparatif des synchronismes de l'histoire des temps héroïques de la Grèce* (Paris: Imprimerie royale, 1827), 91. For a brief (and not entirely reliable) discussion of Petit-Radel's historical claim, see Martin Bernal, *Black Athena: The Afroasiatic Roots of Classical Civilization*, vol. 1, *The Fabrication of Ancient Greece, 1785–1985* (New Brunswick, NJ: Rutgers University Press, 1987), 307–8.

36 Ibid., 208; and in L.C.F. Petit-Radel, "Seconde lettre de M. Petit-Radel à Monsieur Le Duc de Luynes," *Annales de l'Institut de correspondance archéologique de Rome* 6 (1834): 365. In this passage, Petit-Radel compares his "historical lithology" to Cuvier's "terrestrial lithology."

37 On the subject of historical chronicles written on temple walls, see Petit-Radel, "Discours préliminaire," in *Examen analytique*, 1–61.

38 L.C.F. Petit-Radel, *Recherches sur les monuments cyclopéens et description de la collection des modèles en relief composant la galerie pélasgique de la bibliothèque mazarine* (Paris: Imprimerie royale, 1841). The work was published posthumously, five years after the death of its author.

39 Ibid., 42–105.

40 Petit-Radel is particularly explicit on the subject in "Monumens. Topographie. Recherches comparées," *Annales de l'Insitut de correspondance archéologique* 4 (1832): 233–54.

41 Petit-Radel, *Recherches sur les monuments cyclopéens*, 9.

42 See Petit-Radel's extensive collection of "témoignages" in *Recherches sur les monuments cyclopéens*, 60–126.

43 The most explicit articles on the subject are both by Albert Lenoir, an architect close to the circle of Labrouste; see his "Monuments sépulcraux de l'Étrurie moyenne," *Annales de l'Institut de correspondance archéologique* 4 (1832): 254–79; and "Tombeaux de Norchia," *Annales de l'Institut de correspondance archéologique* 4 (1832): 289–95.

44 See the articles by Lenoir cited at note 43. For a more extended discussion, see Bressani, "Projet de Labrouste," 57–9.

45 Petit-Radel refers to the help of Henri Labrouste (with his brother Théodore and Léon Vaudoyer) in "Seconde lettre de Petit-Radel," 363. He also refers to Labrouste and his entourage in his *Recherches sur les monumens cyclopéens*. For the parallel between Etruscan architecture and Gothic architecture, see Lenoir, "Monumens sépulcraux de l'Étrurie moyenne." On the general topic of the meaning of the arch for the Romantics, see Bergdoll, *Léon Vaudoyer*, 85–98, 115–34.

46 Letter from Léon Vaudoyer to A.-L.-T. Vaudoyer, 27 June 1828, quoted in Bergdoll, *Léon Vaudoyer*, 88, 293.

47 This idea is diffused through the writings of the Romantics. Apart from Léon Vaudoyer's letter to his father just quoted, see the article by Pierre Morey, "Temple dit de la Paix à Paestum," in *Nouvelles annales publiées par la section française de l'Institut archéologique* 2 (1838): 98–106 at 98–9.

48 Pierre-Simon Ballanche, "Essai de palingénésie sociale" (1827–29), in *Œuvres complètes* (Geneva: Slatkine Reprint, 1967), 331. Subsequent references to Ballanche will be to the page numbers of the reprint.

49 Charles Lenormant, "Étude de la religion phrygienne," in *Nouvelles annales par la section française de l'Institut de correspondance archéologique de Rome* 1 (1836): 215–72 at 242.

50 Ballanche, *Essai de palingénésie sociale*, 421. The foundation rites in the ancient Latium are a recurrent motif in Ballanche's text.

51 Joseph Rykwert, *The Idea of a Town: The Anthropology of Urban Form in Rome, Italy and the Ancient World* (Cambridge, MA: MIT Press, 1988), 106–44.

52 See Labrouste's sketchbook #329, f. 10, Académie d'architecture, Paris.

53 The two sources dominating the literature, even in France, were Carl Niebuhr, *Römische Geschichte* (1811–12), translated into English as *The History of Rome* (London: Taylor and Walton, 1847); and Karl Ottfried Muller, *Die Etrusker* (Breslau: J. Max and komp., 1828).

54 See Carl Niebuhr, *Römische Geschichte* (1811–12; 2nd rev. ed., Berlin: G. Reimer, 1827–45). With his theory of the conflict between the patricians and plebeians arising from differences in race, Niebuhr drew attention to ethnological distinctions as a key factor in historical development. Generally, Niebuhr was acknowledged in the nineteenth century as the father of the modern critical historical method. Niebuhr compared his own method to anatomy: "I dissect words as the anatomists dissect bodies ... I am trying to separate from foreign matters a skeleton of fossil bones collected too carelessly"; quoted in Antoine Guilland, *Modern Germany and Her Historians* (London: Jarrold, 1915), 52. Niebuhr's influence was momentous for Romantic historiography, not only in Germany but also in France, particularly in the circles around Ballanche. J.J. Ampère studied directly under Niebuhr in Bonn in 1826–27. His friend Charles Lenormant, a key member of the Institut de correspondance archéologique in Rome, showed great interest in Niebuhr's theories. See Amélie Lenormant, *Madame Récamier: Les amis de sa jeunesse et sa correspondance intime* (Paris: Lévy, 1874), 248–55. A review of Ottfried Muller's "Die Etrusker," published anonymously in France in the *Revue française* 13 (Jan. 1830): 80–94, underscores the central importance of the work of Niebuhr (with Creuzer and Muller) in modern historiography.

55 Augustin Thierry, "Sur l'antipathie de race qui divise la nation française," *Dix ans d'études historiques* (Paris: J. Tessier, 1835), 292: "We think we

are one nation, but we are two nations occupying the same land, two nations that are enemies in their memories, irreconcilable in their project: one has once conquered the other, and its goals, its eternal wishes are the reviving of that ancient conquest" (my translation). Thierry's article was originally published in *Le censeur européen* (April 1820).

56 See Ballanche, *Essai de palingénésie sociale*; and Jules Michelet, *Introduction à l'histoire universelle* (Paris: Hachette, 1831).

57 Creuzer, *Religions de l'antiquité*, first part of vol. 2, 150.

58 Ballanche, *Essai de palingénésie sociale*, 331.

59 On Huyot's influence on the Romantic pensionnaires, see Bergdoll, *Léon Vaudoyer*, 88–9.

60 J.-N. Huyot, "Notes on my voyage, 1821," from a draft manuscript of his travels in 1817–21 kept at the Bibliothèque nationale in Paris, partly published in Gabriel Vauthier, "J.-N. Huyot, architecte de l'Arc de triomphe de l'Étoile," *Bulletin de l'histoire de l'art français* (1920): 6–19 at 18.

61 Ibid., 16–19. Charles Texier reports that Huyot was particularly interested by the hybrid Doric temple of Assos that had a bas-relief with sphinxes, presumably of Egyptian influence; see Charles Texier, *Descriptions de l'Asie mineure* (Paris: Didot, 1849), vol. 2, 200.

62 Henri Labrouste, *Mémoire explicatif de la restauration des temples de Paestum près Naples* (1829), École des Beaux-Arts, f. 8.

63 Labrouste, *Mémoire*, f. 6–8. Curiously, the first plate discussed in Labrouste's manuscript bears the number 23, the last in the bounded volume of plates. It is unclear whether this numbering system and the binding of the plates dates from Labrouste's original submission or was added later.

64 Ibid., f. 6–7, emphasis added.

65 See Pedley, *Paestum*, 29.

66 Labrouste's account is practically a carbon copy of the description of the walls of Pompei contained in the first volume of François Mazois's *Les ruines de Pompei* (1812), a book from which he had copied some plates. Mazois had established that the origin of the walls of Pompei was Oscan, with some Etruscan influence. I owe to Brigitte Desrochers the observation that Labrouste copied plates from Mazois. In a public talk at the Study Centre of the Canadian Centre for Architecture in Montreal in February 2002, entitled "Beyond Style: The Birth of Structural Classicism in *Les ruines de Pompei*," Desrochers successfully argued the strong influence of Mazois on Labrouste. According to Desrochers, Labrouste contributed to the last volume published after Mazois's death.

67 Petit-Radel, "Seconde lettre de Petit-Radel," 367.
68 Creuzer, *Religions de l'antiquité*, first part of vol. 2, 324.
69 John Griffiths Pedley has recently described the Temple of Ceres (the Temple of Athena, in his terminology) in a similar way; see his *Paestum*, 54.
70 Labrouste, *Les temples de Paestum*, 13.
71 Ibid.
72 Ballanche, *Essai de palingénésie sociale*, 399, 414. Viollet-le-Duc would later characterize the whole development of Western thought as stemming from a fusion of the Doric and the Ionic, the former "admitting only absolute unity," the later allowing "infinite divisibility, difference without identity"; Viollet-le-Duc, *Entretiens sur l'architecture*, vol. 1, 409–10. For a more extended discussion of the concept of fusion in Viollet-le-Duc's architectural theories, see Martin Bressani, "Science, histoire et archéologie: Sources et généalogie de la pensée organiciste de Viollet-le-Duc" (PhD thesis, Université de Paris-Sorbonne, 1987), 415–70.
73 Ballanche, *Essai de palingénésie sociale*, 411–12, 414.
74 For a recent discussion of the importance of this spatial configuration for French Romantic architects, see Witman, "Félix Duban's Didactic Restoration."
75 Niebuhr, *History of Rome*, 292.
76 Expression used by Van Zanten, *Designing Paris*, 13.
77 See Petit-Radel's very extended discussion on this topic in *Examen analytique*, 33–53.
78 Labrouste, *Mémoire explicatif*, f. 34.
79 Levine, "Architectural Reasoning," 354–8.
80 See David Leroy, *Les ruines des plus beaux monuments de la Grèce*, 2nd ed. (Paris: Musier, 1770), vol. 1, plate 1.
81 Leroy mentions the passage in a footnote already in the first edition of *Les ruines des plus beaux monuments de la Grèce* (Paris: Guerin, Delatour & Nyon, 1758), vol. 1, x.
82 Auguste Choisy, *Histoire de l'architecture* (1899; reprint, Paris: Serg, 1976), vol. 1, 204–8, 224–5.
83 Levine, "Architectural Reasoning," 357.
84 *Iliad*, bk 23, trans. Robert Fagles (Harmondsworth: Penguin Books, 1990), 791–4. To my knowledge, the only reference in nineteenth-century architectural writings to this passage by Homer is in Thomas Hope, *Historical Essay on Architecture*, 21.
85 Levine, "Romantic Idea of Architectural Legibility," 390.

86 The passage that best describes a three-stage evolution is the following from Labrouste, *Mémoire explicatif*, f. 30. I borrow from Levine's translation, "Romantic Idea of Architectural Legibility," 389–90, with only slight modifications to stay closer to the original:

I have assumed already that the first care of the Troezenians, founders of Poseidonia, must have been to erect a temple to Neptune, their protector, to whom the city was dedicated; but one is not able to assume ... that the new colonists set out as zealously to erect temples to other deities.

It was only after a number of years of prosperity that the new colonists must have thought to erect a temple to Ceres, in gratitude to the fertility of their lands.

It was also only after many military successes, and when the colony had acquired a certain degree of stability and power, that the Poseidonians must have thought to construct porticoes for the assemblies gathered to discuss communal business.

The passage does not explicitly describe a three-stage chronological sequence, although it could be implied. Note, however, that Labrouste used the term "also" when dealing with the Portico: "It was also only after a number of years." This implies a parallel rather than chronological sequence. Moreover, that Labrouste positioned the discussion of the Portico before the Temple of Ceres in his original manuscript contradicts the reading of a three-stage chronology that may have been implied earlier. Indeed, when Labrouste summarized his chronology, he named the Portico first: "We must therefore consider the Portico and the Temple of Ceres as posterior to the Temple of Neptune" (f. 31). He repeats that order again a few lines below: "and to consider the Portico and the Temple of Ceres as posterior to the temple of Neptune" (f. 31). He seems to have insisted only on the Temple of Neptune having been built first. These few observations lead me to believe that Labrouste had not categorically given the Temple of Ceres chronological priority over the Portico.

87 Morey, "Temple dit de la Paix à Paestum," 98.

88 Victor Hugo, "Preface," in *Cromwell*, 62–109 (1827; reprint, Paris: GF-Flammarion, 1968), 79.

89 Creuzer, *Religions de l'antiquité*, first part of vol. 2, 429.

90 Bergdoll, *Léon Vaudoyer*, 102.

91 For an excellent recent account of that historical doctrine see Antoine

Picon, *Les Saint-simoniens: Raison, imaginaire et utopie* (Paris: Belin, 2002), 60–4. See also François-André Isambert, "Époques critiques et époques organiques – une contribution de Buchez à l'élaboration de la théorie sociale des saint-simoniens," *Cahiers internationaux de sociologie* 27 (1959): 131–52.

92 Labrouste, *Mémoire explicatif*, f. 32.

93 Ballanche, *Essai de palingénésie sociale*, 402, 405.

94 Levine, "Romantic Idea of Architectural Legibility," 401.

95 See L.A. Holland, *Janus and the Bridge* (Rome: American Academy, 1961).

96 Creuzer, *Religions de l'antiquité*, first part of vol. 2, 432–45.

97 Alan B. Spitzer, *The French Generation of 1820* (Princeton: Princeton University Press, 1987), 10.

98 Alfred de Musset, *La Confession d'un enfant du siècle: Oeuvres complètes en prose* (Paris: Gallimard-Pléiades, 1951), 85, quoted and translated in Spitzer, *French Generation of 1820*, 10–11.

Landscapes of Memory: Philosophical and Experiential *Parcours* at the Musée des monumens français[1]

Jennifer Carter

THE RESURGENCE OF THE ELYSIAN FIELD IN EIGHTEENTH-CENTURY FRANCE

THE THEME OF THE ELYSIUM, or Elysian Field, was a literary and architectural preoccupation in late-eighteenth-century France. Inspired by the Greco-Roman land of the afterlife, writers, philosophers, and architects from Jean-Jacques Rousseau to Alexandre Brongniart conceived of garden utopias that would provide respite from contemporary situations of urban overcrowding and political instability, while offering a space for solitary reflection. Unlike its paradisiacal origins in ancient mythology, in which the Elysium was imagined as the abode of the blessed after death, its modern incarnation in late-eighteenth-century France gave greater latitude to the concept. Influenced by innovations in landscape design, ideals of the Elysium informed a surprising variety of public spaces, from the cemetery to the museum, as these emerged in a newly defined, post-Revolution public sphere.

The most famous of these Elysiums, the Père Lachaise Cemetery, was inaugurated in 1804 following an intensive period of cemetery reform and changes in social attitudes toward death (fig. 5.1). It was designed by the city architect, Alexandre-Théodore Brongniart, under the watchful eyes of the city prefect, Citizen Frochot, and of the critic and historian Quatremère de Quincy, and it was developed throughout the first two decades of the nineteenth century. As Paris's first modern cemetery, the Père Lachaise quite literally realized the theme of the Elysium as a space of death. Unlike the city's earlier burial sites that were haphazard and unkempt outgrowths of local parish churches, the topography of the Père Lachaise followed the popular Romantic and Picturesque principles of English landscape theory then being introduced in France, and, by virtue of the personalities buried within its precinct, the cemetery quickly assumed the qualities of a garden-pantheon. This new social space in Parisian society – the burial ground conceived in the image of a *champs de repos* (field of rest) – emerged as one of the paradoxes in the wake of a bloody and violent French Revolution, as Richard Etlin has observed.[2]

Before the Père Lachaise, the idea of the landscaped cemetery had existed only in project form, such as that envisioned by the Parisian administrator Jacques Cambry (1749–1807) in his *Rapport sur les sépultures: Présenté à l'Administration centrale du Département de la Seine*, published in 1799 (fig. 5.2). Cambry had been instructed to visit the

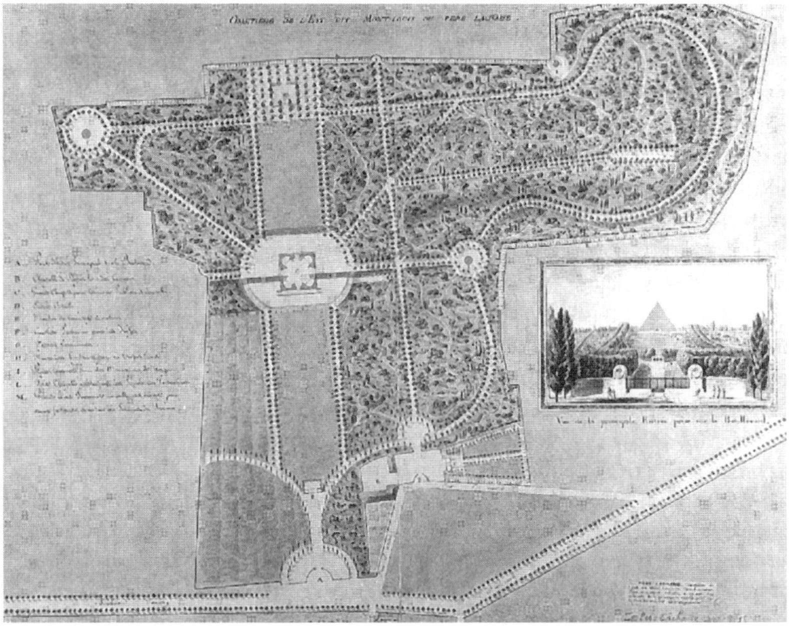

5.1 Plan of the Cemetery of Père Lachaise in Paris, France, by Alexandre-Théodore Brongniart, first project, c. 1812, in Richard Etlin, *Symbolic Space: French Enlightenment Architecture and Its Legacy* (Chicago: University of Chicago Press, 1994), 170.

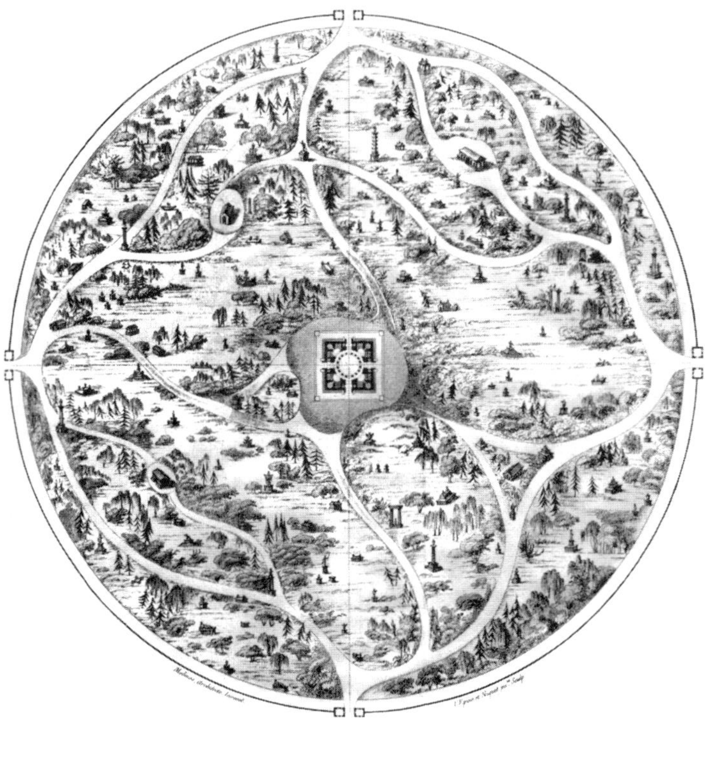

5.2 Plan of the Champs de repos (Field of Rest) proposed by Jacques Cambry, illustrated by Jacques Molinos, in Jacques Cambry, *Rapport sur les sépultures: Présentés à l'Administration centrale du Département de la Seine* (Paris: Impr. de P. Didot, l'aîné, an VII [1799]), plate 1.

cemeteries of Paris and to comment on their condition. His critique was scathing. "No people," he wrote, "no era has left man in such cruel abandon after his death."[3] Cambry's proposed reforms were, in his own words, intended to bring about the cemetery's "return to order, to nature, to gentle sensibility, to the religion of the tomb,"[4] suggesting a romantically inspired vision of death, one advocating that the correct treatment of the dead entailed not only their burial in an idyllic setting, but the philosophical and intellectual dimension that such a setting should and would impart. Throughout his text, Cambry advocated the use of sentimental representations of death, a clear departure from both the neglect and opulence of previous traditions. Nature in this scheme was put to its greatest symbolic potential, with tree species suggesting specific attributes of the dead, such as strength and innocence. Above all, proper burial was to be made a fully public right and expression of Revolutionary ideals. Although Cambry's plan received the city's approbation, it was never realized. We nevertheless detect the genesis of ideas that would be put into effect at the Père Lachaise only a few years later.

The Père Lachaise would become Paris's most famous necropolis, but it was not the city's first Elysian Field. Almost a full decade before its inauguration, Alexandre Lenoir had begun to create his own Elysium, or Elysée, on the grounds of the museum that he founded and administered, the Musée des monumens français, filling it with tombs and monuments dedicated to the memory of famous French artists and intellectuals (figs 5.3 and 5.4). An innovation in its time, this museum presented, through a collection of French monuments, sculpture, and architectural fragments, the history of art in France from the medieval ages to the contemporary moment. Lenoir understood this collection of largely funerary sculpture as representative not only of the nation's artistic production, but also of the history of France itself. Lenoir believed that architecture and the arts adhered to the same laws governing the destiny of empires, a destiny that he viewed as cyclical. Thus the development of empires or nations could be seen through the collection's dual embodiment of the progress and decline of the development of the arts.[5]

Lenoir provided a lengthy historical introduction to the theme of the Elysium in his museum catalogue of 1810, *Musée Impérial des Monumens français: Histoire des arts en France, et description chronologique des statues en marbre et en bronze, bas-reliefs et tombeaux des hommes et des femmes célèbres, qui sont réunis dans ce Musée.*[6] In this essay,

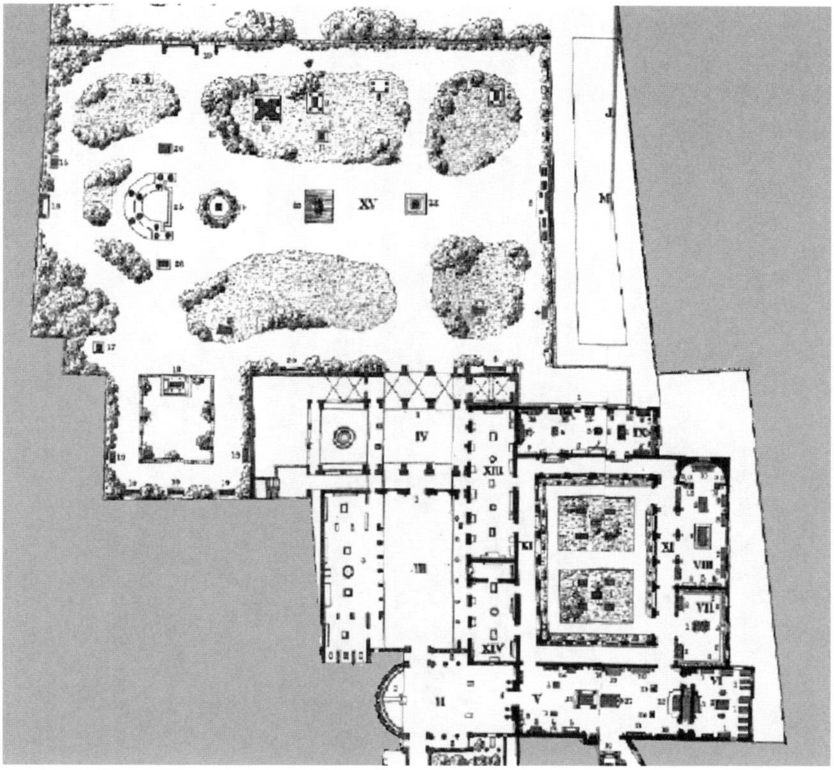

5.3 Plan showing the period halls, cloisters, and Elysium at the Musée des monumens français, Paris, France, 1809, in Ministère de l'instruction publique, *Inventaire général des richesses d'art de la France: Archives du Musée des monumens français* (Paris, 1883–97), vol. 1, in "Avertissement," opposite page x.

Lenoir traced the ancient lineage of the Elysium in diverse cultural practices, noting that in most cases the Elysian Field was a chimeric invention and remained unattainable except to the most virtuous citizens in society: philosophers and poets. In fact, the very idea of the Elysian Field – its function and geographic location and strata – has been interpreted differently by various writers throughout antiquity and the Renaissance. As one of the first writers to locate the afterlife in an Elysian setting, Homer connected the Elysium to the kingdom of Zeus and described in book 4 of the *Odyssey* how Zeus invited those mortal individuals deserving of eternal happiness to the picturesque meadow adjoining the stream of Oceanus, on the western margin of the earth. Menelaus, by

5.4 View of Elysium from cloisters, engraved by Jean Baptiste Réville and Jacques Lavallée, in Jean-Baptiste-Bonaventure de Roquefort, *Vues pittoresques et perspectives des Salles du Musée des monumens français, et des principaux ouvrages d'architecture, de sculpture et de peinture sur verre qu'elles renferment; gravées au burin, en vingt estampes* (Paris: Impr. de P. Didot, l'aîné, 1816), plate 12.

virtue of his marriage to Zeus's daughter Helen, was thus spared the fate of most human bodies in death, where "matter is changed, and varying forms decay." He was sent instead to enjoy Elysium, and

> the blissful pains of utmost earth,
> where Rhadamanthus reigns.
> Joys ever young, unmix'd with pain or fear,
> fill the wide circle of th'eternal year:
> stern winter smiles on that auspicious clime:
> the fields are florid with unfading prime;
> from the bleak pole no winds inclement blow,

mould the round hail, or flake the fleecy snow;
but from the breezy deep the blest inhale
the fragrant murmurs of the western gale.[7]

In Homer's conception of the Elysium, inhabitants are said not to know death *per se*, as they have arrived at this place of immortality without ever having died. This specific designation imbues the Elysium with a liminal quality, for it exists as a transitional domain between life and death.

Conversely, the Roman poet Virgil located the Elysium in the Underworld near Hades, giving form to the setting in the passage where Aeneas encounters his father, Anchises, in book 6 of the *Aeneid*. Virgil described the activities of the dead who engaged in poetry, song, feasting, and dance beneath the setting's own constellations and sun:

> Aeneas enters and sprinkles his body with fresh water and plants the Golden Bough upright upon the threshold ... [In] the happy land of the Elysian Fields, the blessed dwelling places of the Fortunate Groves, Here an ampler air envelops the fields in light ... Some spirits are exercising their limbs on grassy lawns, or vying in games and wrestling on the yellow sand, others are taking part in the dance, and singing songs ... Here are those who were wounded fighting for their country; and those who in their lifetime were pure and pious priests and trusted soothsayers, whose words were meet for Apollo. And those who had made life better with their skill and inventions, and those who were remembered for their kindly deeds.[8]

It was in the writing of his French compatriot, Fénélon, that Lenoir found his most inspirational account of the Elysium. Although he neither identified Fénélon fully nor indicated in which publication the latter mused over the Elysium, I would suggest that Lenoir was referring to François de Salignac de la Mothe-Fénélon, the first and perhaps most famous member in an illustrious line of Fénélons dating back to the mid-seventeenth century from the eponymous château in Périgord. Born in 1651, this Fénélon led a distinguished career as a priest and eventually as archbishop of Cambray,[9] a position to which he was appointed by Louis XIV in 1695 and held until his death in 1715. Fénélon, who pursued an active writing career and published extensively his ideas on education and religion, was posthumously championed by the Encyclopedists for his liberal views and sensibilities and was celebrated as an influence on the Revolution and eighteenth-century utopists.

Lenoir was interested in Fénélon's musings on the Elysium, an account that he quoted at length and appreciated not only for its elegance and simplicity – these were mere stylistic conventions – but equally for the eternal happiness that Fénélon's portrait promised. It was a happiness derived from a sense of unity, the unity of a humankind perfectly and harmoniously engaged in communal activity: "They see, they taste their happiness, and know they will always be this way. They sing the gods' praises, together in a single voice, a single thought, a single heart. A common bliss ebbs and flows in these unified souls."[10] Fénélon's emphasis on the Elysium as a space of unity introduced a new dimension to the eighteenth-century appropriation of the term, and in this particular conception of the Elysium, Lenoir recognized a model for his own society in the aftermath of the French Revolution and its rejection of the Ancien Régime. In previous descriptions, the hero who was sent to the Elysian Fields lived in itinerant leisure, without specific purpose or attachment to place; Virgil described it well: "No one has a fixed home; we live in the shady forests, on the soft river-banks, in meadows fresh with streams."[11] However, when Lenoir adopted the setting for his own ends, there would be a greater unity of purpose and design. Clearly, a different intention inspired his invocation of the Elysium: under him the Elysium became a vehicle of nationalist display that articulated French nationhood as the sum of the accomplishments of a variety of citizens, not simply philosophers but artists and musicians as well.

THE ELYSIUM AT THE MUSÉE DES MONUMENS FRANÇAIS: DEMOCRATIZING HISTORIOGRAPHY

While Lenoir identified with Fénélon and his writing, he still lamented the absence of a real Elysium. To his eighteenth-century sensibilities, such a space would be neither imaginary nor elusive but accessible to the citizen, a space that celebrated good and virtuous deeds in the mortal and moral world: a pantheon of illustrious figures. From his lengthy catalogue exposé, it is clear that Lenoir was justifying the need for his own Elysium – a tangible, sensorial, and evocative Campo Santo[12] – to be realized as an integral component of the philosophical and spatial program at the Musée des monumens français.

Lenoir began to develop plans for this Elysium in 1796, the year following the official inauguration and opening of the museum to the public. In it, he dispersed approximately forty monuments dedicated to the memory of artists, musicians, writers, philosophers, and historians throughout the site, much like in a modern cemetery, without strict chronological or typological structure. These monuments were placed at the edges of pathways, within a tranquil carpet of flowers and lawn. In their seemingly random placement, the monuments in the Elysium were a strong contrast to the inner organization of the museum, with its monuments arranged in chronologically ordered, century-specific halls. Unlike in the interior, one's encounter with the Elysium's monuments was perforce random, episodic, unanticipated. Contemporary representations of this space illustrate this intention. The forty plates on the Musée in Jean-Pierre Brès's evocatively titled *Souvenirs du Musée des monumens français*, published in 1821, present a meandering movement through the garden, unlike the full-frontal depictions of the interior halls (figs 5.5 and 5.6).

Thus, through its different collections and organizations, Lenoir's museum intended visitors to engage with the past in different ways. Inside, the narrative was based on an aesthetics of style and informed by a Hegelian notion of time: linear, rigorously chronological, and progress-oriented. Outside, the narrative was Romantic and far less structured by either the perception of time or style: rather, it was fluid, literary, and free of stylistic associations. Two forms of representation were used to communicate two different historiographies at the Musée des monumens français: one traditional and one emerging. In the Elysium, Lenoir assembled tributes to outstanding citizens, the preferred democratic subjects of an evolving Romantic historiographic narrative and genre, not the kings and queens who were the focus of a Humanist historiography in the Musée's interior.

THE ELYSIUM AND EIGHTEENTH-CENTURY LANDSCAPE THEORY

In a lengthy catalogue essay, Lenoir's discussion of literary precedents for his Elysium provide us with ample insight into how he anticipated his own space of ideal happiness would be experienced and what function this space would serve in a museum dedicated to the display of history and art. Through their individual presence and meaning, as well as

5.5 View of Elysium, drawn by J.-E. Biet, engraved by Normand Père et fils, in Jean-Pierre Brès, *Souvenirs du Musée des monumens français, Collection de 40 dessins perspectifs gravés au trait représentant les principaux aspects sous lesquels on a pu considérer tous les monumens réunis dans ce musée* (Paris: L'auteur, chez Normand fils, P. Didot l'aîné impr. du Roi, 1821–26), plate 37.

5.6 View of the thirteenth-century hall, drawn by J.-E. Biet, engraved by Normand Père et fils, in Jean-Pierre Brès, *Souvenirs du Musée des monumens français, Collection de 40 dessins perspectifs gravés au trait représentant les principaux aspects sous lesquels on a pu considérer tous les monumens réunis dans ce musée* (Paris: L'auteur, chez Normand fils, P. Didot l'aîné impr. du Roi, 1821–26), plate 15.

their assembly in the Elysium, Lenoir believed that these monuments could stimulate the soul, provide useful lessons, and recall touching memories. Lenoir also recognized the potential to give new life to the objects assembled in his garden, invoking the word that he quoted from Fénélon, *félicité*, or bliss: "That one assumes these lifeless remains are receiving a new life to see, to hear and to enjoy a communal and constant bliss ... we are honoured to admit that we experience a gentle and new emotion every time we visit this venerable enclosure; we would add that the greatest reward would be to transmit to the souls of our readers and visitors the saintly respect with which, in making this Elysium, we ourselves were endowed toward enlightenment, talent and virtue."[13]

In his understanding of the Elysium's ability to engage the soul, Lenoir was influenced by Rousseau's philosophical ideas about nature as a stimulus to the imagination and about the role of the imagination in appreciating objects and their evocative potential. Rousseau's proclamation that an object can be a catalyst for memory resonates with Lenoir's own ideas about remembering and engaging the past. As Suzanne Nalbantian has noted in her study of the shape of memory in literature, "Rousseau's memory patterns do not *connect* moments in time but rather *isolate* them as prevailing incidents or what might be termed as Wordsworthian '*spots* of time,' which are building blocks in the formation of that identity considered to be the soul."[14] Lenoir's placement of funerary monuments in the Musée's Elysium themselves created "spots of time" by choreographing historical phenomena in Nature. Like Rousseau, who freely resorted to invention to fill in the gaps, Lenoir used the compositional freedom of the *fabrique*[15] to achieve veracity rather than accuracy in the individual monument, while the narrative of his century-specific halls in the interior of the museum relied on an even greater number of exemplar-objects, such as statues of the monarchy, to illustrate France's official history.

THE OBJECT AND THE FRAGMENT: RECONFIGURING WHOLENESS

Many monuments arrived at the Musée in fragmentary condition, and Lenoir went to great lengths to restore these items before putting them on display. Unlike his contemporary John Soane, in whose museum of architecture in London the fragment was valued precisely for its poetic associations, Lenoir *did not* leave the object in a fragmented state. His obsession with reconfiguring the object to a pristine, although not necessarily "authentic," condition seems to have been informed more by a literary sensibility, such as that of Rousseau, than by the prevailing views of his contemporaries and immediate predecessors in architecture and the fine arts, namely Soane, Giovanni Battista Piranesi, and David LeRoy. Rousseau sought to overcome memory lapses, not to confabulate or to promote falsity: "and if by chance I have used some immaterial embellishment ('quelque ornement indifférent') it has been only to fill a void due to a defect of memory."[16] Likewise, Lenoir's impetus seems to have been a post-Revolution need to fill in the void: to rewrite a cohesive history of France and to render this history visible, tangible, felt, even as the nation itself was revising its own history.

THE ELYSIUM AND CONTEMPORARY LANDSCAPE THEORY

Despite the historiographic and scenographic differences in the two parts of the museum, Lenoir's own writing indicates that he considered the Elysium to be essential in communicating the museum's overall character. Lenoir further claimed in the 1810 edition of his catalogue that the Elysium would be visible from the Introductory Hall of the Musée, establishing from the outset both an agreeable perspective and *the idea* of a sense of movement or trajectory in the space.[17] This is similar to a principle that the marquis and vicomte d'Ermenonville, René-Louis Girardin (1735–1808), inaugurated in his own garden and one by which the French Picturesque landscape movement distinguished itself from earlier English landscape theories. Girardin recognized the importance of treating the landscape as a whole (*un ensemble*) and used this principle to guide his designs for his estate at Ermenonville. Thus, as the writer Mérigot remarked in his narrative walking tour entitled *Promenade ou Itinéraire des jardins d'Ermenonville*, published in 1788,[18] Girardin was the first to compose a garden with a concern for how it would be seen from the interior of the château.

In this respect, I argue that Lenoir's conception of the Elysium was informed by a two-fold interpretation of contemporary garden and landscape theory, both as a theoretical practice and as a literary narrative. The emergence of garden treatises in England and France inaugurated a new genre of writing in the mid to late eighteenth century. Unlike the architectural treatise, the garden treatise was primarily descriptive and experiential in tone, providing a narrative walk-through of the garden as the author had conceived it. As we shall see, only a small number of written passages in Lenoir's catalogue emulated this genre (Lenoir's writing was largely in the tradition of antiquarian literature). However, the similarities are based more on practice and intent than uniquely on the style of writing. The approaches to both the garden and the museum invited visitors to activate their imaginative faculties, to enter a landscape of monuments rich in narrative potential and engage in their stories. The parallels were also compositional: principles of perspective, points of view, use of the *parcours* (or pathway), the heightened concept of space as experiential, and the role of nature and its appeal to the imagination for sustained engagement. All of these elements were theorized in the eighteenth-century French landscape treatise and became integral to the experience of a garden site as well as to Lenoir's compositional interventions at the Musée des monumens français.

Key to the Picturesque garden were philosophical ideals that recognized the potential of the landscape to produce mental sensations through association. They can be traced to John Locke's empirical philosophy that all knowledge of the world derives from sensory awareness and personal experience, displacing the concept of the mind as a receptacle for revealed Truth.[19] As Elizabeth Barlow Rogers has observed in her recent book *Landscape Design*,[20] Lockean empiricism and its literary and political developments in Rousseau would make the various forms of the garden – from the rural cemetery to the public park – the ideal sites for honouring citizens and heroes of state. The "landscape of moral virtue," as Rogers has defined it, could promote solitary contemplation and the idea that perception and intuitive thinking were governed more by sentiment than by Enlightenment's reason.

If we consider how the eighteenth-century landscape treatise provided a model for Lenoir, there are two principal observations to be made. The first, as we have seen, occurs at the level of practice and concerns the elements of landscape design that Lenoir incorporated into his Elysium and period halls. The second was realized on a literary level, and Lenoir's catalogue descriptions provide clues to his intentions. Lenoir seamlessly made the transition from an expository essay on the history and cross-cultural shape of Elysiums – a *parallèle*, if you will – to a description of its actualization in the garden of his Musée by invoking the voice and the role of the storyteller: in other words, by altering the narrative voice in his catalogue from a detached overseer to an engaged visitor. Inviting the reader/visitor to enter his Elysium landscape and partake of its narratives, Lenoir himself guided the tour of the garden: "Let us enter with our readers into this venerable landscape, to examine the monuments that a humble hand dared to dedicate to famous men."[21] This narrative device contrasts markedly with his previous writing style. It prompts the reader to adopt a different relationship with the text by engaging the imaginative faculties and identifying with the textual and spatial narratives. As Elizabeth MacArthur has noted in her study of literary accounts of landscape gardens, the presence of the tomb in the garden (and Lenoir's Elysium was full of them), "makes the garden into a narrative: it arouses the visitor's desire, perhaps even motivating the visit, but it also focuses and orients that desire, and provides a sense of closure."[22]

In effect, Lenoir appropriated the narrative techniques and literary genre of landscape theorists such as Girardin[23] and his contemporary Claude-Henri Watelet.[24] Both authors embarked on a descriptive journey of the site, focusing less on the objects themselves and more on the stories that they evoked, individually and collectively. In his description of the Elysium, Lenoir mentioned his own personal designs for monuments within the garden and the interior. He described the monument of the antiquarian and historian Bernard de Montfauçon, for example, as a composite of "hieroglyphs, Egyptian figures, Greek reliefs, figures from the late Roman Empire and remains of monuments from the first years of the French monarchy" (fig. 5.7).[25] This was one of many monuments that Lenoir created from the remains of others – a curious conservationist practice by our current standards and not without criticism in his own time as well. Although Lenoir insisted that the monuments he fabricated, his *fabriques*, combined only materials from similar historical eras (much like the criteria by which he organized his period halls), he did not always abide by this dictum. In the very popular chapel that he recreated for the medieval lovers Héloïse and Abélard, Lenoir combined a newly commissioned neo-Gothic canopy, the twelfth-century funerary monuments that he had purchased from their original setting at the Abbey of Paraclet near Nogent-sur-Seine, and a contemporary death mask of Héloïse that he commissioned from the sculptor – and later detractor of his practices – Louis-Pierre Deseine (fig. 5.8). Biet described the making of this *fabrique*-installation:

5.7 Lenoir's fabrique and monument to Bernard de Montfauçon, featuring a composite of Egyptian, Greek, and Roman sources, in Alexandre Lenoir, *Recueil de gravures pour servir à l'histoire des arts en France, prouvée par les monumens* (Paris: Chez l'auteur, au Musée, C.L.F. Panckoucke, 1812), image 513.

5.8 Lenoir's installation and monument to Héloïse and Abélard, drawn by J.-E. Biet, engraved by Normand Père et fils, in Jean-Pierre Brès, *Souvenirs du Musée des monumens français, Collection de 40 dessins perspectifs gravés au trait représentant les principaux aspects sous lesquels on a pu considérer tous les monumens réunis dans ce musée* (Paris: L'auteur, chez Normand fils, P. Didot l'aîné impr. du Roi, 1821–26), plate 38.

> The monument of Héloïse and Abélard, as we see it here, was built under the direction of M. Le Noir [*sic*]. In the making of this monument, we used the remains of a chapel from the Church of Saint-Denis, as well as the tomb that Pierre-le-Vénérable had built for his friend Abélard, in the chapel of the infirmary of Saint-Marcel-lez-Châlons [*sic*]. In its ensemble, this monument communicates the character of architecture in the twelfth century ... We were unable to obtain statues or authentic busts of Héloïse and Abélard. The heads of the two statues that we see here are based on the skeletal remains of Héloïse and Abélard, and were sculpted by a contemporary artist.[26]

As Lenoir confessed in his own writing, in the absence of authentic objects, an invention will do, providing that it conforms to the architectural character of the period. This very viewpoint also underlay Lenoir's spatial conceptions of the period halls.

There is perhaps an explanation for Lenoir's unorthodox conservationist attitude toward the very objects that he collected and purported to be "salvaging" from vandals and general neglect. In contemporary landscape theory, the *fabrique* was a garden structure, closely allied with French Picturesque painting and popular in the late eighteenth century, when English garden theory first appeared on the continent. The *fabrique* was likened to another popular garden element of the time, the folly, a structure intended to evoke a poetic past or an exotic place. These architectural constructions varied in form from bridges to huts, grottoes, and Gothic ruins and were placed in select locations throughout the landscape.

Elizabeth Barlow Rogers has claimed that the French landscape theorist Claude-Henri Watelet coined the term *fabrique* in a 1756 entry in the *Encyclopédie*, although his description at the time was confined to the language of painting (*le langage de la Peinture*). The term, if not the object itself, would reappear in Watelet's own treatise of 1774 and in his French garden, Moulin Joli. Watelet concluded his treatise with correspondence to a friend, in which he described a contemplative walk in a pastoral French garden containing the popular features of a deserted island and a building-monument to Héloïse. Celebrating a Romantic appreciation of both the landscape and the solitary promenade, Watelet's work anticipated Rousseau's *Reveries of the Solitary Walker*, a series of ten essays or "walks" composed between late October 1776 and the philosopher's death in July 1778, and published posthumously in 1782. Besides being Rousseau's last written works, these essays are unique in his oeuvre because they were written in a remarkably different voice than earlier publications such as his *Dialogues* and *Confessions*.[27]

As noted at the beginning of this essay, Lenoir's Elysium preceded the Père Lachaise as the first modern cemetery in France, but there was also a philosophical, literary, and formal precedent to Lenoir's work that brings the story of his interest in garden theory full circle. Of all the forays into landscape design and its theories in late-eighteenth-century France, the writing and activities of René-Louis Girardin perhaps most explicitly synthesized the period's interest in the Elysium and its incarnation in the eighteenth-century French garden. An amateur gardener who wished to redesign his estate at Ermenonville in the early 1770s, Girardin originally had sought advice from the renowned Lyonnais landscape architect Jean-Marie Morel (1728–1810), whose treatise *Théorie des jardins, ou L'Art des Jardins de la Nature* was published in Paris in 1774. When Girardin's views on the use of monuments for their associative potential rather than their utilitarian function were not well received by Morel, Girardin dismissed him and proceeded to design his 2,100 acre estate in the manner of the *parc à l'anglaise* on his own over the next decade. In his landscape theories, Girardin espoused close-up views rather than sweeping, panoramic vistas; he composed scenes in the manner of arcadian and rural paintings; and his garden included the final resting place of Rousseau, in a Roman-style tomb designed by Hubert Robert on the picturesque Ile des Peupliers (figs 5.9 and 5.10).

Girardin concurrently wrote and published a garden treatise of his own, *De la composition des paysages, ou Des moyens d'embellir la nature autour des habitations, en y joignant l'agréable à l'utile* (1777), which was heavily indebted to principles of the English *ferme ornée*[28] and French Romanticism. At a time when many English treatises (such as those of Walpole, Whately, and Chamber) were being translated into French, Girardin's treatise was the only French garden treatise to be translated into English. Furthermore, while the origins of the French Picturesque in landscape painting and its subsequent influence on landscape development are often a subject of discussion in the landscape treatise,[29] the connection between garden theory and landscape painting in Girardin's situation is explicit: three contemporary French painters and acquaintances of Girardin – Hubert Robert (1733–1808), François Boucher (1703–70), and Claude-Henri Watelet (1718–86) – were also involved in garden design.

5.9 Left: View of Rousseau's resting place on the Ile des Peupliers, drawn by Mérigot fils, text ascribed to Stanislas Girardin, in *Promenade ou Itinéraire des jardins d'Ermenonville: Auquel on a joint vingt-cinq de leurs principales vues* (Paris: Chez Mérigot, 1788), plate 9.

5.10 Right: View of Rousseau's tomb on the Ile des Peupliers, drawn by Mérigot fils, text ascribed to Stanislas Girardin, in *Promenade ou Itinéraire des jardins d'Ermenonville: Auquel on a joint vingt-cinq de leurs principales vues* (Paris: Chez Mérigot, 1788), plate 10.

In an increasingly secular society, monumental tombs such as Rousseau's on the Ile des Peupliers were designed to honour contemporary national heroes rather than historical, religious, or monarchical figures, thus demonstrating a significant shift in historiographic practices. Rousseau's writing on politics and nature had struck a chord with French Republican sensibilities. Thus it was not surprising that Girardin, a great patron and admirer of Rousseau, chose to pay homage to the exiled Swiss philosopher on his estate. In creating his garden as a meditative itinerary at Ermenonville, Girardin realized Rousseau's philosophical views about man living in unity with nature and showed how the garden could engage the imagination in a space designed for reflection. A meander to the temple of philosophy, the Naïades grotto and waterfall, the arcadian prairie, and the altar of reverie culminated with a view of Rousseau's tomb, a popular pilgrimage site visited by thousands until its reconsecration at the Pantheon in 1794, less than two years before Lenoir began work on his own Elysium.

5.11 Twentieth-century view of Naumachy, Lenoir's *fabrique* at Malmaison, in Bernard Chevallier, *Malmaison Château et domaine des origines à 1904* (Paris: Éditions de la Réunion des musées nationaux, 1989), 431, plate 218.

Whether Lenoir ever visited Ermenonville is not known. What is known is that Lenoir also pursued curatorial activities tied to garden design outside his official duties at the Musée des monumens français. In his role as Conservateur des objets d'art de la Malmaison to Empress Josephine, a curatorial position that he occupied as early as 1801, Lenoir collaborated on a number of *fabriques* and installations for Josephine's garden and principal residence at Château Malmaison (where she resided from 1799 until her death in 1814), including the Temple de l'Amour, the grotto housing a sculpture of St Francis reconfigured as a garden hermit, the stele entitled *Mélancolie*, and the *Naumachie* (fig. 5.11).[30] Coincidentally, Morel, whose position at Ermenonville had been cut short, had also been employed by Josephine for a brief period at Malmaison.[31]

Lenoir's literary and spatial innovations at the Musée des monumens français positioned this eighteenth-century museum in a different light than traditional scholarship would have it. Shortly after the turn of the nineteenth century, the museum institution would emerge as a physical incarnation of prevailing literary models of didacticism, Diderot and d'Alembert's *Encyclopédie* being the most prominent example. Yet in its pre-Revolution form, as Anthony Vidler has noted, the museum institution was much more diverse in scope, ambition, and intention.[32] The garden as an originary site for museological inquiry was an important inspiration for Alexandre Lenoir. Landscape theory was by no means an exclusive source for Lenoir, but it provides an important conceptual framework for considering his highly original creation as something other than a manifestation of the democratization of royal collections after the fall of the Ancien Régime. In its narrative presentation of sepulchral sculptures and its use of early Romantic principles of landscape design, the Elysium at the Musée des monumens français was conceived as a *parcours* and space of memory, a landscape of evocative objects to engage the senses (fig. 5.12).

5.12 Lenoir's monument to himself, in Alexandre Lenoir, *Recueil de gravures pour servir à l'histoire des arts en France, prouvée par les monumens* (Paris: Chez l'auteur, au Musée, C.L.F. Panckoucke, 1812), 11.

NOTES

1 I would like to thank the librarians at the Canadian Centre for Architecture for their research assistance in the preparation of this essay.

2 Richard Etlin traced the tradition of gardens of remembrance in *The Architecture of Death: The Transformation of the Cemetery in Eighteenth-Century Paris* (Cambridge, MA: MIT Press, 1984), ch. 6, 229–301.

3 Jacques Cambry, *Rapport sur les sépultures: Présenté à l'Administration centrale du Département de la Seine* (Paris, 1799), 1, my translation.

4 Ibid., 1.

5 As early as the third edition of his museum catalogue (1796–97), Lenoir claimed that "the arts undergo revolutions just as empires do: they develop successively from childhood to superiority [*sic*], and eventually return to the point at which they began"; see Alexandre Lenoir, *Description historique et chronologique des monumens de sculpture, réunis au musée des monumens français*, 3rd ed. (Paris: Au Musée, rue des Petits-Augustins, an V [1796–97]), 9, my translation.

6 Alexandre Lenoir, *Musée impérial des monumens français: Histoire des arts en France, et description chronologique des statues en marbre et en bronze, bas-reliefs et tombeaux des hommes et des femmes célèbres, qui sont réunis dans ce Musée* (Paris: De l'Imprimerie d'Hacquart, 1810), 277–87. Lenoir also described the Elysée in volume 5 of his eight-volume publication, *Musée des monumens français, ou Description historique et chronologique des statues en marbre et en bronze, bas-reliefs et tombeaux des hommes et des femmes célèbres pour servir à l'histoire de France et à celle de l'art* (Paris: De l'Impr. de Guilleminet, 1800–21).

7 Homer, *The Odyssey of Homer*, trans. Alexander Pope (London: Ingram, Cooke, and Co., 1853), bk 4, 66.

8 Vergil, *The Aeneid*, trans. and intro. James H. Mantinband (New York: Frederick Ungar, 1964), 131–2.

9 In an attempt to enlarge his collection of monuments and "national antiquities" at the Musée, Lenoir presented a report on Cambray Cathedral to the Celtic Society in 1806 and published it as an article, "Rapport sur la cathédrale de Cambray," in 1809. In this report, Lenoir made a case for procuring the remains of Cambray Cathedral, notably its allegorical sculptures, for the reconstruction of the Musée's eleventh-century hall, claiming that he could cull from the cathedral's ruins its most important pieces to add to the collection of the Musée des monumens français; see Alexandre

Lenoir, "Rapport sur la cathédrale de Cambray: Lu à l'Académie celtique, dans la séance du 29 Septembre 1806," in Vaudoyer collection, *Architecture, antiquités, arts, mélangés* (1819), available at the Canadian Centre for Architecture, Montreal.

10 Lenoir, *Musée Impérial*, 282–4.

11 Virgil, *Aeneid*, 132.

12 Ironically, Quatremère de Quincy, with whom Lenoir would have numerous debates about the very existence and survival of the Musée des monumens français, proposed in a letter to the *Moniteur Universel* (13 April 1791) a Parisian version of Pisa's Campo Santo as an alternative to the Panthéon then being planned. Quatremère retracted his views in support of a garden cemetery in a later article on ideal cemeteries published in the *Encyclopédie Méthodique*; see Etlin, *Architecture of Death*, 232.

13 Lenoir, *Musée Impérial*, 293.

14 Suzanne Nalbantian, *Memory in Literature: From Rousseau to Neuroscience* (Houndmills, UK, and New York: Palgrave MacMillan, 2003), 31–2, original emphasis; see esp. ch 2, 24–42.

15 The *fabrique* was a sculptural fabrication by Lenoir, a recomposition of existing "debris," often with contemporary additions.

16 Jean-Jacques Rousseau, quoted in Nalbantian, *Memory in Literature*, 27.

17 Dominique Poulot, "Un jardin de la mémoire," *Jardins et châteaux*; *Dalhousie French Studies* 29 (Winter 1994): 159–68 at 163: "From the Museum's introduction hall, located near the street, we'll see the Elysian garden; this will give a sense of movement to the architecture and will provide a pleasant perspective ... Greenery and trees will dominate the background of the building and will leave openings to allow multiple viewpoints" (my translation).

18 J. Mérigot, with text ascribed to Stanislas Girardin, *Promenade, ou Itinéraire des jardins d'Ermenonville: Auquel on a joint vingt-cinq de leurs principales vues*, designed and engraved by J. Mérigot fils, 1st ed. (Paris: Chez Mérigot, 1788). Mérigot subsequently published a similar descriptive promenade of Chantilly in his *Promenades, ou Itinéraires des jardins de Chantilly: Orné d'un plan et de vingt estampes représentent les principales vues* (Paris: Desenne, 1791).

19 See John Locke, *An Essay Concerning Human Understanding* (New York: Dover Publications, 1959).

20 Elizabeth Barlow Rogers, *Landscape Design: A Cultural and Architectural History* (New York: Stewart, Tabori and Chang; London: Thames and Hudson, 2001).

21 Lenoir, *Musée Impérial*, 286.

22 Elizabeth MacArthur, "The Tomb in the Garden," *Jardins et châteaux*; *Dalhousie French Studies* 29 (Winter 1994): 97–111 at 106.

23 Stanislas Girardin, *De la composition des paysages, ou Des moyens d'embellir la Nature autour des Habitations, en joignant l'agréable à l'utile* (Geneva: n.p., 1777).

24 Claude-Henri Watelet, *Essais sur les jardins* (Paris: Du fonds de Prault père, chez Prault, 1774).

25 Lenoir, *Musée Impérial*, 290.

26 J.-P. Brès, *Souvenirs du Musée des monumens français: Collection de 40 dessins perspectives gravés au trait représentant les principaux aspects sous lesquels on a pu considerer tous les monumens réunis dans ce Musée*, drawn by M. J.-E. Biet, engraved by Mm. Normand père et fils, with commentary by M. J.-P. Brès (Paris: L'auteur, chez Normand fils, P. Didot ainé, impr. du Roi, 1821), 39, my translation.

27 See the Preface and Interpretive Essay by Charles Butterworth in Jean-Jacques Rousseau, *The Reveries of the Solitary Walker*, vii–xix, 145–240 (Indianapolis and Cambridge: Hackett, 1992).

28 *Ferme ornée* is the French term for ornamental farm, used by Stephen Switzer in *The nobleman, gentleman, and gardener's Recreation, or, An introduction to gardening, planting, agriculture, and the other business and pleasures of a country life* (London: Printed for B. Barker and C. King, 1715). The concept advocated the use of aesthetic principles in agricultural practices, such as the incorporation of monuments to provoke poetic associations, the use of the circuit drive for movement throughout the landscape, and the compositional planting of vines, flowers, and hedges between fields.

29 For Watelet's treatise and discussion of *Des Parcs modernes*, see his *Essais sur les jardins*, 55–61, in which he explicitly states that the Picturesque derived its ideas from painting.

30 Josephine assembled an eclectic collection of paintings, antiques, sculptures, curiosities, and ethnographic objects at her chateau, for which she consulted Baron Dominique Vivant Denon, director of the Musée Napoléon,

the dealer Guillaume-Jean Constantin (for paintings), and Lenoir (for antique objects). She regularly transferred objects from the nation's museums to supplement her own developing collection. In 1809 Lenoir compiled for Josephine a *catalogue raisonné* detailing the collection of antiquities and marbles at her imperial palace at Malmaison and, upon her death in 1814, was responsible for the inventory of Josephine's estate. For a comprehensive account of Malmaison in the Napoleonic regime, see Bernard Chevallier, *Malmaison, château et domaine des origines à 1904* (Paris: Editions de la Réunion des musées nationaux, 1989).

31 Josephine officially appointed Morel landscape architect of Malmaison in 1803, although he was involved to a lesser degree as of 1801. In 1802 a second edition of his treatise was published, with a dedication to Josephine. Note that the design for a *jardin à l'anglaise* had already been traced by the chateau's previous owners, M. et Mme. Le Couteulx.

32 Anthony Vidler, *The Writing of the Walls: Architectural Theory in the Late Enlightenment* (Princeton: Princeton Architectural Press, 1987), esp. essay entitled "Architecture in the Museum: Didactic Narratives from Boullée to Lenoir," 165–73.

Looking around the Edge of the World: Contending with the Continuist Principle and the Plenarist Passion

Edward S. Casey

Chora

> Things are no longer there simply according to their projective appearances ... but on the contrary upright, insistent, flaying our glance with their edges.
>
> – Maurice Merleau-Ponty[1]

IN THIS CHAPTER I REFLECT on something that we don't usually pause to consider: edges. Despite their delimited and focal character, edges are found everywhere; little, if anything, in our experience comes unedged, and the range of edges is enormous: from the edge of the earth (and its many regions) to the edge of the most mundane object (these pages). The world as we know it is rarely if ever edgeless. Every thing, every place has its edges. Of very few concepts can such scope be claimed.

Why this extensivity of the edge? What does it signify about our insertion into the spatial world?

Most two-dimensional surfaces end in edges that limit them, and certain edges meet in the corners of solid rectilinear objects, while still others confront us. But any such formal analysis fails to capture the role of edges in ordinary experience. This role is complex and highly ambiguous. Edges act both to protect us (from what threatens from their other side) as well as to block us (e.g., in our forward movement or from getting a straightforward view). For the most part, edges are obstructive, something that we have to get around to get somewhere else. They hold us back, or at the least make us consider what to do next. They are "coefficients of adversity" (in Sartre's term), offering not ease of passage but resistance to motion or sight, what Peirce might call "Secondness."[2] They stand in our way, or else they lead us to change our direction if we are already on our way. The life-world is an edgy place, multiply so and often to our frustration, although sometimes to our delight (as when an architect modulates edges to suit our fancy).

In view of the densely edged character of the world, humans and other creatures have devised special means to cope with the situation – given that any mobile nervous animal must be able to manoeuvre as freely as possible in the larger environment, the place-world. In other current work, I focus on two of these means: the glance and imagination, the first taken from the realm of perception and the other from that of mentation. Imagination is characteristically wayward but with remarkable resources and few limits of inventiveness; the glance is hawklike in its ability to pick out discrete features of things yet possesses few resources of its own, being so outwardly directed. Despite these basic differences, the two acts are closely affiliated in their collusive and constructive dealings with the edge-world. Each gives us decisive assistance in navigating through this world – and doing so swiftly and effectively.[3]

Such motions, endowed with the rapidity of Hermes, occur in very different domains: at home, as we careen from one room to another, not by walking but by looking or phantasying; when we travel, as we project what lies beyond the horizon of today's ventures; indeed, whenever we wish to be located elsewhere without literally taking steps to get there, getting there instead by looking or imagining ahead. I shall consider the predicament of the edge – its virtual tyranny in our ongoing lives – by first considering the circumstance of early exploration beyond the Mediterranean, where the edge rises in an especially dramatic form; then I shall reflect on the role of the edge in architecture, contrasting it with the fold, before ending with some thoughts on the relation between edge and place.

GOING AROUND THE EDGE OF THE EARTH

I

Can we even imagine what it was like to set out on sea voyages in the ancient world – voyages that would take sailors into the heart of darkness and the unknown? Given a lack of reliable maps and adequate navigational devices, the prospect of sailing on a trackless waste of water must have been terrifying. The ancient Greeks even coined a special word for the open sea, *pontos*,[4] and they were terrified of going astray on it, instead preferring to cling to the coastline and to travel from port to port in the cautious manner that came to be called *costagierre*, in which the fearful sailor never lost sight of land. As a recent study of this situation, aptly titled *The Edges of the Earth in Ancient Thought*, puts it: "Greek sailors and seamen felt ill at ease when surrounded by large stretches of open water; they were accustomed, even when sailing the comparatively placid Aegean, to hug the coasts and stay within sight of land at all times. The prospect of sailing in waters so wide that no land could be seen was regarded with great apprehension, and open-sea voyages were attempted only under extreme duress."[5] If the bounded waters of the Mediterranean were felt to be threatening (even the Phoenicians found them so), all the more so was *ōkeanos* – the ocean that surrounded the known world and was thought to begin at the Pillars of Heracles (the Straits of Gibraltar). This was a truly *boundless* body of water, and the very term *to apeiron*, "the boundless," was often applied to it. It was thought to be radically indeterminate in extent and composition: foggy, muddy, "a murky and undifferentiated welter of elements."[6] In its very inchoate state, it was thought to be primeval – to have been there since the origin of the universe and perhaps to *be* this origin. Thus its temporal boundlessness matched its spatial distendedness.

Nevertheless, although unbounded in itself, *ōkeanos* did serve as the boundary of the earth, its extreme limit, its outer edge. This is the primary paradox of ancient Greek geography: what is boundless on its own terms acts as a fiercely delimiting boundary for the very earth that it surrounds. Shapeless in its outer extent, it had shape, *peira*, on its inner edge – like a vast river (and *ōkeanos* was technically a "river," *potamos*) with only one bank. There was an ancient fascination – indeed, an obsession – with the idea of *epi peirasi gaiēs*, being "at the borders of the earth." Such borders were considered "the physical extremities of the earth ... the limit of the human world."[7] A *peirar*, or "boundary," is embodied in a shoreline or coast, and if this latter notion is extended to the inner edge of the world-ocean, then it becomes clear that the "boundaries of Ocean" (*peirata ōkeanoio*) are in effect the edges of continents. Indeed, the etymology of *ōkeanos* itself is "that which encircles" the earth, regarded as an island composed of the continents of Europe, Africa, and Asia. The famous ekphrastic Shield of Achilles in the *Iliad*, book 18, shows the earth as surrounded by Ocean at its outer limit: "Around the rim Ocean flowed, seeming as if in flood, and surrounded the entire much-embellished shield."[8]

Now, the ocean is in effect the earth's edge – the place where the known earth suddenly gives way to *terra incognita*. For the ancient Mediterranean, the most emblematic such edge was that of the Pillars of Heracles, which stood as an ultimate threshold, a "forbidding *non plus ultra*, [in the form of] a warning to mariners not to proceed any further."[9] Pindar has this to say about the Pillars:

> Now Theron, approaching the outer limit in his feats of strength, touches the Pillars of Heracles. What lies beyond cannot be approached by wise men or unwise. I shall not try, or I would be a fool.[10]

> By the uttermost deeds of strength did these men touch the Pillars of Heracles, an achievement all their own; let none pursue valor any farther than that.[11]

Those few who did venture beyond the Pillars either disappeared forever or were forced to turn back after making their way along the African or European coasts. The accounts of Hanno and Himilco, both Carthaginian explorers, spoke of the trials and terrors of their voyages. Avienus, reporting on Himilco's trip, says that "a dark fog enshrouds the air as if in a kind of cloak, and clouds hide the face of the deep always, and this veil remains throughout the whole of the darkened day."[12] Hanno purports to have seen rivers of flame, mountains that catch fire in the night, phantom music, and "hairy wild men."[13] What these reports signify, apocryphal as they may have been, is that once beyond the Pillars one encounters the bizarre and the terrible – a vista so open and indeterminate that only the human imagination can populate it – as it does perforce, if only to fill in the intolerable void of the boundless.

On the basis of this brief sketch, several questions arise immediately: Why is the ocean, particularly as it impinges on a single location such as the Pillars of Heracles, such a challenge to the imagination? What is it about the boundless that calls for its being bound – as soon as possible and at least on one side? What does this circumstance have to teach us about any edge, including those we encounter so often in everyday life? From an extreme case such as this we may have much to learn about the ordinary and less threatening instances that we confront each day and at every turn – instances of edges around which we look and try to go, even if we do not know where we are going or into what we are looking.

II

An edge acts not only to curtail vision and undermine motion, but also to invite exploration of its other side. It is an occasion for ambivalence, for being tempted to go at least two ways: *to go away from*, as when Mediterranean mariners so often turned around when approaching the Pillars of Heracles out of fear and ignorance, but also *to go around*. The other side of the edge beckons. This is so despite the firm belief that the ocean on the other side of the Pillars is abyssal and, indeed, evil: "If it were not an evil thing, it would not lie here at the world's edge," proclaimed one ancient writer.[14] The world's edge, in the guise of the ocean that impinges on the Pillars, occasions not only aversion but attraction

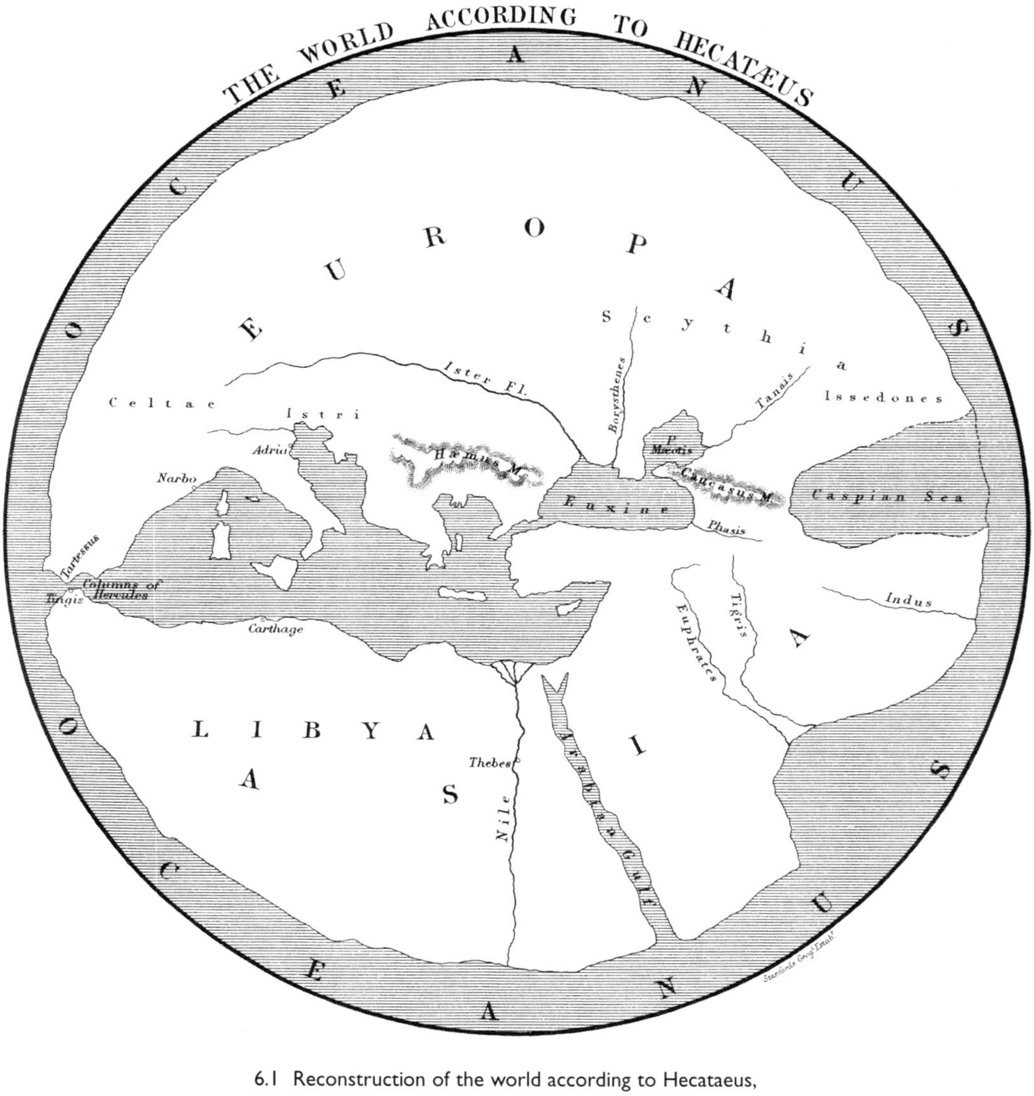

6.1 Reconstruction of the world according to Hecataeus, in Edward Herbert Burnbury, *A History of Ancient Geography among the Greeks and Romans from the Earliest Ages till the Fall of the Roman Empire* (1883; 2nd ed., New York: Dover, 1959), vol. 1.

– hence an entire genre of geographic literature entitled the *periodos gēs*, literally "round-the-earth-journey."[15] Anaximander, the sixth-century B.C. philosopher, wrote the first known treatise with this title, but Hesiod and Democritus, Hecataeus, and a number of Hellenistic poets also wrote books with this same name. These purported to describe journeys of various kinds – the word *hodos*, "path" or "route," is embedded in *periodos* – and they are notable for their combination of fact and fiction, which is to say, experience and imagination.

There are two uses, then, of the ancient geographical imagination. The first is to *fill in* what is otherwise empty. "Empty" is a term of emphasis in early geographical accounts, including that of Herodotus: "As to what lies north of the [Thracian] country, no one can say with any certainty what men dwell there; rather, beyond the Ister the territory seems to be empty (*erēmos*) and unbounded (*apeiros*)."[16] We need not go all the way to the ocean to find unoccupied regions that call for filling-in by the geographical imagination; such imagination has plenty to do right on land.[17]

In contrast to such filling-in at two extremes is the *filling-out* accomplished by journeys around the earth. Since a *periodos gēs*, by its very nature, is a trip from one determinate place to another – typically along a given coast – the geographical imagination here builds on the deliverances of perceptual experience, filling *out* these deliverances, extending while also altering them. But any such alteration or extension is nevertheless *of them*, of certain things seen (or at least reported to have been seen) in a previous journey. This is why Herodotus puts his trust in reliable witnesses wherever possible, thereby inaugurating a new genre of empirical geography. This empiricism represents an effort to curb earlier speculative excesses of the *periodos gēs*.[18]

Excessive or not, the *periodos gēs* is panoramic in character and induces the special form of looking that we call "scanning" in English. In its effort to grasp the "whole earth," it encourages the *looking around* that is the perceptual basis of filling-out. This can be done deliberately and systematically, as when Marduk scans Tiamat's dismembered body in the *Enuma Elish*; or it can be done at a glance, as in a fragment of the *Catalogue of Women*, a *periodos gēs* in the Hesiodic style: the sons of the North Wind race around the entire earth three times looking for the Harpies – in the course of which the reader is taken "aloft to gain a bird's eye view of the earth's perimeter, encompassing in a single glance all four corners of the globe."[19] Such a sweeping glance is to be contrasted with the furtive, fearful looking around the edge of the land into the ocean – a glance as discontinuous as the space that is truncated by the land's edge. The occluded vista (e.g., the Atlantic glimpsed through the Pillars) induces one both to look at and to look away, to look and *not* to look. Thus it reflects the basic ambivalence of the edge itself, its two-sidedness. Between looking and not looking is the sidewise look that tracks – here realized as the glance along the coast, the glance that notes landmarks and other orienting features of the earth as populating the edge of the known world.

Three different circumstances call for three different kinds of looking: the edge that blocks the view occasions the curious or threatened look; the panoramic view (from above) engages the sweeping look; and the view of the earth-as-edge involves the tracking look. Of course, there are intermediate states – for example, the look that tries to peek around a corner, perhaps as timid mariners peered around the Pillars of Heracles without actually sailing around them. Although this was most often a fearful look in the ancient Greek world, it can also be hopeful, as when Phoenicians who had heard of the silver reserves on the western Spanish coast peered ahead to see if they could make it past the Pillars. And there is the glance that refuses to engage the edge at all, that looks away before looking at all, as when a passerby refuses to engage our look, not even for a cursory second. Not to mention looking *over* something (e.g., over a mountain to glimpse the sky above) or *under* (as when I glance at the feet of the person I confront on the street).

But the central action solicited by the edge is the look *around*, the circumambient glance. This need not be comprehensive, much less a matter of scanning – both of which betray a spirit of gravity. To look around is not necessarily to take in (or even to want to take in) *all* that is there to be seen; it is compatible with leaping from one item to another, from one landmark nearby to another far away. As we say in English, to "look around" is often merely to "check out" a given scene, to "size it up." This is compatible with quite discontinuous looking; indeed, it thrives on it as we leap by a *saltus oculorum* between different points of passing interest. Quite different is the more literal looking around of those early earth voyagers who fastened on every detail belonging to the coast of a new continent seen for the first time from the ocean – a kind of intent scanning. One has to be comparatively familiar with a given landscape to engage in casual looking around for newly presented items that pique our curiosity.

The *periodos gēs* and its many modern and postmodern avatars call for two modes of vision: the sweeping scan and the leaping look, both forms of looking out. In contrast, the *peirata gaiēs* encourages two other forms of visual perception: ambivalent looking-away and furtive peeking-around. Just as the essential circularity of the *periodos* (always signifying "encirclement or enclosure")[20] contrasts with the bounded linearity of *peirata* (implying limits that in principle can be traced out in more or less rectilinear forms), so the two former sorts of looking reflect a situation of being surrounded in an arc of some larger whole, while the two latter answer to the more rigid circumstance of being faced with a limit that cuts off rather than opens up.

By the same token, there are two basic kinds of geographical imagination that correspond to – indeed, are constitutive of – the *peirata gaiēs* and the *periodos gēs* and their associated modes of looking. The first imagination fills in a gaping void by sheer discovery, and the second seeks a filling-out that aligns itself with a circular voyage wherein a certain experience has already been gained (by oneself or those who preceded one's own journey). Let us call the first imagination "formative" after Kant's term *abbildende* in his *Anthropology*; if not wholly fictive, it is at least productive and builds on the slightest of clues, often only arbitrarily related to the circumstance (e.g., mythical accounts, hearsay). The second kind of imagination is not reproductive – unlike cartography, the pretension to an exact account of what is already there – but "reformative" since it operates on the basis of a certain empirical knowledge, however imperfect this may be. It supplements such knowledge by adding its own embellishments: it builds *out* just as its two associated forms of vision both look out to what is delivered in perception, whether by scanning or by just looking around.

Going around an edge in geographical imagination, then, means opening out your mind to what lies beyond – to the other side of the edge, past which one must move. Staying at the edge, refusing to go farther, is to remain within the blinders imposed by the edge itself. It is to close down on any collaboration between perceiving and imagining; instead of looking out, it is to stay within the confines of one's own fearful mind, to gain an assurance there that one cannot find without. In the one case, one leaps into and thus looks out; in the other, one stays put and thus looks within. Both are ways of looking around that are occasioned by going around, but the bolder modes of looking around reflect the fact that one is going in a much larger circle: one sails right out into the Atlantic rather than staying within the Pillars and continuing to circumnavigate the familiar coasts of the Mediterranean. Between the delimited *peirata gaiēs* and the open one, there stand the gates of the sea, the *periodos gēs*, the narrow place where sea meets the ocean. This narrows (the *eng-* root of "anxiety" means precisely "narrow") is the isthmus where the geographical imagination was first, and is perhaps still most fully, engaged; narrow is the gate but wide the way.

PHILOSOPHY AT THE EDGE OF THINGS

I

The ancient example points to a larger lesson: *the anxiety of the edge.* Humans not only flee the void and the chaotic (this is a better-known story), but they also flee the edge of these primal phenomena of ontological anxiety, whether this be the edge of land or sea, or just the edge of any door that leads we know not where: "a stone, a leaf, a door." (They also seek edges, such as those of the Grand Canyon, but that is another story.) Faced with the prospect of not knowing what is on the other side, it is all too natural – indeed, it is part and parcel of what Edmund Husserl calls "the natural attitude" – to wish to fill in or fill out the empty prospect. This is not only true of the geographical imagination – which, as we have seen, has recourse to these two primary modes of connection making or replenishment – but also true of what we can only call the philosophical imagination. This is a comparable venture in dealing with the anxiety of the edge, albeit now in a much more conceptual register. Faced with this anxiety, each discipline has recourse to what I shall call the Continuist Principle and the Plenarist Passion. In the case of ancient Greek geography, we have already encountered these in the guise of the imaginal filling-in of empty or unknown spaces – so as to ensure continuity – and of the equally imaginal filling-out, which is to invoke the criterion of maximal fullness or plenitude.[21]

The parallel between geographical and philosophical imagination should not surprise us given the depth of the alliance between geography and philosophy. It was already actively present among the Greeks, who prized geography as a form of orientation in the concrete world of land or sea that is comparable to the orientation provided by conceptual schemes and systems. But the two enterprises are not just parallel; they are crucially convergent. Strabo, for one, maintained at the opening of his *Geography* that "the science of Geography, which I now propose to investigate, is, I think, quite as much as any other science, a concern of the philosopher."[22] This convergence is continually being rediscovered in the West, as we know from the cases of Kant, Husserl, Foucault, and Deleuze.[23] "We think too much in terms of history, whether personal or universal," Deleuze said in an interview, whereas "becomings belong to geography, [for] they are orientations, directions, entries and exits."[24] Directions and orientations, entries and exits: these are the very terms of voyages and of the maps (or other navigational devices) that guide them.

II

This is not to deny the considerable differences that exist between geographic and philosophical imaginaries. Geography is not only a theoretical discipline aimed at devising the most accurate picture of the earth; it is always also geared to eventual practical use in conveying the best routes from one site to another in world-space. Even the most extravagant *periodos gēs* purports to outline a possible route along the coasts of the known world, however treacherous this route may prove to be. Thus the geographical imaginary always has one eye on its possible application in the actual world of exploration and travel. This attentiveness to the practical is notably absent in almost every serious philosophical system, including those which (as we find in Heidegger and Wittgenstein) map out the everyday world in its very particularity. The result is that the philosophical enterprise is free to pursue its own imaginary in a way that is beholden neither to practical use nor to empirical reports of the sort so prized by Herodotus. Even the Homeric world-map builds on the geographic specificity of the Mediterranean world, as we know from the detailed studies of Victor Bérard:[25] the *peirata gaiēs* are embodied in genuine features of that world, including the Pillars of Heracles. This difference remains even if the ultimate motivation of both enterprises hinges on similar modes of response to the threat of the edge in human experience, namely the Continuist Principle and the Plenarist Passion.

EDGING INTO ARCHITECTURE

I

Philosophers since Parmenides have been committed to finding Being wherever possible – either by itself alone, eliminating (as did Parmenides) any form of non-Being or else by imposing Being on Becoming (as happens explicitly in the *Timaeus*). The struggle continues and on quite different fronts: Whitehead's eternal objects structure the Becoming that would be otherwise mere flux; Heidegger, while eschewing Being as such in his later work, reinstates it in the form of the Event of Appropriation (*Ereignis*). This continuing attachment to Being and its avatars bespeaks a tenacious wish to preserve continuity and plenary presence at all costs. The pursuit of this wish is perhaps most conspicuous in Leibniz and Husserl. Leibniz, for his part, acts to assure continuity and plenitude by arguing that, in principle, nature has no gaps. As he puts it, "It is one of my great and best confirmed maxims that *nature never makes leaps.* I called this [i.e., in earlier writings] the Law of Continuity."[26] And because nature brooks no gaps, it is irremediably full, as full as the ocean that is Leibniz's paradigm case of continuity; no longer a threat, it is now an illustration of the plenary presence of the perceived world. The argument runs like this: "*continuity, therefore no gaps, and consequently fullness of the world.*"[27] As a direct result, there can be no real surprises in the world, nor can anything arise altogether suddenly. If the world is indeed wholly dense and gapless – "a continuous world is a dense world"[28] – then it can hold no surprises, nor can anything happen in an utterly sudden manner. This is why Leibniz announces that "*nothing takes place suddenly.*"[29] Yet this claim flies in the face of the most ordinary circumstance of encountering something unanticipated, at once surprising and sudden – as so often occurs when we move around the least edge, only to find what we did not expect.

If Leibniz's laws of continuity and plenitude are metaphysical in status and thus apply to what underlies appearances (for Leibniz, discontinuity and emptiness are wholly matters of mere appearance, thus to be discounted), Husserl seeks the continuous and the full at the level of appearances themselves. In short, he does a phenomenology of perception in which the continuous and the full are to be found everywhere in things as they are *constituted* in our experience. This constitution proceeds by means of time-consciousness (where retentions knit together every appearance in a gapless continuum of sinking-back), active and passive synthesis (which assures the coherence of every object), internal and external horizons (which encircle all perceived things), and adumbration (whereby the already perceived sides of something reliably refer us to the other, not-yet-perceived sides). The result is that every material thing presents itself as a "continuum of appearances" (in Gurwitsch's revealing phrase), as a "referential matrix" (*Verweisungszusammenhang*, in Husserl's term) in which there are no gaps and little room for surprise.[30] We can be "disappointed," admits Husserl, but this disappointment applies only to cognitive intentions, which, nevertheless, expect to be fulfilled eventually in an ideal epistemic moment in which there is a coincidence (*Deckung*) of the given and the intended.

II

It is my audacious claim that the same obsessions with continuity and plenitude are to be found in architectural theory and practice – for much the same reason that they appear in ancient geography and modern philosophy, namely fear of the unknown that looms just beyond every edge. Just as ancient mariners, venturing forth beyond the Pillars, suffered from fearful projections of the end of the world, especially in the form of the earth's edge, so philosophers are afflicted with that "horror of the vacuum" that was arguably the most powerful motivating force in early modern philosophy. So, too, architects seek to populate the open landscape with buildings that render this sparse landscape dense and reassuring – as reassuring as the sheer perceived thing in phenomenologists' accounts or the entire universe in the Leibnizian vision. It's not surprising, then, that architecture and philosophy have had an ancient alliance, as ancient as that between geography and philosophy. Not only are they complementary as modes of production – of materialities in the one case, concepts in the other – but they have often shared an intense commitment to geometry, the "measurement of the earth," which is also at stake in geography. Husserl has even maintained that geometry is the common basis of all three enterprises, albeit pursued in distinctively different ways, as he indicates in his great later essay "The Origin of Geometry," which so much influenced both Merleau-Ponty and Derrida. In the case of architecture and philosophy, the specific link is that of *architectonic*, the "master building" that shows up in philosophical systems (e.g., Kant's *Critique of Pure Reason*) as well as in architectural theory proper.[31]

Now, I am aware that my claim concerning architecture may appear dubious at first blush. Aren't architectural spaces *empty* by their very nature – as empty, in their own limits, as the netherlands described by Herodotus, the *erēmoi*? At least is this so if we reduce architectural structure to the walls and struts, roofs and foundations – leaving the spaces of given rooms unoccupied? Indeed, my own emphasis on edge, once taken over into architecture, would seem to contribute to this essential emptiness of built structures – as in fact it does! It is the comparatively definitive character of edges, their angularity and sheer linearity, that leaves a spatial void around them – and often, as in the case of corners, within them. (This is the point of defining edges in terms of "convex" and "concave" dihedral angles, as is often done in topology texts.) Whether we look into the rooms of a newly constructed (or merely projected) house or look out into its surroundings (as notably in many of Edward Hopper's paintings), we are confronted by a pictorial vacuum that challenges our imagination.

The built structure as such is empty, but it is built with an eye to future inhabitation – to being occupied. From being bereft of bodies – a desert of sorts – it will become an *oikumēnē*, an "inhabited world." These bodies are not just superadded to the void of the building: to think of them in this way is to fall prey to the Plenarist Passion that I am decrying. This is perhaps appropriate to financial considerations: "80 per cent occupancy," we say of an apartment building, thinking only of how many rooms have been rented so far. But inhabitation, *dwelling*, is something else. It is a different kind of fullness. Whereas the economic sort is subject to a simple binary choice of being either occupied or not – with no significant intermediate cases other than "sale pending" (which is still indebted to the logic of either/or; the sale will have to go one way or the other) – the act of dwelling brings together the plenary presence of bodies with discrepancies and differences ("écarts" is Merleau-Ponty's word). The gaps are historical, personal, cultural, all the ways in which human beings do not achieve coincidence. I refer to such things as awkwardness and ineptitude, the process of becoming acquainted with new space, the ever-changing sense of how best to decorate a room, the altercations that happen in any given space when people with divergent interests try to live together, and so forth.

Not only is there no preestablished harmony in living spaces (to cite another theme of Leibniz), nor is there just the discontinuity of the differences to which I have just pointed, but there is also material resistance (the "coefficient of adversity" in Sartre's phrase). This resistance, too, is body-based given the obduracy of our own lived bodies, but it is likewise a function of the built structure itself, the very wall, the floors, the furniture in all of their physicality. Even here, however, there are crucial openings: windows, doors, chimneys, stairways. It is revealing that Leibniz considered monads to be "windowless," even though every monad reflects the entire universe from its own point of view. The continuity and plenitude for which he called could not tolerate breaks of any kind, including the openings that windows represent.

It is all too tempting to think that the world must come as continuous and full or else as radically discontinuous and empty. This was the crux of early modern debate over the vacuum – hence the obsessive concern with atomism and the importance of aligning oneself on one side or the other of the debate. Newton, Gassendi, and others were atomists who believed in strictly empty spaces between atoms, while Descartes and Leibniz were plenarists who would not admit the least crevice of unoccupied space to intrude into the cosmos. While this controversy had its own *raison d'être* at the level of physics and metaphysics – with implications for the fate of place that I have traced elsewhere[32] – at the level of phenomenological description, we are not faced with any such diremptive choice. It was Husserl's mistake to believe that we are engaged, at the level of appearances, with precisely this choice – hence his strenuous efforts to assure continuity at any cost. Not that this was some simple mistake. On the contrary, it is a quite understandable reaction to the problem of the edge – the edge that conceals the unknown other sides of any given object. This is powerfully set forth in de Chirico's *Nostalgia of the Infinite*.

By giving sharp edges to the tower depicted in this celebrated painting, de Chirico heightens the sense of mystery as to what lies on the unseen sides of the structure. Given the tenor of the painting, we feel that almost anything could lurk behind the tower – including nothing in particular. All is uncertain on the other side. The heavy shadows – themselves objects, not just extensions of objects – embody the menace of this far side of things. It is striking that de Chirico painted this work in 1913–14, while Husserl wrote the entirety of *Ideas I* in the summer of 1913. This was the eve of the Great War and a remarkably creative period in the arts, as we know from the book simply entitled *L'année*

6.2 Giorgio de Chirico, *Nostalgia of the Infinite* (1913–14), Museum of Modern Art, New York.

1913.[33] This year itself was an edge, a threshold of the gathering storm of war, and was sensed as such by Joyce and Proust, de Chirico and Picasso – and many others. Husserl reflected this same anxiety, and we can read his resolute will to find determination in the very midst of the indeterminacy of any object as a response to the larger malaise of the time. Disappointment he could allow, but uncertainty behind every edge he could not, yet this is just what de Chirico suggests.

The issue may not any longer be that of absolute emptiness versus complete fullness, or strict discontinuity versus total continuity (although newer cosmological theories keep raising these ancient questions: what lies before the Big Bang but yet another void?), but the phenomenon of the edge, its very appearance, does raise the spectre of the unknown and unexpected in our daily lives. How shall we respond to this spectre? Need we tie down the future of looking by closely knit adumbrations and active syntheses that purport to take us around the edge to the nonvisible other side? Do we have to take recourse to universal laws of continuity and plenitude to fill in what would otherwise be significant gaps in our experience?

I think not. We have other means to deal with the edge-world. Imagining what lies on the other side is one way to cope. So, too, is remembering what is there, in this very case or in similar instances. Or we can glance at the edges and just around them. But these are all spontaneous acts, dependent on immediate inspiration or solicitation. Building is a quite different response. Although its source – in an idea or sketch – may be quite spontaneous (and we should take note that this creative moment is often itself a matter of imagining or remembering or glancing), it is itself an intentional and labour-intensive action. In particular, it constructs edged structures within which a complex interplay of presence and absence, determinacy and indeterminacy takes place. It brings about the material conditions for a veritable scenography of the empty and the full, the discontinuous and the continuous. What is excluded in principle by thinkers committed to the Continuist Principle and the Plenarist Passion is precisely what is realized by the least built space: the intertanglement of flesh and *écart*, difference and repetition, stasis and motion.

III

The remarkable fact is that the edged structures of architecture make possible not just the basis for human habitation – thus for history and tradition, all that we sum up with polyvalent words such as "home-place," "work-place," and "sport-place" – but also for innovation in their very midst – that is, for creative imagining and looking, acting and thinking. Indeed, it is just because the physical structures of the built place shore up the scene of the customary body and collective memory – acting as a support system for them – that they in turn shelter such very different activities as imagining and glancing, those freest forms of thought and perception. None of this would be possible, however, unless built spaces were neither entirely empty nor stock-full, both states that would stultify creative action within. It is their very heterogeneity, their complex composition of the open and the closed, that allows for the engendering of actions that are not beholden to these spaces as such: habitual actions of the body, free-flight actions of the mind.

Even within the well-ordered worlds of architectural works there still looms the dark side of the edge: this cannot be eliminated altogether. Every doorway leads to we know not what; every staircase covers what lies behind it even as it allows movement to another floor; every edge of wall around a window limits the very view that the window affords. Each of these exhibits the portentous sense of edge that we first glimpsed in the world of those who braced their way into the unknown ocean, for it is a sense that remains present even in the humblest dwelling of those who stay at home – of course, not with the melodrama and dire consequences of someone faced with the decision of whether to sail through the Pillars of Heracles but nonetheless with a perceptible anxiety before what covers and conceals. Confronted with the massive natural edge, we have recourse only to imagining what lies on the other side or to glancing anxiously ahead. In the dwelling, I do these things, too, but in addition I can draw upon shared histories of being a body in that place -- that is, upon customary actions and memories that are not available on the exploratory sea voyage.

Just as the natural environment has its own edges – from those belonging to the trees around me and the mountains above me and finally to those of the far horizon – so every built structure is an edge-work, a place of edges. This is so both within and without: edges of rooms, edges of the exterior, edges everywhere, whether hard or soft.

"Folds," so much in discussion today in architectural theory, are certainly not edges in any strict sense. To be an edge at all is to possess a certain angularity – literally, to embody an angle, a convex one.[34] To pass over an edge, or to go around it, one must go over something that has a linear aspect, however blurred or blunted or bevelled this may be, whether it takes the form of a sharp shape, ridge, or external corner. To be on the brink of a peak in the High Sierras is to be on an edge; to be in the bowl of a cirque in the same mountains is to be in a fold. It is just because of this angular and linear character that an edge has the power to block and occlude – to challenge sight and movement. Folds, in contrast, are not just easier to get around and to negotiate; they facilitate motion and vision, and they do so whether they are internal to a given thing or external to it (i.e., lying on its surface). Indeed, being themselves enveloping, folds invite our envelopment in turn: seeing the exterior folds of the Bilbao Guggenheim, we find ourselves wishing to encompass or encircle them from without – to hug them, as it were.

The model of the fold first came to philosophical attention in Merleau-Ponty's celebrated treatment of the Chiasm in his unfinished masterpiece, *The Visible and the Invisible*. According to Merleau-Ponty, the perceived world is not some obdurate Other that we manage to grasp by luck or intelligence; it already envelopes us – "invaginates" us in one of his favourite metaphors. Our own flesh (our lived body with a special focus on its thick surface) is congruent with the world's flesh; the two are irremediably intertangled in a chiasmatic embrace whereby one coils over the other, crosses over into the other, and finally *is* the other. In this context, Merleau-Ponty says that "the flesh we are speaking of is not matter. It is the coiling over of the visible upon the seeing body ... [thereby creating] this magical relation, this pact between [perceived things] and me according to which I lend them my body in order that they inscribe upon it and give me their resemblance, [hence generating] this fold, this central cavity of the visible which is my vision."[35] The fold at stake here is between visible things and my own vision, which criss-cross chiasmatically in the body that I lend to the things that leave their image on me – all this being essential to what Merleau-Ponty calls "a true vision."[36] The true vision of something occurs in the embedding of what is visible into the seer: "In our flesh as in the flesh of things, the actual, empirical, ontic visible, by a sort of folding back, invagination, or padding, exhibits a visibility, a possibility that is not the shadow of the actual but its [very] principle."[37]

Any such fold is like a Moebius strip in that I can pass between two orders of things – the seeing body and the visible things – without ever passing over a determinate edge. The two orders inscribe themselves as one seamless whole in my flesh – as "a return of the visible upon itself, a carnal adherence of the sentient to the sensed and of the sensed to the sentient ... there is a circle of the visible and the seeing, the seeing is not without visible existence."[38] The more we think in this direction, the more we would imagine that Merleau-Ponty is offering us a postmodern recurrence of the Plenarist Passion, now pitched in terms of flesh and world rather than monads and the universe. If we were to take over his thought in this spirit alone, we would not have moved beyond Leibniz in any significant sense, for we would have reinscribed continuity and fullness everywhere.

But the fold of the later Merleau-Ponty, although offering a genuine alternative to the edge, is not a plenary presence. One of the most remarkable twists of the text in *The Visible and the Invisible* is his claim that the fold of flesh itself is shot through with "discrepancy" (*écart*) and "difference" – with "fission" and "segregation" – thereby rendering our relationship to the world a radically heterogeneous one, an ineluctable mixture of presence and absence. In a working note of December 1960, Merleau-Ponty proclaims that "the fabric of possibilities that closes the exterior visible in upon the seeing body maintains between them a certain *divergence* (*écart*). But this divergence is not a *void*, it is filled precisely by the flesh as the place of emergence of a vision, a passivity that bears an activity – and so also the divergence between the exterior visible and the body."[39] Here, Merleau-Ponty refuses the either/or logic of early modernism: there is not a straightforward choice between utter void (emptiness, nothingness) and utter plenitude (Being, the One, physical things). Rather, there is an indecomposable and uneasy mixture between my flesh (a certain kind of fullness) and the world's flesh (another kind of fullness) – and between the two a divergence that is no kind of fullness at all. Merleau-Ponty extends the idea of such an uneliminable *écart* to include the still more radical nonplenarist notion of "fission," for the lived body, once inscribed with the resemblances of things – once it has entered into the circle of vision and the visible – draws away from itself by an act of self-segregation. In the simplest act of seeing myself (in the mirror, or when I notice another seeing myself), my flesh "draws this relationship and even this double relationship from itself, by dehiscence or fission of its own mass."[40] There is, then, a "fundamental fission or segregation of the sentient and the sensible"[41] – not just their merging or union. Rather than a single continuous mass, there is "overlapping and fission, identity and difference."[42]

In this last formula, Merleau-Ponty manages to evade the trap of having to choose between plenum and void – that ultimate ontological binary that has held thinkers from Parmenides to Sartre in its thrall – by suggesting that the best model for human being-in-the-world is one that respects a factor both of fullness (i.e., flesh in its double format) *and* of emptiness (i.e., as divergence between seeing and things seen). Moreover, it is a matter of the empty *in the full* – its riddling with pockmarks – and the full *in the empty*: the cavity that is occupied. Like the body, it is always at once empty and full, both within (the gut, the heart) and without (my skin). In particular, the folds of my flesh are not made up of voids or vacua but act as dynamic containers for many kinds of things, human and nonhuman, that coil up within it, just as the world's flesh is a plenary presence which is nonetheless indefinitely elastic and all-absorptive, taking things and events into its ever-expanding maw. Henry Moore's female bodies are enactments of this elusive logic of the full-empty that defies the strict binary oppositions between which philosophical thought so often forces us to choose.

6.3 Henry Moore, *Reclining Figure: External Form* (1953–54), Israel Museum, Jerusalem.

This is not to say, however, that folds are the only agents of inclusion or that edges are entirely exclusive in their action. Edges bring together both of the basic parameters described by Merleau-Ponty: they conjoin *and* separate (one side with/from the other), and they are at once linked (both sides are sides of the same edge) and disjoined (as seen versus unseen sides). They are factors of fusion as well as fission. Indeed, the paradox of edges is precisely that, for all their occlusive power, they manage not just to foil and frighten us but also to open the way to what we want: they certainly do stand in the way, but they promise vistas on their other side that we may very well wish to see. Some of the sailors who went through the Pillars were seeking silver on the western shores of Spain; for them, these colossal edges of land were ways to get to the metal that they sought. It is as though, once past the Pillars, there was still another choice to make: to go south to the unknown western coast of Africa or north to an area of reputed wealth. Moreover, every body needs an edge to delimit what might otherwise be an altogether confusing scene – as when we are lost in a blizzard, at bay in fog, or escaping from the black smoke of Ground Zero on 11 September 2001. We need this edge more than we need a fold, which acts less to delimit than to merge, more to encompass than to delineate. It may be delightful and mellow to do without a determinate edge at times – to follow the flow of the fold; hence the sheer delight of watching rivers roll by – but the edge calls us back to order, reminds us of the coefficient of adversity in our lives, the irremissible rigour of fact or law, history or concept.

CONCLUSION

In *Rooms by the Sea*, Edward Hopper's late masterwork, the edge of the door leads directly to the ocean (presumably the Atlantic Ocean), without any intermediary beach or lawn to temper this drastic transition. The building does not merely have an edge but, more crucially, *is* an edge. It is an edge on the untamed natural world in the guise of ocean – a civilized but brute presence, a constructed Pillar, beyond which the unknown lurks.

Strangely, we are looking at the very Atlantic Ocean so feared and sought by the earlier Greek, Carthaginian, and Phoenician explorers with whose travels and travails I began. We are seeing it now from *the other side*: not just the other side of an object or thing but the other side of the

6.4 Edward Hopper, *Rooms by the Sea* (1951), Yale University Art Gallery, New Haven.

world – from another edge of the earth, one wholly unknown in earlier eras. If only those adventurers could have looked outward far enough over the western horizon, they might have glimpsed the continent from which Hopper is looking back in an easterly direction. If only they could have seen "around the edge of the world," they might have seen this part of the world. As it was, they could only imagine it (e.g., in the form of the myth of Atlantis) – or glance out keenly toward it, without ever perceiving it. It is not surprising that they were so anxious: they were looking from the narrows of the Pillars to the broadness of the earth.

Hopper's seaside cottage constructs an edge against which the water-world stands out in contrast. It blocks a full view of this world but becomes all the more effective in its mystery and its power. The ocean looms from behind the edges of the built structure, at once resident and menacing, like every backside of every edge.

The edge is at once the emblem and the concretization of the radical contingency of our lives. It is the ultimate face of this contingency, the one that shows itself most often and most conspicuously (providing we take the time to notice). Despite the folds that comfort and protect us, the edge remains, if only to remind us of the limits of our knowledge and action. Edges don't tell us everything, but they do tell us that little is certain in the next spatial or temporal phase; they also tell us that we should expect neither a plenum nor a void on the other side. Rather than presenting us with these false options, edges reveal a chancy world whose very fullness is shot through with gaps, whose certainties are themselves uncertain, whose near side is already far, and whose places cannot be taken for granted. An edge shows us – indeed, it finally *is* – the acute limit of the place-world itself. It gives us the place-world's endgame right up front since its beginning is our own end. The other side that it starts to show accentuates our ignorance, the end of perception, and in some cases it is the very end of a life.

NOTES

1 Maurice Merleau-Ponty, "The Philosopher and his Shadow," in *Signs*, trans. Richard C. McCleary, 159–81 (Evanston: Northwestern University Press, 1964), 181.

2 The "coefficient of adversity," originally Gaston Bachelard's phrase, is taken over by Sartre in *Being and Nothingness*, trans. H. Barnes (New York: Washington Square Press, 1992), 619–20, 628. On "Secondness," see Charles S. Pierce, *Collected Papers*, ed. C. Hartshorne and P. Weiss (Cambridge, MA: Harvard University Press, 1935), vol. 6, par. 95.

3 See Edward S. Casey, *Imagining: A Phenomenological Study*, 2nd ed. (Bloomington: Indiana University Press, 2000); Edward S. Casey, *The World at a Glance* (Bloomington: Indiana University Press, forthcoming).

4 Benveniste points out that *pontos* derives from an etymon signifying "path in a region off-limits to normal travel." Cited from *Problèmes de linguistique générale* (Paris: Gallimard, 1966), 296–98, in James S. Romm, *The Edges of the Earth in Ancient Thought: Geography, Exploration, and Fiction* (Princeton: Princeton University Press, 1992), 16n.

5 Ibid., 16.

6 Ibid., 22.

7 Ann L.T. Bergren, *The Etymology and Usage of 'Peirar' in Early Greek Poetry*, American Classical Studies, no. 2 (N.p., 1975), 22–3. Cited in Romm, *Edges of the Earth*, 12.

8 From Hesiod's *Shield*, lines 314–15. See also this line from the *Iliad*, bk 18, 607–8: "And thereon Hephaestus set the great strength of river Ocean,

beside the outermost rim of the shield [of earth] so cleverly made." Both cited in Romm, *Edges of the Earth*, 17.

9 Romm, *Edges of the Earth*, 20.

10 Pindar, *Olympians*, bk 3, 43–5. See also these lines from Pindar, *Nemean*, bk 3, 20–3: "As a man of beauty, who accomplishes feats beautiful as himself, the son of Aristophanes may set forth on supreme, manly endeavors; but not easily across the untrodden sea, beyond the Pillars of Heracles, which that hero-god set in place, as a famed witness of the furthest limit of seafaring." Both cited in Romm, *Edges of the Earth*, 21.

11 Pindar, *Isthmean Odes*, bk 4, 11–14. Cited in Romm, *Edges of the Earth*, 22.

12 Cited in Romm, *Edges of the Earth*, 21.

13 Ibid., 19.

14 The full statement by Glycon is: "This is not the river Simois, nor the Grancius [scenes of Alexander's earlier victories]; if it were not an evil thing, it would not lie here at the world's edge." Cited in Romm, *Edges of the Earth*, 26.

15 Again, I follow Romm; see his *The Edges of the Earth*, 26ff.

16 Cited from Herodotus, *Histories*, bk 5, 9. Herodotus also remarks in *Histories*, bk 4, 8, that "they *say* that Ocean runs around the whole earth, starting from the eastern horizon; but they don't show any evidence for it." Both cited in Romm, *Edges of the Earth*, 34, 36. From the latter statement, we see that Herodotus was skeptical of the idea of an all-encompassing ocean.

17 Perhaps we can detect a sliding scale here, ranging from the absolute void of ocean to the comparative emptiness of *terrae incognitae*. The oceanic end of the spectrum is the ultimate challenge to such imagination, as suggested in a fragment from Plution: "[Ocean] is greatest because of this: It is beyond all things, but beyond it is nothing." Cited in Romm, *Edges of the Earth*, 26. To be "beyond all things" is to defy description in terms of such *concreta* as rivers and hills, trees and valleys. These latter, however, are the staple of descriptions of the other end of this same spectrum: however empty the country north of Thrace may be, the geographer (and his reader) are certain that they will yield *some such items* as grass or dirt, bushes or buildings, specifiable "things" in any case. There is a geographical assurance in such specifiability that is absent from oceanic descriptions – hence the recourse to "wild descriptions" in the latter case, to sea monsters and hairy monsters (wilder in any case than the at least humanoid Hyper-

boreans posited as inhabiting the country north of Greece). On the Hyperboreans, see Romm, *Edges of the Earth*, ch. 3.

18 Romm, *Edges of the Earth*, 32, designates the *periodos gēs* as "the most panoramic genre of geographic writing" in the ancient world. Indeed, the Herodotian revolution can be seen as the empiricizing of both the *peirata gaiēs* and the *periodos gēs*, each of which is highly theoretical in character: the first in regard to the limits of the known world; the second with respect to a projected journey around this same world.

19 Romm, *Edges of the Earth*, 30.

20 Ibid., 27. Thus Hecataeus's classical *periodos gēs* was in effect a tour from the Pillars of Heracles into the Atlantic and then back again, all in a circle that may have been less than the author wished for but nonetheless preserved the basic structure of the *periodos*; see ibid., 29n.

21 It also illustrates the two extremities that we have observed in ancient Greek geography: an alternation between a fascination with a world-whole, best exemplified by the belief in an all-encompassing ocean, as we have seen with Homer and Strabo and exemplified in Parmenidean and Platonic monism; and a fascination with the particularities of the empirical world, most evident in Herodotus's recourse to special regions of the earth and in Aristotle's concern with the precise ratio of the earth's overall shape.

22 Strabo, *The Geography of Strabo*, trans. H.L. Jones (New York: Putnam's, 1917), 4.

23 Kant's lectures on geography, delivered over a period of more than forty years, were at the core of his teaching. Husserl, in his later writings, found the earth to be the "primal Home-place" (*Urheimstätte*) in relation to all other "basis-bodies" and to be the ground for the moving human body in particular. More recently, Foucault has famously declared the close affiliation of his work with genealogy, recommending that the emphasis on time and history so characteristic of nineteenth-century thought needs to be replaced with a new appreciation of spatiality and spatial networks; see Michel Foucault, "Of Other Spaces," trans. J. Miskowiec, *Diacritics* 16, no. 1 (Spring 1986): 22–7. Deleuze proposes that philosophy is ultimately "geophilosophy" and, more systematically than Foucault, has examined what it would mean if we were to think in terms of "nomadology" – of "smooth" versus "striated" space – rather than in strictly temporal categories; see Mark Bonta and John Protevi, *Deleuze and Geophilosophy: A Guide and Glossary* (Edinburgh: Edinburgh University Press, 2004).

24 Gilles Deleuze, interview with Anne Parnet, *Pourparlers: 1972–1990* (Paris: Minuit, 1990), 67. Deleuze and Guattari also say that "history is always written from the sedentary point of view and in the name of a unitary State apparatus ... What is lacking is a Nomadology, the opposite of a history"; see Gilles Deleuze and Felix Guattari, *A Thousand Plateaus*, trans. Brian Massumi (Minneapolis: University of Minnesota Press, 1987), 23.

25 Victor Bérard, *Les navigations d'Ulysse* (Paris: A. Colin, 1971).

26 Gottfried Leibniz, *New Essays on Human Understanding*, ed. P. Remnant and J. Bennett (Cambridge, UK: Cambridge University Press, 1981), 56, original emphasis.

27 Dionysius A. Anapolitanos, *Leibniz: Representation, Continuity, and the Spatiotemporal* (Dordrecht: Kluwer, 1999), 63, original emphasis. The same argument can be stated in reverse: "If the principle of plenitude did not hold, then the world would contain vacua. But vacua are gaps in the order of the world, and such a thing would contradict the maxim that 'nature never makes leaps'"; ibid., 62.

28 Ibid., 62; the full statement is: "A continuous world is a dense world, i.e., it is a world characterized by the existence of intermediaries between any two different elements of a chain (substantial or other) in the world." Leibniz characterizes such density in this way: "all the species which border on or dwell, so to speak, in regions of inflection or singularity are bound to be ambiguous and endowed with characters related equally well to neighboring species"; Letter to Varignon of 1702, cited in Gottfried Leibniz, *Leibniz: Selections*, ed. Philip Wiener (New York: Scribner's, 1951), 185.

29 Leibniz, *New Essays*, 56, original emphasis.

30 Aaron Gurwitsch, *The Field of Consciousness* (Pittsburgh: Duquesne University Press, 1964), 227. Edmund Husserl's phrase occurs in his *Experience of Judgement*, ed. L. Landgrebe, trans. J. Churchill and K. Ameriks (Evanston: Northwestern University Press, 1973), 44.

31 See Edward S. Casey, "Place, Form, and Identity in Postmodern Architecture and Philosophy," in G. Shapiro, ed., *After the Future*, 42–58 (Albany: State University Press of New York, 1990).

32 See Edward S. Casey, *The Fire of Place: A Philosophical History* (Berkeley: University of California Press, 1997).

33 Liliane Brion-Guerry, *L'année 1913: Les formes esthétiques de l'oeuvre d'art à la veille de la Première Guerre mondiale: Travaux et documents*

inédits réunis sous la direction de L. Brion-Guerry (Paris: Klincksieck, 1971).

34 Topologically regarded, an edge is "a junction of two surfaces that make a convex dihedral angle"; J.J. Gibson, *The Ecological Approach to Visual Perception* (Hillsdale, NJ: Lawrence Erlbaum, 1986), 308. Folds, however, can be concave as well as convex.

35 Maurice Merleau-Ponty, *The Visible and the Invisible*, trans. A. Lingis (Evanston: Northwestern University Press, 1968), 146.

36 Ibid., original emphasis.

37 Ibid., 152.

38 Ibid., 142–3.

39 Ibid., 272, original emphasis.

40 Ibid., 146.

41 Ibid., 143.

42 Ibid., 142.

Horizons at the Drafting Table: Filarete and Steinberg

Marco Frascari

Chora

WHEN WORKING ON PAPER, ARCHITECTS trace horizons within the horizons of their drafting tables. The tracings carried out on drafting surfaces are not merely supports for architectural ideas; they become the eidetic surfaces and vital instrumental plans to sustain architects' individual and communal cosmologies. These inscriptions of individual and societal representations give evidence to their conscious and unconscious orientation toward the world, together with the intersecting regions of architectural intentionality. As cosmographers, they render in graphic form the merging of cultural and individual cosmologies. These cosmological tracings are the real drawings of architecture. They are not prescriptive but descriptive instructions for constructions within a horizon, resolving the contrast between the immediate intuition of the imaginative world and the mediate materiality of architectural practice.

Perhaps now, more than ever, we need to better understand architectural drawing. Forced and circumscribed by prescriptions and codifications, the power of electronic imaging traps architectural imagination; architects must search once again for essence in their drawings. What is the role of drawing in architectural perception, memory, and empathy?

Ambiguously paradoxical and paradoxically ambiguous, architectural drawings are *ontophanies*, graphic manifestations of the essence connecting the visible to the invisible. A humorous view of architecture is essential to decipher how architectural intelligence and imagination operate. Architecture cannot exist within a ponderous and weightily grave context; it exists essentially in humour since every portion of it is built to fight solemn gravity. A humorous view of architecture is achieved not in the prosaic blueprints and renderings that flood a wasteful profession but in the authentic domain of construction documents, which are not prescriptive but eidetic presences that can be transformed into built bodies of knowledge.

The problem is in the locution "humorous" or comic architecture, which carries in itself an unfortunate semantic confusion. When the word "humorous" is mentioned, we seek a comic artefact, a building element that should make us laugh or smile, but this deplorable confusion regards the instrumental cause of a design as its final cause. Comic is an instrumental cause that can include satire, parody, mockery, lampoonery, farce, comedy, and jocularity, but in itself, it is not a laughing or smiling matter since it allows designing for the unknown "other."

We know that architecture can be sublime, grave, terrifying, glorious, grandiose, tragic, astonishing, and magnificent, but can architecture be wonderfully comic? If architecture can fit into these other aesthetic categories, why can it not also be comic? Most aesthetic and philosophical manuals and most architectural treatises present architecture as a very severe and grave enterprise. To be proper and dignified, buildings, *edifices*, must be emphatically serious; they are grave expressions of humanity. It is true that an integral part of architectural design is to deal with gravity, but this means not to *accept* gravity but to fight it structurally, as cosmopoietically Carnival fights Lent and as light fights darkness at the beginning and end of the day.

Humorously attentive architects know that architecture echoes nature since both act at a fundamental level of eidetic cogency: nature produces horizons, while architecture captures them. Joining the rhythm of the universe through a conscious tracing of drawings, architects perform a constructive vision that operates within genetically rhythmic processes unique to architecture. In this cadenced milieu, architects tell graphic tales that mark places by discovering, drawing, and building horizons.

To further explain the "horizon-tale" essence of architectural drawings, I will analyze the work on paper of two humorous, comic architects. A span of centuries exists between their tracings on paper, but they have a marked place and a set of horizons in common. One began his architectural labour in Milan, Italy, and the other concluded his architectural career in this same city. This is not a fundamental and decisive event for standard historical narration, but it is crucial to their phenomenologically intersecting horizons. The commonality of place is an essential notion that uses one architect's horizons in understanding another architect's horizons.

The historical relationship between these two architects is analogous to the droll one that connects the two leading characters in Raymond Queneau's *Les fleurs bleues* (1963). Milan is the common place, as Paris is the common place in Queneau's story.[1] Like Queneau's characters, the two architects are virtual *doppelgangers* whose drawings have a symmetric relationship. This construct of historical telling, at the same time, keeps its distance and dissolves in a slight puff of air, not only in theoretical abstractions, but also in confronting the apparent concreteness of the present horizonless reality of architectural drawings.

One of these two individuals is Antonio Averlino (1400–c.1465), a Renaissance architect known as Filarete, an illustrative name of Greek origin, meaning "lover of virtue." His construction record is modest, but he wrote and illustrated an astonishing treatise. The other character is Saul Steinberg (1914–99), a superb twentieth-century architect with an even scantier construction record: he built but a few pieces of furniture. However, Steinberg is known to most of us as one of the powerful cartoonists working for the *New Yorker* magazine.

A Florentine sculptor, Antonio Averlino moved to Rome during the 1430s to study the monuments of antiquity in his preparation to become an architect. The bronze doors of St Peter's are his celebrated project of the period. Although somewhat original in style, he was more a skilful metal caster than a sculptor.[2] In 1451 Francesco Sforza summoned Filarete to Milan to work for him as an architect. During his Milanese stay, Filarete wrote the twenty-five books of a *Libro architettonico*[3] and built a few pieces of architecture, among them the initial portion of Ca' Granda, or Spedale de'Poveri, Milan's hospital for the poor.[4]

In *Lives of the Painters, Sculptors and Architects*, Vasari disapproves of Filarete's bronze doors but highly praises the hospital built in Milan: "To say it in a few words, this place is so well built and ordered that there is no other place similar in all Europe." In addition, Vasari emphasizes that Filarete's treatise is a preposterous and asinine work: "And however there is hardly any good thing that can be found in it ... it is a ridiculous and silly work and nothing more than an antic storytelling."[5]

Organized as a scientific storytelling, Filarete's treatise portrays the relationship between Francesco Sforza (1401–66), who was Duke of Milan from 1450 until his death, and the architect Onitoan (anagram of Antonio), who has been given the task of building a new city with the sycophantic name of Sforzinda. The new city is mirrored in a mythical ancient city, described in a gold book found in a stone time capsule during the excavation for the foundations. The mythical city is Plusiapolis, which was ruled by King Zogalia (anagram of Galiazo [Galeazzo] Maria Sforza, son of Francesco, 1444–76).

Although translated from Latin by the great scholar Antonio Bonfini for the use of Matthias Corvinus, the famous humanist king of Pannonia (Hungary), Filarete's treatise had been viewed by many historians and critics through the coolly negative Vasarian lens. The drawings illustrating the treatise have been deemed comically droll, a hybrid notation of Renaissance ideas unsystematically mixed with flavours and resemblances of medieval sketchbooks.[6]

Romanian-born Saul Steinberg arrived in America in 1942 after fleeing Italy, where he had completed his degree in architecture at the Polytechnic Institute of Milan in 1940, and began his graphic recording of the life and times of the United States. As many great literary critics have pointed out, Steinberg's cartoons combine an acute perception of people and situations with a highly original and evocative way of graphically demonstrating his observations. Nevertheless, Steinberg's drawings are expressions of an architect, although many literary critics have dreamed of using their overconfident pens to force Steinberg's calligrams into Procrustean literary lines.[7] Steinberg's graphic expression has an essence that is typical of architectural drawings. As Ernst H. Gombrich points out, Steinberg is an artist "who knows ... about the philosophy of representation."[8] I would add that Steinberg is also an architect who knows about the horizon of architectural representation. However, I am not going to force his work into architecture because I am a biased architect who sees architecture in everything and everybody. I am doing it because Steinberg himself was an architect. Furthermore, Steinberg gives a curious and elliptical definition of the role of architects by affirming that in the Faculty of Architecture they were teaching everything *but* architecture. This definition makes architects "curious intellectuals" who deal not with the *vane curiositas, turpis curiositas* castigated by atomist philosophers but with the potential curiosity that originates in the Latin *cur(i)a*, meaning "care," and to be more precise, in one meaning of *curiositas*, a unique curiosity, employed to motivate both the action and the frame of the action.[9] This curiosity is the transformation of temporality from the mode of mystery into the feeling of invention. Steinberg's curious and elegant drawings cut the Gordian knot that normally binds the emotional foundation of one's judgment and intellectual pursuits to preconceived cultural and visual data. They also show "free association" of the data provided by the "agent." By beginning to drift and by setting new grafting points, they demonstrate that curiosity kills cats, not architects.

In their drawings, Filarete and Steinberg tie the place-time of drawing in bundles of practices within the horizon of a region. These drawings do not belong to geographical positions in projective space but create specific time-place sections through habitual social practices. Their details systemically bind specific locations through the overlapping of time-horizons. These horizons make possible the understanding of being, which in turn makes possible individual constructive attitudes. However, time is to be understood not as a series of "nows" but as a temporal "extantness" that makes past, present, and future coexist in a possible architecture. The drawings represent, on the one hand, a field of action by offering extension to the deployment of projects and practical intentions and, on the other, a source of action by presenting a set of places from which energies are derived and toward which they are directed. The image does not speak, but the essence of its graphic marks brings into our perception the nature of a place. Interfacing between the generating movements and the boundaries within which they have been performed, a comparison of two orphic palaces drawn by the two architects can facilitate an understanding of the temporal "extantness" of their drawing. The word "palace" comes from Rome's founding place, the Palatine Hill, an urbane region whose name comes from being enclosed by an artificial horizon defined by a palisade. A palace is a place with a specific regional horizon; in the case of an orphic palace, the place is set in temporal "extantness," coupled above and below to a cosmological framework.

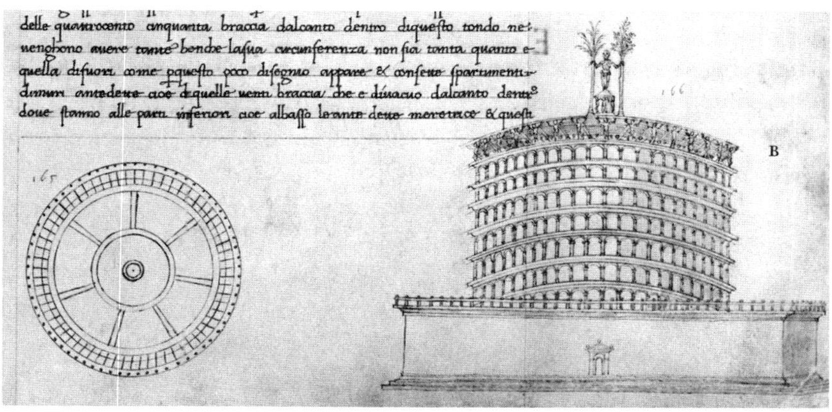

7.1 Antonio Averlino (Il Filarete), plan and elevation sketch of the Palace of Vice and Virtue, n *Trattato di architettura* (Milan: Il Polifilo, 1972).

7.2 Saul Steinberg, "Prosperity" (1991). Pencil, colored pencil, and pastel on canvas backed paper, 56½ x 72½ inches. Private collection. © The Saul Steinberg Foundation/Artists Rights Society (ARS), New York/SODRAC, Montreal

Filarete drafted the Palace of Vice and Virtue as the central piece of Sforzinda (fig. 7.1); Steinberg located his Palace of Prosperity in Manhattan (fig. 7.2). Filarete describes his palace as an artificial mountain; Steinberg presents his palace as a ziggurat. Artificial mountains have been a major emblematic presence denoting the structure of a phenomenological universe, from the erection of pyramids and ziggurats to the construction of great temples, churches, and palaces. Two gates, the Porta Areti (the upright gate of virtues) and the Porta Cacchia (the cacophonic gate of vices) mark the entrances to Filarete's cosmological palace, a building that accommodates a brothel on the ground floor and an astronomical observatory at the top and that is mostly a seat for university teaching. Filarete mirrors this *fantasia*[10] on a Dedalic crossing of boundaries, similar to the one told by Virgil in the *Aeneid*.[11] There are two possible exits from Virgil's underworld: the gates of horn (true shades) and the gates of ivory (false dreams), an allegorical connection between the figures of Sleep and his brother, Death.[12]

Known as the Lord of the Two Gates, son of Night, little brother of Death, and father of Dreams, the sandman Morpheus (he who forms or molds) is also the crucial image of the American Dream cosmology embodied in Steinberg's Palace of Prosperity on the threshold between Lexington and Madison Avenues. The two main gates fall under the oppositions of Law and Order, Fame and Fortune, and other innumerable allegories and emblems of duality, such as Beauty and Power, Dogma and Taxes, that lead to the pursuit of happiness. The top figure in Steinberg's palace is the personification of Prosperity: a businessman with broken shekels who is flanked by tall and slender twin columns holding the busts of Santa and Freud. Correspondingly, the figure at the top of

7.3 Antonio Averlino (Il Filarete), sketch of Virtue, in *Trattato di architettura* (Milan: Il Polifilo, 1972).

Filarete's palace is an armoured personification of Virtue located between a willowy sanctifying palm and a Freudian tall laurel (fig. 7.3).

If architects do not trace their drawings within horizons, they leave conventional readers and interpreters of plans, sections, elevations, perspectives, and other architectural drawings in a condition comparable to that of the inhabitants of Abbott's Flatland, for whom the activity of higher-dimensional creatures is incomprehensible, although perfectly visible. Readers of architectural drawings cannot reach the eidetic essence embodied in the graphic representation unless they are given the means to enter the horizons within which the drawings have been traced. A constructive examination of Steinberg's morphic views of drafting tables, followed by an analysis of Filarete's instruction on how to trace a drawing, might help to explain this phenomenon of nonseparation between horizons and the tales traced on architects' tables. In these drawings transpires an embodied cultural calling-into-being of experience. They frame the spirit of drawing in relation to tales that link horizons of perception, memory, and empathy.

The first portrayal of Steinberg's many reflections on drawing tables embodies an act of tracing in which the drawing of the line generates a cloud of twirling marks (fig. 7.4). It is a negation of the rational geometry of Flatland in the essence of drafting. The motion of the line reveals the mark within the land of drafting by also making clear that the relationship between imagining and imagination can be developed only in such a cryptogram. The movements of drafting convey an alien knowledge by bridging the shadowy and mysterious world of architectural design with the clean, well-lit world of the intelligibles.

A virtuoso masterpiece, a drawing of multiple overlying edges made with only one line, the second image shows a drafting table with scattered leaves of paper overlapping ambiguously between drawing and boundaries of the drawing surfaces (fig. 7.5). By pointing out how an ambiguous notion of the drawing surface is not only appropriate but also crucial, this drawing is a technogram that reveals how architects are compelled and bounded by images locked in a hall of mirroring horizons. Another image shows a drafting table in a room, a technographic elaboration on the horizon, moving from the edge of the drawing to the sheet of paper, to the table, to the vertical and horizontal. It shows the importance and unification of horizons that exist within architectural delineations. A watercolour rendering of a drafting table holding a flowerpot, a shell, a bot-

7.4 Saul Steinberg, Untitled (c. 1965). Ink on paper. Originally published in *The New Yorker*, 31 July 1965. © The Saul Steinberg Foundation/Artists Rights Society (ARS), New York/SODRAC, Montreal

7.5 Saul Steinberg, Untitled (c. 1965). Ink on paper. From Steinberg, *The Inspector*, 1973. © The Saul Steinberg Foundation/Artists Rights Society (ARS), New York/SODRAC, Montreal

tle of ink, a razor blade, a postcard, a water bottle, a match box, a ruler, a spiral notebook, a pencil, and three similar pencil squiggles, the fourth image is a calligram indicative of how the understanding made flesh in the drawing consists of accumulated personal and cultural histories, combined with systematically manifested communications.

Proofs of ontological validity, these demonstrations of architects' graphic tripartite mergings of technograms, calligrams, and cryptograms take place beyond the mere representation of nature, even though it remains consciously inscribed within a tale of horizons. This accurately imprecise nature of drawing manifests itself in a stubborn struggle between the celebration of form and the diffusion of its parts, between a will to represent and the evanescence of representations, between a search for certainties and an awareness of their relativity in a comic, graphic undertaking that is necessarily autobiographical, displaying the other as self. The essence transforms the usual opposition between high and low with the introduction of a *tertium comparationis* and advocates a science of hybrids, of mixed bodies, a comparative knowledge and compound sapience in which any practice of purification is regarded with suspicion. These drawings call for a novel yet traditional hybrid form of knowledge.

In the twenty-third book of his treatise, with instructions on how to make a drawing for a future building, Filarete deals with the same ontological question and solves, in analogous hybrid settings, his horizon's tales. Filarete's instructions have always been regarded as an awkward application of perspective, a retelling of the *costruzione legittima* worked out by the Florentine lineage of Filippo Brunelleschi and Leon Battista Alberti. Filarete acknowledges both Ser Pippo and Ser Battista, but the suggested drafting procedure for casting a building is presented with a peculiar cosmopoietic twist: the viewpoint of the perspective is not placed in front of the usual perspectival window, a *lucida*, but curiously is located above the drafting table, making completely different the subsequent translation of the constructive diagram within the horizon of a buildable space. The horizon line does not cross the visual window horizontally; it becomes the edge of the drafting tablet, which then becomes the horizon of the site. Using a figurative anachronism, Filarete's construction of the horizon seems analogous to the view of the horizon from the berth of a rising hot-air balloon. In another drawing, a plan of a church is drafted within a perspectival rendering of a site, a *lucus*, a clearing in a forest, showing how the drawing generates a *lucus lucendo*.[13] Twisted cosmopoietic drawings contribute to the interaction between the imaginative consciousness and the images themselves by making them aesthetically crucial and ethically indispensable. They are a negation of the real, but at the same time, they hold open the possible as poetic reality. This condition makes drawings a vital process of communication whereby we pass beyond ourselves toward what is *other* than ourselves.

Filarete graphically describes the outline of Sforzinda as a perfect octagon, the result of two superimposed squares, with inserted details of fortifications and gates (fig. 7.6). At its centre (fig. 7.7) is a set of three geometrically related squares, where the most significant municipal buildings are located:

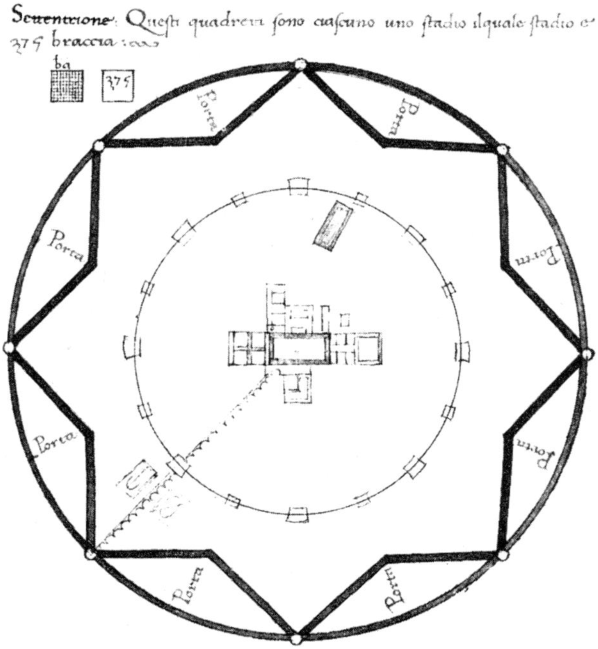

7.6 Antonio Averlino (Il Filarete), plan of the city of Sforzinda, in *Trattato di Architettura* (Milan: Il Polifilo, 1972).

The piazza is in the middle of the city. As I said above, its width is 150 braccia and its length 300; the latter runs from east to west, the former from south to north. Each of these little squares is one stadium or 375 braccia. At the eastern end I will build the cathedral, and the royal court at the western ... In the northern part of the piazza I will make the merchant's piazza, which will be a quarter of a stadium wide, that is 93 3/4 braccia, and one-half stadium long. On the southern side of the piazza I will make another piazza that will be a seat of market where edibles can be sold, for example, meat, fruit, vegetables and other things necessary to the life of man. This will be one-third of a stadium wide and two-thirds long, or about 250 braccia ... In the merchant's market I will make, on one end, the Palazzo del Pedestal and opposite it the law courts. On the northern part, I will make the municipal prison. This will be directly behind the law courts. On the eastern part, at the corner of the piazza, I will make the mint, where money is made and stored, and near it the customs house. In the merchant's piazza ... will be the Palazzo del Capitan and on the other side the butcher, chicken and fish shops, and the latter in season. Behind this piazza toward the south will be the bordellos, the public baths, and inns, or taverns.[14]

Nevertheless, within the two interlocking squares circumscribed by a circle delineating the Sforzinda plan, radial and Cartesian coordinates do not locate or relate public squares, gates, or streets, nor do they lo-

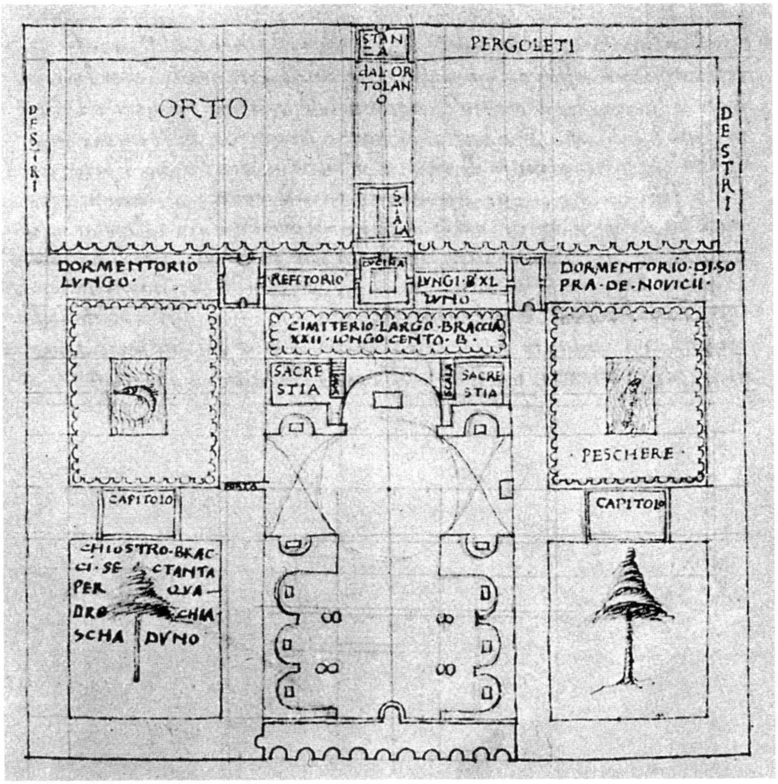

7.7 Antonio Averlino (Il Filarete), plan of the city centre of Sforzinda, in *Trattato di architettura* (Milan: Il Polifilo, 1972).

cate or relate sacred and private buildings. No graphically detailed depiction maps the whole city, which is given only in fragments of urban plans based on orthogonal grids that cannot fit the radial nature of the basic diagram. Nevertheless, another drawing shows the city as a conceptual diagram on the site, using the technique of the horizon tale. Carefully reading the text and the fragments of plans of the urban building assemblies presented in the manuscripts reveals that Sforzinda, a city described by many – including ordinary architectural history surveys – as an Ideal City, is in reality an amalgam of actual cities.[15] Urban fragments of Milan, Vigevano, Bergamo, and Venice, together with their medieval cartographic representations, make up the essence of Sforzinda and the mirroring Plusiapolis; fragments of mythical cities such as Atlantis and the platonic Athens make up the model city. Furthermore, Filarete's tracings do not stop at the immediate surrounding built environment; his tracings, mediated by cultural rediscoveries, amplify the design horizon of his two cities – at least to the river Indus. This cosmopoietic attitude makes architectural drawings a *sui generis* representation that is its own beast, distinct from perception and necessary for sensing essential truths. Located at the hub of time and place dialectics, an architect's drafting gathers up its past and projects itself into the future. In these dialectical tracings, drawing links the visible and the invisible, rescuing images from an alienated, perceptual world that skilfully negates their cosmopoietic status by emphasizing functions and ridiculing drawings as mere traces of traces. The conventional notion of image is destabilized by emphasizing the difference between the traces of drawings and the so-called photographic "real world."

In one of the copies of the manuscript are plans for the urban assembly of the *Terme* (public baths), the *Casa di Venere* (brothel Venus), the *Osterie* (pubs), and the *Casa Usoraria* (loan-shark house). These Latin marginalia by an earnestly serious pundit attempted to rationalize Filarete's cosmopoietic and humorous naming. They indicate a typical disregard for the humorously illuminating condition of cosmopoiesis that makes architectural drawings a *sui generis* expression of humanity.

Steinberg's "View of the World from 9th Avenue," the famous cover of the *New Yorker*, is a powerful manifestation of a cosmopoietic point of view (fig. 7.8). It presents the graphical essence necessary to give reality, shape, and meaning to the world and to the horizon. The popularity of the drawing is evident in numerous translations of other cosmologies that attempt to imitate its cosmographic tracings and reach its powerful cosmological qualities.[16] Cities, colleges, states, and nations throughout the world, often in postcard size, have copied the tongue-in-cheek "view of the world" that Steinberg invented. However, the real thing, drafted on 26″ x 19″ paper, resulted from a series of preparatory drawings that began with a perspectival view, a *costruzione legittima*, and ended with a cosmopoietic urban macro-micro view that relates building details and ecumenical realities, explaining complex situations much better than a normal perspective view.[17] To set a horizon tale, an eidetic delight is essential for relating collective heritage and quotidian identity. As a consequence, architectural drawings become places of urbane and elegantly complex human inventions at the confluence of nature and artefacts, myth and history, past and future.

A different view, looking toward the east side of Manhattan, offers a new focus to Steinberg's eidetic delight by adding a drafting table that reveals the foundation of the horizon tale (fig. 7.9). The faraway edge of the table has disappeared from the actuality of the perception, and the

7.8 Saul Steinberg, "View of the World from 9th Avenue," cover of *The New Yorker*, 29 March 1976.

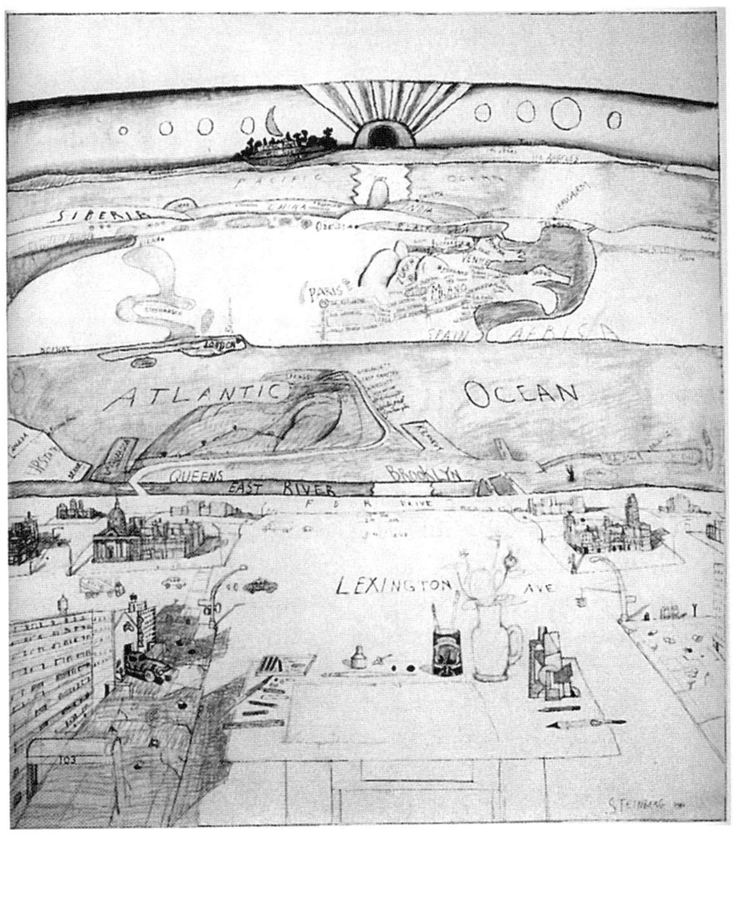

7.9 Saul Steinberg, "Looking East (from Lexington Avenue)" (1986). Pencil, crayon, watercolor, and oil pastel on paper, 67 x 62½ inches. Private collection.

7.10 Saul Steinberg, "Bucharest in 1924" (1970). Ink, pencil, and colored pencil on paper, 23 1/8 x 23 inches. Private collection. © The Saul Steinberg Foundation/ Artists Rights Society (ARS), New York/ SODRAC, Montreal

horizon is centred on an uptown crossing of Lexington Avenue. In this view, the memory-zoom goes from the traditional notation of small dots that indicate cities to the representation of clusters of streets in specific cities. As in Sforzinda, the lack of recognized geometric ruling allows geographical anachronisms in which the streets of Paris connect to the streets of Milan. Furthermore, in the faraway sky the multiple presence of the moon in its different phases marks the temporal "extantness" that makes past, present, and future coexist in the drawing.

Recognizing the role of description in universal "eidetic" terms as an explanation by means of causes, purposes, or grounded human existence, cosmography maps the entire universe – stars, planets, sun, moon, oceans, and continents, as well as the countryside and urban landscapes – within the same set of images. This confused but ambitious mapping program relies on an awareness of several seemingly disparate disciplines, including astronomy, astrology, cartography, navigation, surveying, dialing (sun shadow-casting), architecture, and instrument making. The interpretive mapping makes drawings manifest what is hidden in the ordinary experience of the structure of everydayness, or being-in-the-world: an interconnected system of equipment, social roles, and purposes.

A memory drawing of Steinberg gives us a further clue for understanding the labyrinthine nature of the horizon of wonder. Drafted in 1970, it is a view of Bucharest in 1924 (fig. 7.10). The drawing is constructed with several drafting media: coloured pencils, watercolours, inks, and graphite, eidetically related to the representation. In the background is a transparent building full of amazing mechanical devices, a drafting table, a paper cutter, a printing machine, and so on, and on top of the façade is decoration representing a rainbow; resting on it is a female figure holding a wreath of laurel. It is the bow of Iris, the daughter of Thauma (Father Wonder), that is bracketing the attitude of taken-for-grantedness and aiming to awaken a profound sense of wonder in this phenomenon.

The same power of wonder is evoked in other drawings showing a drafting table in a summer still life (1974). On the table an open sketchbook presents a watercolour of a Dutch landscape with a rainbow reflected in the water (fig. 7.11). Objects of the everyday life of a drafter surround the sketchbook. The drawing, a phenomenological reduction, shows an attitude toward the mood of wonder by implying an approach that can shatter the taken-for-grantedness of our everyday reality. Wonder is the unwilled willingness to meet what is utterly strange in what is most familiar. It is the willingness to step back and let things speak to us, a passive receptivity to let the things of the world present themselves in their own terms. When we are struck with wonder, our minds are suddenly cleared of the clutter of everyday concerns that otherwise constantly occupy us. The thing, the phenomenon in all of its strangeness and uniqueness, confronts us. The wonder of that thing takes us in and renders us temporarily speechless.

7.11 Saul Steinberg, "Summer Still Life" (1974). Watercolor, colored pencil, collage, and pencil on paper, 28 3/4 x 38 3/4 inches. Private collection. © The Saul Steinberg Foundation/ Artists Rights Society (ARS), New York/SODRAC, Montreal

Perhaps it is strange to speak of wonder as a method. Nevertheless, drawing renews wonder (*admiratio*) and points to wonders (*admirabilis*). Architects Steinberg and Filarete understand wonder as cognitive, non-appropriative, perspectival, and particular. Not merely a physiological response, wonder recognizes the singularity and significance of the thing encountered. Only what is different from the knower can trigger wonder, yet wonder will always be perceived in a context and from a particular point of view. From this moment of wonder, a question may emerge that addresses us and is addressed by us. It should animate one's questioning of the meaning of some aspect of lived experience. It also should challenge the architect to draw in such a way that the reader of the phenomenological drawing is stirred to the same sense of wondering attentiveness to the subject under examination.

The wonder of architects is not the one displayed in the *Wunderkammer*; it is a tracing of horizons in graphic wonders. With the architectural draftsperson's mode of being-in-the-world, architects live in a world that invites them to explore, to seek, to search. Architects are authentically present in the world and live directly in the world. By living directly in the world, architects allow things to disclose themselves. In this disclosure, things invite architects to play. Thus a drawing table is no longer a support but an alluring surface, a place for a willing suspension of disbelief that invites architects to draw. A white board provokes architects to reach out with pens and pencils and to disrupt the white surface by drawing across it. Three essential building blocks come together when an architect draws: the observation of the representation, the memory of all other representations and people, and the architect's imagination, which searches for meaning. Architects can make sense by combining this experience with all other experiences that they have had. Steinberg's and Filarete's drawings demonstrate that perception and drawing in *real* architectural drawings do not differ in their intentional structure but in the "modes" in which drawing posits its objects. In so doing, a thin transparent sliver of consciousness is forced between perception and drawing: the object of perception mirrors consciousness constantly; the object of the image is that of consciousness; nothing can be learned from an image that is not already there. Hence drawing is, for Filarete and Steinberg, a realization of reality; to posit the imaginary is ipso facto to realize actual images.

To make architectural representations effective, it is necessary to increase the intelligible nexuses linking architectural objects since, for architects, architecture is not in itself a subject of knowledge but simply a knowledge of objects. The misconception of architectural representation as an independent instrument is not only deceptive and misleading, but also seriously dangerous. The essence of representation is not a relationship with a substance; it is a simple, material reevocation of a relation between two terms: a horizon and a tale. Sitting at their drawing boards, Steinberg and Filarete act like the Roman god Janus. On the one hand – or better, with one face – they observe the physical world of human constructions; with the other face, they observe their own hypothetical, internal world of construing. The former experimentation takes place between the site of a construction and the construing of it in an architectural survey that takes place simply on the drawing board. On the drawing board it is an experiment done with diagrams and graphic constructions of their own. As cosmographers, they render in graphic form the merging of cultural and individual cosmologies. The tracings performed on the drafting surfaces are eidetic records and vital instrumental plans necessary to sustain architects' individual and communal cosmologies. These inscriptions of individual and societal horizons, as cosmographies, corroborate the intersecting regions of architectural intentionality with conscious and unconscious courses of action, which in turn resolve the contrast between the immediate intuition of the imaginative world and the mediate materiality of architectural practice. Actual drawings of architecture, these cosmologically nonprescriptive tracings are evocative directions for constructions within a horizon.

NOTES

1 Raymond Queneau (1903–76), who selected manuscripts for the French publishing firm Gallimard, in his free time became a most interesting author. Raymond Queneau, *Les fleurs bleues* (Paris: Gallimard, 1965), trans. Barbara Wright, *The Blue Flowers* (New York: New Directions, 1967), tells the story of two dreamers: the fiercely feudal Duke of Auge and Cidrolin, a peace-loving citizen who is living on his barge, moored on the outskirts of Paris. In *Les fleurs bleues*, Queneau indulged his passion for history. The story starts in 1264, when the duke appears at the summit of the keep

of his castle in Normandy: "There to consider, be it ever so little, the historical situation. It was somewhat confused." After two and a half pages, we make the acquaintance of Cidrolin minding his own business – in 1964. The story unobtrusively jumps back and forth every so often, which means that we realize that the Duke and Cidrolin are each the dream of the other, and when they finally meet on Cidrolin's barge in 1964, they, too, begin to sort and to realize: "Rêver et révéler, c'est à peu près le même mot" (*Les fleurs bleues*, 159).

2 Cyril Stanley Smith, "Granulating Iron in Filarete's Smelter," *Technology and Culture* 5 (1964): 386–90; John Spencer, "Filarete's Description of a Fifteenth Century Iron Smelter at Ferrière," *Technology and Culture* 4 (1963): 201-5.

3 Antonio Filarete, *Treatise on Architecture*, ed. John R. Spencer (New Haven and London: Yale University Press, 1965); Antonio Filarete, *Trattato di architettura* (Florence: Biblioteca Nazionale), Codex Magliabechianus 2.1.140, reprint ed. Anna Maria Finoli and Liliana Grassi, 2 vols (Milan: Il Polifilo, 1972); Luisa Giordano, "Il trattato del Filarete e l'architettura lombarda," in *Les Traités d'architecture de la Renaissance: Actes du colloque tenu á Tours ... 1981*, 115–28 (Paris: Piccard, 1988); Luisa Giordano, "On Filarete's *Libro architettonico*," in Vaughan Hart, with Peter Hicks, eds, *Paper Palaces*, 51–65 (New Haven and London: Yale University Press, 1998); Howard Saalman, "Early Renaissance Architectural Theory and Practice in Antonio Filarete's *Trattato di architettura*," *Art Bulletin* 41, no. 1 (1979): 89–106; Peter Tigler, *Die Architekturtheorie des Filarete* (Berlin: De Gruyter, 1963).

4 Michele Lazzaroni and Antonio Muñoz, *Filarete scultore e architetto del secolo XV* (Rome: W. Modes, 1908).

5 Giorgio Vasari, *Le Vite dè più eccellenti architetti, scultori e pittori* (Florence: Giuntina, 1568), vol. 3, 245–7.

6 Maria Beltramini, "Le illustrazioni del trattato d'architettura di Filarete: Storia, analisi e fortuna," *Annali di architettura: Revista del Centro internazionale di studi architettura Andrea Palladio* 13 (2001): 25–52.

7 Many great writers have used their sharp and incisive pens to comment on the work of Saul Steinberg. To name a few, Italo Calvino, John Hollander, and Arthur Danto have written superb, elegiac, and rhapsodic lines to celebrate the graphic lines of Steinberg's amazing imaginative world. For them, Steinberg is a colleague using a pen in a graphic manner – not meant

metaphorically – to make epic elegiac and idyllic statements about the everyday American way of life. They praise the muse that gave him such magnificent tracing techniques. This graphic art is able to elaborate bodies of lines, capturing the essence of his visual, critical experience. These masters of language honour his amazing command of visual language and his ability to distil the ethereal, the sublime, the secular, and the grotesque embodied in common existence. These masters of critical and brilliant wording adore Steinberg's command of pens, brushes, crayons, pencils, and meanings. In Steinberg's work, a sharp and piercing critical eye is coupled with a sensitive and sensible hand that transforms ink-graphite-watercolour washes into a configuration rich with puns, barbs, jests, epigrams, aphorisms, adages, and anecdotes that appeal to literary sensibilities.

8 E.H. Gombrich, "The Wit of Saul Steinberg," *Art Journal* 43, no. 4 (Winter 1983): 377-80 at 377.

9 See Alexander Scobie, "El Curioso impertinente and Apuleius," *Romanisches Forschungen* 88 (1976): 75–6; and Joseph DeFilippo, "*Curiositas* and the Platonism of Apuleius' *Golden Ass*," *American Journal of Philology* 111 (1990): 471–92.

10 The word *fantasia* is used by Filarete to mean a drawing.

11 Virgil, *Aeneid*, bk 6, 14–41.

12 The nature of the first gate most likely reflects a classical belief in rebirth, the gates having the specific purpose, then, of allowing shades to return to our world, to a new body. Anchises, Aeneas's father, earlier explains the cycles of a soul and its final stage, when some souls, after drinking from the water of the river Lethe to forget the past, "return again to the upper hollows of the world" ("supera ut convexa revisant / rursus"); *Aeneid*, bk 6, 750-1. Having both an entrance (the *vestibulum*) and designated exits, Virgil's underworld is a place where only a few individuals are fully permitted both to enter and to leave, indicating the important role of reincarnation in the classical scheme of man and the soul.

13 *Lucus* is the sacred clearing in the forest full of light. The well-known *verbis verberare,* "Lucus a non Lucendo" (dark grove), gets it completely wrong.

14 Filarete, *Trattato di architettura*, reprint, vol. 1, 25v, my translation.

15 Luigi Firpo, "La citta ideale del Filarete," in *Studi in memoria di Gioele Solari*, 11–59 (Turin: Ramella, 1954).

16 The word "cosmography" is ancient, whereas the term "cosmology" is of

recent origin. It was coined by Christian Wolff in 1730, when he entitled one of his works *Cosmologia generalis* (Frankfurt and Leipzig: n.p., 1737); see esp. sections 176–221. Wolff's work marks a turning point in the perception of cosmology as an intellectual activity in its own right.

17 See *Saul Steinberg: Fifty Works from the Collection of Jeffrey and Sivia Loria*, exhibition catalogue (New York): Jeffrey H. Loria 1995).

Opening the Eye: "Seeing" as "Knowing" in *Vastusastra* (Indian Architectural Theory) According to the Treatise *Manasara*

Jose Jacob

Chora

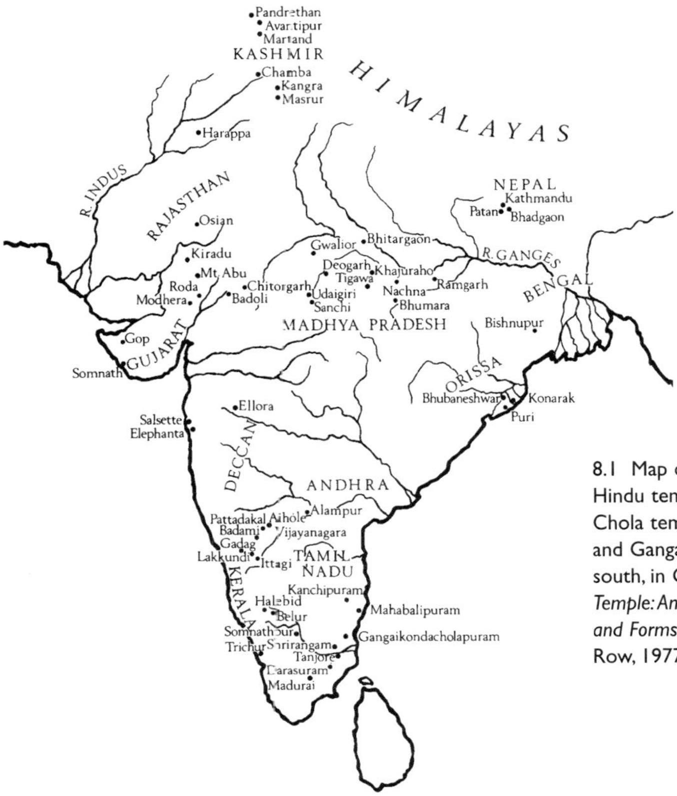

8.1 Map of India showing principal Hindu temple sites, including the Chola temples in Tanjavur (Tanjore) and Gangaikondacholapuram in the south, in George Michell, *The Hindu Temple: An Introduction to Its Meaning and Forms* (London: Harper and Row, 1977).

INTRODUCTION: THE *MANASARA*

THE FOLLOWING ESSAY IS BASED on an exegesis of the *Manasara*, a treatise belonging to the Indian architectural tradition of *vastusastra*. The *Manasara* is a Sanskrit text with seventy chapters in which architectural and iconographic topics are discussed comprehensively. These topics encompass principles of composition of buildings and images of deities, systems of measurement, technical instructions on building procedure, prescriptions for rituals associated with construction, classification of buildings, the nature and quality of building materials, such as wood and stone, and characteristic features of deities. The *Manasara* has no individual author, nor a specific historical date. Rather, it is a compilation that emerged out of the fluid interactions among oral, written, and craft traditions of premodern architectural practice in India. Based on rough correspondences between internal evidence in the text and archaeological information on extant temples, an approximate date of the original compilation of the text may be assumed as the tenth or eleventh century of the common era (C.E.), and its geo-political context as the Chola kingdom, which had its capital in Tanjavur (Tanjore) on the banks of River Kaveri in southern India.[1]

8.2 Brihadesvara Temple, Tanjavur (1000 C.E.), in Percy Brown, *Indian Architecture: Buddhist and Hindu Periods* (Bombay: D.B. Taraporevala Sons, 1965), plate 67, fig. 1.

8.3 *Vimana* (tower above adytum) of Brihadesvara Temple, Tanjavur, in Percy Brown, *Indian Architecture: Buddhist and Hindu Periods* (Bombay: D.B. Taraporevala Sons, 1965), plate 67, fig. 2.

8.4 Siva Temple, Gangaikondacholapuram (1025 C.E.), in Percy Brown, *Indian Architecture: Buddhist and Hindu Periods* (Bombay: D.B. Taraporevala Sons, 1965), plate 68, fig. 1.

Again, evidence in the text points to its religious affiliation with the devotional Saiva sect within Hinduism, which worships Siva as the supreme deity. The Chola kings were professed Saivites who built several major temples dedicated to Siva in their kingdom (fig. 8.2–8.4).[2]

8.5 Cover of *Manasara*, critical edition in Sanskrit, prepared by P.K. Acharya (reprint, Delhi: Low Price Publications, 1995).

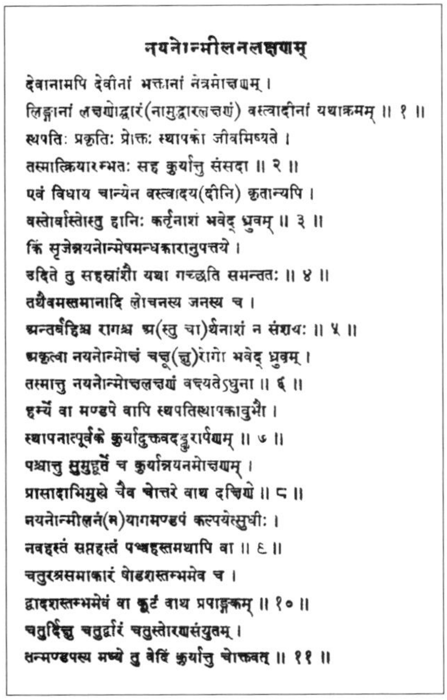

नयनोन्मीलनलक्षणम्

देवानामपि देवीनां भक्तानां नेत्रमोक्षणम् ।
लिङ्गानां लक्षणोद्धारं(नामुद्धारलक्षणं) वस्त्वादीनां यथाक्रमम् ॥ १ ॥
स्थपतिः प्रकृतिः प्रोक्तः स्थापको जीवमिष्यते ।
तस्मात्क्रियारम्भतः सह कुर्यात्तु संसदा ॥ २ ॥
एवं विधाय चान्येन वस्त्वादय(दीनि) कृतान्यपि ।
वस्तोर्वास्तोस्तु हानिः कर्तृनाशं भवेद् ध्रुवम् ॥ ३ ॥
किं सृजेन्नयनोन्मेषमन्धकारानुपत्तये ।
उदिते तु सहस्रांशौ यथा गच्छति समन्ततः ॥ ४ ॥
तथैवमस्तमानादि लोचनस्य जनस्य च ।
अन्तर्बहिश्च रागश्च अ(स्तु चा)र्थनाशं न संशयः ॥ ५ ॥
अकृत्वा नयनोन्मोक्षं चक्षू(क्षु)रोगो भवेद् ध्रुवम् ।
तस्मात्तु नयनोन्मोक्षलक्षणं वक्ष्यतेऽधुना ॥ ६ ॥
हर्म्ये वा मण्डपे वापि स्थपतिस्थापकावुभौ ।
स्थापनात्पूर्वके कुर्यादुक्तवदङ्कुरार्पणम् ॥ ७ ॥
पश्चात्तु सुमुहूर्ते च कुर्यान्नयनमोक्षणम् ।
प्रासादाभिमुखे चैव चोत्तरे वाथ दक्षिणे ॥ ८ ॥
नयनोन्मीलनं(न)यागमण्डपं कल्पयेत्सुधीः ।
नवहस्तं सप्तहस्तं पञ्चहस्तमथापि वा ॥ ९ ॥
चतुरश्रसमाकारं षोडशस्तम्भमेव च ।
द्वादशस्तम्भमेवं वा कूटं वाथ प्रपाङ्गकम् ॥ १० ॥
चतुर्दिक्षु चतुर्द्वारं चतुस्तोरणसंयुतम् ।
तन्मण्डपस्य मध्ये तु वेदिं कुर्यात्तु चोक्तवत् ॥ ११ ॥

8.6 Page from *Manasara*, critical edition in Sanskrit, prepared by P.K. Acharya (reprint, Delhi: Low Price Publications, 1995), ch. 70, "Nayanonmilanalakshanam" [Description of opening the eye (of the image of the deity)], 414.

The *Manasara* survives today in the form of eleven manuscripts written in five scripts: Tamil, Grantha, Telugu, Malayalam, and Devanagari. These manuscripts are all transcriptions of a later date – the eighteenth and early nineteenth centuries C.E. – and are held by various libraries in India and England. There also exist a critical edition of the text and an English translation of this edition, both prepared in the early twentieth century by P.K. Acharya, a professor of Sanskrit (fig. 8.5, 8.6). Acharya also wrote a short summary of the work and an extensive commentary on it, both in English.[3]

Theory, as it pertains directly to making, is outlined in the *Manasara* principally as a series of injunctions. These injunctions direct the *sthapati* (master builder) and his guild to carry out technical operations of building and rituals associated with key stages during construction.[4] The injunctive form of theory derives from its theological foundation, which the *Manasara* establishes in the opening chapter by claiming that *vastusastra* (architectural theory) has a divine origin.[5] The claim of divine provenance and the injunctive form are concrete expressions of the understanding of theory as a priori with respect to practice. In turn, this understanding lays such an emphasis on the instrumental dimension of theory that the nature of theory seems purely instrumental. This mentality is captured well in the Sanskrit term for theory, *sastra*, which derives from √*sas* (to chastise, control, regulate). Practice, then, is understood as mere application of theory-as-rules. However, such an understanding of architectural theory and practice and their interrelationship is not quite accurate; it accounts only partially for the nature and constitution of the traditional paradigm.[6] A closer hermeneutical reading of the text reveals that theory-as-rules is infused with a symbolic intent, the source of which is the same theological foundation of theory. This symbolic intent is present throughout the *Manasara* as it elaborates the making of the temple (the paradigmatic architectural object), understood in the Saiva theological scheme as the abode as well as manifestation of the deity. To the nature and constitution of theory, this symbolic intent contributes a non-instrumental dimension. Thus it modifies the very understanding of the relationship between theory and practice, allowing a certain reciprocity between the two.

The final chapter of the *Manasara*, titled "Nayanonmilanalakshanam" (Description of opening the eye [of the image of the deity]), presents an especially dramatic convergence of symbolic intent, ritual proceedings, and technical operations in temple architecture and iconography. It gives a detailed account of the iconographic operation of chiselling the eye of the image of the deity (Siva) and its installation in the adytum of the completed temple in their ceremonial setting.[7] Pronounced as "opening the eye" (a rendition that is at once theologically valid and poetically revealing), this ceremony is a poignant moment: it completes the manifestation of the divine in the image and temple. The entire project of making the temple and image is directed toward this instance of epiphany. The same sense of "epiphanic completion" is reflected in the text, where it dedicates its concluding chapter to the ceremony of "opening the eye." One might well speak of such a manner of "completion" or "conclusion" of theory (writing the text) and practice (making the temple and image) as their "consummation."

"Opening the eye" implies not only a "seeing" but also a "knowing." Within the Saiva theological horizon and owing to its specific characteristics,[8] these two aspects are necessarily interrelated, and their relationship is one of identity and reciprocity. In other words, "seeing" is "knowing," and "knowing" is "seeing." In this essay, using key verses from the final chapter as windows,[9] I seek to fully draw out the aspect of "seeing" (or better, "seeing-as-knowing"), as it pertains to making the temple and image, in the architectural theory of the *Manasara*. This aspect of "seeing" signifies the symbolic intent within theory and its noninstrumental dimension. The first two of the following sections show how perception and meditation, each on a plane proper to its nature,[10] are engaged as overarching modes of "seeing" in making the temple and image. The third section shows how the symbolic intent in *vastusastra* serves the spiritual realization of the *sthapati*, in addition to making the temple and image and investing them with theological meaning. Here, the noninstrumental nature of theory paradoxically becomes "instrumental" in the process of spiritual realization (that is, union with the deity) of the maker-as-devotee.

SEEING THE TEMPLE: PERCEPTION IN *VASTUSASTRA*

> If the opening of the eye is done wrongly, not only internal and external *raga* as well as wealth will doubtless be destroyed, but also disease of the eye contracted.
>
> – *Manasara*, ch. 70, 10–11

The caveat issued through these verses is directed at ensuring the "observance" of rules by the *sthapati* (master builder) in both ritual and iconographic procedures of opening the eyes of the image of the deity. The consequences of transgression are serious: loss of health (that is, loss of sight through disease of the eye) and wealth, but more direly, loss of *raga*. Within the scheme of Saiva theology, *raga* is one of the thirty-six principles and connotes *eros*, the creative passion of the self that encompasses an entire range of emotions: desire, affection, delight, charm, joy.[11] In addition to these psychological "emotions," the semantic horizon of *raga* includes also physiological "modalities" based on the visual and aural senses.[12] Taking all these aspects into consideration, *raga* can be understood as a passionate, sonorous "seeing." For the *sthapati*, the key principles of creativity are *raga*, *kala* (aptitude), and *vidya* (knowledge with a basis in skill of craft).[13] Loss of *raga* thus implies the very deprivation of passion and imagination for artistic creation.

The verse mentions two kinds of *raga*: internal and external. It is by engaging both internal and external *raga* that architectural and iconographic making proceeds. For the *sthapati*, building the temple and making the image are, so to speak, "seeing" them into being. "Seeing" in architectural and iconographic making involves interaction with the material world through perception and observation as well as exploration of the inner realm by imagination and conception. Among these, perception and imagination are eidetic and poetic modes of "seeing," whereas observation and conception are empirical and rational modes. These modes of seeing are, respectively, synthetic and analytic by nature. While acknowledging this duality of synthesis and analysis in "seeing," it must be noted that in the framework of traditional architectural theory and practice, a Cartesian dualism does not exist between the two. Here, the analytic mode of "seeing" always operates within the synthetic mode. One might characterize such a "seeing" as an aspect of the "phenomenological" (that is, distinct from the modern scientific) mindset.[14]

In the *Manasara*, the most frequent words that denote the "seeing" of the *sthapati* as he engages in the making of temple and image are *prekshana* and *parikshana*. They conjoin respectively the prefixes *pra* (before, in front of) and *pari* (around) to the verb √*iksh* (to see). These prefixes are "analytic" (as distinct from both "pleonastic" and "idiomatic") by function, in that they have a particular semantic value of their own that modifies or qualifies the meaning of the verb-root.[15] Thus *prekshana* (looking at) and *parikshana* (looking around) connote a "seeing" that is primarily synthetic. There is also an analytic dimension contained within *prekshana* and *parikshana* that "verifies" perceptions against the precepts of theory. Thus the semantic horizon of the two terms also includes the meaning "examination."

The text often uses another term, *samgrahana*, in conjunction with the above terms. The basic verb-root of *samgrahana* is √*grah*, which has a set of meanings denoting activities that range from the mental to the physical: "to grasp, seize, lay hold of, claim, marry, receive, perceive, observe, recognize." The prefix *sam* (together), when added to the verb-root, points again to the synthetic nature of these acts. Thus, in architectural and iconographic making, *samgrahana* is the psycho-physical act of the *sthapati* by which he "grasps around" the object before him – in other words, a phenomenological mode of knowing that combines the immediate mental apprehension of the object and its perception through the senses.

Sacred architecture begins by identifying an auspicious site for the dwelling of the deity. The *Manasara* states that the site is to be "examined" in terms of its physical characteristics of contour, form, colour, sound, odour, taste, and touch.[16] The terms in the text that denote this activity are *pariksha* and *samgrahana*. First, the site is perceived through the senses. This perception is then tested against the stipulations of theory to ascertain the auspiciousness and fitness of the site for building, with respect to its physical characteristics as well as habitant flora and fauna. Thus the first "selection" of the site involves the phenomenological apperception, appreciation, and appropriation of the site.

Once the site is selected, it is demarcated by ritual furrowing. It is then subjected to further examination to test the quality of its soil. The text uses the same term, *pariksha*, to denote the overall examination of the site. It involves conducting certain tests and observing their results. By sowing seeds of barley in the site and observing their growth, some primary conclusions are drawn regarding the quality of the soil. Then the sprouts are allowed to be grazed upon by cattle. By observing the dung of the cattle, the first conclusions are verified. The permeability of the soil is tested by filling a pit dug in the site with water and checking the water level on the following day. The "observation" of these test results is denoted in the text by the term *prekshana*. Specific results lead to specific conclusions regarding the nature of the soil and fitness of the site.[17] The structure of test, observation of result, and inference in the above proceedings has a quasi-empirical dimension. Nevertheless, the process itself is phenomenological because the qualities of the site are evaluated experientially at the site itself.[18]

Using a gnomon, the site is oriented to the path of the sun. The shadow of the gnomon "sights" the sun, albeit inversely. A circle is drawn on the site with the gnomon as centre. The points at which the shadow of the gnomon touches the circle in the morning and in the afternoon are marked. The line connecting these two points gives the east-west direction, and its perpendicular gives the north-south direction.[19] The delineation of the site follows. At this stage, the actual extent of the building, its geometrical form and physical dimensions, exists only as abstract relations that are

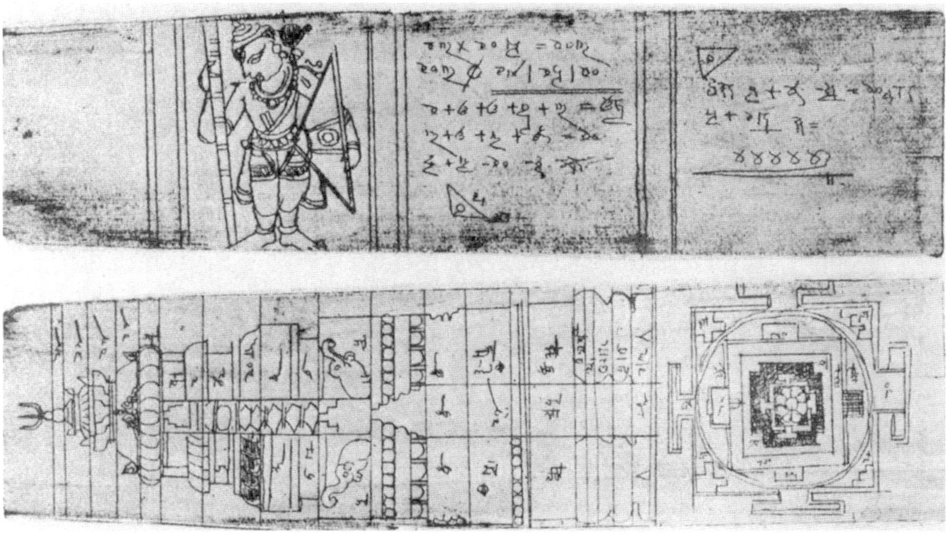

8.7 Two sides of a palm leaf taken from a manuscript on temple building (Orissa, eastern India, seventeenth century C.E.), in George Michell, *The Hindu Temple: An Introduction to Its Meaning and Forms* (London: Harper and Row, 1977), 56. The roles of number and geometry in temple building are depicted: the *sthapati* holds measuring rod and level; the calculation of proportions is presented; the geometry of the *mandala* generates and regulates the plan and elevation of the temple.

"conceived" in the mind of the *sthapati*. Initiating the process of realization of the "idea" (here, in the mathematical sense) of the building requires the aid of instruments, both conceptual and physical.

It is the act of measurement that initiates the architectural translation of the ideal into the real. Indeed, the *Manasara* understands "measure" as the essence of the science or theory of architecture.[20] Hence, the system of units of measurement is considered as the most basic conceptual instrument that aids the construction process. Chapter 2 of the *Manasara* outlines the system of measurement:

8 atoms = 1 chariot-dust particle
8 chariot-dust particles = 1 hair-end
8 hair-ends = 1 nit
8 nits = 1 louse
8 lice = 1 barley-corn
8 barley-corns = 1 digit (finger-breadth)
12 digits = 1 span (distance between thumb and middle finger when stretched)
2 spans = 1 cubit (distance from elbow to tip of middle finger)
4 cubits = 1 rod
8 rods = 1 rope.[21]

The text states that the smallest and "fundamental" unit, the *paramanu* (atom), is seen (only) by the sages.[22] The verb used in the text for this "seeing" is *ud√viksh* (to perceive). The basic verb root again is √*viksh* (to see), to which two prefixes, *ud* and *vi*, are attached. The prefix *ud* has the sense of "arising," and *vi* that of "asunder." When attached to the verb-root √*viksh*, they indicate that this "seeing" is of a "higher" and yet "analytical" kind. In the phenomenological sense, this "higher analytical seeing" is an exercise of the eidetic faculty that enables both a direct intuitive grasp of its (necessarily supersensuous) object and a process of bracketing and reduction of tangible objects and their perception to their most "essential" constitutive element.[23] The system of measurement, then, can be understood in two ways: (1) as constructed upward (that is, from small to large units) based on the first and immediate perception of the atom; and (2) as based on the digit, the "pivotal" unit (being the first to refer to the human body), from which smaller units down to the atom are derived by division, and larger units up to the rope by aggregation. Thus, even though the system of measurement is a "conceptual tool" (with an instrumental dimension) at one level, it originates from a "seeing" that is phenomenological.

The way materials are selected, collected, and used is also governed by a phenomenological "seeing." The procedure of collecting wood from the forest, a potentially dangerous task, demands that perceptual acumen be particularly sharp. The text gives an elaborate list of sensate phenomena – sight, sound, and occurrence (for instance, a tree falling in a particular direction when cut) – as good or bad omens.[24] While collecting wood, the *sthapati* and his retinue use their knowledge of these omens (which is part of theory) to seek out and "sight" the good omens and avoid the bad ones.

The *sthapati* ascertains the quality (expressed in terms of gender – male, female, or neuter) of the wood pieced and prepared for assembly by *prekshana* (that is, examining it by touch and feel, "turning it again and again [in his hands] from left to right").[25] Similarly, when selecting stone for iconography, its gender (again, male, female, or neuter) is ascertained by its form, colour, the sound it produces, how it is found lying on the ground, and so on.[26]

SEEING THE DIVINE: MEDITATION IN *VASTUSASTRA*

> Regarding opening the eye, it is to dispel darkness. Just as when the sun rises, spreading its myriad rays around, so also the opening of the eyes of the people.
>
> – *Manasara*, ch. 70, 7–9

These preambulary verses of the final chapter make explicit the symbolism of chiselling the eye of the image and its significance to the devotee.[27] The simile in the above verses is rather poorly constructed against the measures of poetics; nevertheless, it captures the dynamic of reciprocal sight-giving that underlies the whole event, which unfolds in a series of rituals. The invocatory rituals preceding the marking of the eye prepare the image for its "enlivening" with divine presence. The *sthapati* then "writes" its eyes by chiselling them[28] and covers them with cloth. When the enlivening of the image is completed through subsequent rituals, the cloth is removed so that the deity offers *darsana* (auspicious sight) to the devotee. The light of divine manifestation shines forth through the eyes of the image and is received into the heart of the devotee through his own eyes. Thus the darkness pervading his heart is dispelled by the light of divine manifestation, just as the night is dispelled when the sun rises and spreads its rays. In short, chiselling the eyes of the image of the deity, and thus opening them, grants "insight" to the devotee. *Darsana*, this mutual "seeing" of deity and devotee,[29] is also a "union" between them, the culmination of devotional worship in Saivism.

The underlying program of sacred architecture (making temple and image) is to manifest the divine and thus to facilitate *darsana*. Each aspect of construction has a "theological" dimension (oscillating between mythical and metaphysical), which the *sthapati* accesses through a spiritual "seeing" while conducting the technical operation or performing the ritual. This is *dhyana* (meditation, contemplation). *Dhyana* derives from √*dhya* (to think, contemplate), etymologically "a perfectly normal variant of the root from √*dhi* ['to see, perceive']."[30] The principle behind *dhyana* in artistic and architectural making is that of visualization, association, and identification.[31] The *sthapati*, while conducting a particular technical operation, visualizes the object at hand (for instance, a component of the structure such as a column) as a particular deity (among the lesser deities) or as a particular aspect of Siva, the supreme deity.[32] He associates the object with the deity and identifies them as one through himself (being the agent of the operation). The association and identification of object, deity, and maker are effected through a dialectical interplay between two modes of spiritual seeing: the yogic technique of intense-yet-restrained meditation employed by the sages; and the ecstatic vision resulting from the rapture of devotional love experienced by the saints. Meditation as a mental visualization of the form of the deity is accompanied by a vocalization of its name (that is, recital of *mantra*, a sacred formula containing the name of the deity), rendering the association and identification even more efficacious.

Thus, while making the tools of measurement, the *sthapati* meditates upon Vishnu as the tutelary deity of the cubit scale and the measuring rod, and upon Vasuki, the serpent deity, as the deity of the measuring rope. Brahma, as creator, is meditated upon as the presiding deity of measurement itself.[33] After the site is taken possession of, it is imagined as Kamadhenu, the mythical all-giving cow.[34] The site is meditated upon also as the goddess Ambika.[35] While furrowing the site, the *sthapati* meditates upon himself as Brahma, upon the plough as Varaha (the incarnation of Vishnu as Boar, who, using his horn, rescued the earth from the bottom of the sea), and upon the pair of oxen yoked to the plough as sun and moon, the eye and mind respectively of the deity.[36] During the ritual marking of plots in the delineated site, the *sthapati* visualizes the form of *vastupurusha* (man or "spirit" of the site who "inhabits" it) as lying face down and stretched out across it while reciting the sacred formula of obeisance to him.[37] He also visualizes the *vastumandala*, a cluster of forty-five deities who subjugate *vastupurusha* by sitting on his limbs and thus occupy plots in the four quarters of the site (fig. 8.8). He invokes the deity corresponding to each plot and "situates" it by touching the plot while visualizing its form in all iconic detail and vocalizing its specific formula of veneration.[38] While conducting the ritual of sacrificial offerings to the deities of the *vastumandala*, the *sthapati* meditates upon himself as Siva.[39]

Similarly, by meditation and recitation, the *sthapati* unites symbolic meaning with the compositional or structural function of each building component of the temple, thereby "establishing" it firmly in its proper place in the overall program of divine manifestation. The conception of the temple's foundation in the mind of the *sthapati* finds concretion

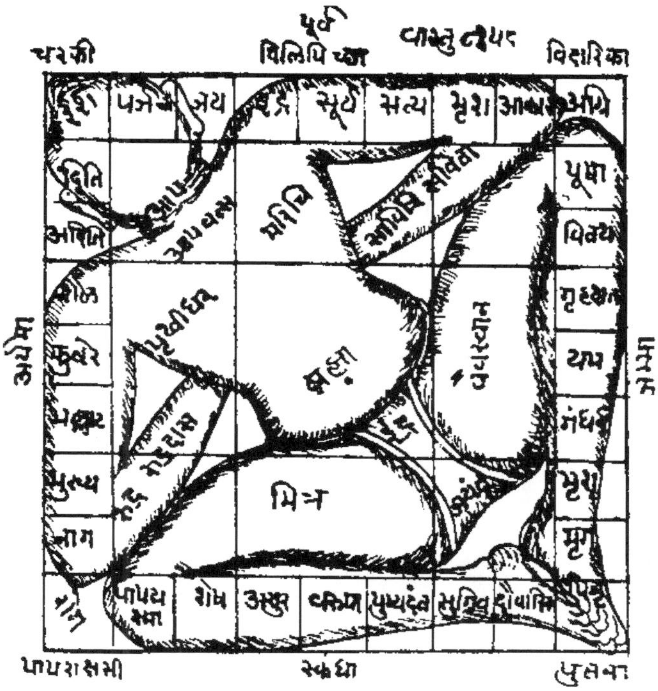

8.8 *Vastupurushamandala* depicted in an ancient manuscript, reproduced in George Michell, *The Hindu Temple: An Introduction to Its Meaning and Forms* (London: Harper and Row, 1977), 72.

when it is firmly installed in place by meditating on it as upheld by the eight mountains and guarded by the eight quarter-lords on the firm surface of the earth, which in turn rests upon the primordial waters and upon Ananta (Vasuki), the serpent deity.[40] While laying the foundation, he meditates upon Siva in his emanate form of Visvakarman (creator) and as lord of the universe, who is the ground of creation, preservation, and dissolution.[41] In other words, the laying of foundation is meditated upon as a reenactment of cosmic creation. The *sthapati* visualizes the column first as the Himalaya mountain and then as the mythical Mount Meru (upon which rests the abode of the gods).[42] He meditates on the last four stones of the assemblage of the superstructure (which, together, hold the finial in place upon the domical crown of the tower above the adytum) as seats of the lords of the cardinal directions.[43] The finial (dome-nail) itself is meditated upon as the transcendent form of the deity who is to be installed in the temple (in this case, Siva).[44]

The theme of meditation is even more persuasive in iconography. In chapters 51 to 67, on iconography, the *Manasara* gives vivid descriptions of characteristic features of the various deities. These iconic representations, divinely revealed to sages of the hoary antiquity, are not to be subjected to artistic caprice. Hence the text qualifies the imagination of the iconographer as *murtidhyana* (meditation of [the form of] the deity).[45] In addition to knowing and employing the theory of iconography, iconographers often made use of the visions of saints (recorded in their hymnal compositions, which are also part of the body of Saiva sacred scripture) as "meditational verses," reciting them while sculpting the image (fig. 8.9).[46] The final iconographic operation is chiselling the eyes of the image. The chiselling is also conducted in a meditative mode with the intent of opening the eyes of the deity, thus completing its manifestation.

8.9 Siva as Enchanting Mendicant on the outer wall of the adytum of Brihadesvara Temple, Tanjavur (1000 C.E.), in Vidya Dehejiya, *Indian Art* (London: Phaidon, 1997), 216.

8.10 Siva as King of the Dance, bronze (c. 970 C.E.), in Vidya Dehejiya, *Indian Art* (London: Phaidon, 1997), 12.

SEEING, KNOWING, MAKING: *VASTUSASTRA* AS MEANS TO SPIRITUAL REALIZATION

> In the centre of the lotus-heart of the devotee, the deity should be the supreme object, and like a lamp.
>
> – *Manasara*, ch. 70, 111

In Saiva theism, *darsana* is orchestrated in the context of ritual worship of Siva in the temple. Daily worship is conducted at dawn and dusk, the two conjunctions between night and day, and also at noon. The "event" of *darsana*, as a thickened spatio-temporal "presence" and "present," is announced in the temple by singing, playing musical instruments, bell-chimes, and loud recital of the sacred formulas. For the devotee, *darsana* is a sensuous, wholesome experience: he sees and is seen by the deity, hears its name being recited in sacred formulas and recites them himself, inhales the aroma of the incense, tastes the ambrosia. By such elemental mingling, divine immanence extends into the territory of the devotee's heart in a pronounced way. The verse cited above exhorts the *sthapati*, after he has opened the eyes of the image of the deity, to install the radiant deity in his heart. The heart is the centre of being, so to speak, where the cognitive and affective faculties of the self meet. Thus the act of installing the deity therein perspicuously connects divine seeing and knowing.

In chapter 59 of the *Manasara*, in the section on iconography, a fourfold classification of devotees is mentioned: (1) *salokya*, (2) *samipya*, (3) *sarupya*, and (4) *sayujya*. The names of these classes evince a hierarchical grade of spiritual ascent, or degrees in the state of union with the deity. Thus *salokya* is "being in the world"; *samipya* is "being near [the deity]"; *sarupya* is "assuming [divine] form or likeness"; and *sayujya* is "consummate union [with the deity]."[47] The four classes of devotees or states of spiritual life correspond somewhat to the four divisions of the *Agamas* (Saiva religious texts containing theology and rubrics of ritual) and, in turn, to the four modes of *sadhana* (religious practice): (1) *carya* (ritual and moral conduct), (2) *kriya* (architectural and iconographic making), (3) *yoga* (meditation), and (4) *jnana* (gnosis). Thus being in the world corresponds to ritual and moral conduct, divine proximity to architectural and iconographic making, divine likeness to meditation, and divine union with gnosis.[48] Since the distinction between *carya* (ritual conduct) and *kriya* (making of temple and image) in the Agamic scheme is not always clear,[49] the latter may be seen as encompassing both modes. Making is the primary and most accessible mode of *sadhana* (religious practice) for the *sthapati* and his guild, being makers of temple and image. This does not necessarily mean that the higher modes of *yoga* and *jnana* are a priori inaccessible to the *sthapati*. In fact, employing yogic meditation and discipline, as well as knowledge of the science or theory of architecture in the process of making, prepares the *sthapati* to access the higher modes. Regarding yogic meditation, the exercises conducted by the *sthapati* to visualize the particular forms, manifestations, and attributes of the divine in connection with specific architectural components have already been mentioned. With respect to his yogic discipline and concentration, evidence is found in the text in the several ascriptions of the *sthapati*: as *niyatah* (he who restrains self), *samahitamanah* (he who has undissipated mind), *vicaksanah* (he who has discerning sight), and *ekacittavat* (he who possesses single-mindedness), to mention a few.

Regarding the role of *jnana* (gnosis) in the *sadhana* (religious practice) of architectural and iconographic making, the following points may be observed. First of all, this *jnana* is specifically architectural knowledge, which in turn can be distinguished as skills of the craft ("the how") and its theoretical principles ("the what").[50] The *sthapati* learns these in his young age through apprenticeship at the workshop and work-site. At this stage, he is simultaneously a *bhakta* (devotee) and *sadhaka* (aspirant). During his apprenticeship, while undertaking architectural and iconographic operations, he simultaneously engages *bhakti* (devotion), which in turn incites *raga* (desire) and *bhava* (imagination), *vairagya* (dispassion), which is part of yogic discipline, and *jnana* (knowledge of the how; skills of the craft). In the course of his "graduation" as *sthapati* (indeed, a gradual process), he masters the theoretical principles of architecture and iconography to receive the titles of *sarvasastrajnah* (he who is knowledgeable in all theory), *sastraparagah* (he who has reached the other shore of theory), and *acarya* (preceptor). Also, he is imparted metaphysical and theological knowledge (the "why") of architecture by the *sthapaka* (priest).[51] In the *Manasara*, the *sthapati* is also called *vedavid* (knower of Veda; that is, one who possesses sacred knowledge). The instruction of the *sthapati* by the *sthapaka* in metaphysical and theological knowledge is not limited strictly to the context of construction, even though its primary occasion is the construction of the temple itself, nor to construction's specific means: the building rituals and associated meditations.[52]

The instruction of the *sthapati* by the *sthapaka* also implies an initiation of the former through the categories of the Saiva theological system. The objective categories – the five gross and five subtle elements[53] – are understood as together constituting the media or material of making. The subjective categories – the five faculties of action, the five faculties of perception, and the five faculties of cognition[54] – together enable the *sthapati* to engage in the activity of making. The categories of experiential and existential contingencies constitute the setting in which the making unfolds.[55] Having been initiated into the realm of theological knowledge – through the architecture of the temple and the image as the manifestation of the deity – he is sufficiently prepared to leave the phenomenal realm behind. The culmination of this stage is *darsana*, the auspicious seeing of Siva, at the completion and consecration of temple and image. *Darsana* illuminates his lotus-heart, removes its taints of ignorance (thus purifying it), and grants him self-insight.[56] He installs Siva in the sanctuary of his heart and worships him therein. Now an adept, he ascends to the state of *sarupya* (divine likeness) by exercises in visualization and to *sayujya* (divine union) by reaching the realm of transcendent knowledge. The "space" of this consummate experience of divine union (knowing and relishing) is, again, his lotus-heart.

CONCLUSION

The foregoing focuses on the particular aspect of "seeing" as it pertains to making in *vastusastra* (architectural theory) according to the treatise *Manasara*. The insights gained in this exposition throw significant light upon the nature of traditional theory and its relationship to traditional practice as well as upon how the traditional paradigm of architectural theory and practice is ontologically different from the modern one. These insights are primary and propitious aids in addressing the question faced by modern Indian architects regarding the role of traditional theory in contemporary practice constituted in the modern scientific and technological mode.

NOTES

1 See Bruno Dagens, "Introduction," in Bruno Dagens, ed. and trans., *Mayamatam: Treatise of Housing, Architecture and Iconography*, xxxix–ci (New Delhi: Indira Gandhi National Centre for the Arts; Delhi: Motilal Banarsidass Publishers, 1994), xliv–xlv. The *Mayamata* is also a southern Indian treatise and may be considered a "sister treatise" of the *Manasara* with respect to form and content. Dagens's statement regarding the date of the *Manasara* occurs while comparing the contents and contexts of the two texts. According to Dagens, the *Mayamata* predates the *Manasara*.

2 The period of roughly 400 years of reign of the Chola dynasty (850–1270 C.E.) witnessed illustrious temple-building activity in the region of the Kaveri basin and the refinement of what architectural historians have called the "Dravidian style" of temple architecture; see Percy Brown, *Indian Architecture: Buddhist and Hindu Periods* (Bombay: D.B. Taraporevala Sons, 1965), 84–8. One of the main features of this refinement was a tall *vimana* (tower above the adytum), which consisted of an upright base (comprised by the walls of the adytum, single- or double-storey in height), a tapering body of several (false) storeys, and a domical crown. This is seen especially in the two most important temples built by the Cholas: the Brihadesvara Temple in Tanjavur (built c. 1000 C.E. by king Rajaraja Chola) and the Siva Temple at Gangaikondacholapuram (built c. 1025 C.E. by king Rajendra Chola, son of Rajaraja). In the former, the *vimana* had fifteen storeys (excluding the crown) and in the latter, ten. For a detailed morphological analysis of these two temples, see Pierre Pichard, *Tanjavur Brhadisvara: An Architectural Study* (New Delhi: Indira Gandhi National Centre for the Arts; Pondicherry: École française d'Extrême-Orient, 1995).

The construction of the temples was carried out by hierarchically ordered guilds of builders whose members specialized in the various crafts associated with building, such as masonry, carpentry, and metal work. According to the *Manasara*, critical edition in Sanskrit, prepared by P.K. Acharya (reprint, Delhi: Low Price Publications, 1995), ch. 2, 17–35, the guild was comprised of four members: (1) *sthapati* (master builder), who possessed comprehensive theoretical knowledge in all the branches of the science of architecture; (2) *sutragrahin* (measurer), who was knowledgeable in measurement and proportions; (3) *vardhaki* (stonecutter and iconographer); and (4) *takshaka* (carpenter). For a brief account of the rules of organization and the functioning of a typical guild, see George Michell, *The Hindu Temple: An Introduction to Its Meaning and Form* (New York: Harper and Row, 1977), 55–7.

3 The complete body of Acharya's work on the *Manasara*, including the critical edition, translation into English, and commentary, has been reprinted in seven volumes; see P.K. Acharya, *Manasara Series*, nos 1–7 (reprint, Delhi: Low Price Publications, 1995). Four of the eleven extant manuscripts of the *Manasara* are owned by the Library of India Office in London, two each by the Palace Estate of Tanjavur and the Government Oriental Library in Madras, and the rest by Deccan College in Poona, the Oriental Library of the Asiatic Society of Bengal in Calcutta, and the Palace Library of Trivandrum; see Acharya, "Preface," in *Manasara Series*, no. 3, *Manasara on Architecture and Sculpture*, vii–xxii at ix–xvi.

4 The Sanskrit term for the injunctive form is *vidhi*; it is characterized in grammatical construction by the optative mood of verbal conjugation.

5 *Manasara*, ch. 1, 3–4. Architectural theory was first enunciated by Siva, the supreme deity, and "heard" by other deities and sages of antiquity, who, in turn, passed it on to the sage Manasara, the purported "author" of the treatise. The text also claims a divine origin for the four-tiered builders' guild in the account of its genealogy; see ch. 2, 2–20.

6 This projection by the treatise of the instrumental dimension of its theory by means of the injunctive form does not warrant the reading of the traditional paradigm as being in accordance with the modernist framework of functionalist tenets dictating technological production. This reading of traditional theory and practice as identical in essence to the modern paradigm is a common tendency in contemporary Indian architectural discourse and practice. The historical roots of this misreading can be traced back to P.K. Acharya himself. Acharya conducted an "architectural experiment" in 1935 by conceiving and building a guest house (which he named the Svastika Mansion) in the city of Allahabad that "demonstrate[d] a residential design from the *Manasara*" (fig. 8.11); see Acharya, "Preface," in *Manasara Series*, no. 6, *Hindu Architecture in India and Abroad*, ix–xxviii at xiii–xiv. According to Acharya, this "demonstration" verified and proved the relevance and applicability of traditional theory in modern practice. Despite Acharya's claim about the success of the experiment, the Svastika Mansion failed to capture the attention of wider architectural cir-

cles at the time or thereafter and was never listed among significant works in any contemporary account of Indian architectural history. It is no surprise, then, that the above tendency has never really risen beyond an easy syncretism to produce a meaningful synthesis of the traditional and the modern in contemporary architectural practice in India.

8.11 Front view of the Svastika Mansion, Allahabad (1935–36 C.E.), built by P.K. Acharya "according to the Manasara," in P.K. Acharya, *Manasara Series*, no. 6, *Hindu Architecture in India and Abroad* (reprint, Delhi: Low Price Publications, 1995), plate 4 (b).

7 In brief, a summary of the rituals that make up this ceremony, as described in *Manasara*, ch. 70, 13–110, can be paraphrased as follows:

First, the ritual of *ankurarpana* (offering of sprouts) is conducted. The *sthapati* builds the sacrificial pavilion and altar. He marks a pattern of plot-disposition (in which a deity presides over each plot) on the floor of the pavilion and on the altar. Pitchers filled with pure water, corresponding in number to the number of plots in the pattern, are brought and placed on the altar. The main pitcher occupies the central plot and is believed to contain the yet unmanifested deity. The image whose eyes are to be chiseled is also brought into the pavilion and placed on the floor. Following this, *ashtamangala* (eight auspicious objects) are placed on the altar.

The *sthapati* then purifies himself by ablution and conducts a joint offering of all objects. He waves incense and lamp, recites *mantras* (sacred formulae) and shows *mudras* (hand gestures of magical efficacy), all before the main water-pitcher amidst song and dance. Offerings of food items such as rice and milk are made. He then performs *homa* (sacrifice) by offering rice, clarified butter and water to the consecrated fire. He sprinkles the image with water and thereby prepares it for the chiseling of its eyes. He uses a sharp needle to "write" the eyes, washes the eyes with water and clarified butter, and then covers them with cloth.

In the next stage, the *sthapati* and his retinue carry the water-pitchers in procession around the temple. Returning to the pavilion, he pours water from the main pitcher upon the image. This ritual, called *kumbhabhisheka* (anointing with water), marks the transference of the unmanifested deity from the water-pitcher to the image. The deity now has manifested himself in the image. The *sthapati* then worships the deity in the image with incense and lamp and offerings of food, flowers, etc., amidst song and dance. With his retinue, he carries the image through the village and brings it back to the temple. Next, he conducts *ratnavinyasa* (placing of the nine precious stones in the pedestal in the adytum of the temple). Finally, he installs the image of the deity upon the pedestal, thus completing the ceremony.

8 The basic contours of Saiva theology are drawn along the lines of the principle of emanation. Siva is the supreme deity who begets, preserves, and dissolves the cosmos through the processes of evolution and involution. A set of thirty-six categories marks the stages of these processes. These categories range from subtle to gross and encompass the modes of divinity (deity), humanity (self), and the world of matter. The notion of a creation *ex nihilo* is absent, and consequently the ultimate ground for a real ontological distinction between categories is also lacking. Moreover, temporality is comprehended more as a cosmological than a historical experience. For a comprehensive account of Saiva theology, see K. Sivaraman, *Saivism in Philosophical Perspective* (Varanasi: Motilal Banarsidass Publishers, 1973).

9 This is a rhetorical strategy and structure that I employ in the essay. A verse from the chapter of the *Manasara* that is pertinent to the theme under discussion in a particular section is first cited at the beginning of the section. The text that immediately follows the verse is dedicated to the explication of its meaning. In the course of this explication, the connection to the theme is brought to light. Thus a way is opened through the verse to delve into the theme in depth. The translations of the verses are my own.

10 Perception, being the mode of "seeing" by which the outer world is apprehended, operates on the "ontological" plane, whereas meditation, exploring the realms of the divine, operates on a "theological" plane.

11 Monier Monier-Williams, *A Sanskrit-English Dictionary* (reprint, Delhi: Motilal Banarsidass Publishers, 1995), 872. The word *raga* derives from √*ranj*, which means "to glow," and also "to be affected, excited."

12 To vision, *raga* is "colour, hue, tint, dye, (especially) red colour"; to hearing, it is "a musical note, harmony, melody"; see ibid.

13 In Saiva theology, these three principles pertain to the self; see Sivaraman, *Saivism*, 237–42.

14 To be more accurate, the traditional mode of seeing and mental disposition is "proto-phenomenological" because phenomenology, as a conscious philosophical enterprise, is indeed modern and has Cartesian roots that it sought to overcome; see Edmund Husserl, *Cartesian Meditations: An Introduction to Phenomenology*, trans. Dorion Cairns (The Hague: Martinus Nijhoff, 1960). However, the ascription of the traditional Indian mindset as "phenomenological" (with the above-stated qualification) is plausible insofar as "logic" (or better, "reason [as] a broad title," as Husserl puts it) was engaged therein as it encountered reality given through phenomena and attempted to provide a coherent account of the experience. On this point, see J.N. Mohanty, "Phenomenology and Indian Philosophy: The Concept of Rationality," and Karl Schuhmann, "Husserl and Indian Thought," both in D.P. Chattopadhyaya, Lester Embree, and J.N. Mohanty, eds, *Phenomenology and Indian Philosophy*, 8–19, 20–43 (New Delhi: Indian Council for Philosophical Research and Motilal Banarsidass Publishers, 1992).

15 Robert P. Goldman and Sally J. Sutherland Goldman, *Devavanipravesika: An Introduction to the Sanskrit Language* (Berkeley, CA: Center for South Asia Studies, University of California, 1999), 145.

16 *Manasara*, ch. 3, 15–34; see also ch. 4.

17 *Manasara*, ch. 5.

18 Obviously, this process is distinct from a modern scientific experiment, which, in the rarefied environment of a laboratory, abstracts and quantifies the object under scrutiny.

19 *Manasara*, ch. 6, 22–8.

20 This is evident from the title of the treatise, which translates as both "the essence of measurement" and "the essence that is measure."

21 *Manasara*, ch. 2, 41–53.

22 *Manasara*, ch. 2, 40.

23 The notion of eidetic intuition and that of bracketing and reduction as

constituting the phenomenological sense are drawn from Edmund Husserl, *Phenomenology and the Foundations of the Sciences*, bk 3, *Ideas Pertaining to a Pure Phenomenology and to a Phenomenological Philosophy*, trans. Ted E. Klein and William E. Pohl (The Hague: Martinus Nijhoff, 1980).

24 *Manasara*, ch. 15, 257–339.

25 *Manasara*, ch. 17, 27–30.

26 *Manasara*, ch. 52, 183–215.

27 The "devotee" is anyone who follows the Saiva tradition of theology and religious practice. In the context of this discussion, however, the devotee is primarily the *sthapati* himself, whose basic emotional state as he undertakes the commission of temple building and image making is that of devotional love toward the deity (Siva).

28 The verb used in the text to denote the operation of chiselling is √*likh* (to write).

29 The term *darsana* derives from √*drs* (to see).

30 Jan Gonda, *The Vision of the Vedic Poets* (The Hague: Mouton, 1963), 289.

31 Several scholars have sought to extract the spiritual and technical senses in which the concept of *dhyana* was applied in religious and artistic practices by translating it as "meditation," "meditative contemplation," "concentrated meditation through visualization," "inner absorption," "penetration of real essences and mysteries," "undistracted attention," and so on; see ibid., 289–90. One might consider *dhyana* as "disciplined imagination" that is open to receiving impressions of transcendent realities.

32 In ibid., 61–2, Gonda offers a more "essentialist" interpretation of the same process; as does Ananda Coomaraswamy, *Transformation of Nature in Art* (reprint, New York: Dover, 1956), 166.

33 *Manasara*, ch. 2, 68, 75.

34 *Manasara*, ch. 5, 37.

35 *Manasara*, ch. 5, 23–5.

36 *Manasara*, ch. 5, 80–2.

37 *Manasara*, ch. 7, 253–69.

38 *Manasara*, ch. 7, 155–252.

39 *Manasara*, ch. 8, 60. The specific verb-root used here to denote "meditation" is √*smr* (to remember). According to Saiva theology with its emanationist slant, the self is ontologically divine in its inner essence but ignorant

of it, being fettered by the world of the flesh. Thus meditation as "remembrance" is the process of "re-cognition" by the self of its divine nature, thereby bringing about its identification or union with the divine.

40 *Manasara*, ch. 12, 108–9.

41 *Manasara*, ch. 12, 112–14.

42 *Manasara*, ch. 15, 409, 430–1.

43 *Manasara*, ch. 18, 371.

44 The identification and worship of the finial as the transcendent form of Siva is not stated directly; it is inferred from the account of the elaborate ritual that accompanies the technical act of erection of the dome-nail; see *Manasara*, ch. 18, 340–413.

45 *Manasara*, ch. 51, 25. The iconological details of deities, together with the system of proportional measurement for images, constituted the "theory" of iconography.

46 Dehejiya mentions one such instance in which the iconographer made use of the Tamil saint Appar's vision, recorded in his poem *Tevaram*, of Siva as the Enchanting Mendicant with a swaying gait as the meditational verse while sculpting that image; see Vidya Dehejiya, *Art of the Imperial Cholas* (New York: Columbia University Press, 1990), 115–16.

47 *Manasara*, ch. 59, 1–4. In the Saiva tradition, these four states are explained not only in abstract, philosophical terms, but also in concrete, relational terms. In *salokya* the relationship of devotee to deity is servile (between servant and master), in *samipya* it is filial (between son and father or between disciple and teacher), in *sarupya* it is fraternal (between friends), and in *sayujya* it is amorous (between lovers).

48 Sivaraman, *Saivism*, 393.

49 Jan Gonda, *A History of Indian Literature*, vol. 2, fasc. 1, *Medieval Religious Literature in Sanskrit* (Wiesbaden: Otto Harrassowitz, 1977), 2–3.

50 From a strictly epistemological point of view, knowledge of the "how" is "tacit knowledge"; knowledge of the "what" can be further distinguished as "explicit" and "systematic" knowledge; see Michael Polanyi, "The Logic of Tacit Inference" and "Tacit Knowing: Its Bearing on Some Problems of Philosophy," both in Marjorie Grene, ed., *Knowing and Being: Essays by Michael Polanyi*, 138–58, 159–80 (London, Routledge and Kegan Paul, 1969). The term "explicit" need not imply a propositional or even aphoristic structure; such knowledge can be in the form of narratives as well. On the other hand, knowledge that is "systematic" is "theoretical" in the full contemporary sense of the term.

51 The medieval *sthapaka* (officiating priest in temple-building rituals) is the successor of the *sthapaka* of a much earlier period, mentioned in the text *Vastusutra Upanisad*. The *Vastusutra Upanisad* deals with making divine form; see Alice Boner, Bettina Baumer, and Sadasiva Rath Sarma, trans and eds, *Vastusutra Upanisad: The Essence of Form in Sacred Art*, Sanskrit text with English translation and notes, 3rd rev. ed. (Delhi: Motilal Banarsidass Publishers, 1996). This text is a unique instance in the history of Indian architectural theory where the "how," "what," and "why" of making are set in delicate balance. Its date, although still in dispute, may be posited tentatively as ca. 200 B.C.E. In the *Vastusutra Upanisad*, the *sthapaka* is the maker of divine form; he also "attends to" it and thus also exercises a priestly function. He defends his practice against the attacks of brahmanical priests of the fire-sacrifice cult who privilege divine name over divine form (and therefore hold a certain iconoclastic grudge). The text claims that liberation (as the ultimate goal of the individual) is possible through knowledge and practice of the craft of image making. The text makes the following assertion in chapter 1, sutra 4:

> Who has the knowledge of circle and line is a *sthapaka*.
>
> Holding in hand a measuring rod of *khadira* wood and a cord of *darbha* grass fitted with a ring, that is his outer aspect. This knowledge is the knowledge of Art (*silpajnana*). From this knowledge arises divine knowledge, and such knowledge leads to liberation. This [liberation] is verily the essence of the knowledge of Art. He who knows this [attains the essence].

52 The *Manasara* stresses the necessity and importance of collaboration between *sthapati* and *sthapaka* throughout the temple-building and image-making procedure. According to the text, ch. 70, 3–4, "the *sthapati* is the 'source' of the temple and image and the *sthapaka* its 'life-principle.'" The "collaboration" is, of course, hierarchical in structure: the *sthapati* is the disciple of the *sthapaka*.

53 The five gross elements are space (ether), air, fire, water, and earth; the five subtle elements are sound, touch, sight, taste, and smell.

54 The five faculties of action are voice (speech), hands, feet, anus, and genitals; the five faculties of perception are ear, skin, eye, tongue, and nose; the faculties of cognition are consciousness, corporeality, intellect, mind, and self-hood.

55 These categories are aptitude, knowledge, desire (affection), time, and fate (necessity).

56 As a theological category within the scheme of the thirty-six principles, this "state" of self-insight (which, paradoxically, is also self-obscuration) constitutes the threshold between the phenomenal and the transcendent realms.

Projecting Utopia: The Refortification of Nicosia, 1567–70

Panos Leventis

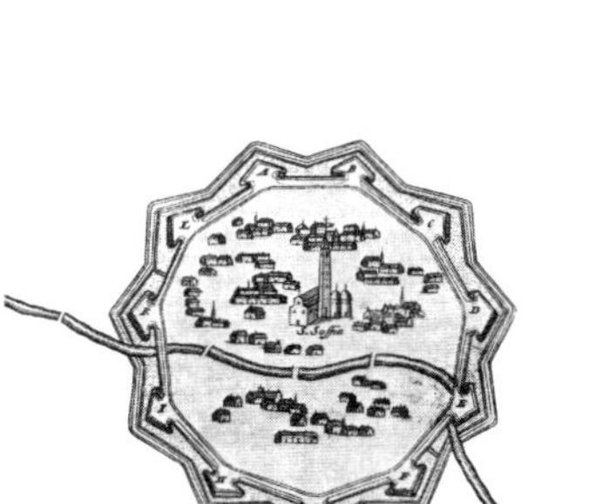

Chora

INTRODUCTION[1]

IN THE EARLY HOURS of 9 September 1570, following seven weeks of siege and fifteen major assaults, Ottoman mercenaries succeeded in scaling the Podocataro bastion of the recently refortified city of Nicosia, the capital of Cyprus and centre of the Serenissima's militarily most significant colony. The entire city was taken, most of its buildings were set on fire, and most of its citizens were put to death. For the following three centuries, Nicosia would lie dormant as an insignificant post in a corner of the vast Ottoman Empire, a place of exile for those unfavoured by the Sultan in Constantinople. Her circular walls and eleven bastions would remain rare reminders of her past lives.

This essay describes the conception and construction of Nicosia's Renaissance fortifications and discusses theoretical and practical issues of ideal cities and fortifications from the late fifteenth to the late sixteenth centuries. Nicosia was the first city to fuse an ideal city plan with a bastioned fortress. The essay shows that this urban and military experiment was developed with theoretical and philosophical considerations, contrary to previous claims, and that it was the fall of Nicosia that prompted the radial street plan in ideal city designs. This change led urban fortification to lose its multifaceted symbolism. Preconfigured urban grid patterns would thus become mere tools to fortify edges during military operations, while cities within would become poor social and cultural environments.

The space was hazy and dark. A trembling ray of September sun managed to find its way through the cracks of the roof. It hit his thinning, grey hair, moved slowly down and glittered on his sweaty forehead, and finally completed its path by attacking his tired eyes.

Blinded momentarily, he raised his head and gave a fleeting look toward the open window. The hot breeze was pursuing its monotone effort, carrying patches of dust and thick smoke inside. Uninvited, the thoughts entered along with the haze: Could they have advanced again? Were they threatening the heart of the city?

No. He was certain that the walls would push them back. Their stones would hold for a few more hours. He did not require but those few, precious hours. Afterwards, they would all be spared.

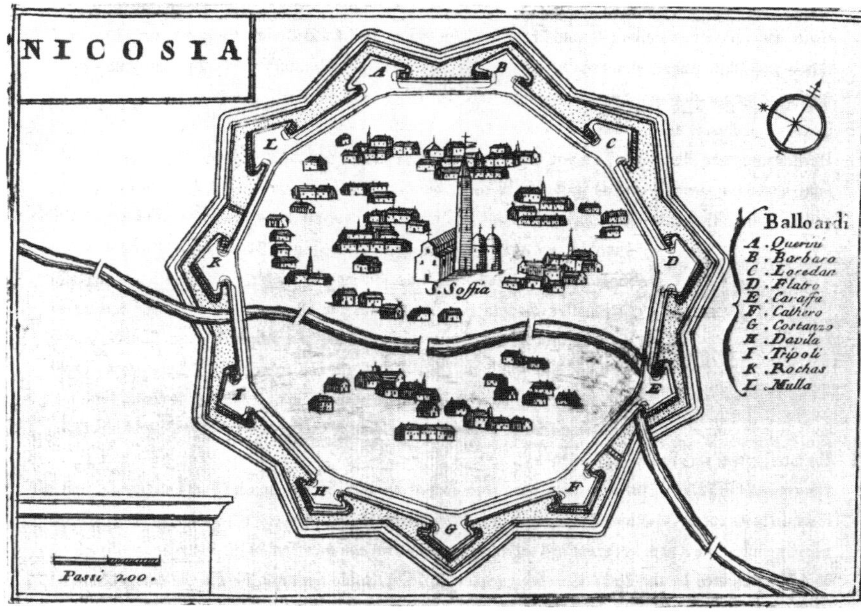

9.1 Vincenzo Maria Coronelli, "Nicosia," in *Il Mediterraneo Descritto Dal Padre Maestro Coronelli Cosmografo dalla Serenissima Republica di Venetia* (Venice: Gli Argonauti, 1706). Courtesy of the Bank of Cyprus Cultural Foundation, Map Collection, Nicosia. Based on the second of two woodcuts published by Giovanni Francesco Camocio in Venice following the 1570 fall of the city. The bastions are correctly placed and named, but the river is shown crossing the city, despite its earlier diversion. The fabric within the walls, depicted conventionally except for the intriguing double cathedral, remained unaltered during the construction of the Renaissance fortress.

BETWEEN *MEDIOEVO* AND *RINASCIMENTO*

It was not unexpected that Nicosia provided a theoretical *and* topographic ground for this experiment in fortification. For the city, that fateful day in 1570 was the end of 500 years of urban life as the capital of a rich Byzantine province, the royal and religious seat of a late medieval kingdom, and the administrative and cultural centre of a Renaissance Venetian colony.

For millennia, geography had given Cyprus and her cities the privilege to lie at the crossroads of religious, ethnic, and economic development. In 1191, when Richard the Lionheart captured Cyprus from an unruly Byzantine lord,[2] Nicosia became the seat of the Lusignan, an old crusading family from France.[3]

In the thirteenth century the city was a safe haven at the western edge of the contested Holy Land. It was one of the stops on Saint Francis's journey to the Terra Santa in 1221,[4] as well as the adopted home of crusading Saint Louis for most of 1248.[5] Nicosia thus was adorned with a large religious core of *two* cathedrals and bishoprics (Latin and Greek)[6] and many Cistercian,[7] Franciscan, and Dominican establishments.[8] The city attracted the attention of Saint Thomas Aquinas, who dedicated his *De Regno, ad Regem Cypri*[9] to young King Hugh II in 1265. Raised in Nicosia, Hugh would rule over a kingdom essential to the West, a kingdom whose capital city was to be refounded and reshaped by superimposing Christian *and* Vitruvian principles, as Aquinas advised young Hugh.[10] Nicosia would thus be the reason for the first use of Vitruvius's text, two centuries *before* its (re)publication.

In the fourteenth century Nicosia received many refugees from the Holy Land's collapsed kingdoms. It grew in size and in social and ethnic diversity. Humanism found fertile ground in its courts, loggias, and schools, synthesizing influences from Constantinople with those from Italy's early Renaissance centres. In the mid-fourteenth century a request by Hugh IV of Cyprus led Boccaccio to write the *Genealogia Deorum Gentilium*,[11] one of the first works to describe the Greco-Roman cosmos of myth to the early Renaissance world.

Under Hugh and his son Peter, the city refurbished its royal courts and built large stone walls.[12] In the 1370s Peter II constructed an extensive citadel at the southwestern edge for defence from the outside and as a

With both his fists swaying through the heavy air surrounding him, as if attempting to alter the path of the sun's rays, he found himself angrily murmuring sets of reassuring sounds.

Slowly becoming aware and calm, he stopped and looked down with a rejuvenated boldness.

His body was now hunched over a large table in the middle of the dusty room. His hands were resisting the trembling, fighting as they were against merciless Time. His fingers continued undeterred, in their delicate task.

Of this he was certain: With his help, Nicosia itself would soon take charge. The city would rise and encounter destiny once again. The noble city that he worshipped would complete the task that all those miserable men could not accomplish.

refuge for his family in times of urban discontent. These defences protected Nicosia from the 1360s to the 1560s, until a century of fortification theory and practice would use its fabric as an ultimate testing ground.

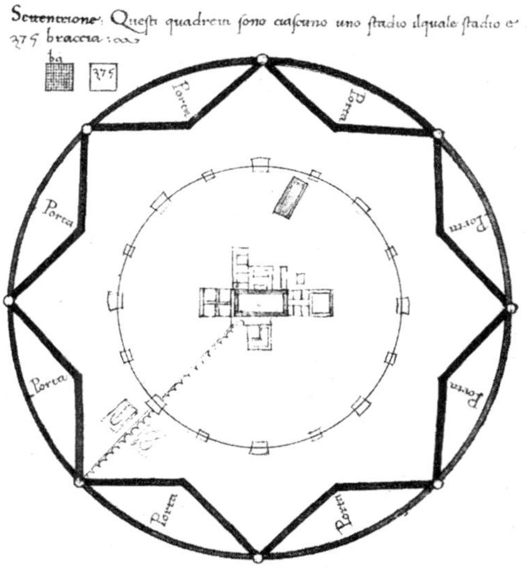

9.2 Antonio Averlino (Il Filarete), plan of the city of Sforzinda, in *Trattato di Architettura* (Milan, 1464), detail of fol. 43r°. Courtesy of McGill University Library, Blackader-Lauterman Art and Architecture Collection, Montreal. The octagonal ideal city has eight protrusions with round towers and gates in the middle distance pointing to the direction of the winds, following the rediscovered Vitruvian tradition.

> Stopping for a moment and wiping his palms with an old piece of cloth, he measured the space in a quick glance.
>
> He was not alone.
>
> One after another, appearing out of dark corners, a parade of eyes was staring at him in a perplexed gaze.
>
> A rising tide of hands slowly reached out and surrounded him in silent implore.

THE CONTEXT OF THEORY AND PRACTICE, PART I

At the apogee of humanism in the fifteenth century, the treatises of Alberti, Filarete, and di Giorgio,[13] as well as da Veroli's first edition of the "rediscovered" Vitruvius, pointedly focused on harmony, proportions, and the human body. These topics were symbolized in their discussion of defensive constructions but were not always literally translated.

Between 1477 and 1482, di Giorgio designed fortifications for various localities in the Duchy of Urbino. His anthropomorphic designs for forts are well known, as are his presentations of ideal city projects, along with those of Filarete. Anthropomorphic concerns are also evident in other fortifications, such as Baccio Pontelli's 1485 design and construction of Ostia Antica's fort and Giuliano da Sangallo's 1487 designs for Poggio Imperiale.[14]

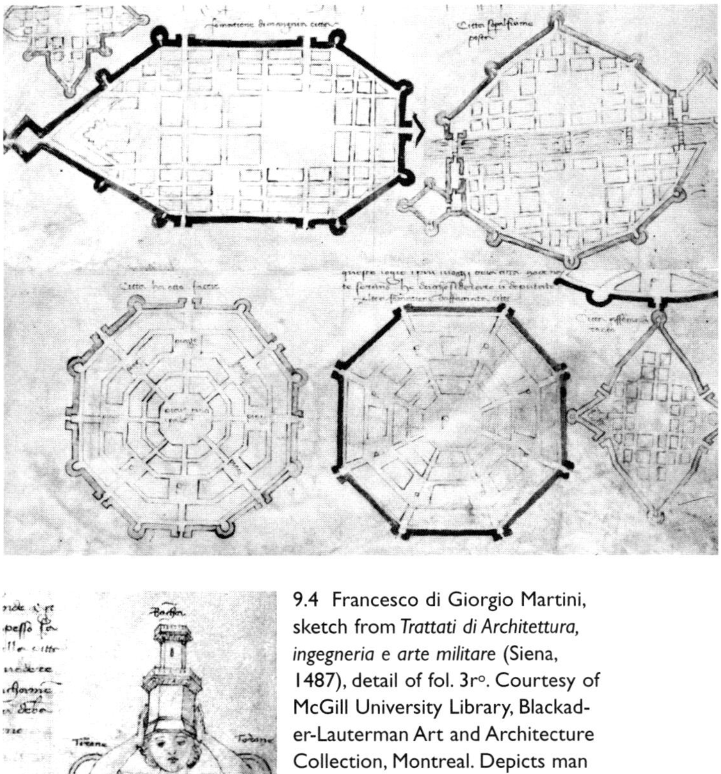

9.3 Francesco di Giorgio Martini, sketch from *Trattati di Architettura, ingegneria e arte militare* (Siena, 1487), details of fols 7r° and 7v°. Courtesy of McGill University Library, Blackader-Lauterman Art and Architecture Collection, Montreal. Depicts contemplations on ideal city geometries.

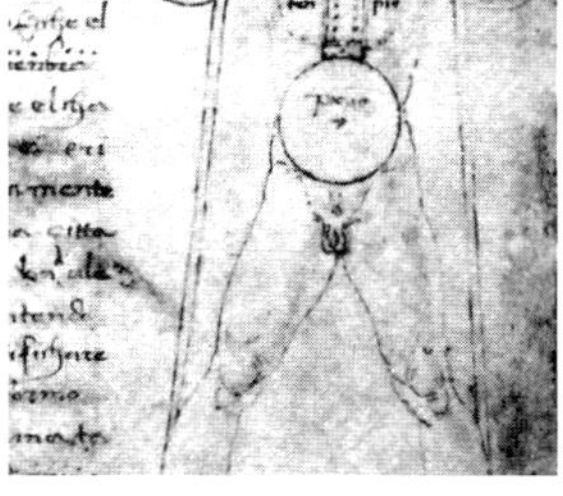

9.4 Francesco di Giorgio Martini, sketch from *Trattati di Architettura, ingegneria e arte militare* (Siena, 1487), detail of fol. 3r°. Courtesy of McGill University Library, Blackader-Lauterman Art and Architecture Collection, Montreal. Depicts man as a fortified city, with the citadel at the head, the central piazza at the belly, the cathedral at the heart, round towers at the limbs, and a lobed bastion foreshadowing at the projection of the genitals.

The presence of anthropomorphic principles in early fortification design has often been viewed with suspicion or outright rejection, including the claim that it "reside[s] solely in the evidence it provides of a desire to add a non-engineering element to the reappraisal of Renaissance fortifications."[15] However, hadn't fortifications *already* been reappraised as mere "elements of engineering," instruments of defence in the late and post-Renaissance world? The intentions, at the origin of Renaissance fortification design, of Di Giorgio and even of Leonardo – whose 1480s fortification sketches appear to be based on Di Giorgio[16] – should not be forgotten. While late-fifteenth-century designs maintained the basic form of medieval fortifications, they introduced humanist ideals and symbols and also experimented with lower heights and differentiated tower forms.

This "foreshadowing" of the bastion, however, did not provide an effective defence against the new, formidable machine of war: the cannon. By the 1490s, French cannons led to victories against the most resilient fortifications and demonstrated the need for a new approach to fortification design.[17] Sangallo's 1501 design and construction of the Nettuno fort was one significant response.

In the undivorced realms of theory and practice of the early sixteenth century, work on bastion forms progressed quickly. Simultaneously, fortifications were endowed with the same Vitruvian principles of beauty, harmony, and proportion as in the new "temples": the Renaissance cathedrals and palaces. In 1502 the Sanzarello fortress was declared "very strong and beautiful," while Vasari described the fort of S. Andrea as "marvelous ... with the beauty of its walls represent[ing] the grandeur

Against all four walls of the room, pieces and blocks of unfinished statues jolted violently on the blast of each firing and on the crash of each cannonball.

For the past few years and through the last difficult weeks, those pieces of stone, his incomplete creations and dedicated companions, gave him unconditional encouragement. Why were they so different today?

He resumed his work.

Although on that afternoon the attacks were more frequent and sounded louder, this was a work that he would complete.

The enemies were attempting to penetrate through his focused mind and rip his dedication apart.

They would not succeed.

and majesty of the most famous buildings of Roman greatness."[18] It would be inappropriate to superimpose an anachronistic "art versus engineering" opposition onto this mid-Renaissance understanding of fortifications[19] since the two were inseparable in the design and construction of religious, civic, *and* defensive buildings.

During this age, anthropocentrism elevated man to an unprecedented status, and anthropomorphic designs were applied to churches, cities, and fortifications. Discussing architecture in conjunction with astrology and mathematics, studies such as Pacioli's *On Divine Proportion*[20] and the 1521 and 1522 editions of Vitruvius's text by Cesariano[21] and Fra Giocondo[22] further translated the body's proportions into architectural proportions and established the symbolic basis for subsequent fortification treatises and designs.

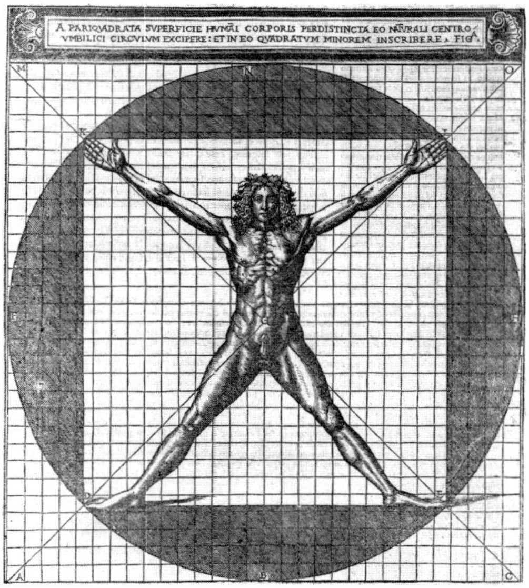

9.5 The human body's proportions predestined for and inscribed in the circle and square, in Cesare Cesariano, *Di Lucio Vitruuio Pollione De Architectura Libri dece traducti de Latino in vulgare affigurati commentati et con mirando ordine insigniti* (Como: Gotardo da Ponte, 1521), bk 3, ch. 1, detail of fol. 50v°. Courtesy of McGill University Library, Rare Books and Special Collections Division, Montreal.

A deafening blast shook the workshop. The far corner of the ceiling gave in, and cries from neighbouring buildings filled the rotten haze.

He did not raise his head. No cannon was strong enough to alter or prohibit the passing of Fate. And today, Fate stood firmly on the inside of Nicosia's strong and beautiful fortress.

This more-than-human world surrounded and protected the city and was manifested in architectural, urban, and political forms. Even in the cruelly pragmatic world of Macchiavelli,[23] the encounter between the human and the divine in the form of *Fortuna* provided a necessary safeguard for the fortresses and cities of every self-respecting Prince. Alongside the practical ambition to develop anti-artillery bastion and moat forms, the human body was superimposed onto the celestial and "perfect" body of the stars and of geometry, and aided by Fortuna herself, it provided the theoretical and symbolic terrain for conceiving, designing, and building fortifications.

THE CROSSING TO VENICE

Meanwhile, by the fifteenth century, Nicosia's fortunes had reversed. Two destructive attacks, one by the Genoese army in 1373 and the other by the Mamelukes of Egypt in 1426, left the once wealthy capital in ruins. However, the subsequent reconstruction, the influx of refugees and logians from the fallen capital of the Byzantine Empire, and the increasing power of the city's Italian *comuni* contributed to the city's cultural and architectural production in the mid-fifteenth century. The art of Palaiologan Constantinople and the architecture of the Italian Renaissance were superimposed onto Nicosia's rejuvenated, but more modest, hybrid urban fabric.

In the 1450s the city also received attention from the Vatican. Recognizing the significance of Cyprus's loss to the advancing Ottomans, Pope Nicolas V issued indulgences to reconstruct Nicosia's half-de-

The small, round surface that was gradually taking shape between his fingers echoed the story of his city.

Just as he fondly remembered and could easily trace every demolished corner of Nicosia, he was convinced that all the pieces being chiselled away, broken, thrown to the ground under his table, and forever separated from the remaining substance, could still reveal the meaning of the completed work.

Still, he was uncertain and uneasy of other thoughts persisting in his mind. Was this true for the city itself?

Would all the destruction that Nicosia suffered bear fruit?

Would the harmony and perfection of its new form prove effective against this powerful enemy standing before its gates?

stroyed fortifications.[24] It remains unclear whether these funds ever reached the Cypriot capital or were used for this purpose.

The 1473 wedding of King James II to the noble Venetian Caterina Cornaro was a clever political move on Venice's part. James's death and Caterina's 1489 abdication effortlessly ended the 300-year Lusignan reign and added the island to Venetian possessions.

During the 1490s and 1500s, and following a destructive earthquake, the new proveditors of the capital attentively fixed the cathedrals and other damaged structures but did little for the city's castles, citadels, or walls. Not until 1567, when faced with immediate danger, did Venice urgently but belatedly reconstruct the crumbling defences, destroying more than a third of the city itself.

THE CONTEXT OF THEORY AND PRACTICE, PART 2

Nicosia was not the first Venetian possession to be partially demolished to permit the construction of new defences. In 1509–11 Fra Giocondo had designed and supervised the refortification of Treviso and Padova. At Treviso, he encountered a medieval core with crumbling fortifications that provided a buffer between the core and the growing Renaissance *borghi* that housed most public buildings and citizens. The project included the removal of all structures within a 500-metre zone beyond the proposed defences so that attackers would be exposed and the defenders would have a clear line of fire. The proposed demolition of so many buildings was intensely opposed by Treviso's hesitant citizens, and months of negotiations with the Venetian Senate were needed to gain approval.[25]

Was it only in his clouded mind that the bastions were twisting, holding, and pushing the attackers away?

He did not have answers. He knew only that while Nicosia had been fighting bravely for weeks, the enemy was slowly carving away at its defences and the resolve of those who, in hope and desperation, had enclosed themselves within its walls.

However, the invaders could not, and would not, dismantle his determination. As his friends in Rome would testify, Alessandro was a man of legendary stubbornness. If there ever was a time to hold true to his fame, that time had now arrived. The city was calling for his help, and he was coming to the rescue. The Florentine master undoubtedly would have been content.

Four years later, Civitavecchia was reconstructed by Antonio da Sangallo (Giuliano's nephew), who surrounded the city, the harbour, and Michelangelo's fort with bastions of varying shape. This project demonstrated that the newly conceived succession of bastions and walls would be more useful for larger urban fortifications than for smaller fortresses.[26]

Concurrently, Michelangelo's 1528 Prato d'Ognissanti studies in Florence further verified both the ongoing concern for *disegno* in fortifications and the symbolic association of defensive architecture with the human body. Although economic and political concerns prevented its realization,[27] the project demonstrated Michelangelo's ingenuity and knowledge and showed that he regarded fortification as a meaningful military, artistic, and symbolic operation.

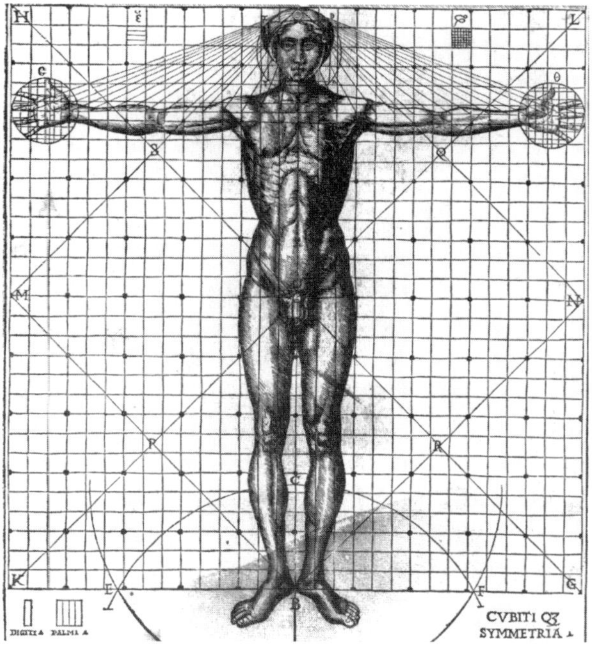

9.6 The human body understood as the origin of symmetry, eurhythmy, and proportion, in Cesare Cesariano, *Di Lucio Vitruuio Pollione De Architectura Libri dece traducti de Latino in vulgare affigurati commentati et con mirando ordine insigniti* (Como: Gotardo da Ponte, 1521), bk 3, ch. 1, detail of fol. 49v°. Courtesy of McGill University Library, Rare Books and Special Collections Division, Montreal.

He could not recall when he had last eaten, let alone when he had last slept, but none of that was his concern. The last medal was finally complete.

Clearing away the dust and revealing its depiction, he carefully set it on the table, at the centre of a circle formed by eleven other medals.

Rising up in reserved and almost ceremonial satisfaction, he prepared.

Following the Ottoman capture of Rhodes, Cyprus became the eastern Mediterranean's sole Christian outpost. The Venetian Senate considered the urgent need for new defences on Corfu, Crete, and Cyprus. Michele Sanmicheli, colleague of Antonio da Sangallo and pupil of his uncle Giuliano, was thus dispatched in 1538, first to Crete and then to Cyprus.

The Sanmicheli "school" of fortification, like the Sangallo "school" that preceded it, was concerned not only with military and economic considerations. While designing enceintes for Crete's three main cities, Sanmicheli also conceived and realized projects for public health and civil architecture.[28] Similarly, while refortifying Civitavecchia in 1515, the "pragmatist and realist" Antonio da Sangallo had begun the symbolically charged pentagonal fortified basement of the Caprarola Palazzo. Their concerns thus were not confined to "practical engineering" nor to financial affairs. As Renaissance architects, they drew inspiration from contemporary religious and even mystical sources.[29]

By the 1550s Sanmicheli's refortification designs were also carried out in Corfu, in Zara, and in Famagusta, Cyprus, by his nephew, Gian Girolamo. Gian Girolamo died while overseeing the Famagusta works in 1558, and Michele fell ill and followed his nephew a few months later. Their family of prolific fortification builders, rivals of Michelangelo and his followers, had now come to a close.[30]

The proliferation of treatises on architecture and fortification in the 1550s provided additional theory with which designs were realized.[31] "There was a significant shift in practice and values between the middle of the Quattrocento and the middle of the Cinquecento. In the former, the notion of military architecture assumed that *disegno* was the prompting talent of its practitioners, and that its exponents were at least touched by the hem of Vitruvian respectability. In

Stretching the dirty piece of cloth, he placed on it the medals, gathered in a careful, predetermined order. He wrapped the cloth around them and tied it in the form of a pouch. The ammunition was complete. Now Alessandro was ready to fight for his life and for his city.

Coming out into the street, he started walking quickly toward the west, gracelessly dragging his bare feet on the cobblestones. He was blinded by the fiery colours of the sky and the horizontal rays of the setting sun.

The enduring heat and swirling dust of the afternoon mixed with the smoke and powder from the explosions to fill Alessandro's world with a thick, scarlet haze.

Never before had Nicosia seen such a blood-red sunset.

the latter ... shelter beneath Vitruvius' mantle became a last and self-conscious resort."[32] While this statement is generally true, its historical boundaries need to be shifted. The mid-Quattrocento had not yet seen Alberti's treatise nor Vitruvius's first edition. "Vitruvian respectability" certainly would permeate treatises until the 1560s, and concerns beyond military practices would be evident in treatises long afterward. During Nicosia's reconstruction in 1567, the fortification project in both theory and practice was not merely an act of engineering. A few of these treatise writers would find themselves in Cyprus between 1570 and 1571 and perish inside the fortresses of Famagusta and Nicosia.[33]

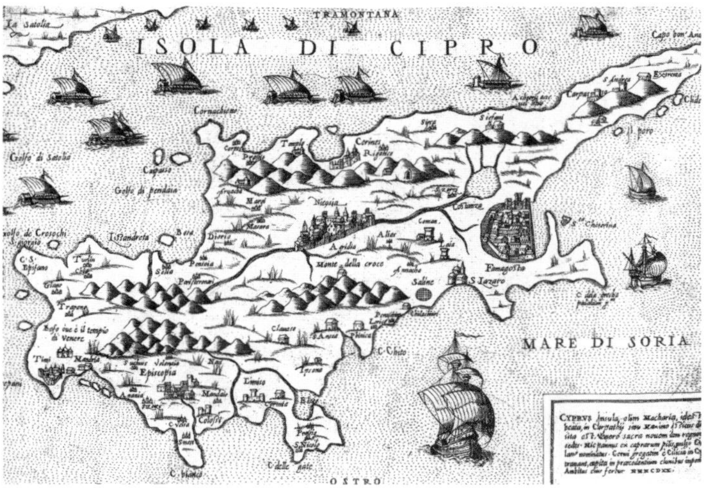

9.7 Mario Kartaro, *Isola di Cipro* (c. 1562), engraved in Rome and published by Ferrando Bertelli in Venice. Courtesy of the Bank of Cyprus Cultural Foundation, Michaelides Collection, Nicosia.

As he overtook the half-destroyed wall of a garden, a tree lying barren caught his attention. He kneeled and filled his grip with dry soil. "Soon, you will all have water," he shouted, with the echo of his voice resounding in the middle of the deserted street. "Soon, you will all be free."

Through the winding alley, the hovering dust caused him to become all but a fleeting shadow, slowly dissappearing beyond the misery of the urban haze.

NICOSIA BEFORE ITS REFORTIFICATION

By the mid-sixteenth century the capital of Venetian Cyprus was immersed in decadence. In 1553 the traveller John Locke commented that Nicosia, "the ancientest citie of the Island ... is walled about, but it is not strong neither of walles nor situation," and he found that "there hath every Cavallier or Conte of the Island an habitation."[34] As in Treviso, gardens and large suburbs around the perimeter of the city reduced the defensive capability of its walls.[35] A 1562 engraving depicted the city with elongated walls and orthogonal towers[36] as a fruitless debate was taking place over the future of the island's weak defensive system. Between 1558 and 1566 various proposals led to no results.[37] Cyprus was now surrounded by the Ottoman Empire.

The pessimism of the time is illustrated in a 1562 report by the engineer Ascanio Savorgnano on the condition of the city and its defences, proclaiming that "the civic disposition is one of a disorganized city, without public squares and with narrow and dusty streets."[38] Savorgnano added that the walls had fallen to the ground, that the fortifications were obsolete and weakened by vegetation in the gardens, and that they were not terraplained and had towers rising out "in the old manner."[39]

Two events ended the indecision. Drained of resources by the continuous export of products to the Venetian mainland, Nicosia's population (except the nobility) had been on the verge of starvation, saved only by emergency grain imports in 1561 and 1562. Poor and undernourished, the urban and suburban masses revolted in 1565 over the deteriorating conditions and the proveditors' oppressive rule.[40] This prompted a further investigation into the condition of the walls; again, they were found to be in almost com-

A cannon blast fell close enough and shook the ground under his feet. Alessandro stumbled, grabbed firmly against a sidewall, regained his balance, but did not once look down. He resumed his pace undeterred.

The towers and roofs of the cathedrals appeared in the red horizon.

He came out of the alley and faced the piazza. His fear of open spaces and crowds was overpowered by his sense of responsibility. He walked directly into the deserted, hazy openness, with his gaze wandering through the space. Only vague silhouettes of buildings appeared, surrounding the square at an indeterminate distance. The shadows of the two cathedrals stood side by side in silence.

Distant cries were heard from all directions. A dog was quietly lamenting.

plete ruin, inadequate to defend the old urban core even from its own discontents. Commander Bernardo Sagredo's 1565 report to the Venetian Senate recommended the refortification of Nicosia "in a few months," not only to defend the island, but also to respond to the demands of its nobility and feudal lords. Surprisingly, Sagredo found the city's wall "good and sufficient." He stated that the refortification process would simply reuse stones from the old walls to construct the new fortress and would require only "a few more stones" to complete the work.[41]

When the ambitious Selim II became Sultan in September 1566, the next focus of his powerful army immediately became clear. The decision was finally made, and in March 1567, Doge Girolamo Priuli named Giulio Savorgnano (brother of Ascanio) the new general governor of Cyprus's army and assigned him to complete the fortifications of Famagusta and to build a new fortress in either Keryneia or Nicosia. After weeks of negotiations with the *università*, the consulting body of the city's governors and nobility, Savorgnano decided against constructing a new fortress. Instead, the task would be much larger: the whole capital was to be refortified, testing the recent theories of urban fortification, and the project would be completed in less than one year.[42]

9.8 Giovanni Francesco Camocio, "Nicosia" (c. 1570), in *Civitatum Aliquot, insigniorum et locorum, magis munitorum exact delineatio* (Venice: Donato Bertelli, 1574), plate 50. Courtesy of the Bank of Cyprus Cultural Foundation, Map Collection, Nicosia. This woodcut, executed after the fall of Nicosia, offers its first large-scale depiction.

The debates preceding construction indicate a priority to protect the city from cannon fire from the hills along its southern edges. However, prominent Nicosians such as the nobleman Florio Bustron had suggested including the southern hills and boroughs *within* the city by extending the medieval *enceinte* around them.[43] In the end, symbolism prevailed over topography, and continuous bombardment from those hills irrevocably weakened the geometrically perfect circular defences of the city.

UTOPIA REALIZED?

The refortification project required 5,000 to 6,000 workers. The river crossing Nicosia was diverted to flow into the new moat surrounding the city. The old walls and all structures lying outside the new *enceinte* (1,800 houses, eighty churches and chapels, two monasteries, and numerous gardens) were demolished, and a smaller, circular fortress with eleven bastions was constructed. The nobility funded Savorgnano's project in exchange for dedicating the bastions with the names of the largest contributors. The rich families of Nicosia eagerly accepted and were assigned to supervise the construction of their respective bastions. The masses were easily recruited as labourers, assuring them a minimal income during this desperate time.[44] Supported by the funds of the nobility, the blessing of the clergy, and the hands of the poor, work commenced on 1 June 1567.

He focused in an attempt to overcome his sadness and reassert his determination. This was the time. He looked around and weighed the distances as well as he could.

In the middle of the hazy upper square, with the cathedrals to his one side and the old river course to the other, Alessandro first turned toward the sky with an inquisitive gaze, and then kneeled.

He was attempting to remove a cracked cobblestone from the old paving of the square when a company of armed men traversed the open space in anxious haste, heading for one of the bastions. "Is not that man crazy old Alessandro?" exclaimed one. Without turning to face them, he replied, "Tomorrow you will be a salvaged but still ungrateful man."

Shelter was not provided for the 10,000 people whose homes were demolished. Most of them worked on the project and constructed makeshift wooden rooms to live in. From 500 to 800 men and women worked on each bastion from 6 A.M. to 1 P.M. and from 7 P.M. to midnight or 1 A.M. Groups shifted every two weeks, and music, dance, and entertainment were provided each night for the workers. Savorgnano departed in December 1568 from what he described as his "Purgatorio, o per dir meglio casa del Diavolo," leaving behind a largely realized yet still incomplete fortification.[45] His deputy Nicolò Dandolo assumed charge of the project, but due to inefficient handling, the walls were not faced with stone and the moat was not completely dug when the Ottoman army landed on Cyprus in the summer of 1570.

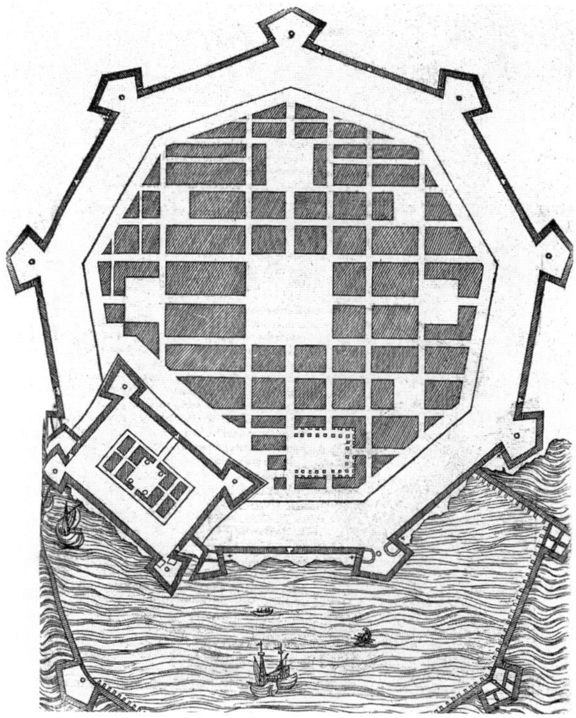

9.9 Pietro Cataneo, ideal city, in *I Quattro Primi Libri di Architettura di Pietro Cataneo Senese* (Venice: Aldo, 1554), bk 1, ch. 18, fol. 22v°. Courtesy of McGill University Library, Rare Books and Special Collections Division, Montreal. In Cataneo's treatise, cities have from four to eleven bastions, and the orthogonal street system's centre is always the open piazza. This coastal town possesses a fortified jetty and a large citadel on its southwestern edge. Nicosia's old citadel, also at the city's southwestern edge, was demolished during construction of the circular fortifications.

Out of the pouch he took the first medal, the one he had just completed. On its edge, the plan of the city's new walls surrounded two figures. Above, a figure of the Virgin Mary, with her hands stretched to embrace Nicosia, appeared, but unclearly, as if doubly engraved.

The location of the new *enceinte*'s geographic centre has been a frequent subject of speculation. Certainly, the aim was not to place the centre at the geographic middle of the medieval conglomeration, as this lay much farther east of the eventual centre of the new walls.[46] Theoretical designs for ideal fortified cities in the 1550s and 1560s had an open piazza at their geometric centre. In designs of the 1570s and 1580s, this piazza was bounded on one side by the cathedral's façade.[47] Of course, this was no novelty, as Francesco di Giorgio's drawings attest. For Nicosia, "while the Latin archbishop donated the *place* of the archiepiscopal palace so that the piazza could be the geographic centre of the city, the prevailing spirit of profit negated Savorgnan's modern urbanistic concepts."[48]

However, it is not certain that these "modern urbanistic concepts" remained unrealized.[49] Was the *place* of the archiepiscopal palace an open space northwest of the Latin cathedral, as research would suggest? It appears that Nicosia's fortification design took advantage of a different open space, the *piazza di sopra*, or Upper Square, that lies approximately at the geometric centre of the new *enceinte*.

Despite Savorgano's alleged "theoretical failure" to align the old Royal Cathedral of the Latins at Sainte Sophia with a new piazza at the geometric centre of the new fortification, he inadvertently established a new centre near or within the existing upper square, and on its northeast edge was the cathedral of the city's silent majority, the Greeks.

In the centre, Aphrodite the Cypria, or perhaps a mermaid, emerged out of a flowing stream.

He carefully set the medal into the hole and then filled the space around it with dry ground. He stood up, slowly completed a full circle above the medal, then started running, tracing the soldiers' path south.

The medals of the Elements had to be placed where danger was most imminent.

He attempted to follow the soldiers into the fortifications as they headed for the bastion of the Podocataros.

He was swiftly pushed back.

"Go to your house, Alessandro, be on your way," shouted the one who had recognized him in the town centre.

There was no time to explain and certainly no one there who would understand.

THE BASTIONS: TOPOGRAPHY AND SYMBOLISM

The significance of eleven for the number of bastions has eluded researchers but can be explained. While the Renaissance was preoccupied with arithmology, divine numbers, and mysticism, another form of symbolism seems to have governed this decision: during the period of Venetian rule, Cyprus was divided into eleven administrative provinces, or *contrade*. The new *enceinte* of the capital would thus incorporate the island and its provinces allegorically in the number of its new bastions. A comment in Captain Nogiero's letter of the 1567 demolitions supports this hypothesis. Before mentioning that 500 to 800 paid women and men would work on each bastion, Nogiero claimed that "the eleven provinces of the island *fussero distribuite* to the eleven bastions."[50]

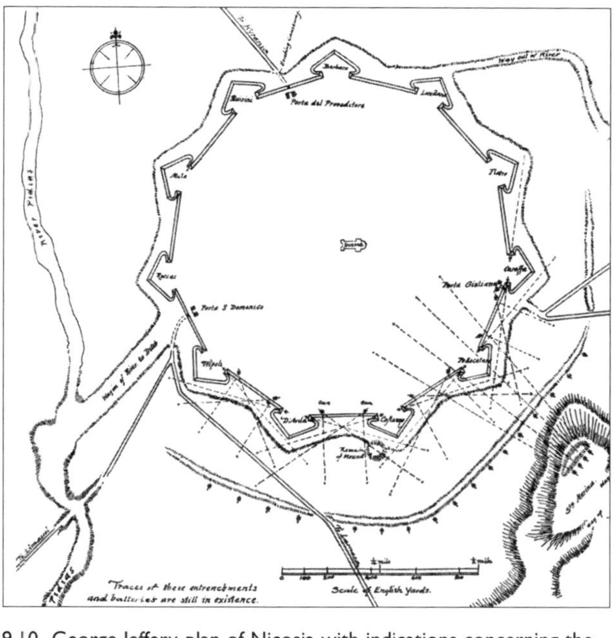

9.10 George Jeffery, plan of Nicosia with indications concerning the 1570 siege, in "The XVIth-Century Fortress of Nicosia," *The Builder* (London) 92 (1907): 51–5. Courtesy of McGill University Library, Blackader-Lauterman Art and Architecture Collection, Montreal. A similar plan, dated 1899, was included in Claude Delaval Cobham, *Excerpta Cypria: Materials for a History of Cyprus* (Cambridge, UK: Cambridge University Press, 1908), facing page 87. The entrenchments encircling the eastern and southern sections of the city, "still in existence in 1899" as Jeffery remarked on the plan, appear to be the trace of the medieval walls.

Heading west to the Costanzos's bastion, he glanced at the second medal, firmly nestled in his grasp. A slightly deformed Winged Messenger was commanding the Air.

By the time a fighter attempted to halt his path, he had reached the front of the bastion.

Beyond this initial allegory of the number of bastions, their dedications would have reinforced the symbolic meaning of the fortress through topographic, ethnic, and class references to Nicosia. Seven bastions were named after prominent Latin and Greek families in Nicosia's nobility, and the remaining four carried the names of the city's contemporary Venetian rulers. All the bastions were dedicated with reference to their location in the city and what had existed there before the demolitions of 1567.

THE SOUTHERN BASTIONS

The Podocataro,[51] Costanzo,[52] and Davila[53] bastions, named after Cypriot noble families, were constructed along the southern edges of the city, previously occupied by working-class neighbourhoods of its largest ethnic group, the Greeks. Names of localities, churches, and monasteries demolished outside these bastions help to define the pre-1567 ethnic character of the area.

After arriving on the outskirts of Nicosia on 26 July 1570, the Ottomans began to construct earthen forts on the hills south of the city. The first fort was set up on the hill of Santa Marina,[54] across from Podocataro bastion. The second fort was at the foot of the same hill, and from here the lobe, or *orecchion*, of the bastion was bombarded.[55]

Farther west, toward a certain "San Zorzi" and slightly farther away from the city walls, a third fort was built to attack Podocataro bastion *and* to strike Costanzo bastion at its front edge, or *ponta*.[56] It is probably the same fort that was constructed "on the little hill called Margheriti ... between Costanzo and Podocataro bastions."[57]

He pushed the medal into the parched ground and ran back, accompanied by angry shouts of disapproval.

It was impossible to approach his next destination. He asked a soldier to take the third medal into the bastion of the Davilas. The soldier examined the medal, on which a bearded man holding a trident was riding a chariot pulled by dolphins emerging out of angry Waters, and responded, "Certainly, old man. With the blessing of Saint Nicholas we will be victorious." Alessandro smiled as he ran across the piazza.

The fourth medal, showing an anvil under a burning bush surrounded by towering Fires, he threw as close as possible to the edge of the Count of Tripoli's bastion.

A fourth fort was constructed "in certain houses where they dyed leather," to bombard the front of Davila bastion and the connecting wall, or *cortina*, leading to the adjoining bastions, but it was destroyed four days later by strikes from the *cortina* of Costanzo bastion. This confirms the location of the city's old dye-work factories.[58] The historic Greek nuns' monastery of Palluriotissa had been demolished in 1567 outside Costanzo bastion.[59] Finally, a fifth fort, west of the other forts, was located at "S. Giorgio di Magniana."[60] This name was later corrupted into "la collina di San Zorzi Maggiore." That the fort struck at Tripoli bastion and at the piazza of Davila bastion[61] places the old Greek monks' monastery of Mangana on a hilltop southwest of the city.

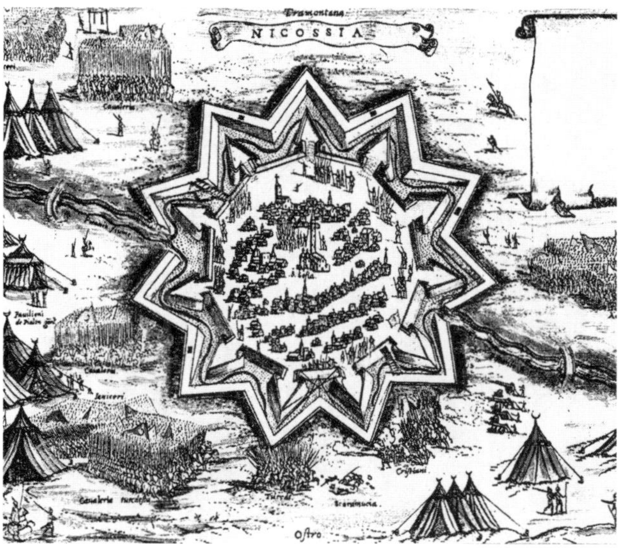

9.11 Giovanni Francesco Camocio, "Nicossia" (c. 1571), in *Isole famose, porti, fortezze e terre maritime sottoposte alla Ser.ma Sig.ria di Venetia* (Venice: Donato Bertelli, 1574), plate 72. Courtesy of the Bank of Cyprus Cultural Foundation, Map Collection, Nicosia. The siege of the city was mounted against its four southern bastions of (from east to west) Podocataro, Costanzo, Davila, and Tripoli.

The fifth medal, with an engraving of a shining sword, he set at Count Roccas's bastion. The sixth medal, which he inserted into the ground on Counselor Mula's bastion, showed an olive tree with interweaving branches.

From there, Alessandro was certain that the brave siblings would fight well. The divine commanders of War and Wisdom would be aided by the old monasteries. Their stones would take revenge.

THE WESTERN BASTIONS AND GATE

Two more of the seven "Cypriot" bastions – Tripoli[62] and Roccas[63] – were dedicated to the two titular counts of the island. It is significant that they were located where the city's extensive citadel had stood before its demolition in 1567. The citadel was built in the 1370s on the site of the residential quarter of the counts, the Kountiatika.[64]

Roccas and the adjoining Mula bastions were constructed in the heart of the Latin monastic area. They required the demolition of the monastery of Saint Dominic, the church of Santa Barbara, the convent of Saint Mamas, the church and convent of the Carmelites, and, farther out, the church of San Giovanni, the old Cistercian monastery of Beaulieu.[65] The unassuming gate created south of Roccas bastion was named San Domenico, undoubtedly to preserve the memory of the capital's most illustrious monastery.

THE NORTHERN BASTIONS AND GATE

Mula,[66] Querini,[67] Barbaro,[68] and Loredano,[69] commanding Nicosia's north and northwestern edges, were bastions dedicated to the Venetian rulers of Cyprus in 1565–67, the two *luocotenenti*, or *proveditori*, and their *conseglieri*. The symbolism of the "Venetian" bastions is evident: the seat of government, the "Third Royal Court," and the old Venetian quarter were located there. The new *enceinte* included the *entirety* of these localities, for obvious political reasons.

In his tired hands he was now holding three medals. Two of them depicted bare-breasted, seated female figures, while on the third was an erect man, or a God, whose stare commanded unimaginable power.

He set the first female figure at the Querini bastion and the male figure on Proveditor Barbaro's bastion.

"The Life and Death of this city meet here, under your gaze," he shouted. "Have mercy on us."

By the time he reached Counselor Loredano's bastion and set the second female figure, his legs were weakened and his breathing heavy.

He opened the pouch under Segnor Flatro's bastion and removed the tenth and eleventh medals, the first he had completed and his most cherished ones. The commanding bow and the beautiful lyre that adorned them he had lovingly carved.

On 15 August 1570 the besieged Nicosians attempted a surprise attack through the Porta Bemba.[70] Researchers have mistakenly identified this as Porta San Domenico, the western gate.[71] Proveditor Lorenzo Bembo[72] would be honoured by the naming of Porta del Proveditore, the northern opening facing the extensive Villa Traceona and the Campo Santo, the old cemetery of Nicosia.[73] Thus this gate was to be the point of exit for the Cypriots' surprise attack, as it was distant from the Ottoman forces along the southern edges.

East of Barbaro lay Loredano bastion, beyond which "many houses of the poor," large mansions belonging to Venetians, and three churches had been demolished in 1567.[74]

THE EASTERN BASTION AND GATE

The two remaining bastions, the Flatro[75] and Caraffa,[76] faced east. The Porta Caraffa, through which the infantry eventually exited for their surprise attack on 15 August 1570,[77] is in fact Porta Giulia, named after Giulio Savorgnano, at the southern edge of Caraffa bastion. In 1567 the largest number of "houses of the poor," mansions, and churches had been demolished outside these bastions and the Porta Giulia.[78] The largest area of urban fabric destroyed to permit the refortification of Nicosia had been located east of the present walled city.

FALL AND AFTERMATH

On 9 September the Ottomans succeeded in breaking through Nicosia's defence. Although later accounts maintained that they first captured Costanzo bastion before proceeding through the fortifications and into the city,[79] earlier texts state that the assailants first gained entry through neighbouring Podocataro bastion.[80] The later accounts, reinforced by the Ottoman monument that was erected after the fall of the city and that is still standing on Costanzo bastion, prompted some scholars to side with the former interpretation.[81] Instead, although it remained unknown to the narrators "from what lack of arrangement,"[82] it appears that the fortifications and their demoralized defenders first gave way at Podocataro bastion.

The fall of Nicosia prompted fortification planners to abandon tradition and embrace the "ideal" radial city plan for the urban fabric inside

He gasped as he simply laid the medal of the bow at the slope leading to the bastion, and shortly afterward the double-sided medal of the lyre under Segnor Caraffa's bastion, by the side of the eastern gate.

The sole medal left in his hand, the one he had not been able to place earlier, was destined for the Podocataros's bastion. For the protective circle to be complete, the image of the Earth had to be present there.

There was no one around the backworks. He was crawling to the edge when he saw enemy soldiers cheering and taking over the ridges.

This was the end. He had not completed the circle in time.

A sudden blast shook him. Blood gushed from his sides. He moved two paces forward and then collapsed onto the ground. He was still holding the medal.

the new fortresses. Although scholars proclaimed that "only when the fall of Nicosia demonstrated how dangerous it was to separate the habitation from the defenses ... would these experiments be epitomized in the renovated town plan of Palmanova, and the habitation would at last be used to support the defenses," we can ask whether the fall of Nicosia should be blamed solely on the alleged adoption of an "entirely abstract concept, with regards to the urban conditions of the existing town, [which] created many obstacles to an efficient [defence]."[83] This hypothesis is not a certainty. Famagusta, Cyprus's main port, withstood the Ottoman siege for more than a year despite its less developed fortifications and its medieval, *unplanned* urban fabric.

Instead, a careful reading of descriptions of the siege suggests that disagreements between factions of defenders contributed to the city's fall: rivalries between noble clans defending different bastions, broken promises on the granting of freedom to the serf population, and a hysterical fear of domestic uprising that occasionally prompted the government not to provide ammunition to the defenders finally achieved what the Ottoman army had been unable to accomplish for weeks.[84]

These scandalous events were not emphasized in reports to the Venetian Senate. Instead, the loss of Nicosia was blamed on the failure of the fortification due to the city's "unplanned" fabric. The radial city plan was thus adopted by military architects in Venice and in the emerging French and Dutch schools, with the bastions linked to each other and to the town centre with direct, unimpeded traffic arteries. The supposed advantages of this plan were assumed to be so obvious that theoreticians would not even consider commenting on them.[85]

Evidence is telling: two years after Nicosia's fall, Savorgnano adopted a radial street pattern for the fortress of San Niccolò del Lido in Venice. The streets and the urban fabric were now aligned directly with the bastions.[86] Two decades later, in 1593, Savorgnano, Lorini, and Scamozzi designed Palmanova, the world's "largest and most powerful fortress," which manifested "the military ideal in its most frigidly functional severity."[87] Thus, "in fusing bastioned fortifications with the radial city plan, the military architect converted into a functional tool a plan that had embodied the ideals of Renaissance urbanism. He not only trimmed it of all symbolic and most aesthetic qualities, but even disregarded the needs of the civilian populations that were to inhabit his protected fortress cities."[88]

The "gigantic snowflake"[89] of Palmanova never attracted a population for its sustenance and remained a sparsely manned military outpost on the edge of Venetian lands.

Nicosia's ambitious refortification experiment had failed. The momentous but momentary union of its symbolic bastioned defences and its living

Alessandro stood up as suddenly as he had fallen. A bright light travelled through the medal in his hand. Under his tired feet, the ground and the bastion started trembling, shaken under its very foundations. He must have been wounded and hallucinating, for it appeared that the whole bastion began to turn.

He looked around, first on one side, then the other. The two neighbouring bastions were now slowly moving along in the same direction.

With a progressively faster pace, the whole fortress was revolving around the city. Nicosia, surrounded by magic and wonder, was no longer attached to the Earth.

The fortress lifted the city high above the ground. Alessandro turned into a transparent shadow and joined others in that swirling, circular cloud.

Everyone was there: Builders were scaling construction sites. Servants and nobles appeared out of baths and mansions. Rows of shops hovered above their owners. Kings and fairies burst out of palaces and castles. Churches and chapels surrounded priests and nuns. Streets, bridges, and a flowing river joined in the procession.

Along with its fortress, Nicosia was migrating toward the heavens. Below, a lifeless urban corpse remained.

urban core was not given the opportunity to flourish and perhaps prove more protective and symbiotic than Renaissance and contemporary theorists would care to admit.

The "ideal" fortress instead would rely once again on pure theory. Its circular fortifications and radial street plans would be implemented often during the following three centuries. These constructions were highly successful military tools but shamefully poor urban and cultural environments.

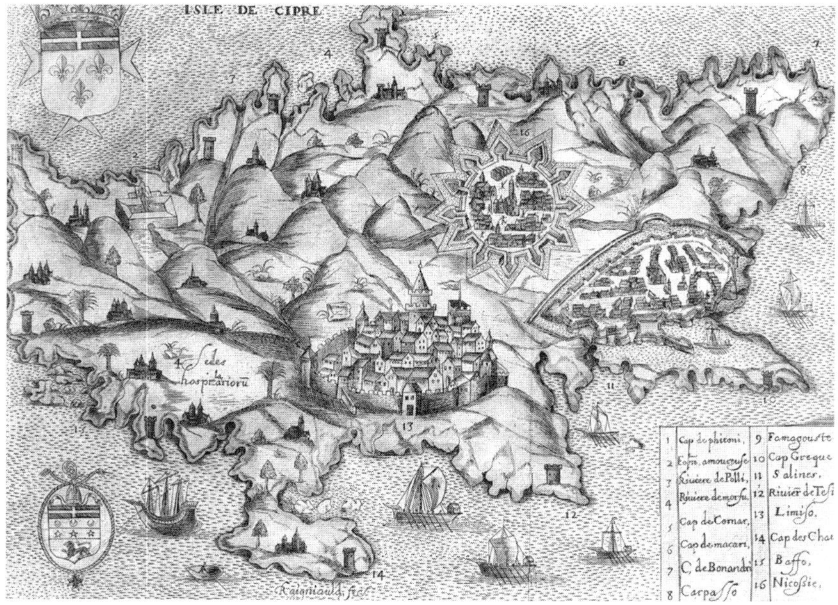

9.12 François-Antoine de Naberat, "Isle de Cipre," in *Histoire des Chevaliers de l'Ordre de S. Jean de Hierusalem par I. Baudoin* (Paris: Michael Soly, 1629). Courtesy of the Bank of Cyprus Cultural Foundation, Map Collection, Nicosia. The engraver Henry Raigniauld depicted Nicosia possessing twelve, rather than eleven, bastions.

NOTES

1 The main text is accompanied by a brief narrative in which the protagonist is Alessandro Cesati, one of the most significant medal and gem engravers of the Renaissance. Cesati was born in Nicosia in the 1520s to a Greek (Cypriot) mother and an Italian (Milanese) father. He moved at an

early age to Rome and, after being introduced to pontifical circles and to the Farneses, was appointed Incisore e Maestro delle Stampe at the papal mint, where he remained for most of the 1540s and 1550s, becoming known as Il Grecchetto or Il Greco.

On seeing one of Cesati's medals, depicting Alessandro Farnese as Pope Paul III and, on the reverse, Alexander the Great greeting the high priest of Jerusalem, Michelangelo reportedly proclaimed that "the hour of art's death had arrived, because a better one could not exist" (see Varsari text cited below). Other medal themes by Cesati, evidencing his Renaissance education, include Athena, Priam, Dido, Phocion, Augustus, and Apollo shooting at Python. Scholars think that Michelangelo knew personally and admired Il Grecchetto, although this remains to be verified. In 1564, the year of Michelangelo's death, Cesati returned to Nicosia, continuing his work until his traces were lost after the 1570 fall of the city.

The narrative follows Cesati along a fictional journey in the final hours of Nicosia's siege on 9 September 1570, as he attempts to aid the defence of his city by "using" his art.

On Cesati, see Giorgio Vasari, *La Vita di Michelangelo nelle Redazioni del 1550 e del 1568*, ed. Paola Barocchi (Milan and Naples: Riccardo Ricciardi, 1962), vol. 1, 232–3; Camille Enlart, *L'Art Gothique et la Renaissance en Chypre* (Paris: Ernest Leroux, 1899), vol. 1, 65–6; Camille Enlart, *Gothic Art and the Renaissance in Cyprus*, ed. and trans. David Hunt (London: Trigraph, 1987), 71; George Jeffery, *A Description of the Historic Monuments of Cyprus* (Nicosia, 1918; reprint, London: Zeno, 1983), 88; Antonia Boström, "Alessandro Cesati," *The Dictionary of Art*, ed. J. Turner (London and New York: Macmillan, 1996), vol. 6, 360.

2 T.S.R. Boase, *Kingdoms and Strongholds of the Crusaders* (London: Thames and Hudson, 1971), 167; Nicholas Coureas, "To What Extent Was the Crusaders' Capture of Cyprus Impelled by Strategic Considerations," *Epetiris* (Nicosia) 19 (1992): 197–202.

3 For a Lusignan prosopography, see Wipertus-Hugo Rudt de Collenberg, "Les Lusignan de Chypre," *Epetiris* (Nicosia) 10 (1980): 85–319.

4 On the Franciscans in Nicosia, see John Hackett, *A History of the Orthodox Church of Cyprus* (London: Methuen, 1901), 600–2; Jeffery, *Historic Monuments*, 48; Girolamo Golubovich, "Cipro Francescana," in *Biblioteca Bio-Bibliografica della Terra Santa e dell'Oriente Francescano* (Florence: Coll. di S. Bonaventura, 1906–27); Martiniano Rincaglia, *St. Francis of Assisi and the Middle East* (Cairo: Franciscan Center of Orien-

tal Studies, 1954), 37, 55–8, 61–2; Sylvain Beraud, "Terre Sainte de Chypre: L'Ordre des Frères Mineurs: Églises et Couvents," *Kypriakai Spoudai* (Nicosia) 40 (1987): 135–53; Nicholas Coureas, *The Latin Church in Cyprus, 1195–1312* (Aldershot: Ashgate, 1997), 205–9.

5 See Georges Duby, *Saint Louis à Chypre* (Nicosia: Leventis Museum, 1991).

6 On the Greek cathedral, see Enlart, *L'Art Gothique*, vol. 1, 150–62; Enlart, *Gothic Art*, 136–47; Jeffery, *Historic Monuments*, 84–9; George Francis Hill, *A History of Cyprus* (Cambridge, UK: Cambridge University Press, 1948), vol. 3, 1129–31; Robert B. Francis, *The Medieval Churches of Cyprus* (London: Ecclesiological Society, 1949), 37; Michael Willis, "Byzantine Beginnings of the Bedesten," *Kypriakai Spoudai* (Nicosia) 50 (1987): 185–92. On the Latin cathedral, see Enlart, *L'Art Gothique*, vol. 1, 78–141; Enlart, *Gothic Art*, 82–130; Hackett, *Orthodox Church*, 490–500; Jeffery, *Historic Monuments*, 64–80; Francis, *Medieval Churches*, 31–4; Nicholas Coureas and Christopher Schabel, eds, *The Cartulary of the Cathedral of Holy Wisdom of Nicosia* (Nicosia: Cyprus Research Centre, 1997), 48–54.

7 On the Cistercians in Nicosia, see Hackett, *Orthodox Church*, 602–5; Jean Richard, "The Cistercians in Cyprus," in Michael Gervers, ed., *The Second Crusade and the Cistercians*, 199–209 (New York: St Martin's Press, 1992); Coureas, *Latin Church*, 191–9; Jean Richard, "La Levée des Décimes sur l'Église Latine de Chypre: Documents Comptables de 1363–1371," *Epetiris* (Nicosia) 25 (1999): 11–15.

8 On the Dominicans in Nicosia, see Enlart, *Gothic Art*, 77–8; Hackett, *Orthodox Church*, 592–9; Jeffery, *Historic Monuments*, 21; Hill, *History*, vol. 2, 27; Coureas, *Latin Church*, 211–15.

9 Saint Thomas Aquinas, *De Regno, ad Regem Cypri* (c. 1260–65), published as *On the Governance of Rulers*, ed. and trans. Gerald B. Phelan (Toronto: St Michael's College, 1935); also published as *On Kingship: To the King of Cyprus*, ed. and intro. I.Th. Eschmann (Toronto: Pontifical Institute of Medieval Studies, 1949).

10 Aquinas, *On Kingship*, ed. Eschmann, bk 2, ch. 5, 68–71; bk 2, ch. 6, 71–4; bk 2, ch. 7, 74–8; bk 2, ch. 8, 78–80. Most passages are taken directly from Vitruvius, *De architectura*, bk 2, intro. and 1.4.

11 Giovanni Boccaccio, *Genealogiae deorum gentilium* (c. 1347–71), in Vincenzo Romano, ed., *Scrittori d'Italia n.200: Giovanni Boccaccio Opere X* (Bari: Giuz. Laterza and Figli, 1951).

12 See the four main chronicles of late medieval Cyprus: (1) Leontios Makhairas, *Exegesis tis glykeias choras Kyprou, i poia legetai Kronaka toutestin Chronikon* (c. 1440), in R.M. Dawkins, ed. and trans., *Recital Concerning the Sweet Land of Cyprus Entitled "Chronicle,"* 42, 56, 70 (Oxford: Clarendon, 1932); (2) Diomedes Strambaldi, *Cronicha del Regno di Cypro di Diomede Strambaldi Ciprioto* (c. 1440), in René de Mas-Latrie, ed., *Collection de documents inédits sur l'histoire de France: Histoire politique: Chronique de Strambaldi*, vol. 2, 18, 25 (Paris: Imprimerie Nationale, 1893); (3) Francesco Amadi, *Cronaca di Cipro* (c. 1450), in René de Mas-Latrie, ed., *Collection de documents inédits sur l'histoire de France: Histoire politique: Chronique d'Amadi*, vol. 1, 253 (Paris: Imprimerie Nationale, 1891); and (4) Florio Bustron, *Historia Overo Commentarii de Cipro* (c. 1568), in René de Mas-Latrie, ed., *Collection des documents inédits sur l'histoire de France: Mélanges historiques, Tome Cinquième: Chronique de l'île de Chypre*, 26, 224 (Paris: n.p., 1886).

13 Leon Battista Alberti, *De re aedificatoria* (Florence, 1452); Antonio Averlino (Il Filarete), *Trattato di Architettura* (Milan, 1464); Francesco di Giorgio Martini, *Trattati di Architettura, ingegneria e arte militare* (Siena, 1487).

14 J.R. Hale, *Renaissance Fortification: Art or Engineering?* (London: Thames and Hudson, 1977), 43.

15 Ibid., 44.

16 Amelio Fara, *Il Systema e la Città: Architettura fortificata dell'Europa moderna dai trattati alle realizzazioni, 1464–1794* (Genoa: Sagep Editrice, 1989), 152–3.

17 Host de la Croix, *Military Considerations in City Planning: Fortifications* (New York: George Braziller, 1972), 41.

18 Hale, *Renaissance Fortification*, 7.

19 See title and discussion in ibid.

20 Luca Pacioli, *La Divina Proportione* (Venice, 1509).

21 Cesare di Lorenzo Cesariano, *Di Lucio Vitruuio Pollione de architectura libri dece traducti de Latino in vulgare affigurati commentati et con mirando ordine insigniti* (Como: Gotardus De Ponte, 1521), vol. 2, 29r°–30v°.

22 Fra Giovanni Giocondo, *M. Vitruuii De Architectura libri decem: Nuper maxima diligentia castigati atq(ue) excusi ...* (c. 1511; Florence, 1522).

23 See Macchiavelli's *I Discorsi* (1513), *Il Principe* (1514), and even *Arte della Guerra* (1522).

24 Louis de Mas-Latrie, *Histoire de l'Ile de Chypre sous le Règne des Princes de la Maison de Lusignan* (Paris: Imprimerie Nationale, 1852–61), vol. 3, 67n, 76.
25 De la Croix, *Military Considerations*, 42–3.
26 Ibid., 45.
27 Fara, *Il Systema e la Città*, 105–6.
28 Christopher Duffy, *Siege Warfare: The Fortress in the Early Modern World, 1494–1660* (London and New York: Routledge, 1996), 32.
29 Popular treatises, including Henricus Cornelius Agrippa's *De occulta philosophia* (1533), Tartaglia's *Quesiti et Inventioni* (c. 1538; Venice, 1556), and even Vesalius's *Anatomia* (1543), further illustrate the symbolic and mystical concerns of the time.
30 For Italian fortification families, see Duffy, *Siege Warfare*, 38–9.
31 Prominent among them were the Cataneos; see Pietro, *I Quattro Primi Libri di Architettura* (Venice, 1554); and Girolamo, *Dell'Arte Militare* (Brescia, 1559). See also Giacomo Lanteri, *Il Modo di fare le fortificazioni* (Venice, 1559); Giambattista Zanchi, *Del Modo di Fortificar le Città* (Venice, 1560); and Girolamo Maggi, *Della Fortificazione delle Città* (Venice, 1564).
32 Hale, *Renaissance Fortifications*, 35–6.
33 Girolamo Maggi died during the siege of Famagusta.
34 John Locke, *Voyage to Jerusalem* (1553), quoted in Richard Haklyut, *The Principal Navigations, Voyages, Traffiques and Discoveries of the English Nation* (London, 1589; reprint, Glasgow: J. MacLehose, 1903–05), vol. 5, 97–8. For a variation, see Claude Delaval Cobham, *Excerpta Cypria: Materials for a History of Cyprus* (Cambridge, UK: Cambridge University Press, 1908), 71.
35 Gilles Grivaud, "Aux Confins de l'Empire Colonial Vénitien: Nicosie et ses Fortifications (1567–1568)," *Epetiris* (Nicosia) 13–14, no. 1 (1987): 269–79 at 271.
36 Andreas Stylianou and Judith Stylianou, eds, *The History of the Cartography of Nicosia* (Nicosia: Leventis Museum, 1989), 22–3.
37 Grivaud, "Aux confins de l'empire," 272–3.
38 Ascanio Savorgnano, *Coppiosa Descrittione delle cose di Cipro e le reggione in favor o contra diverse opinione e delle prouvisioni necessarie per quel regno* (c. 1562), quoted in Gianni Perbellini, "Le Fortificazioni di Cipro dal X al XV Sec.," *Castellum* (Rome) 17 (1973): 7–58 at 55; Gianni Perbellini, *The Fortress of Nicosia, a Prototype of European Renaissance Military Architecture* (Nicosia: Leventis Museum, 1994), 9.

39 Savorgnano, *Coppiosa Descrittione*, quoted in Perbellini, "Le Fortificazioni," 55; Perbellini, *The Fortress of Nicosia*, 9.
40 Grivaud, "Aux confins de l'empire," 272.
41 Bernardo Sagredo, [*Report to the Senate*] (c. 1565), quoted in Mas-Latrie, *Histoire*, vol. 3, 556.
42 Grivaud, "Aux confins de l'empire," 273–4.
43 Bustron, *Historia*, 27; Bustron refrains from further elaboration, as "that was not the time."
44 Grivaud, "Aux confins de l'empire," 273–5.
45 Ibid., 276–8.
46 Perbellini, "Le Fortificazioni," 56.
47 Among others, see Pietro Cataneo, *I Quattro Primi Libri di Architettura di Pietro Cataneo Senese* (Venice: Aldus, 1554); Girolamo Maggi and Giacomo Fusto, *Della Fortificazione delle Città* (Venice: Rutilio Borgominiero, 1564).
48 Grivaud, "Aux confins de l'empire," 277–8.
49 It has not yet been possible to consult the important Archivio Proprio Conrarini 4 in the Archivio di Stato di Venezia, on which Grivaud's article was largely based.
50 Nogiero, quoted in Gilles Grivaud, "Nicosie Remodelée (1567): Contribution à la topographie de la ville médievale," *Epetiris* (Nicosia) 19 (1992): 281–306 at 306.
51 Named after a Livio or a Giulio Podocataro; ibid., 300, 302.
52 Named after Tutio Costanzo, cavalry commander; ibid., 301.
53 Named after Constable Antonio Davila; ibid., 302, 306.
54 Ibid., 300–1; Giovanni Sozomeno estimates the distance at 270 paces in his *Narratione della Guerra di Nicosia fatta nel Regno di Cipro da Turchi l'Anno 1570* (Bologna, 1571), cited in Cobham, *Excerpta Cypria*, 82.
55 Pietro Valderio, *La Guerra di Cipro* (c. 1570–73), ed. and trans. Gilles Grivaud and Nasa Patapiou (Nicosia: Cyprus Research Centre, 1996), 54.
56 Valderio, *La Guerra di Cipro*, 54.
57 Sozomeno, *Narratione della Guerra di Nicosia*, 83.
58 Valderio, *La Guerra di Cipro*, 54, 218.
59 Grivaud, "Nicosie Remodelée," 305.
60 Sozomeno, *Narratione della Guerra di Nicosia*, 82.
61 Valderio, *La Guerra di Cipro*, 54, 218.
62 Named after James de Nores, titular Count of Tripoli; Grivaud, "Nicosie Remodelée," 300.

63 Named after the Count of Rochas, a title held from 1502 to 1570 by the Syncliticoi family.
64 Makhairas, *Exegesis*, 88; Strambaldi, *Cronicha*, 35.
65 Nogiero, cited in Grivaud, "Nicosie Remodelée," 305, 306.
66 Named after *consegliero* (counsellor) Mula; Grivaud, "Nicosie Remodelée," 302, 306.
67 Leutenant Querini died in July 1567 and was replaced by counsellor Mula; Grivaud, "Nicosie Remodelée," 306.
68 Named after Proveditor Francesco Barbaro (1565–67).
69 Named after "Clarissimo. Loredano consegliero"; Grivaud, "Nicosie Remodelée," 304.
70 Valderio, *La Guerra di Cipro*, 56.
71 Ibid., 118, 276.
72 Ibid., 99, 118.
73 Grivaud, "Nicosie Remodelée," 304.
74 Ibid., 304.
75 Named after Ugo Flatro, *visconte* of Nicosia; ibid., 303.
76 Named after Scipio Caraffa; ibid., 300.
77 Valderio, *La Guerra di Cipro*, 56.
78 Nogiero, cited in Grivaud, "Nicosie Remodelée," 304–5.
79 Paolo Paruta, *Storia* (1605), and Giacomo Diedo, *Storia* (1751), cited in Cobham, *Excerpta Cypria*, 95, 107.
80 Sozomeno, *Narratione della Guerra di Nicosia*, 84–5; Valderio, *La Guerra di Cipro*, 59, 224; Calepio, cited in Cobham, *Excerpta Cypria*, 138–9, is clear that the Turks attacked the defenders of Costanzo bastion from inside the city.
81 Stylianou, *History of the Cartography of Nicosia*, 32.
82 Sozomeno, *Narratione della Guerra di Nicosia*, 84.
83 Perbellini, *The Fortress of Nicosia*, 8, 11.
84 Enlart, *Gothic Art*, 25.
85 De la Croix, *Military Considerations*, 50.
86 Perbellini, *The Fortress of Nicosia*, 11.
87 De la Croix, *Military Considerations*, 51.
88 Ibid., 50.
89 As dubbed in Hale, *Renaissance Fortifications*, 37–8.

Vitruvius and the French Landscape of Ruins: On Jean Gardet and Dominique Bertin's 1559 Annotations of *De Architectura*

Daniel M. Millette

Chora

INTRODUCTION[1]

JAN MARTIN[2] AND JEAN GOUJON'S[3] translation of *De architectura* from Latin into French became one of the most influential renditions of Vitruvius's treatise in Renaissance France.[4] Martin had translated other works before this one[5] – texts related to his employment as secretary to the humanist and promoter of arts Cardinal Robert de Lenoncourt (1498–1561)[6] – yet with this particular focus on architecture, his aim was more than translation per se: he wanted to provide practical knowledge for French builders so that they could be better equipped to compete with the Italian craftspeople settling in France. His partner in the project, Goujon, prepared many of the illustrations and addressed the reader in the book's final pages.[7] Martin and Goujon introduced a non-Latin readership to a particular version of Vitruvius's architecture and to their interpretation of newly popularized drawing techniques and related geometrical applications.

This was not the first time that French architects had been exposed to Vitruvius; Fra Giovanni Giocondo da Verona (c.1435–c.1514)[8] had sojourned in Paris from 1495 to 1505, teaching, among other subjects, a course on Vitruvius and classical architecture.[9] At least one partial French edition of *De architectura* had been accessible to architects and builders,[10] and the treatise was also available, in Latin, in a host of libraries.[11] Martin and Goujon's appeal to French architects and humanists was probably enhanced by passages where Vitruvius seemed to allude to first-hand experiences of Gaul.[12] The book's completion also coincided roughly with the annotations of Vitruvius's treatise[13] by Guillaume Philandrier (1505–65),[14] which certainly helped popularize *Vitruve*. The success of Martin and Goujon's book, if measured by subsequent commentaries, is certain.[15] With its numerous illustrations and its lexicon of technical terms and authors – the "explanation of proper names and difficult words contained in Vitruvius"[16] – the work became an architectural standard in sixteenth-century France.[17]

Nonetheless, the Martin and Goujon edition was not unchallenged. In the mid-1550s, Jean Gardet and Dominique Bertin[18] were in Toulouse, preparing their own rendition, complete with a set of illustrations and annotations that would, if we are to judge from the comments in the annotations, compete with the earlier interpretation (fig. 10.1).[19] The idea

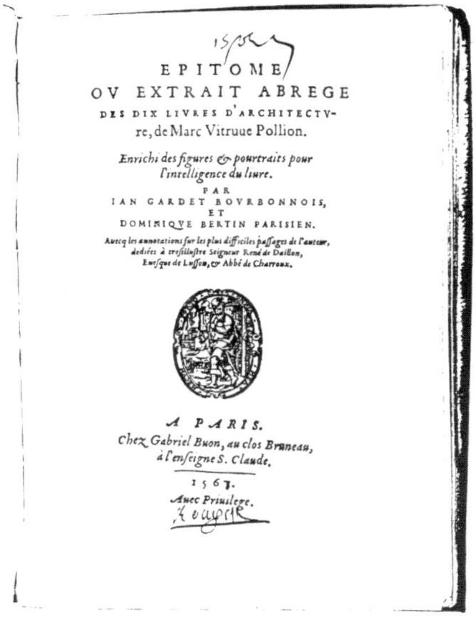

EPITOME
OV EXTRAIT ABREGE
DES DIX LIVRES D'ARCHITECTVRE, de Marc Vitruue Pollion.
Enrichi des figures & pourtraits pour l'intelligence du liure.
PAR
IAN GARDET BOVRBONNOIS,
ET
DOMINIQVE BERTIN PARISIEN.
Auecq les annotations sur les plus difficiles passages de l'auteur, dediées à tresillustre Seigneur René de Daillon, Euesque de Lusson, & Abbé de Charroux.
A PARIS.
Chez Gabriel Buon, au clos Bruneau, à l'enseigne S. Claude.
1567.
Auec Priuilege.

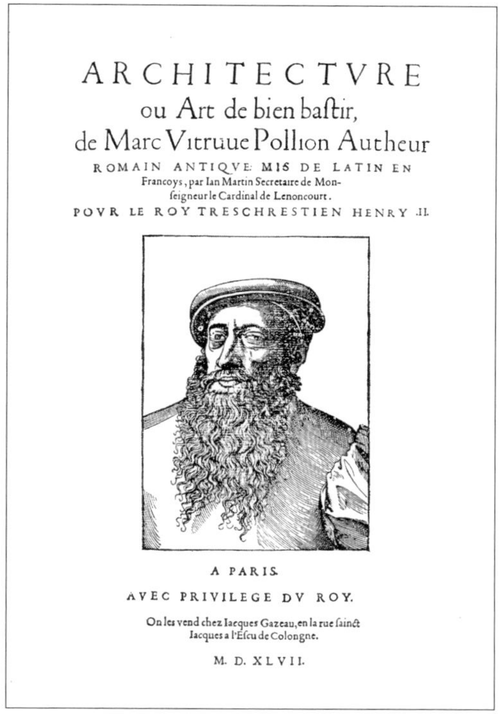

ARCHITECTVRE
ou Art de bien baſtir,
de Marc Vitruue Pollion Autheur
ROMAIN ANTIQVE: MIS DE LATIN EN Francoys, par Ian Martin Secretaire de Monſeigneur le Cardinal de Lenoncourt.
POVR LE ROY TRESCHRESTIEN HENRY .II.
A PARIS.
AVEC PRIVILEGE DV ROY.
On les vend chez Iacques Gazeau, en la rue ſainct Iacques a l'Eſcu de Colongne.
M. D. XLVII.

10.1 Left: Title page of Jean Gardet and Dominique Bertin, trans., *Epitome ov Extrait Abrege des dix livres d'architectvre de Marc Vitruue Pollion. Enrichi des figures & pourtraits pour l'intelligence du liure. Par Ian Gardet Bovrbonnois, et Dominiqve Bertin Parisien. Auecq les annotations sur les plus difficiles passages de l'auteur, dediées à tresillustre Seigneur René de Daillon, Euesque de Lusson, & Abbé de Charroux. A Paris. Chez Gabriel Buon, au clos Bruneau, à l'enseigne S. Claude. 1567.* Avec Priuilege.

10.2 Right: Title page of Jan Martin and Jean Goujon, trans., *Architectvre ou Art de bien bastir, de Marc Vitruue Pollion Autheur romain antiqve: mis de latin en Francoys, par Ian Martin Secretaire de Monseigneur le Cardinal de Lenoncourt. Povr le roy treschrestien Henry II. A Paris avec privilege du roy. On les vend chez Iacques Gazeau, en la rue Sainct Iacques a l'Escu de Colongne. M.D. XLVII.*

of providing annotations undoubtedly was sparked by Philandrier's work, but the project appears motivated by a different impetus than the latter's or Martin and Goujon's (fig. 10.2). Aside from purporting to bring Latin (and Greek) closer to the French builder,[20] the project does not appear to have been a direct response to the incoming Italians and their design methods, as had been the case with Martin and Goujon's book.[21] Its close reading suggests that it was a reaction to the Martin and Goujon treatise and that it proposed a relation between *De architectura* and the classical monument remnants lying in the French countryside.

While their readership would have been generally the same as that of the earlier edition – builders and students of classical architecture – the work appears to have been triggered by a deeper need to reconcile personal classical architectural imaginations (derived at least partly from the panorama of ruins in southern France) to Vitruvius's set of classical precepts. In this sense at least, the immediate textual, visual, and philosophical landscapes in Toulouse, which would have been different from Martin and Goujon's in Paris, closely informed the new edition. While the Martin and Goujon translation had provided an initial link between the classical architectures of France and Italy, it was with the interpretation of Gardet and Bertin that the association of French antiquities with Roman classical monuments would begin to be connected textually.

GARDET AND BERTIN AS HUMANISTS

Very little is known of Gardet and Bertin. The first was a Bourbon and the second a Parisian. Both spent some years in Toulouse, and Bertin worked on sculpture at the Auch cathedral in the early 1550s. He was later named lieutenant under the *général des oeuvres* in charge of the king's masonry and fortifications projects.[22] It is significant that the general was Jean Delorme, brother of the architect Philibert Delorme (1510–70);[23] Bertin would thus have been well connected to French architectural circles, and he may have been aware of the important work being prepared by Delorme.[24] The partnership between Gardet and Bertin undoubtedly was born out of a shared task of locating marble quarries necessitated by the Louvre alterations and similar projects in Paris. As they mapped and assessed sites, and eventually oversaw shipments of marble to Paris,[25] the two came across ruins scattered throughout the Midi area (fig. 10.3). Among other places, they refer to Saint-Bertrand-de-Comminges, where remnants of the hillside Gallo-Roman theatre would have been apparent from a considerable distance, and sections of a first century B.C. aqueduct were visible in their fallen state.[26] Around the time of these travels, they set out to provide the French builder with a new translation of *De architectura*.

As was customary during the Renaissance, the two architects interpreted classical architecture through Vitruvius and therefore would have noticed the differences between the old text and the surrounding ruins. With Martin and Goujon's edition[27] in hand, along with their own work-in-

10.3 Sepulchres at Saint-Rémy (ancient Glanum), as depicted by Jean-Honoré Fragonard in 1760. Archives des Monuments Historiques, Paris.

progress on Midi antiquities,[28] it would have been relatively straightforward to identify discrepancies between Vitruvius's prescriptions and the built realities of Gaul. Among other books, they mention those of Philandrier[29] and Guillaume Budé (1467–1540),[30] as well as the books by Leon Battista Alberti (1404–75) and Fra Giocondo.[31] The two certainly were influenced by the humanists and especially by Fra Giocondo; his earlier restoration of *De architectura* was still popular in the 1550s and was the principal one to which they would turn for their translation.[32]

Fra Giocondo had completed his fully illustrated edition of Vitruvius's treatise by 1511.[33] The book included 138 drawings, a glossary, and a chart of mathematics-related symbols employed by Vitruvius that would be echoed by Gardet and Bertin.[34] Prior to the friar's work, renditions of the treatise had very few, if any, illustrations; copyists and translators rarely made corrections, editorial alterations, or adjustments to counter the inevitable corruptions acquired from repeated transcriptions. Furthermore, the reading of *De architectura* had been confused, due partially to

Vitruvius's ambiguous phraseology and Greek terms[35] and also to the fact that words, phrases, and even an entire page had been out of sequence.[36] Fra Giocondo had ensured that his text was clear, comparing different versions and including the combinations that he felt best reflected Vitruvius's words.[37] He was explicit about his rationale for the emendations and alterations, stating in his title: "ut iam legi et intelligi posit"[38] (so that it can be read and understood). Indeed, having practised architecture and engineering under several rulers in both France and Italy, he was well equipped to render a more clearly legible and understandable edition. His interests in philology, archaeology, numismatics, and epigraphy added to his interpretation, and his knowledge of antiquities was particularly appealing for humanists: he provided an almost reverential text that subsequent translators, including Gardet and Bertin, would emulate in their quest for textual rapprochements to classical antiquity.[39]

Recall that prior to the Renaissance, the monuments of antiquity – its treatises, buildings, and ideas – had not been temporally separated from the immediate past. They were utilized at specific moments when solutions to arguments or problems were needed. Humanists began distinguishing classical antiquity from the present. As antiquity was extended back in time, it became part of a revised collective memory, was idealized, and in turn provided a template with which new monuments – textual, architectural, and ideological – could be modelled and ultimately assessed. A new class of intelligentsia, learned in ancient thought, classical languages, and the new temporal realities, became experts in philology and especially in the archaeological thought of the moment, which concerned unearthed monuments and treasure and comparisons to the rediscovered classical texts.[40] Between 1450 and 1600, ancient Rome was unearthed by learned individuals such as Alberti, who drew, studied, and identified monuments, all the while reinterpreting *De architectura* according to their observations.[41] This practice soon became entrenched in architecture and archaeology; Fra Giocondo, Martin and Goujon, and Gardet and Bertin would use it in their own training and intellectual development. When Fra Giocondo temporarily relocated to France, he reinforced humanist notions in the minds of his students. Similarly, Martin and Goujon encouraged a humanist approach for interpreting classical architecture in the 1540s. As Gardet and Bertin navigated through the landscapes and ruins of the Midi, they, too, would have been preoccupied with the idea of temporally distancing classical antiquity through the study of texts and monuments. This permeated their *vécu*, shaped their outlook, and ultimately manifested itself in their translation and its annotations.

THE PARTIAL TRANSLATION AND ANNOTATIONS OF GARDET AND BERTIN

Although never presented in a completed form,[42] the translation and accompanying annotations constitute an incredibly candid – if not altogether bold – commentary on previous interpretations of *De architectura*.[43] The work took considerable time to reach publication, and with the exception of sporadic references to later books, only the first three of Vitruvius's books are discussed. Judging by the errors in the page headers[44] and pagination,[45] the publisher may have been in a rush to print.[46] Regardless, from the eighty-seven pages of comments, it is possible to glimpse the thoughts of Gardet and Bertin on Vitruvius, his treatise, their personal classical architectural imaginations, and most certainly, the earlier translation by Martin and Goujon.

Written by Gardet,[47] the annotations begin with a dedication to René de Daillon, bishop of Luçon, followed by polite praise for Martin and Goujon and a four-page introduction in which Vitruvius is carefully recalled: "Marcus Vitruvius Pollio, author of ancient stature, in the course of his ten books, if not amply and with such facility as one might well desire, at least with great testimony to his erudition and knowledge of many disciplines, with all of which he had accompanied the experience of this art."[48] And as with previous translations, the importance of *De architectura* is stressed by Gardet, who states that "the writings of such importance ... belong more to the instruction of the architect than the episodes ... belong to the farces and fables of the ancients."[49] The section is followed by an additional three-page message to the reader. The long passage has a personal tone, and its position in the work suggests that it was probably added after the initial drafting of the main text. One sentence is particularly revealing, where Gardet underscores, "Because it is such that common utility must be preferred over singular affections, and that these issues must be judged by the ways of the severe and incorruptible Athenian areopagites, I agree willingly that my fantasies be placed on the same balance in which I have placed the work of others."[50] Gardet acknowledges that a certain amount of imagination influenced his interpretation. This is not unusual, of course; who does not incorporate personal meanings and mental images when reading a text? However, the comment reveals a self-awareness of having incorporated "fantasies" in the translation. While all translations are interpretations and thus alter earlier versions, here he seems to imply a level of inventiveness.

At the same time, it is ironic that, while admitting to the liberal interpretation of some passages, Gardet repeatedly refers to words in Martin's text as erroneous.[51] Further, Gardet's partner uses the drawings provided by the earlier translators as models for his own; figures 10.4–10.5 and 10.6–10.7, for example, show how the capital and theatre engravings of the Martin and Goujon edition were reversed and only slightly altered for the new book. The two "revised" engravings offer no corrections and, by being transposed and rotated 180 degrees, suggest a deliberate attempt to mask their source. From early on, and despite acknowledging that translations involve inventiveness, a subtle critique of the earlier edition begins to emerge. The critique is relentless; consider the following examples of how Gardet questions Martin's interpretive abilities.

The first term discussed in the annotations is *graphis*, and Gardet carefully presents it with its related vocabulary.[52] The discussion focuses on the importance of providing graphic depictions for buildings. Gardet writes: "He makes the plan and the elevation of one of the façades, and then shows it from its sides, foreshortened by the art of perspective."[53] Once the basic instruction is given, the text states the need for a wooden model. To Gardet, Vitruvius was calling for such a model in book I, and Martin did not interpret it as such.[54] To fully convince the reader, Gardet suggests that the Elder Pliny had also intended this in his book XXXV.[55] Gardet here is reverting to a familiar device that was employed repeatedly by Vitruvius: turning to ancient sources for authority. While this is probably how Pliny had interpreted Vitruvius, it is not necessarily more accurate.[56]

As Gardet continues with the argument for a wooden model, he shifts the emphasis from *graphis* to *exemplar*: to him, *exemplar* is similar to *forma* and *formare*, and it signifies *pour faire modelle* (to make a model).[57] Gardet includes other terms such as *graphicè*, *grammicè*, and *formatio*, all

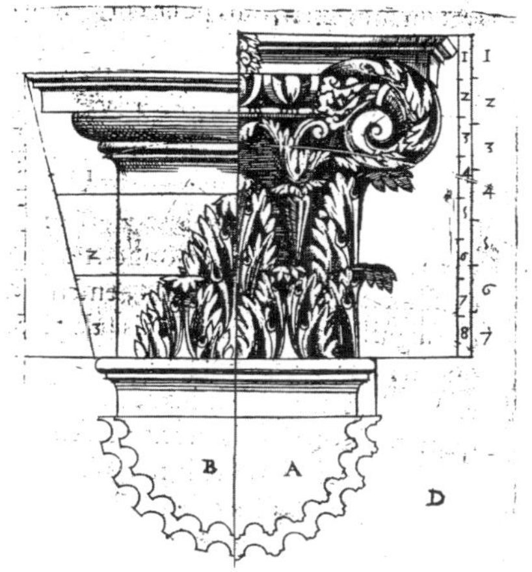

10.4 Composite capital, in Jean Gardet and Dominique Bertin, trans., *Epitome ov Extrait Abrege des dix livres d'architectvre de Marc Vitruue Pollion*, 87.

10.5 Theatre, in Jean Gardet and Dominique Bertin, trans., *Epitome ov Extrait Abrege des dix livres d'architectvre de Marc Vitruue Pollion*, 141.

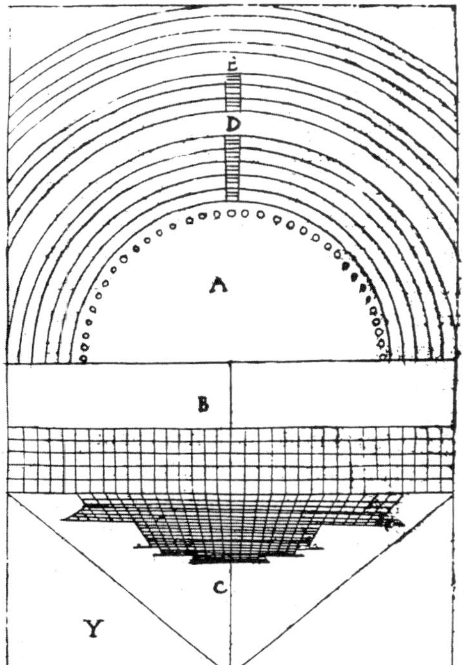

10.6 Composite capital, in Jan Martin and Jean Goujon, trans., *Architectvre ou Art de bein bastir, de Marc Vitruue Pollion Autheur romain antiqve*, 48.

10.7 Theatre, in Jan Martin and Jean Goujon, trans., *Architectvre ou Art de bien bastir, de Marc Vitruue Pollion Autheur romain antiqve*, 75 verso.

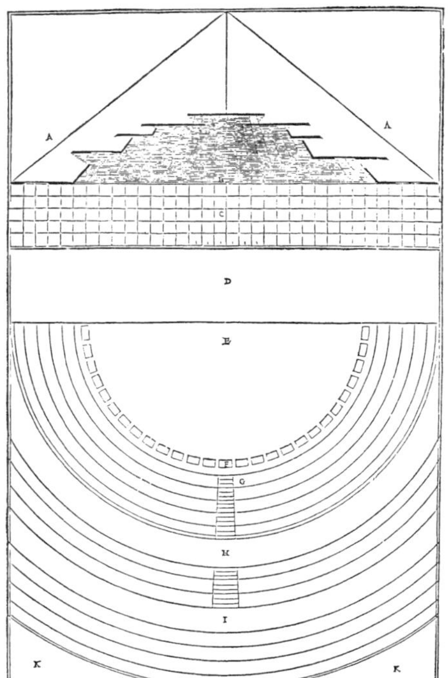

incorporated in a complex and circular discussion of *graphis*.[58] In the end, the reader has to take his word for it, yet Martin did not mention a wooden model at all but wrote *modelle faict apart* (model made separately).[59] Nor did Vitruvius, who probably used *exemplaribus pictis* (painted examples).[60] It would seem, at least in this case, that it is Gardet who misinterprets Vitruvius's manuscript as he switches from a painted model to a wooden one.

Because the Martin annotations are comprised of relatively short entries that, for the most part, explicate geographical terms and identify classical personages, Gardet probably wants to fill in what he regards as gaps. His references to "errors," however, often seem without sound basis. For instance, in a later annotation on timber use by the Colchian people, Gardet records that "Jan Martin has not sufficiently understood the way of building in Colchis: neither the drawing of Giocondo, nor that of the Italian [Alberti], nor that of the Frenchman [Martin] are able in any way to go back to the intent of the author. For this reason, I shall put here the Latin text for you, so that you may compare it, if you wish, to the French version."[61]

Here, Gardet points out that Martin and others erred in their pictorial and textual interpretations, and he inserts the Latin version of the passage. He then recounts the story of timber construction among the Colchian people.[62] Although the Latin quotation obviously lends an air of authority, there is no reason for him to include it; if he is translating it correctly, as he says he is, why reproduce it in his text?[63] It is also puzzling that he offers no drawing to clarify the apparently confused visual representation presented by Martin and others.[64] He simply repeats the story and leaves the reader with the impression that his is the most correct and credible.[65]

Consider another example of the criticism. In his discussion of the Circle of the Winds,[66] Gardet writes that "if one works with the translation of our volume on the basis of the figure of page 16, it will be easy to escape the confusion which is in Jan Martin's text."[67] Here, we begin to suspect that the Gardet commentary is based on professional jealousy. To Gardet, Martin's translation is confused and the diagram is inadequate, resulting in interpretive error in the section on winds. He provides a diagram of his own, presumably to offset Martin's "ambiguity" (fig. 10.8, 10.9). At first reading, Gardet's criticism seems fair, as Martin does not provide any nomenclature to link the drawing in his translation to the text. However, closer perusal of Martin's drawing suggests that it is well integrated with his discussion of the winds' relation to town planning. While the cardinal directions are not explicit in his drawing, the governing grid in his illustration suggests a meaning to the reader. In Gardet's translation, the drawing becomes confusing because of its placement: while there is a reference to it on page 26 of the annotations, it is not presented until page 40. The placement of the diagram and its references to the text interpret the Circle of the Winds in a way that is much more confused than Martin's passages.

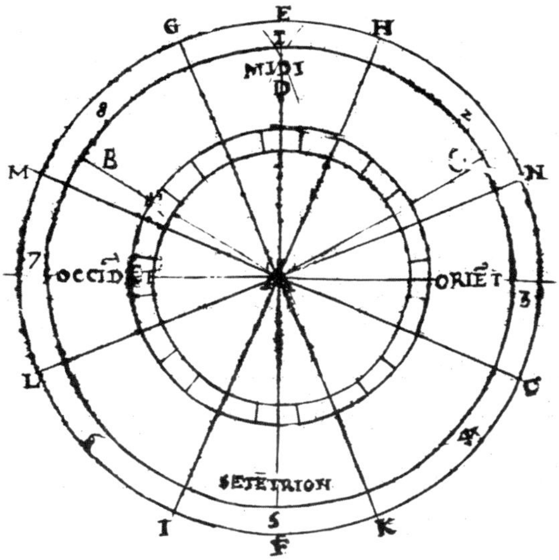

10.8 Circle of the Winds, in Jean Gardet and Dominique Bertin, trans., *Epitome ov Extrait Abrege des dix livres d'architectvre de Marc Vitruue Pollion*, 16.

10.9 Right: Circle of the Winds, in Jan Martin and Jean Goujon, trans., *Architectvre ou Art de bien bastir, de Marc Vitruue Pollion Autheur romain antiqve*, 12 verso.

In the annotations to book II, the critique continues in the passages on the use of wall surfacing and stucco or plaster.[68] Gardet writes, "Note that in three areas of this chapter, and in one of the following chapter, Jan Martin has given the wrong meaning to *tectorium*, taking it for a covering."[69] The purported misinterpretation centres on "wall covering" versus "plaster" or "stucco." Gardet indicates that Vitruvius himself refers to it in book VII, *de opere tectorio*, as a way of plastering walls.[70]

On the one hand, Gardet asserts that *tectorium* was employed by Vitruvius to mean a method of applying wall covering, while he sees Martin translating the word to mean covering. The usual authorities are invoked to buttress the argument: "Pliny makes mention, in the place just recalled, and Palladius speaks of it in chapter 15 of book I."[71] He implies that Pliny and Palladius are more correct than Martin.[72] Again, the only proof of the flaw is the citation of authorities. While Martin does not refer directly to wall coverings such as plaster in any related passages, he does allude to the poor quality resulting from an inappropriate method of applying mortar to brick walls.[73] The lines in Martin's book are relatively clear and do relate to "method." Unless one compares the two versions, Gardet's account seems more authoritative than Martin's.

As a final example, consider Gardet's criticism of Martin's discussion of construction details and, to some extent, *moellons* (squared building stones).[74] He disagrees with Martin: "Of this tender building stone, Vitruvius does not employ *polita* to signify elegant or polished; he employs it to denote a structure which is united and squared and in this sense we have to correct in Jan Martin."[75] The note seems trivial; Vitruvius was discussing Greek methods, and while Martin does write *blocage poly ny délicat*,[76] the interpretation is not altogether erroneous; Callebat, for instance, uses the term *plastique*, among others, in his translation of Vitruvius.[77]

Martin's errata are highlighted throughout the annotations of Gardet and Bertin, even though Vitruvius's tenets are general and his language is sometimes obscured by Greek terms and his own style of writing. Martin, like other translators, was simply making the best out of the transcriptions that came down to him. No translation of *De architectura* is without its ambiguities, and each translator brings a personal imagination based on current styles, impressions, and preferences.[78] Why, then, were the two architect-translators from Toulouse so intent on "correcting" the earlier work? Perhaps it was professional jealousy or an attempt to legitimize their own work. It was probably a combination of the two. Nevertheless, this authoritative tone in their version of Vitruvius would have been convincing to their contemporaries, eventually lending credence to their linking of Vitruvius's treatise to the ruins in the French countryside.

CONNECTING VITRUVIUS TO THE FRENCH LANDSCAPE

Another trend emerges in the pages of the annotations. Within the set of examples that Gardet provides, he repeatedly invokes the notion of memory as he turns to Midi antiquities. That he highlights memory should not be surprising; Vitruvius certainly had done so in several places.[79] The latter alluded to the architectural memory of his readership when he mentioned *memoria*[80] and *memoratur*.[81] In his book I, for example, he evoked memory in referring to his own "zeal ... which had remained faithful to ... [the emperor's father's] memory"[82] before mentioning that the emperor's monuments were "a memorial to future ages."[83] He was fully aware of the posterity, legacy, and meaning of Republican architecture, and he was cognizant of cultural memory, the recording of history (oral or otherwise), and the reliance on tradition. The three were in fact juxtaposed in his notion of the "old ways." Earlier in the same book, he underscored the importance of the architect keeping track of "useful [architectural] precedents"[84] and remembering historical antecedents.[85] Later, Vitruvius reminded the reader of previous textual and memorized works,[86] and he noted the importance of recording *memorentur antiquitus*, his own antiquity, as he wrote about Mount Vesuvius.[87] What Vitruvius did, in fact, was link built monuments to cultural memory.

Of course, Vitruvius's memory of the past would not have been necessarily synonymous with Gardet and Bertin's memory of classical antiquity; Renaissance humanists were just beginning to differentiate "recent" from "distant" pasts. However, recall that one of the humanists' main preoccupations was to connect "present" thought to notions of classical antiquity. In this light, linking their built and cultural landscapes to ancient Rome would have been fundamental. For French humanists geographically removed from Rome, this task would have been amplified. In the case of Gardet and Bertin, their day-to-day exposure to Vitruvius's text would have been a constant reminder of the grandeur of Rome. Their regular contact with the antiquities of the Midi also would have hinted at the grandeur of Gaul. Therefore, it is no leap to say that they would have linked the monuments of the Midi to Vitruvius.

In their annotations to book III, Gardet and Bertin include a detailed discussion of some of the sepulchres that they had observed during their travels (fig. 10.10).[88] They transcribe and reproduce inscriptions and provide detailed explanations for their examples.[89] The locations of the monuments in the vicinity of Narbonne and Saint Girons along the east-west transect of the Midi reflect the marble-seeking mandate of the two architects (fig. 10.11). Their itineraries would have traced a path from Narbonne through the early Roman route to Tolosa (Toulouse) as well as dozens of villas, military camps, marble quarries, and, of course, the sepulchres and monuments along the way. They also travelled farther south, probably examining the monuments at places such as Orange (fig. 10.12).[90] The two studied a variety of ruins as they travelled throughout the region and worked on their now-lost "Antiquities Commentary." The monuments in these places remained unexcavated and "unrevived" during their lifetimes, and it is only through their collective imagination that they could have interpreted them.

The latter is connected to the discussion of the term *sepulcrum*, where Gardet digresses on monuments, memory, and how they are related.[91] He writes: "The phrase *de nonnullis monumentis* 'concerning several monuments' in the Latin text ... Jan Martin has translated it as 'certain relics of antiquity,' and in the earlier chapter 7, he said 'fragments of antiquity.' But here we take *monumenta* to signify sepulchres or monuments, following the evidence/authority of Terence Varro, who, in his *On the Latin Language*, outlines these words *memoria*, *manimoria*, *mamuria*, *monere*, *monimenta* as derived from a single lineage."[92] Now that he has invoked the writings of Varro, he immediately quotes him: "The monuments of the sepulchres, he says, are for this reason located along the roads, so that they may remind those passing by that they are mortal, and those who are there buried, that they were once mortal. And from thence all things written or made in the memory of someone were called *monimenta*."[93] Here, Gardet seems right. He is saying that *nonnullis monumentis* – the many monuments in the landscape – should not

10.10 Partial map of southern France, etched by Cundier, 1664. Archives des Monuments Historiques, Paris. Note Orange to the north, along the eastern bank of the river.

10.11 Theatre at Orange (Arausio). Musée Départementale, Orange.

10.12 Below: Triumphal arch at Orange (Arausio). Musée Départementale, Orange.

be interpreted as relics of classical antiquity (as Martin had done) but that they should be understood as the monuments that Varro had written about: *sépulchres*. By insisting that Vitruvius was writing about "monument" in terms of memory (which is obvious) and that the sepulchres of the Midi are typical monuments of memory, he establishes a link between the word "monument" in *De architectura* and the monuments of the Midi. After this point, the references to monuments in the annotations refer to both Rome and the Midi.

As Gardet and Bertin were humanists, it is reasonable to assume that they were familiar with the classical art of memory. Those who practised this art planted cues, represented as images installed in specific (imaginary) places, to be recalled in sequence. Certainly, the technique continued to be used in the monastic tradition and elsewhere.[94] The idea of placing pictorial cues in particular locations – *loci* – is interesting in this context. Is it possible that Gardet and Bertin were deliberately installing cues in their readers' minds, using French monuments as memory aids, as was done in classical times? Probably not, but the effect would have been similar. Placing Gallo-Roman monuments in their discussion of memory would leave memory cues for the reader to connect Vitruvius and monument remnants.

Once the memory of classical antiquity and the monuments of the Midi are partnered, Gardet is free to infer that the classical monuments of southern France are part of the panoply of monuments to which Vitruvius refers. Gardet uses his immediate surroundings to define what is meant by "monument" in *De architectura*, although Vitruvius was not writing about the sepulchres of Gaul. To these translators, *De architectura* was not only about the grandeur of Rome's monuments but also about the grandeur of Midi antiquities.

CONCLUSION

At first reading, the project of Gardet and Bertin appears to have been prompted by the Martin and Goujon book. The two architects in Toulouse undoubtedly had a very different set of realities in the Midi and aimed to provide their own reading of Vitruvius's treatise. Aside from purporting to bring the classical treatise closer to a non-Latin readership of architects and builders, Gardet and Bertin may have had other objectives in mind. By underscoring interpretive errors in other versions, they sought authority. They offered a set of annotations that extended well beyond the lexicon-like commentaries of some earlier editions, undertaking what would have been an early version of an *apparatus criticus.* This is noteworthy: no one else had been so critical of Martin's passages.

Gardet and Bertin's project also may have been precipitated by a need to reconcile their immediate landscapes and architectural ideals with Vitruvius's set of classical precepts. What Martin and Goujon had not done (directly link the Gallo-Roman landscape to the Roman panorama), Gardet and Bertin would begin to do with their annotations. They lured the reader toward their interpretation and implicitly toward themselves as purveyors of a more accurate *De architectura.* The open critique of Martin and Goujon's translation reminded readers that theirs was more correct. As Vitruvius had done, they turned to classical "authorities" to strengthen their case. The inheritance of classical antiquity, shown in the textual renditions of Fra Giocondo's book (the *texte de base* for Gardet and Bertin) and also in the visual remnants of the Midi, provided them with vignettes that were juxtaposed with the annotations to provide a set of classical models within the French architect's geographical reach. Now that the monuments of the Midi were textually tied to those of Rome, the former could be more readily accepted as classical models, to be reconstructed later by combining Vitruvius's prescriptions and examples of Rome.

NOTES

1 I am indebted to Dr Gerald Sandy and Dr Sherry McKay for their suggestions in reviewing an earlier version of this essay. I am also most grateful to Dr Wolfgang Haase for his close reading and thoughtful advice and to Dr Pérez-Gómez and this volume's anonymous reviewer for suggestions leading to a clearer text.

2 On Jan Martin (1500–53), see Françoise Fichet, *La théorie architecturale à l'âge classique: Essai d'anthologie critique* (Paris: Pierre Mardaga, 1979), 55–76.

3 On Jean Goujon (1515–68), see Pierre du Colombier, "Jean Goujon et le Vitruve de 1547," *Gazette des Beaux Arts* (March 1931): 155–78.

4 Jan Martin and Jean Goujon's full title is: *Architectvre ou Art de bien bastir, de Marc Vitruue Pollion Autheur romain antiqve: mis de latin en Francoys, par Ian Martin Secretaire de Monseigneur le Cardinal de Lenoncourt.*

Povr le roy treschrestien Henry II. A Paris avec privilege du roy (Paris, 1547). Until Claude Perrault's translation of 1673, Martin's was one of the key bridges between Roman classical architecture and French architectural practice. The link held until at least the mid-eighteenth century, when Diderot published his *Encyclopédie* (Paris, 1751); for a discussion of the decline in use of *De architectura* during the late eighteenth century, see Vaughan Hart, "Introduction: 'Paper Palaces' from Alberti to Scamozzi," in Vaughan Hart and Peter Hicks, eds, *Paper Palaces: The Rise of the Renaissance Architectural Treatise*, 1–32 (New Haven and London: Yale University Press, 1998).

5 Among other treatises, Martin had translated the first two books by Serlio in 1545. Serlio himself supervised the accompanying illustrative work. For a listing of other works translated by Martin, see Fichet, *La théorie architecturale*, 56.

6 For a brief biographical note on the Lenoncourt family, see *Biographie Universelle, ancienne et moderne* (Paris: Desplaces, 1856), vol. 24, 137.

7 Goujon's commentary title is *Svr Vitrvve. Ian Govion Stvdievx d'architectvre avx lectevrs. Salvt.* He prepared 40 of the approximately 155 illustrations in the translation; the balance came from other sources, including four from Serlio's treatise.

8 On Fra Giocondo, see L.A. Ciappini, "Appunti per una biografia di Giovanni Gicondo da Verona," *Italia Medioevale e Umanistica* 14 (1961): 131–58.

9 See Vladimir Juren, "Fra Giovanni Giocondo et le début des études vitruviennes en France," *Rinascimento* 14 (1974): 101–15, and Lucia A. Ciapponi, "Fra Giocondo Da Verona and His Edition of Vitruvius," *Journal of the Warburg and Courtauld Institutes* 47 (1984): 72–90. Printed editions of *De architectura* had been available since 1486.

10 A French-language summary of *De architectura* had been available in the 1526 work of Diego de Sagredo, translated from Spanish into French around 1530 as *Raison d'architecture antique, extraite de Vitruve et autres anciens architectes, nouvellement traduit de l'espagnol en français à l'utilité de ceux qui se délectent en edifices.*

11 See Louis Callebat, "La Tradition Vitruvienne au Moyen Age et à la Renaissance," *International Journal of the Classical Tradition* 1, no. 2 (1994): 3–14.

12 Vitruvius probably travelled to Gaul; in *De architectura* he hinted at stays in bk II, 1.4; bk VII, 13.2; bk VIII, 2.6; and bk X, 16.11–12.

13 On Guillaume Philandrier, see Frédérique Lemerle, "Introduction," in *Les Annotations de Guillaume Philandrier sur le De architectura de Vitruve – Livres I à IV*, 11–47 (Paris: Picard, 2000); as well as his "On Guillaume Philandrier: Forms and Norms," in Hart and Hicks, eds, *Paper Palaces*, 186–98.

14 Guillaume Philandrier, *Premier livre des annotations sur les dix livres du De architectura de Marc Vitruve Pollion par Guillaume Philandrier, Français de Châtillon, citoyen romain* (Lyon: Jean de Tournes, 1552). Philandrier had released an earlier version in Rome in 1544.

15 For a partial list of commentary authors, see Fichet, *La théorie architecturale*, 56.

16 Jean Gardet and Dominique Bertin, trans., *Epitome ov Extrait Abrege des dix livres d'architectvre de Marc Vitruue Pollion. Enrichi des figures & pourtraits pour l'intelligence du liure. Par Ian Gardet Bovrbonnois, et Dominiqve Bertin Parisien. Auecq les annotations sur les plus difficiles passages de l'auteur, dediées à tresillustre Seigneur René de Daillon, Euesque de Lusson, & Abbé de Charroux* (Toulouse: Guion Boudeville, 1559): "Declaration des noms propres. Et motz difficiles contenvz en Vitrvve." All quotations are from this edition. All translations are mine.

17 Other treatises, such as Philibert Delorme, *Premier tome de l'architecture* (Paris: Frédéric Morel, 1567), were equally important, but it was as a *translation* of Vitruvius that Martin and Goujon's book dominated.

18 For biographical notes on Gardet and Bertin, see Henri Graillot, "Deux architectes-archéologues du XVIe siècle dans le midi de la France," *Revue des Études Anciennes* 21 (1919): 290–4.

19 At least three editions of Gardet and Bertin's translation were published: one in Toulouse, by Guion Boudeville in 1559; and two in Paris, by G. Buon in 1567 and 1568. Original copies of the three are located, among other places, at the Bibliothèque Nationale in Paris. A further copy of the 1567 edition is located at the Canadian Centre for Architecture in Montreal. I am grateful to both institutions for making these available for the present research.

20 In his annotations, 51, Gardet writes: "nous ne deuions regarder à autre chose, qu'à l'auancement de notre langue, & à l'instruction des moins exercés aux lettres Grécques & Latines: ausquels il facheroit beaucoup de les apprendre maintenant" (we did not have to look at anything but the advancement of our own language and the instruction of those less experienced in Greek and Latin literature, to whom it would cause much annoyance to learn them now).

21 Italians continued to move to France under the protection of the Valois. The appearance of a new French edition no doubt would have further informed French builders.

22 Bertin held other positions, including *architecte du roi*, *capitaine de Bagnères-de-Luchon*, *garde des mines pour le roi*, and *conducteur des marbres* for the royal estates; see Graillot, "Deux architectes-archéologues," 291.

23 On Philibert Delorme, see Fichet, *La théorie architecturale*, 77–9.

24 Delorme's *Nouvelles inventions pour bien bâtir à petits frais* was published in 1561; his more famous *Premier tome de l'architecture* appeared in 1567.

25 See Graillot, "Deux architectes-archéologues," 291.

26 Gardet's comments on the ruins at Saint-Bertrand-de-Comminges are the earliest mention of the site. The note is contained in his annotations, 67: "auons nous veu aux monts pyrenées, tout auprés de la ville de Saint Bertrand, le plat fons, & lacunaire d'un grand conduit qui est sous terre" (we have observed in the Pyrenees, close to the town of Saint-Bertrand, upper and missing sections of a large conduit which is underground). He comments especially on the qualities of masonry and mortar but is clearly impressed by remnants such as the aqueduct that he and Bertin observed. Other monument traces would have been visible: the baths, theatre, temple, and so on.

27 Martin is referred to in a variety of passages in the book; see, for example, annotations, 26, 41, 42, 61, 62, 66, 73, and 81.

28 Although there is no known copy of Gardet and Bertin's commentary on Midi antiquities, they refer to it in the dedications of both the text and the annotations; see, for example, annotations, 70: "duquel nous auons parlé en noz commentaires d'architecture, poursuiuans vne bonne partie des choses mémorables, qui se treuuent de par de la" (of which we spoke in our commentaries on architecture, following a great many of the memorable things, that can be found there).

29 Philandrier is mentioned less than Martin; see, for example, annotations, 10, 84; the latter is wrongly paginated as 66.

30 See, for example, annotations, 49. For a relevant biographical sketch of Guillaume Budé, see J. Plattard, *G. Budé et les origins de l'humanisme français* (Paris: n.p., 1923).

31 For a discussion of the links between Budé and Fra Giocondo, see Juren, "Fra Giovanni Giocondo," 101–15.

32 For a discussion on treatise translations of the Renaissance, see Alina A. Payne, *The Architectural Treatise in the Italian Renaissance: Architectural*

Invention, Ornament and Literary Culture (Cambridge, UK, and New York: Cambridge University Press, 1999).

33 On early transcriptions of *De architectura*, see the introductory paragraphs in Gustina Scaglia, "A Translation of Vitruvius and Copies of Late Antique Drawings in Buonaccorso Ghiberti's Zibaldone," *Transactions of the American Philosophical Society at Philadelphia* 69, part 1 (1979): 3–30.

34 Annotations, 39.

35 See Carol H. Krinsky, "Seventy-Eight Vitruvius Manuscripts," *Journal of the Warburg and Courtauld Institutes* 30 (1967): 36–70.

36 Ingrid D. Rowland discusses the problems in her "Introduction" to *Vitruvius: Ten Books on Architecture*, 1–18 (Cambridge, UK: Cambridge University Press, 1999).

37 Not everyone agrees with Fra Giocondo's emendations; see, for example, T.L. Donaldson, "Some Particulars Relating to Manuscripts Preserved in Various European Libraries," *Royal Institute of British Architects, Transactions* 1 (1835–36): 114–22.

38 Fra Giocondo, quoted in Ciapponi, "Appunti," 74.

39 See Donaldson, "Some Particulars," 115.

40 On Renaissance thought, see especially Paul Oskar Kristeller, *Renaissance Thought: The Classic, Scholastic, and Humanist Strains* (New York and Evanston: Harper Row Publishers, 1961). For a more recent evaluation, see Ingrid D. Rowland, *The Culture of the High Renaissance: Ancients and Moderns in Sixteenth-Century Rome* (Cambridge, UK: Cambridge University Press, 1998).

41 On the practices associated with architectural training and its relationship to Vitruvius during the period, see Hanno-Walter Kruft, *Geschichte der Architekturtheorie: Von der Antike bis zur Gegenwart* (Munich: C.H. Beck'sche Verlagsbuchhandlung, 1985); translated into English by Ronald Taylor, Elsie Callander, and Antony Wood as *A History of Architectural Theory from Vitruvius to the Present* (New York: Princeton Architectural Press, 1994), 73–92.

42 The translation is complete; the annotations are incomplete.

43 While there are annotations only for the first three books, the plan seems to have been to cover the entire treatise. In his annotations, 26, Gardet writes: "C'est la … come nous montrerons ci apres sur le 7. chap. du 9. livre" (It is there … as we will show hereafter in chapter 7 of book IX), suggesting that discussion will take place at a later point.

44 For instance, the header of page 47 refers to book II, although the discussion relates to book I.

45 For example, page 84 is numbered as page 66.

46 A rush to publish would explain the book's unfinished state.

47 Bertin drew the illustrations.

48 Annotations, 2: "M. Vitruue Pollion, autheur d'anciéne marque, en la suite de ses dix liures: Si non si amplement, & par telle facilité qu'on desireroit bien, aumoins aueq' grand témoignage de son érudition, & connoissance de maintes disciplines, desquelles il auoit acompagné l'expérience de cét art."

49 Annotations, 3: "les écris de telle importance & qui apartiénent plus à l`institvtion d`vn architecte, que les épisodies aux farces & fables des anciens."

50 Annotations, 6. "Or puis qu'il est ainsi, que l'vtilité commune doit étre préférée aux particuliéres affections, & que ces choses se doiuent iuger à la mode des Séuéres, & incorruptibles aréopagites athéniens, ie consens volontiers que mes fantaisies soient mises en la méme balance, ou i'ai poisé le labeur d'autrui."

51 Gardet and Bertin would not have known the extent to which Martin and Goujon were turning to their own *fantaisies* in translating *De architectura*. It is difficult to conceive, however, of the two not assuming that Martin and Goujon were delving into their own imaginations, as they were architects.

52 Annotations, 7.

53 Annotations, 7, "il fait le plan, & la montée d'vne des faces, & la montre des cotés r'acourcis par l'art de perspective."

54 See Vitruvius's use of "exemplaribus" in *De architectura*, bk I, 1.4.

55 Pliny, *Historia Naturalis*, bk XXXV, 12.

56 Pliny mentions *De architectura* in books XVI, XXXV, and XXXVI of his *Historia Naturalis*.

57 Annotations, 7.

58 Annotations, 7–10.

59 Jan Martin and Jean Goujon, trans., *Architectvre ou Art de bien bastir, de Marc Vitruue Pollion Autheur romain antiqve: Mis de latin en Francoys* (Paris: Venue & Heritiers de Jan Barbé, 1547), 5 verso.

60 The words are translated as "modèles peints" in Philippe Fleury, trans., *Vitruve: De l'architecture, Livre I* (Paris: Collection des Universités de France, Les Belles Lettres, 1990), 5.

61 Annotations, 42: "Ian Martin n'a pas assez entendu quelle étoit la maniére de batir en Colchis: voire que ni la figure de Iaconde, ni celle de l'italien, ni du françois, ne peuuent point reuenir au sens de l'auteur: à raison dequoi, ie te mettrai le texte latin, afin que tu le collationnes s'il te semble bon à la version françoise."

62 Here, Gardet is referring to the narrative in bk II, 1.4.

63 Annotations, 51.

64 The drawing to which Gardet is referring is in Martin and Goujon, trans., *Architectvre ou Art de bien bastir*, 16 recto.

65 In Martin and Goujon's annotations, Colchi is included and geographically situated in a brief entry; no discussion related to the narrative of the Chalcidian timber construction is provided.

66 The Circle of the Winds passage is in Vitruvius, *De architectura*, bk I, 6.4–13.

67 Annotations, 26: "Si lon pratique la traduction de notre epitome, sur la figure du 16. feuillet, il sera facile de sortir de la confusion qui est au texte de Ian Martin."

68 References to wall and *revêtement* are made in other books of Vitruvius's *De architectura*. For example, aside from book II, 3.2, 4.3, 5.1, and 8.20, there are sections in books VII, II, III, IV, V, and VI.

69 Annotations, 54: "Nottez qu'en trois endrois de ce chapitre, & en vn de celui qui vient apres, Ian Martin a mal tourné, tectorium, pour vne couuerture."

70 Annotations, 54: "traitte au 7. livre, de oper & tectorio, qui est la maniére d'enduire les murailles"; *tectorio* appears in no fewer than six places in Vitruvius's treatise, while other grammatical cases and/or genders related to *tectorius* appear throughout.

71 Annotations, 54: "de quoi Pline fait mention, au lieu dernirement allégué, & Palladius en parle, au 15. chap. du I. Livre."

72 Gardet constantly evokes "authorities"; Cato, Pliny, Aristotle, Theophrastus, and many others are referenced throughout his commentary. The pattern culminates with Gardet's reference to Exodus (ch. 5, where Moses speaks to the Israelites) in dealing with straw and its use in brickmaking; see annotations, 47.

73 Martin and Goujon, trans., *Architectvre ou Art de bien bastir*, bk II, 17 verso. See *Vitruve de l'architecture, livre II,* trans. Louis Callebat, with commentary by Pierre Gros, vol. 1 (Paris: Collection des universités de France, Les Belles Lettres, 1999).

74 Vitruvius, *De architectura*, bk II, 8.5.

75 Annotations, 66: "De ce tendre moëllon Vitruue ne prend point en ce lieu, polita, pour signifier élégante ni polie, mais pour denoter vne structure vnie & à l'équierre, pource faut il corriger dans Ian Martin, de blocage poli ni délicat."

76 Martin and Goujon, trans., *Architectvre ou Art de bien bastir*, 21 verso.

77 See *Vitruve de l'architecture*, trans. Callebat, bk I, 25.

78 Others have highlighted this phenomenon; see, for example, Alberto Pérez-Gómez, "Juan Bautista Villalpando's Divine Model in Architectural Theory," in A. Pérez-Gómez and S. Parcell, eds, *Chora*, vol. 3, 125–56 (Montreal and Kingston: McGill-Queen's University Press, 1999).

79 Martin and Goujon had echoed Vitruvius's words in their translation, but they had not given memory any attention in their commentary.

80 Vitruvius mentioned *memoria* in *De architectura*, bks I, III, V, VII, IX, and X.

81 Vitruvius alluded to *memoratur* in all books of *De architectura* except I, V, and VI.

82 Vitruvius, *De architectura*, bk I, preface, 2: "Cum autem concilium caelestium in sedibus inmortalitatis eum dedicavisset et imperium parentis in tuam potestatem transtulisset, idem studium meum in eius memoria permanens in te contulit favorem" (Thus, when the council of the Olympians consecrated him among the abodes of immortality and passed his sovereignty into your own jurisdiction, this same devotion of mine[,] fixed upon his memory, naturally transferred allegiance to you). In this note and those that follow, I turn to Ingrid D. Rowland, trans., *Vitruvius: Ten Books on Architecture* (Cambridge, UK: Cambridge University Press, 1999).

83 Vitruvius, *De architectura*, bk I, preface, 3: "Cum ergo eo beneficio essem obligatus, ut ad exitum vitae non haberem inopiae timorem, haec tibi scribere coepi, quod animadverti multa te aedificavisse et nunc aedificare, reliquo quoque tempore et publicorum et privatorum aedificiorum, pro amplitudine rerum gestarum ut posteris memoriae traderentur, curam habiturum. Conscripsi praescriptiones terminates, ut eas adtendens et ante facta et futura qualia sint opera, per te posses nota habere" (Therefore, because I had been put in your debt for the favour whereby I will never harbour the fear of want for the rest of my life, I began these matters for you. For I perceived that you had already built extensively, were building now and would be doing so in the future: public as well as private constructions, all scaled to the amplitude of your own achievements so that these

would be handed down to future generations. I have set down these instructions, complete with technical terms, so that by observing them you could teach yourself how to evaluate the works already brought into being and those yet to be).

84 Vitruvius, *De architectura*, bk I, 1.4: "Litteras architectum scire oportet, uti commentariis memoriam firmiorem efficere possit" (An architect should understand *letters* so that he may strengthen his own memory by reading what has been written in the field); emphasis in Rowland's translation.

85 Vitruvius, *De architectura*, bk I, 1.5: "Historias autem plures novisse oportet, quod multa ornamenta saepe in operibus architecti designant, de quibus argumentis rationem, cur fecerint, quaerentibus reddere debent" (He should know a great deal of *history* because architects often include ornaments in their work, and ought to be able to supply anyone who asks with an explanation why they have introduced certain motifs); emphasis in Rowland's translation.

86 Vitruvius, *De architectura*, bk VII, preface, 1: "Maiores cum sapienter tum etiam utiliter instituerunt, per commentariorum relationes cogitata tradere posteris, ut ea non interirent, sed singulis aetatibus crescentia voluminibus edita gradatim pervenirent vetustatibus ad summam doctrinarum subtilitatem" (Our ancestors, not only wisely but also usefully, established the practice of transmitting their ideas to posterity through the reports of treatises, so that these ideas would not perish, but instead, as they grew with each passing age and were published in books, they would arrive, step by step, at the utmost refinement of learning).

87 Vitruvius, *De architectura*, bk II, 6.2: "Non minus etiam memorentur antiquitus crevisse ardores et abundavisse sub Vesuvio monte et inde evomuisse circa agros flammam" (Antiquity records that fires cropped up in greater abundance under Mount Vesuvius and that flames vomited forth from thence into the surrounding countryside).

88 Annotations, 65.

89 The inscriptions are reproduced in Graillot, "Deux architectes-archéologues," 292–3.

90 Gardet and Bertin went at least as far east as Saint-Bertrand-de-Comminges.

91 See Gardet's text, page 32.

92 Annotations, 62–3: "ce qui est au texte latin, de nonnullis monumentis … Ian Martin l'a traduit, Par certaines reliques d'antiquité, & au parauant au 7. chapitre, il auoit dit, fragmens d'antiquité: mais nous prenons ici monu-

menta pour les sépulchres, ou monumens, suivant le témoignage de Térence Varron, qui au livre de la langue Latine montre ces mots, *memoria, manimoria, mamuria, monere, monimenta*, étre sortis tous d'une lignée."

93 Annotations, 63: "Les monumens des sépultures, dit-il, sont pour cette cause, sur le chemin, à fin qu'ils amonétent les passans d'étre mortels, et qu' ceux qui ont été là enséuelis, ont été quelque fois: et de la est venu qu' toutes autres choses écrites ou faites en memoire de quelqu'un ont été apellées *monimenta*."

94 On the art of rhetoric after classical antiquity, see Mary Carruthers, *The Craft of Thought: Meditation, Rhetoric, and the Making of Images, 400–1200* (Cambridge UK: Cambridge University Press, 2000).

Ruskin and Viollet-le-Duc: Figures of Ruin and Restoration

David Spurr

Chora

THE TWO MOST PROMINENT ARCHITECTURAL theorists of the nineteenth century – Eugène-Emmanuel Viollet-le-Duc and John Ruskin, both champions of the Gothic – held diametrically opposed ideas on the question of architectural restoration. Viollet-le-Duc devoted a successful career to restoring many of France's great architectural monuments of the Middle Ages and wrote extensively in defence of his practices. Ruskin, on the other hand, abhorred restoration of any kind and defended the aesthetic value of ruins. The reason for this difference in architectural doctrine has been put down to one of temperament between the rational *architecte de terrain* and the eccentric Oxford aesthete. However, in attempting to go beyond these stereotypes, I have found that the question of architectural restoration rather quickly opens out onto a wider field of inquiry that includes the relation of nineteenth-century architecture to the other arts. My approach to these two writers will propose the notion that the opposition between an aesthetics of architectural ruin and one of restoration bears comparison with another burning issue in nineteenth-century art: the opposition between allegory and symbol. At the same time, I will suggest that both of these oppositions are symptomatic of a condition marking the advent of modernity: its complex and unstable relation to the historical past.

The aesthetic of ruins in the late eighteenth and early nineteenth centuries needs to be understood as part of the emerging distinction between the figures of allegory and symbol, as defined by Romantic writers such as Samuel Taylor Coleridge and Georg Friedrich Creuzer. At the risk of covering some familiar territory, allow me to recall some of their formulations. For Coleridge, "an allegory is but a translation of abstract notions into a picture-language, which is itself nothing but an abstraction from objects of the senses."[1] A symbol, on the other hand, unifies the material object with the metaphysical, the phenomenon with its essence. Coleridge thus speaks of "the translucence of the Eternal in and through the Temporal," while Creuzer speaks of the instantaneousness, the totality, and the unfathomable origins of the symbol.[2] The unity of the symbol is above all a temporal unity: eternity manifests itself in the instantaneous.

It is useful, however, to understand these theories not only in their Romantic formulations, but also in their redefinitions by a twentieth-century theorist such as Walter Benjamin. Coleridge sees allegory, in its purely conventional relation between the sensible and the abstract, as only an artificial and degraded form of the symbol, but it is something else entirely for Benjamin. In *The Origin of German Tragic Drama* (1925), Benjamin overturns the Romantic primacy of the symbol in favour of allegory. For him, allegory is the figure that rigorously refuses the sublimation of the Fall, that resists the illusory reconciliation of the temporal with the eternal, and that insists on the ontological difference between the object and its meaning. Benjamin offers an emblematic image of this aesthetic of negation and difference: "Whereas in the symbol destruction is idealized and the transfigured face of nature is fleetingly revealed in the light of redemption, in allegory the observer is confronted with the *facies hippocratica* [the death-face] of history as a petrified, primordial landscape. Everything about history that, from the very beginning, has been untimely, sorrowful, unsuccessful, is expressed in a face – or rather in a death's head."[3]

This is a powerful figuration of the two opposing rhetorical figures, and in each case there figures a face (*ein Antlitz*). In the symbol, it is the face of nature that is transfigured, its destruction idealized by the light of redemption (*Erlösung*) from the metaphysical realm. In allegory, no such redemption takes place; the face is instead that of history, and its countenance consists of the petrified features of the death's head. The death's head is, in other words, the allegory of allegory – the figure of the allegorical relation that insists on the death of the past, on the temporal distance between signifier and signified, on the ontological difference between the natural and the spiritual.

Paul de Man, who has pushed this distinction as far as seems possible, defines it quite clearly: "Whereas the symbol postulates the possibility of an identity or identification, allegory designates primarily a distance in relation to its origin, and, renouncing the nostalgia and the desire to coincide, it establishes itself in the void of this temporal difference."[4] De Man speaks here of the inauthentic or false nostalgia that seeks to relive the past by abstracting it from any historical reality. Allegory, on the contrary, is without illusion and inconsolable; based on the principle of disunity and discontinuity in its form of representation, it marks a permanent exile from the past and in this way acquires for the modern world a kind of authenticity that is lacking in the symbol.

For Benjamin, allegory is to the realm of thought what ruins are to the realm of things. In both cases, the rupture between the material signifier and the ideal signified appears irreconcilable. The parallel traditions of allegory and ruin come together, however, in the fragment, a figure both literary and architectural. Benjamin likens baroque writing to the process of ceaselessly piling up fragments, as opposed to a more organic model of literary creation, so that "the perfect vision of this new [literary] phenomenon was the ruin."[5] Baroque writing is "constructed" (*baut*), a quality that the writer does not attempt to conceal under the sign of genius or heavenly inspiration. "Hence the display of the craftsmanship, which, in Calderón especially, shows through like the masonry in a building whose rendering [*Verputz*] has broken away."[6] The recurring image here is one of brokenness and fragmentation, both in the relation of the parts of the composition to one another and in the relation of the composition to its ostensible origin. According to Benjamin, this notion of an irreconcilable rupture lies at the heart of the cult of ruins in the baroque aesthetic of the seventeenth and eighteenth centuries, for ruins testify to the irreversible effects of time even as they mark the rupture of the object with its origins.

The aesthetic of ruins can thus be seen as an authentic nostalgia, as the melancholy cult of the past arising out of the space of rupture, and conscious of the irremediable absence of its object. Diderot writes in his *Salons de 1767*: "Great are the ideas that ruins awaken in me. Everything is annihilated, everything perishes, everything passes away. There is only the world that remains. There is only time that endures. How old this world is! I walk between two eternities."[7] What perishes is history and its transcendental meaning; what remains are merely the physical existence and temporal phenomena of the world. The two eternities between which Diderot walks are not those of heaven and hell; they are those of the void. These reflections belong to the more general baroque cult of ruins as a cult of absence. As Jean Starobinski describes it, "The ruin *par excellence* is the sign of a deserted cult, a neglected god. It expresses abandonment and desertion ... Its melancholy lies in the fact that it has become a monument to lost meaning. To dream in the ruins is to feel that our existence no longer belongs to us, and that it is already part of the immense oblivion."[8]

In speaking of the dreamlike aspect of the aesthetic of ruins, Starobinski reminds us that, even if ruins are seen as testimony to the ravages of time, the cult of ruins should not be confused with any sort of historical realism. He notes that "the sacrilege, in the eyes of those who remain attached to this feeling, is to wish to *date* that which should remain *immemorial.*"[9] There would thus appear to be a historical abstraction even in the aesthetic that sees architectural ruin as the negation of any metaphysical transcendence and as the sign of the inescapable immanence of the world in time. However, if this is one form of historical abstraction, it should not be confused with what comes into play with the aesthetic of architectural restoration, at least as it will be put into practice by Viollet-le-Duc and his followers. Restoration implies another kind of abstraction, a different dream. Where the aesthetic of ruins fetishizes the marks of time, restoration seeks to erase them. In this respect, restoration belongs to the form of nostalgia that dreams of the timeless unity of the object with its ideal origins – the unity of the *symbol* – whereas the ruin, as we have just seen, expresses the temporal disunity proper to *allegory*. In the sense that the nineteenth century gave to these terms, restoration is symbolic, while ruins are allegorical.

This excursion into an episode of the history of aesthetics is meant to prepare the ground for a more direct comparison between Viollet-le-Duc and Ruskin, as the two principal nineteenth-century apologists of architectural restoration and ruins, respectively. We have Viollet-le-Duc to thank for the fact that many of the most important buildings of medieval France remain more or less intact today. He began his career of restoration in 1840 with the Church of the Madeleine at Vézelay in Burgundy. In the same year, with Jean-Baptiste Lassus, he undertook the restoration of the Sainte-Chapelle in Paris. He achieved national prominence in 1844 by winning the competition, with Lassus, to restore Notre-Dame de Paris. The projects of the basilicas of Saint-Denis and of Saint-Sernin in Toulouse also belong to this period. Following the fall of the July monarchy, the revolution of 1848, and the coup d'état of Louis-Napoléon, Viollet continued to enjoy the favour of the ruling regime. He oversaw the work of restoration at Amiens and Chartres. In the 1850s he turned to secular architecture by rebuilding the citadel and ramparts of Carcassonne and by restoring the Château de Pierrefonds at Compiègne as an imperial residence. His last major architectural restoration was the Cathedral of Lausanne in 1874. Apart from this extremely active architectural career, Viollet-le-Duc sought to provide a theory for his practice in several major works. We will be concerned chiefly with the *Dictionnaire raisonné de l'architecture française du XI au XVI siécle*

(1854) and with the two volumes of *Entretiens* (Discussions), published respectively in 1863 and 1872. Because of the rational approach to function and structural unity taken in these works, Viollet-le-Duc has often been considered the first modernist architect.[10] Ruskin of course was not an architect, but through his writings and lectures he had a profound effect on Victorian ideas of art in general and of architecture in particular. This chapter is mainly concerned with his two major works of architectural theory, both written from the experience of his voyages to Italy as a fairly young man in mid-century: *The Seven Lamps of Architecture*, 1849; and *The Stones of Venice*, published in three volumes between 1851 and 1853.

A general comparison between Ruskin and Viollet-le-Duc has been made by Nikolaus Pevsner, who remarks on several points in common between the two figures: their celebration of the Gothic art of the thirteenth century, of course, and the importance that both of them attach to a certain notion of truth in architecture in which the appearance of a building corresponds to its actual structure and material composition. In *The Seven Lamps*, for example, Ruskin tells us that the architect must avoid the suggestion of a means of structural support other than the real one, as well as the painting of surfaces to represent a material other than that of which they are made. Likewise, Viollet-le-Duc insists in the *Entretiens* that "stone appear really as stone, iron as iron, wood as wood," and so forth.[11] Both writers seem to agree on the role of the people in constructing Gothic architecture. For Viollet-le-Duc, it is to the common people of the thirteenth century that we owe the great monuments of that age, while for Ruskin these buildings represent the work of an entire race.[12] In his last major work, *The Bible of Amiens* (1880-85), Ruskin several times cites Viollet-le-Duc as an authority on French medieval architecture.

The common ground ends just about there, however, and the differences between these two figures are much more significant than any points of convergence. Viollet-le-Duc, for example, privileges architectural structure, whereas Ruskin gives a greater importance to decoration. We must keep in mind that Viollet-le-Duc, as an active architect, is primarily concerned to justify the methods that he had put into practice, whereas Ruskin, even more than a theorist, is above all a stylist and connoisseur who has little interest or experience in the practice of building. For Pevsner, however, the difference comes down to one of sensibility: in Viollet-le-Duc, he sees a French rationalism that favours the concrete and empirical; in Ruskin, a supposedly English emotivity that privileges suggestion and evocation. In this rather facile analysis, however, Pevsner reduces important aesthetic and theoretical differences to the banal question of national temperament. Let us attempt a deeper appreciation of these two theorists by looking more closely at their respective ideas on ruin and restoration.

In the article on restoration in Viollet-le-Duc's *Dictionnaire raisonné*, we read: "The works of restoration undertaken in France … have rescued from ruin a number of works of undisputed value … These buildings, part of the glory of our country preserved from ruin, will remain standing for centuries as a testimony to the devotion of a few men motivated more by the perpetuation of that glory than by their private interests."[13] These last few words make a thrust at the architects of the Ecole des Beaux-Arts, and at their supposed disdain for the practical work of restorers working in the provinces. Viollet-le-Duc was to be associated with the Ecole only briefly; appointed controversially to a professorship in 1863, he was prevented from teaching his courses by his "classical" colleagues and students. For my purposes, however, it is more important to note that for Viollet-le-Duc, contrary to the baroque and Romantic traditions, ruins have no value as such. On the contrary, the ruin of ancient buildings is to be avoided at all costs because their restoration can transform them into monuments to the perpetual glory of the French nation. This idealized and transcendent notion conforms to the famous definition with which Viollet-le-Duc begins his dictionary article on restoration: "The word [restoration] and the thing are modern: to restore a building is not to maintain it, repair it, or rebuild it; it is to reestablish it in a complete state that might never have existed at any given moment."[14]

For Viollet-le-Duc, architectural restoration was a new science, like those of comparative anatomy, philology, ethnology, and archaeology. Laurent Baridon has shown how the architect's ideas incorporate the scientific concept of organicism characteristic of the mid-nineteenth century: the architectural restorer is to the medieval building what the paleontologist is to the remains of a prehistoric animal; each of them seeks to reconstitute an organism. This theory presupposes a number of qualities in the object to be reconstituted: its unity, its internal logic, its visibility. Like the paleontologist Georges Cuvier, Viollet-le-Duc saw in the object of his study a "correlation of organs" and the subordination of its different elements, so every element could be understood in terms of its function within the overall structure. The point, however, was not merely to recreate a building by imitating medieval practices but to find the solutions to architectural problems that medieval artisans would have adopted had they the technical means available to the nineteenth century.[15] For Viollet-le-Duc, medieval architecture is not essentially a multiple series of historical phenomena rooted in distinct and local contexts. Rather, his theory implies the existence of an ideal form of the building independent of its concrete realization at any given historical moment.

In other words, Viollet-le-Duc reached into the art of the Middle Ages for a certain number of a priori principles, an architectural grammar that guided his projects even where the work of restoration went consciously against the historical realities of a given edifice. As the studies of Viollet-le-Duc are full of examples of this controversial practice in his major projects, I shall cite a relatively minor but nonetheless instructive example from his project for the restoration of the Chapelle des Macchabées in Geneva, built in 1405 by Jean de Brogny as an annex to the twelfth-century Cathédrale de Saint Pierre. The chapel had been converted into a storeroom by Calvin's reformers and later had been used as a lecture hall by the Académie de Genève (today, the University of Geneva). Leila El Wakil has shown how Viollet-le-Duc, based on his own understanding of Gothic principles, proposed the "restoration" of several elements that in fact had never belonged to the building. Among these was the erection of a spire that Viollet-le-Duc freely admitted might never have existed. Nonetheless, he argued, it ought to have existed even if it never had because such a spire conformed to "accepted practice in all independently built chapels" ("l'usage admis dans toutes les chapelles isolées"). Similarly, he proposed to create a rose window in the otherwise intact façade of the western gable, a pure invention justified on the aesthetic grounds that "an intact gable over the architecture of the ground-level story will appear overly heavy" ("un pignon plein sur l'architecture du rez-de-chaussée paraîtra fort lourd"). Characteristically conservative, the city of Geneva rejected these innovative features of the project, judging that "one should put aside those things which, while they might beautify the building, one cannot claim to have ever existed."[16] Although Viollet-le-Duc withdrew from this project after an administrative disagreement, the city went ahead with the restoration of the chapel on the basis of his plans but without the spire, the rose-window, and other innovative features. Viollet-le-Duc's original plans are reproduced in figures 11.1 and 11.2. Figure 11.3 shows the chapel as it appears today, adjacent to the neoclassical façade of the cathedral designed by Benedetto Alfieri in 1752.

11.1 Viollet-le-Duc, plan for the restoration of the Chapelle des Macchabées, west face, 1875. Centre d'Iconographie Genevoise, Geneva.

11.2 Viollet-le-Duc, plan for the restoration of the Chapelle des Macchabées, south face, 1875. Centre d'Iconographie Genevoise, Geneva.

11.3 Chapelle des Macchabées, west face. Photograph by Michael Röösli.

A few years later, in restoring the cathedral adjacent to the chapel, Geneva had to fend off pressure from a very different quarter. A sense of the intense polemic surrounding the question of restoration is given in the official report of the Association for the Restoration of Saint Pierre, which took on the task of restoring the cathedral proper in 1891. Having caught wind of the new plans, William Morris's Society for the Protection of Ancient Buildings had made an urgent appeal to Geneva to abandon its plans to restore Saint Pierre on the grounds that any such work would destroy the work of time and would risk betraying the ideas of the original builders. Morris's society recommended instead that the protection of the cathedral be limited to the simple reinforcement of those parts of the building that were falling into ruin. The response of the Geneva association was unambiguous: "To give in to theories so subversive of our reason for being would be to commit suicide. We preferred to live, and to reply to our correspondents that we do not share their point of view."[17] In other words, Geneva sought a middle way between the conservative movement, which, following the principles of Ruskin, opposed restoration of any kind, and the radical restorations of Viollet-le-Duc.

Viollet-le-Duc's practice of restoring buildings from a priori principles rather than historical evidence continues to attract controversy today. One of his more severe critics finds that his theory amounts to a "delirium" founded on a fundamental tautology: "[his] observations allow the definition of a law, but the law preexists, so the observations conform to the law."[18] Despite the often brilliant investigations that Viollet-le-Duc conducted in order to discover the history of a building, his principles tend to make an abstraction of history in two ways: first, he idealizes a given period, the Gothic era, as the privileged moment of all architectural history.[19] Second, by consciously reconstructing a building into a form that does not correspond to any of the building's past forms, he refuses a rigorously historical approach in favour of an aesthetic of timeless unity. Of course, one might ask how it could be otherwise, once one has started down the path of restoration. Given a building such as Notre-Dame de Paris, which has undergone continual transformation from the twelfth to the seventeenth centuries, how does one decide which of its many forms to restore it to unless one has, for example, an ideal notion of what it might have been in the thirteenth century? The point is, however, that for Viollet-le-Duc Gothic architectural form is not primarily historical; rather, it consists of an ideal unity that is structurally analogous to the unity of the Romantic symbol, even if its content is different.

By its very nature, the Romantic symbol represents the secularization of the metaphysical qualities once attributed to the sacred object. Given the declining authority of religious institutions, the symbol responds to a demand in the nineteenth century for a language that would bring material being into harmony with spiritual being in atemporal but secular terms. In Viollet-le-Duc the Gothic cathedral, like the Romantic symbol, is secularized as an aesthetic object.[20] Neither his writings nor his architectural practice takes seriously the status of the medieval Gothic church as an edifice designed for the ritual of worship and for administering the holy sacraments. On the contrary, he writes in the *Entretiens* that the great Gothic cathedrals of medieval France are essentially the work of lay craftsmen organized into guilds. While employed by the bishops, these craftsmen worked independently, adopting a new system of construction and new forms in architecture and sculpture. Whereas the religious institutions of the early Middle Ages could reproduce only designs in the Romanesque and Byzantine traditions, the "lay school" of the late twelfth century made a complete break from these traditions, replacing them by principles founded on reason – that is, the principles of Gothic architecture. Only at this point, argues Viollet-le-Duc, did there emerge "the special genius of the French nation" ("le génie propre à la nation française").[21] From here, it is a relatively short step to the national ideology that Viollet-le-Duc invokes in support of his projects of restoration. In this way, the metaphysical dimension of the symbol, traditionally given the name of the infinite, the eternal, and the like, acquires an identity rather more specific but equally eternal: the glory of France. This is a rhetorical strategy that we might call the appropriation of the symbolic structure by ideology.

In order to understand Viollet-le-Duc's aesthetic, we need to see it in the context of France's Second Empire and its ideology, which, while aspiring to recover the imperial glories of the first Napoleonic era, nonetheless embraced the values of industrial progress that it had inherited from the bourgeois monarchy of Louis-Philippe. We see both elements in the discourse of Viollet-le-Duc, who pays homage to Napoleon I while insisting on the progress made in the artisanal industries of the provinces thanks to the works of architectural restoration under way all over France. To take up just the first of these elements, we note that for Viollet-le-Duc restoration is above all a national project whose origins lie in the First Empire and in "the will of the Emperor Napoleon I, who was ahead of his times in all things, and who understood the importance of restoration."[22] Viollet-le-Duc's politics, however, are not a simple matter, for they suggest a certain discrepancy between his personal convictions and his public discourse. If, after the fall of the Second Empire, he showed himself to be an ardent republican, there was little to suggest such a conviction in his close connections to the authoritarian regime of Napoleon III, connections that he needed for the support of his architectural projects. By no means the least of these was his restoration of the fourteenth-century Château de Pierrefonds into an imperial residence, where his energetic direction of court entertainments earned him the nickname of "the stage-prompter of Compiègne."[23]

Viollet-le-Duc's discourse on art, however, is not predominantly royalist. It is instead a texture of theories and observations that reflects all of the tensions inherent in mid-nineteenth-century aesthetics. This tension is evident from the very first of the *Entretiens*. On the one hand, in keeping with the emerging Symbolist aesthetics of his age, Viollet-le-Duc argues for the essential unity of art and its value as independent of historical circumstances: "Art has its value independently of the milieu in which it is born and grows up."[24] On the other hand, and in keeping with the scientific humanism of Charles-Augustin de Sainte-Beuve, Viollet-le-Duc sees the *form* if not the *essence* of art as intimately tied to the way of life of a people: "the arts of the Middle Ages follow step by step the manners and customs of the people in the midst of which they develop."[25] This double discourse allows Viollet-le-Duc to argue both for an ideal Gothic, independent of historical specificity, and for the revival of the Gothic as an expression of national unity and character. Thus, in the seventh *Entretien*, Viollet-le-Duc claims that "art in France, from the early years of the thirteenth century, has been an instrument used by royal power in its efforts to develop national unity."[26] This is not offered as a critique of the instrumentalization of art for political ends. On the contrary, Viollet-le-Duc is citing the precedent of the thirteenth century as an argument for the continued support of his various projects of restoration by the imperial regime. National unity is offered as a political justification for the pursuit of an essentially aesthetic ideal.

Like Viollet-le-Duc, Ruskin defends the Gothic against architectural classicism but with a very different declared ideology. For Ruskin, the individual freedom inherent in the Gothic style stands in opposition to the authoritarian classicism of the *ancien régime*, while the nineteenth-century revival of the Gothic marks a parallel revival of Christian faith in reaction to the declining authority of religious institutions in modern life. When Ruskin first went to Oxford in 1836, the Oxford movement of John Keble and John Henry Newman had already begun. It helped to create an intellectual climate in which Ruskin could write of art and architecture in strongly ethical terms that, in his work, resonated with the egalitarianism of the equally important political movement that produced three Reform Bills between 1832 and 1884.

Like Viollet-le-Duc, Ruskin also speaks of a national architecture, declaring, for example, in *The Crown of Wild Olive* (1866), that "all good architecture is the expression of national life and character; and it is produced by a prevalent and eager national taste."[27] But this national character is to be distinguished from Viollet-le-Duc's discourse of national unity. For Ruskin, it is a matter of the impact of architecture on public life, of the manner in which a building becomes a permanent part of the landscape, and of a certain ethical responsibility of the architect toward the people. The monumental character of the Gothic building resides in its capacity to bear witness to the history of a people, which it does through the richness of documentation contained in its ornamentation: "Its minute and multitudinous sculptural decorations afford means of expressing, either symbolically or literally, all that need be known of national feeling or achievement … Better the rudest work that tells a story or records a fact, than the richest without meaning."[28] Already, we may note two points on which Ruskin's discourse differs from Viollet-le-Duc's. First, although he speaks of feeling and national achievement, Ruskin does not privilege any nation in particular. Whereas Ruskin affirms the style and the moral force of what he calls the Goth (the Englishman, the Frenchman, the Dane, the German) against the supposed languor and subjection of Mediterranean peoples, his use of "nation" is essentially racial and has little to do with the meaning given this word by the nationalism of the modern state. Second, Ruskin wishes to affirm the *memorial* function of the Gothic building: if poetry constitutes what a people has thought and felt, then architecture constitutes "what their hands have handled, and their strength wrought, and their eyes beheld, all the days of their life."[29] For Ruskin, the Gothic building has the same *aura* that Benjamin will attribute to the work of art that still bears the marks of the artist's hands, a quality lost in reproduction. In general, Ruskin's notion of the memorial function of the Gothic contrasts with Viollet-le-Duc's ideas, which are both more abstract and more pragmatic. Stephen Bayley has remarked that for the French architect, the Gothic is made into "a flexible system adapted to all needs and their changing nature. The Gothic describes a language of many words."[30]

For Ruskin, ruins also have a memorial function, but they are distinguished from other architectural formations by the quality of what he calls "parasitical sublimity," the sublime that derives from accident or from the nonessential character of the object. This particularly fortuitous form of the sublime corresponds, for Ruskin, to a certain sense of the picturesque. He finds it in the accessory details of a painting by Tintoretto or Rubens: "in the clefts and folds of shaggy hair, or in the chasms and rents of rocks, or in the hanging of thickets or hill sides, or in the alternations of gaiety and gloom in the variegation of the shell, the plume, or the cloud."[31] Here, there is an echo of the baroque poetics of a seventeenth-century poet such as William D'Avenant. Defending the style of his epic poem *Gondibert* (1651), D'Avenant calls attention precisely to its ephemeral, aleatory, and indistinct qualities: "the shadowings, happy strokes, secret graces, and even the drapery, which together make the second beauty."[32] Similarly, for Ruskin, his sense of the sublime is independent of the main lines and principal substance of the object as such. In architecture in particular this fortuitous beauty, this sublime of the supplement, takes the form of the ruin. There is, then, a sublime that resides in ruptures, fissures, stains, and moss – in everything that marks the effects of nature and of time on the architectural work.

The striking quality of such effects had been appreciated by Victor Hugo in *Notre-Dame de Paris* (1831), where, in condemning the various attempts at architectural restoration of that cathedral – attempts to be once more taken up by Viollet-le-Duc in 1845 – he notes that "time has perhaps given the church more than it has taken away, as it is time that has spread over the façade that dark colour of the centuries that makes the old age of monuments the age of their beauty."[33] Similarly, Ruskin holds that "it is in the golden stain of time, that we are look for the real light, and colour, and preciousness of architecture."[34]

Ruskin's own rendering of Kenilworth Castle, done in 1847 (fig. 11.4),[35] shows the Great Hall shorn of its roof, the crumbling masonry overgrown with ivy. Stone and vegetation alike are subject to the variegated effects of light and shadow. The picture retains the strong sense of verticality belonging to the Gothic elements of the building, but these are set in stark contrast to a gray and empty sky. Just enough of Gothic tracery remains in one of the windows to recall the splendour of this edifice in the days of John of Gaunt, in the fourteenth century. From reading Walter Scott's novel *Kenilworth* (1821), Ruskin would have known the rich descriptions of this castle as it stood in Elizabethan days. His sense of the ruin's sublimity, however, would have come from the visible effects of time's ravages in the margins and interstices of the weakening stone.

11.4 Ruskin, Kenilworth Castle, 1847, in John Ruskin, *Diaries* (Oxford: Clarendon, 1956), vol. 1, plate 31.

According to Ruskin, Gothic architecture creates conditions that are particularly advantageous to this external or parasitical sublime because the effects of the Gothic that depend on the play of shadow and light are enhanced by the partial wearing away of sculptural detail. Ruskin denounces architectural restoration, then, because it effaces the sublime effects of time. If Hugo attacks specific projects of restoration on the grounds of their incompetence or lack of architectural understanding, Ruskin's condemnation is more categorical and even more impassioned: "Restoration, so called, is the worst manner of Destruction. It means the most total destruction which a building can suffer: a destruction out of which no remnants can be gathered ... It is *impossible*, as impossible as to raise the dead, to restore anything that has ever been great or beautiful in architecture."[36] The dominant figure in this discourse is that of death. Ruskin declares the impossibility of summoning back to life the spirit of the dead artisan and commanding him to direct other hands and other thoughts. The very concept of restoration is "a lie from beginning to end": "You may make a model of a building as you would of a corpse, and your model may have the shell of the old walls within it as your cast might have the skeleton, with what advantage I neither see nor care."[37] As for those monuments that fall into ruin: "*We have no right to touch them*. They are not ours. They belong partly to those who built them, and partly to the generations of mankind who are to follow us. The dead still have their right in them."[38] It is as though ruins were still the dwelling places of the dead, such that to restore them would be to destroy the eloquent means by which the dead, or death itself, makes itself understood.[39] To declare that "we have no right to touch them" implies the kind of veneration for architectural ruins that is felt for mortal human remains, which, for profoundly emotional and cultural reasons, cannot be disinterred or displaced. This insistence on the presence of death in ruins recalls Benjamin's notion that the emblem of allegory is the *facies hippocratica*, the pale and shrivelled aspect of the human face just before the moment of death.

Ruskin's ideas on death and ruins force us to revise the common understanding that for him the Gothic is a primarily organic art, in both its structural principles and its resemblance to vegetation. In fact, his essay on "The Lamp of Power" finds that one of the elements of sublime architecture is precisely its *inorganic* character, found in the geometric form of the wall and other "wide, bold, and unbroken" surfaces. Both the organic and the inorganic principles are found in nature, "the one in her woods and thickets, the other in her plains and cliffs and waters."[40] If the former "gives grace to every pulse that agitates animal organisation," the latter "reproves the pillars of the earth, and builds up her barren precipices into the coldness of the clouds": "the grey cliff loses not its nobleness when it reminds us of some Cyclopean waste of mural stone … even the awful cone of the far-off mountain has a melancholy mixed with … that of its own solitude, which is cast from the images of nameless tumuli on and of the heaps of reedy clay, into which chambered cities melt in their mortality."[41] As Andrea Pinotti suggests, Ruskin expresses a nostalgia for death and mineral stillness.[42] The language of melancholy, solitude, and mortality with which he contemplates the mountains and cliffs belongs also to the discourse of ruins. In the ruin, where climbing vegetation meets the resistance of ancient stone, we witness the same eternal struggle between the organic and the inorganic principles of nature. The stone, in its hardness and coldness, but also in its marred and worn condition, has the awesome aspect of death itself. It evokes the melancholy, "dead" relation of the allegorical sign to its object, in contrast to the living, organic nature of the symbol.

This identification of Ruskin with allegory is bound to surprise those who read too literally his insistence on "naturalism" in architectural representation. There is, for example, the passage in "The Nature of the Gothic" where Ruskin contrasts the representations of purgatorial fire in two different churches. One of these, in the mosaic of the Romanesque cathedral of Torcello, is purely allegorical. The fire takes the form of a red stream that descends from the throne of Christ and extends itself to envelop the wicked. The other, in the Gothic porch of St Maclou in Rouen, is strongly naturalistic: "The sculptured flames burst out of the Hades gate, and flicker up, in writhing tongues of stone, through the interstices of the niches, as if the church itself were on fire." Ruskin offers this as a demonstration of the "love of veracity" reflected in Gothic design, by which he means a faithful imitation of natural form. As always in Ruskin, however, there is a difference between factual representation and truth. He goes on to say that, on reflection, one will perhaps find more truth in the allegorical figure, "in that blood-red stream, flowing between definite shores, and out of God's throne, and expanding, as if fed by a perpetual current, into the lake wherein the wicked are cast," than in the "torch-flickerings" of the Gothic, naturalistic figure.[43] The point is that for Ruskin allegory represents a deeper truth than naturalistic imitation. A similar point has been made by Gary Wihl, who writes that for Ruskin "sincerity is increasingly figured as allegory, as a writer's or sculptor's self-consciousness about the fictiveness ... of his idealizations."[44] The allegorical figure acknowledges the gap between signifier and signified, and this implicit acknowledgement of the inadequacy of signification is itself the sign of a truth.

In general, we could say that Viollet-le-Duc's aesthetic is to Ruskin's what symbol is to allegory: on the one hand, the timeless unity of the object with its ideal essence; on the other hand, rupture, disunity, and the pathos evoked by the material remains of an irrecoverable past. Here, it might be useful to point out the affinity between the aesthetic of ruins and that of the monument. The monument does not claim to evoke the totality of what it commemorates. It signifies its object only allegorically and by convention; it presents itself as the dead letter of a departed spirit, and its affective power resides precisely in this ontological difference.

Ruskin's implacable rejection of modern architecture for a long time caused him to be seen as an incurable nostalgic, devoted to a regressive pastoralism in the face of modernity.[45] But there is in Ruskin's particular form of nostalgia a certain resistance to nostalgia, just as, conversely, there is nostalgia in Viollet-le-Duc's particular form of modernism. To the extent that the work of each of these figures resonates in the twentieth century, Viollet-le-Duc's impact is on architectural modernism, whereas Ruskin's is on literary modernism. It is on this latter point that I would like to conclude.

The aesthetic of the ruin and of the fragment would be taken up, if transformed, by poets such as T.S. Eliot and René Char in their fragmentation of the word and of literary form. This textual fragmentation would be justified in terms identical to those that Benjamin uses to justify the allegorical fragment – that is, in a discourse that privileges rupture and exteriority. Thus Maurice Blanchot writes of what he calls the *parole du fragment* (fragment word) in Char: "a new kind of arrangement not entailing harmony, concordance, or reconciliation, but that accepts disjunction or divergence as the infinite center from out of which, through speech, relation is to be created."[46] Other elements of Ruskin's work can be seen as a renewal of the baroque spirit in the modern context. There is, for example, the idea of perpetual movement, which Benjamin sees as a constituent element of baroque allegory. In contrast to the Romantic symbol, which remains "persistently the same," allegory, "if it is to hold its own against the tendency to absorption [*Versenkung*], must constantly unfold in new and surprising ways."[47] One can compare this remark to Ruskin's insistence on "changefulness" as one of the essential qualities of the Gothic, as well as on its "disquietude": "It is that strange *disquietude* of the Gothic spirit that is its greatness; that restlessness of the dreaming mind, that wanders hither and thither among the niches, and flickers feverishly around the pinnacles, and frets and fades in labyrinthine knots and shadows along wall and roof, and yet is not satisfied, nor shall be satisfied."[48]

That is, the Gothic spirit is not satisfied in its ceaseless search for a reconciliation of body and spirit, of temporal and eternal, of signifier and signified. This dissatisfaction corresponds to the allegory rather than the symbol, the architectural ruin rather than its restoration, the fragment rather than the whole. The paradox of Ruskin is that his baroque definition of the Gothic gives rise to a certain modernism; in recovering a neglected aesthetic of the past, he looks forward to the new forms of art announced by Eliot's *The Waste Land* (1922): "These fragments I have shored against my ruin."[49]

NOTES

1 Samuel Taylor Coleridge, *Lay Sermons*, in *The Major Works*, 660–5, (Oxford: Oxford University Press, 1985), 661.

2 Cited in Walter Benjamin, *Ursprung des deutschen Trauerspiels. Gesammelte Schriften*, vol. 1 (Frankfurt am Main: Suhrkamp, 1991), 343; trans. John Osborne, *The Origin of German Tragic Drama* (London: Verso, 1998), 166.

3 Benjamin, *Ursprung*, 343: "Während im Symbol mit der Verklärung des Unterganges das transfigurierte Antlitz der Natur im Lichte der Erlösung flüchtig sich offenbart, liegt in der Allegorie die facies hippocratica der Geschichte als erstarrte Urlandschaft dem Betrachter vor Augen"; trans. Osborne, *Origin*, 166.

4 Paul de Man, "The Rhetoric of Temporality," in *Blindness and Insight: Essays in the Rhetoric of Contemporary Criticism*, 187–228 (Minneapolis: University of Minnesota Press, 1983), 207.

5 Benjamin, *Ursprung*, 354; trans. Osborne, *Origin*, 178.

6 Ibid., 355; trans. 179.

7 Denis Diderot, *Ruines et paysages: Salons de 1767*, quoted in Roger Mortier, *La poétique des ruines en France* (Geneva: Droz, 1974), 94: "Les idées que les ruines éveillent en moi sont grandes. Tout s'anéantit,tout périt, tout passe. Il n'y a que le monde qui reste. Il n'y a que le temps qui dure. Qu'il est vieux ce monde! Je marche entre deux éternités." Translations from the French are my own, except where otherwise indicated.

8 Jean Starobinski, *L'Invention de la liberté: 1700–1789* (Geneva: A. Skira, 1987), 180: "La ruine par excellence signale un culte déserté, un dieu négligé. Elle exprime l'abandon et le délaissement ... Sa mélancolie réside dans le fait qu'elle est devenue un monument de la signification perdue. Rêver dans les ruines, c'est sentir que notre existence cesse de nous appartenir et rejoint déjà l'immense oubli."

9 Ibid., 181, original emphasis.

10 See, for example, Jean-François Revel, "Viollet-le-Duc, précurseur de l'architecture moderne," and Hubert Damisch, "Du Structuralisme au fonctionalisme," both in Geert Bekaert, ed., *A la recherche de Viollet-le-Duc*, 130–41, 239–53 (Brussels: Pierre Mardaga, 1980).

11 Eugène-Emmanuel Viollet-le-Duc, *Entretiens* (Brussels: Pierre Mardaga, 1977), vol. 1, 472.

12 Nikolaus Pevsner, *Ruskin and Viollet-le-Duc: Englishness and Frenchness in the Appreciation of Gothic Architecture* (London: Thames and Hudson, 1969), 18.

13 Eugène-Emmanuel Viollet-le-Duc, "Restauration," in *Dictionnaire raisonné de l'architecture française du XI au XVI siècle*, 14–34 (Paris: A. Morel, 1875–89), 31: "Les travaux de restauration entrepris en France ... ont sauvé de la ruine des œuvres d'une valeur incontestable ... Ces édifices, une des gloires de notre pays, préservés de la ruine, resteront encore debout pendant des siècles, pour témoigner du dévouement de quelques hommes plus attachés à perpétuer cette gloire qu'à leurs intérêts particuliers."

14 Viollet-le-Duc, "Restauration," in *Dictionnaire*, 14: "Le mot [restauration] et la chose sont modernes: restaurer un édifice, ce n'est pas l'entretenir, le réparer ou le refaire, c'est le rétablir dans un état complet qui peut n'avoir jamais existé à un moment donné."

15 Laurent Baridon, *L'Imaginaire scientifique de Viollet-le-Duc* (Paris: L'Harmattan, 1996), 18–20.

16 Cited in Leila El Wakil, "Viollet-le-Duc à Genève," in Paul Auberson, ed., *Viollet-le-Duc: Centenaire de la mort à Lausanne: Exposition au Musée historique de l'Ancien-Evêché*, 48–55 (Lausanne: Musée historique de l'Ancien-Evêché, 1979), 54.

17 Association pour la Restauration de St-Pierre, *Rapport administratif et financier* (Geneva: Ville de Genève, 1891), 12: "Donner satisfaction à des théories aussi subversives de notre raison d'être, c'était nous suicider; nous avons préféré vivre et répondre à nos correspondants que nous ne partageons pas leur manière de voir." See also Livio Fornio, "A propos de la restauration de 1889–1913," in *Saint-Pierre, Cathédrale de Genève: Un monument, une exposition*, 103–5 (Geneva: Musée Rath, 1982).

18 Jean-Michel Leniaud, *Viollet-le-Duc ou les délires du système* (Paris: Mengès, 1994), 91.

19 Ibid., 72.

20 I am aware that the analogy proposed here between Viollet-le-Duc's ideal Gothic cathedral and the Romantic symbol risks an oversimplification of the latter, which has a highly complex history and a variety of manifestations. In particular, the rationalism of Viollet-le-Duc's approach has little in common with the Romantic symbol as it is found in literature. It also contrasts with the strain of Romanticism that, rather than "collapsing" the metaphysical dimension of transcendence into the material object, insists on the indefinite deferral of transcendental value. The proposed analogy should therefore be understood as limited to the qualities of atemporality and secularity, which the symbol has in common with the work of Viollet-le-Duc.

21 Viollet-le-Duc, *Entretiens*, vol. 1, 265.

22 Viollet-le-Duc, "Restauration," in *Dictionnaire*, 22: "par la volonté de l'empéreur Napoléon I, qui en toute chose devançait son temps, et qui comoprenait l'importance des restaurations."

23 Paul Gout, *Viollet-le-Duc* (Paris: Edouard Champion, 1914), 51.

24 Viollet-le-Duc, *Entretiens*, vol. 1, 11: "L'art a sa valeur indépendamment du milieu dans lequel il naît et grandit."

25 Viollet-le-Duc, *Entretiens*, vol. 1, 32: "les arts du moyen âge suivent pas à pas les moeurs des peuples au milieu duquels ils se développent."

26 Ibid., vol. 1, 282: "l'art en France, dès les premières années du XIIIe siècle, est un instrument dont le pouvoir royal se sert pour développer ses efforts vers l'unité nationale."

27 John Ruskin, *The Crown of Wild Olive*, in *John Ruskin's Works*, Venice edition (St Louis and Chicago: Holdoway, n.d.), vol. 15, 45.

28 John Ruskin, *The Seven Lamps of Architecture* (New York: Dover, 1989), 183.

29 Ibid., 178.

30 Stephen Bayley, "Viollet-le-Duc et la restauration," in Auberson, ed., *Viollet-le-Duc*, 26–35 at 32.

31 Ruskin, *Seven Lamps*, 192.

32 William D'Avenant, "Preface," in *Gondibert, an Heroick Poem*, i-xlvi (Oxford: Clarendon, 1971), xii.

33 Victor Hugo, *Notre-Dame de Paris* (Paris: Gallimard, Pléiade, 1975), 107–8: "le temps a rendu à l'église plus peut-être qu'il ne lui a ôté, car c'est le temps qui a répandu sur la façade cette sombre couleur des siècles qui fait de la vieillesse des monuments l'âge de leur beauté."

34 Ruskin, *Seven Lamps*, 187.

35 John Ruskin, *Diaries* (Oxford: Clarendon, 1956), vol. 1, plate 31.
36 Ruskin, *Seven Lamps*, 194, original emphasis.
37 Ibid., 196.
38 Ibid., 197, original emphasis.
39 Ruskin's active opposition to architectural restoration lasted well into his mature years. In 1877, for example, he wrote letters to the editors of provincial English newspapers to oppose projects of restoration then being undertaken. His letter of 9 June to the *Liverpool Daily Post* opens with the following words: "My Dear Sir: It is impossible for any one to know the horror and contempt with which I regard modern restoration – but it is so great that it simply paralyzes me in despair."
40 Ruskin, *Seven Lamps*, 78.
41 Ibid., 73.
42 Andrea Pinotti, "Gothic as Leaf, Gothic as Crystal: John Ruskin and Wilhelm Worringer," in Giovanni Cianci and Peter Nicholls, eds, *Ruskin and Modernism*, 17–31 (Houndmills, Basingstoke: Palgrave, 2001).
43 John Ruskin, "The Nature of Gothic," in *The Stones of Venice*, vol. 2, 165–251 (London: Routledge, 1853), 216–17, §§65–6.
44 Gary Wihl, *Ruskin and the Rhetoric of Infallibility* (New Haven: Yale University Press, 1985), 113.
45 For a recent revision of this view, see the collection of essays in Cianci and Nicholls, eds, *Ruskin and Modernism*. Also of interest is Toni Cerutti, ed., *Ruskin and the Twentieth Century* (Vercelli: Mercurio, 2000).
46 Maurice Blanchot, *L'Entretien infini* (Paris: Gallimard, 1969), 453: "un arrangement d'une sorte nouvelle, qui ne sera pas celui d'une harmonie, d'une concorde ou d'une conciliation, mais qui acceptera la disjonction ou la divergence comme le centre infini à partir duquel, par la parole, un rapport doit s'établir"; trans. Susan Hanson, *The Infinite Conversation* (Minneapolis: University of Minnesota Press, 1993), 308.
47 Benjamin, *Ursprung*, 359; trans. Osborne, Origin, 183.
48 Ruskin, *Stones of Venice*, vol. 2, 198, §40, original emphasis.
49 T.S. Eliot, *Collected Poems, 1909–1962* (New York: Harcourt Brace, 1970), 69.

The Enigma of Pyramids: Measuring Salvation in Renaissance Rome

Nick Temple

Chora

BACKGROUND

THE BIRTH OF CONSCIOUS URBAN planning in Rome during the Renaissance coincided with the emergence of a particular historiographical view of topography that saw ancient monuments and venerated Christian sites as metaphorical signifiers of a larger narrative of mytho-historic events. Underlying this understanding of topography was a fervent belief in a preordained providential plan that was sustained by a dynamic relationship between antiquity and present circumstances. Accordingly, the initiatives of *renovatio* (urban and cultural renewal) were deemed part of a larger redemptive project that centred on the hope, or expectation, of a Golden Age. Manifested in the actions of the pope and his curia, Rome became the setting in which *translatio imperii* and *respublica christiana* were actively implemented through urban/architectural development and ritual.

Both humanist and antiquarian interpretations of topography played a key role in this enterprise. This was based on the understanding that certain "distant" mytho-historic events could be made accessible for creative reinterpretation to those who were hermeneutically attuned.[1] It was on the basis of this relationship between historical interpretation and topography that many of the projects of *renovatio urbis* were conceived.

This chapter examines the theme of topography as providential narrative by taking a particular ancient motif, the pyramid, as a symbolic reference. I will argue that the locations and settings of the venerated pyramids of ancient Rome provided the basis for a complex iconographic program that encompassed the mytho-history of the east and west banks of the Tiber River.

ROMULI E REMI

In December 1499 via Alessandrina-Borgo Nuovo was formally opened in the Leonine City in time for the Jubilee celebrations of 1500. Executed under Pope Alexander VI, its layout, which consisted of a wide and straight passage linking St Peter's Basilica to the Castel Sant'Angelo, was a partial implementation of the unexecuted urban scheme for the Borgo envisaged by the earlier Parentucelli pope, Nicholas V. The purpose of via Alessandrina was to facilitate direct access to the Borgo and St Peter's Basilica for pilgrims coming from the east bank of the Tiber River.[2] Also, the street was to function as the first stage in the processional route – the via Papale – for the papal coronation. This linked the Vatican to St John the Lateran, which was located to the east on the Caelian Hill. One obvious feature of via Alessandrina was to have important implications in later urban developments: it formed a crucial link between the Petrine shrine to the west and the bridgehead to the east bank of the Tiber River at Castel Sant'Angelo.[3]

In order to implement the new urban intervention of Pope Alexander VI it was necessary to undertake substantial demolitions of existing buildings in the vicinity of the Mole Adriana (Castel Sant'Angelo). These included the partial removal of an important ancient pyramid located in the path of the new street. Described in a sixteenth-century account, this colossal structure is thought to have been built in the Augustan period and became popularly known as the *meta Romuli* (fig. 12.1).[4] The attribution of this funerary monument to Romulus relates to a long-held belief that the mythical founder of Rome was buried here.[5] It later acquired a special symbolic significance in early Christianity when it became associated with the nearby tomb of St Peter, apostle and founder of the Roman Church. This connection formed part of a contrived ancestral link between Romulus and St Peter that was probably cultivated to emphasize a special concordance between the origins of ancient Rome and the beginnings of the Roman Church.[6] Interpreted in Augustinian terms, however, this apparent concordance would have been construed in eschatological terms as signalling the subordination of ancient classical tradition by a new and urgent Christian order.

Historical and religious comparisons between pagan and Christian traditions were underscored by the belief in generic and symbolic connections between the *meta Romuli* and the other, still extant, Pyramid of Gaius Cestius (fig. 12.2). Located adjacent to the Porta San Paolo to the south, within the ancient Aurelian walls, this second pyramid served a similar function to its Vatican counterpart during the Middle Ages as a giant urban marker for pilgrims proceeding to the nearby shrine of the other prince of the Roman Church, St Paul, located *fuori le mura*.[7]

Moreover, the association of Peter with Romulus in the Vatican was mirrored, so to speak, on the east bank of the Tiber River by the adoption of the name *meta Remi* for the Pyramid of Gaius Cestius during the early Middle Ages.[8] By ensuring the status of Romulus and Remus as legitimate pagan precursors to the princes of the Roman Church, the names

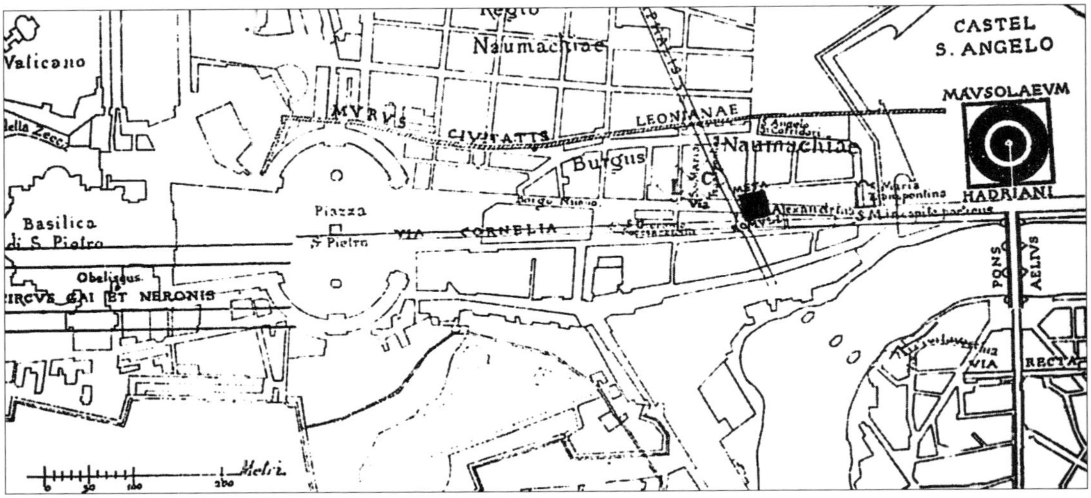

12.1 Plan of the Borgo, showing the location of the *meta Romuli* in relation to via Alessandrina, based on M.B. Peebles, "La 'Meta Romuli' e una lettera di Michele Ferno," in *Atti della Pontificia Accademia Romana di Archeologia Rendiconti*, vol. 12, 21–36 (Citta del Vaticano: Tipografia Poliglotta Vaticana, 1936), 21.

given to the two pyramids also allude to a symmetrical relationship in the mytho-historical narrative of Rome's topography.[9] As prominent markers to the basilicas of Peter and Paul, the pyramids also signal important ancient gateways into old Rome: from the via Triumphalis in the Vatican to the north and the via Ostiensis to the south. This Janus-like relationship highlights in topographical terms the symbolism of Romulus and Remus simultaneously as founders of old Rome and as pagan antecedents to Christian Rome, the latter exemplified by the extraterritorial sites of Peter and Paul.

The idea of a pyramid functioning as a sign-post to a venerated sanctuary reminds one of the urban transformations of Rome under Sixtus V in the late sixteenth century. These entailed the relocation of the ancient obelisks of imperial Rome to positions in front of or near the principal pilgrimage churches, thereby providing beacons for visiting pilgrims proceeding along the new arterial routes.[10] However, unlike the Roman emulation of Egyptian pyramids that were purpose-built as private tombs or monuments on sites in Rome, the ancient obelisks were imported relics from a distant land, reused as totems of imperialism. The subsequent reappropriation of these monuments under Sixtus V for the more specific purpose of signalling important religious establishments reinforces their portability and reusability as urban artefacts.[11] This difference between the Roman pyramids and the Egyptian obelisks is important since it un-

12.2 View of the Pyramid of Gaio Cestio (*meta Remi*) in Rome during the late nineteenth century. Photograph by E. Richter, Vera Fotografia.

derlines the accumulated symbolic meanings in the *meta Romuli* and *meta Remi*. By the Renaissance, this accumulation of meanings was given a distinctly humanistic bias, as the pyramids become crucial references in papal programs of *renovatio urbis*.

In view of the strategic and symbolic importance of the *meta Romuli*, situated near the river crossing and St Peter's Basilica, it is surprising that Pope Alexander VI chose to demolish part of it to make way for his new ceremonial passage.[12] This highlights a contradiction in conscious urban planning in the Renaissance in how it sought to construct a city *de novo* – upon the disorderly layout of its medieval predecessor – and at the same time to respond to existing topographical conditions and symbolic references. Under Pope Alexander VI, this problem demanded certain priorities that were based in part on a new rational understanding of the existing topography of the Vatican and Borgo: namely, the connecting nodes of St Peter's Basilica and the Ponte Sant'Angelo. The *meta Romuli* could not be incorporated easily into this new urban design and consequently was discarded.

This would seem surprising in view of the historical importance of the monument as a symbol for pilgrims crossing the Tiber River at Ponte

Sant'Angelo. It is all the more ironic that Alexander VI had an interest in Egyptian iconography. This was based on the belief, cultivated by his court humanists, that his forbears were the wise sages of ancient Egypt.[13] This is highlighted most clearly in the famous frescos, painted by Pinturicchio, for the pope's Borgia Apartment in the Vatican Palace. The iconography of this fresco cycle was a celebration of syncretism, with references to great classical works such as Apuleius's *Golden Ass*. Among the array of motifs in the frescos is a representation of a pyramid, in the scene of the exploits of Osiris, that is shown with a geometric relief adorned with precious stones. The decoration of this monument is reminiscent of the original marble relief-work of the *meta Romuli*, later removed and reused for the paving of Old St Peter's Basilica. A clearer indication of the original appearance of the *meta Romuli*, as it was understood in the Renaissance, can be seen in the earlier bronze relief of the martyrdom of St Peter by Filarete, executed under Pope Eugenius IV as part of a larger scheme for the doors of the basilica (fig. 12.9). On the lower right of the relief appears a reconstruction of the pyramid, which, like the Pinturicchio fresco, shows elaborate geometrical relief-work.

Given Alexander VI's cultivation of an Egyptian ancestry, it is remarkable that he chose to demolish part of the *meta Romuli*. An explicit reference to his Egyptian ancestry was acceptable in the relative privacy of his apartment but would have been controversial in an urban context. However, the pyramid clearly did not allude to Egyptian ancestry, at least in its historical context, as this study has indicated. The partial demolition of the pyramid may have resulted from an indifference toward the idea of continuity between the founders of Rome and the founders of the Roman Church or may simply have provided the much needed access for pilgrims to St Peter's Basilica from the Ponte Sant'Angelo. The development in conscious urban planning in the mid to late fifteenth century tended to give due priority to a strategic overview of the city – in this case, the Vatican and Borgo – over the symbolic specificity of its parts. While this understanding of urban planning was not fully developed until the eighteenth century, its origins can be traced clearly to this period.[14]

However we attempt to explain the reasons behind the partial demolition of the *meta Romuli*, it is clear that this did not signal the effective redundancy of the *meta Romuli* as a symbol of Roman and Christian traditions. On the contrary, the ruins of the pyramid continued to exercise

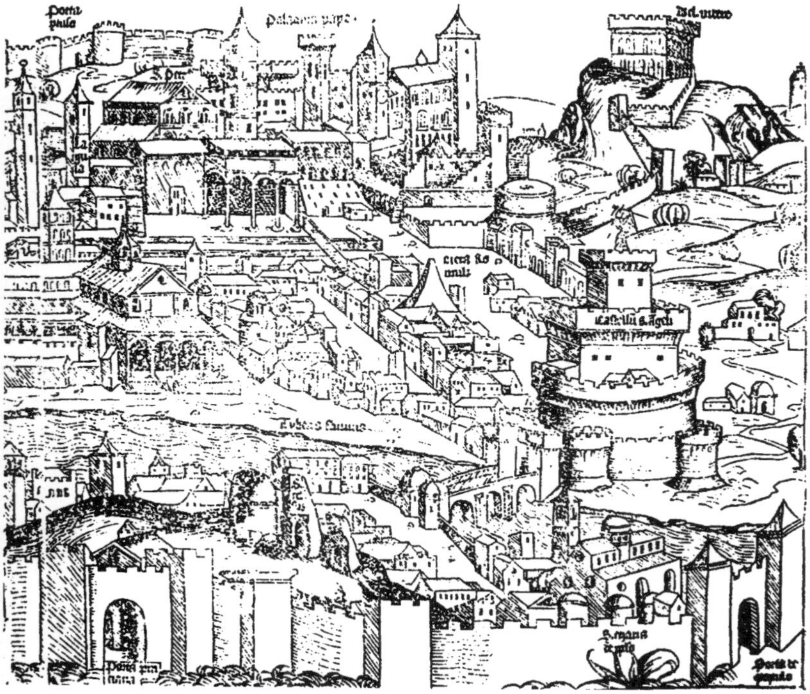

12.3 Sebastiano Münster, detail of engraving of Rome at the end of the fifteenth century, showing partly truncated *meta Romuli* near the Castel Sant'Angelo, in *Cosmographiae universalis* (Basileae, 1550).

12.4 Giulio Romano, detail from the sixteenth-century fresco *Adlocutio di Costantino* in the Sala Costantino, Vatican Apartments, showing the *meta Romuli* on the left next to the Mausoleum of Hadrian. Courtesy of Pinacoteca, Musei Vaticani.

an important influence, both ritually and urbanistically, on the Borgo and Vatican. This should be seen in the context of an increasing antiquarian interest in the symbolism of ancient monuments in the early sixteenth century that was to have a significant impact on papal programs of *renovatio*.

THE VANISHING POINT

From textual and pictorial evidence, we know that a large portion of the pyramid remained standing until the second decade of the sixteenth century, when it was finally removed under Leo X, much to the consternation of antiquarians and artists.[15] In the broader context of urban developments in the early sixteenth century, the *meta Romuli* would have maintained, at least in part, its historical function as a beacon to the Petrine basilica. This is highlighted in the design and orientation of via Giulia, along with the redevelopment of adjacent streets, during the Pontificate of Julius II (fig. 12.5). Designed by Donato Bramante, this urban project formed part of an ambitious program to enlarge the administrative structure of the papacy by constructing a number of papal institutions – such as a mint and a palace of justice – across the Tiber River on the east bank.[16] Like the earlier via Alessandrina, on which it was almost certainly modelled, via Giulia unfolds as a straight and formal urban thoroughfare. Oriented on the north-south axis, it passes through the Regola, Parione, and Ponte quarters of Rome on the east bank.

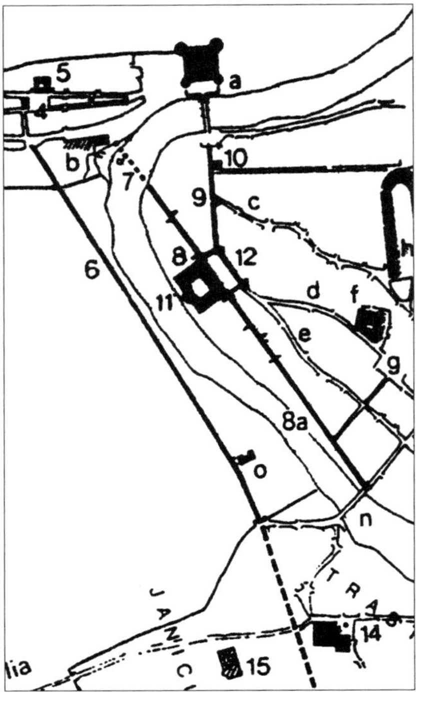

12.5 Plan showing the parallel axes of via Giulia on the east bank of the Tiber River and via della Lungara on the west bank, in Arnaldo Bruschi, *Bramante Architetto* (Bari: Editore Laterza, 1973), 611.

In contrast to the southern end of via Giulia, which concludes at the junction with Ponte Sisto, the street's northern termination was left incomplete at the end of Julius II's pontificate. Consequently, this has led to much debate among architectural historians about Bramante's original proposals for the area.[17] One determining factor in the design of the termination of via Giulia would have been its relationship to the Borgo across the Tiber River.[18] The design of via Giulia and adjacent streets incorporated the proposal to reinstate the Pons Neronianus (or Pons Triumphalis), an ancient bridge that originally spanned the Tiber River at its bend. Thought to have been used in antiquity as a ceremonial crossing from the Vatican hill – as part of the extended triumphal route of the via Triumphalis – it is likely that the bridge's reconstruction was intended to emulate the symbolism of its ancient Roman predecessor. According to archaeological evidence, the axis of the northern part of via Triumphalis, on the east bank of the Tiber, aligns approximately with the ancient pyramid on the west bank (fig. 12.6). This suggests that the monument formed a prominent visual focus during antiquity for armies proceeding north out of the city on military campaigns. Indeed, it is likely that the martial symbolism of Romulus played a part in this axial relationship.[19]

In an attempt to emulate the triumphal symbolism of via Triumphalis, Julius II's program of *translatio imperii* entailed the construction of via Giulia so that it would partially retrace the route of the ancient road. While attempts were made during the Renaissance to locate the original path of the via Triumphalis in relation to existing streets and buildings, it is unlikely that Bramante would have had a clear idea of its precise location.[20] One obvious clue would have been the orientation of the ancient street toward the pyramid, whose symbolic associations with Romulus were well known. Therefore, this may have contributed in some way to Bramante's decision to align via Giulia with the *meta Romuli*.[21] Not all commentators concur with this view, however, as seen in Manfredo Tafuri's examination of modern archaeological evidence.[22] According to excavations carried out in 1948, the *meta Romuli* was located under the Casa del Pellegrino, at the opening of the via della Conciliazione. This position is not completely on the axis of via Giulia, although the pyramid still would have been clearly visible from the street. While this casts some doubt on the relationship, the colossal size of the pyramid, even in its ruined state, would have created a monumental focus.[23] For this reason alone, it

12.6 Archaeological map of the east and west banks of the Tiber River, showing the supposed route of via Triumphalis (in bold) on approximate axis with the "Pyramis (meta Romuli)" across the Tiber River, in Filippo Coarelli, *Roma: Guide archeologiche Laterza* (Rome: Editore Laterza. 1985), 265.

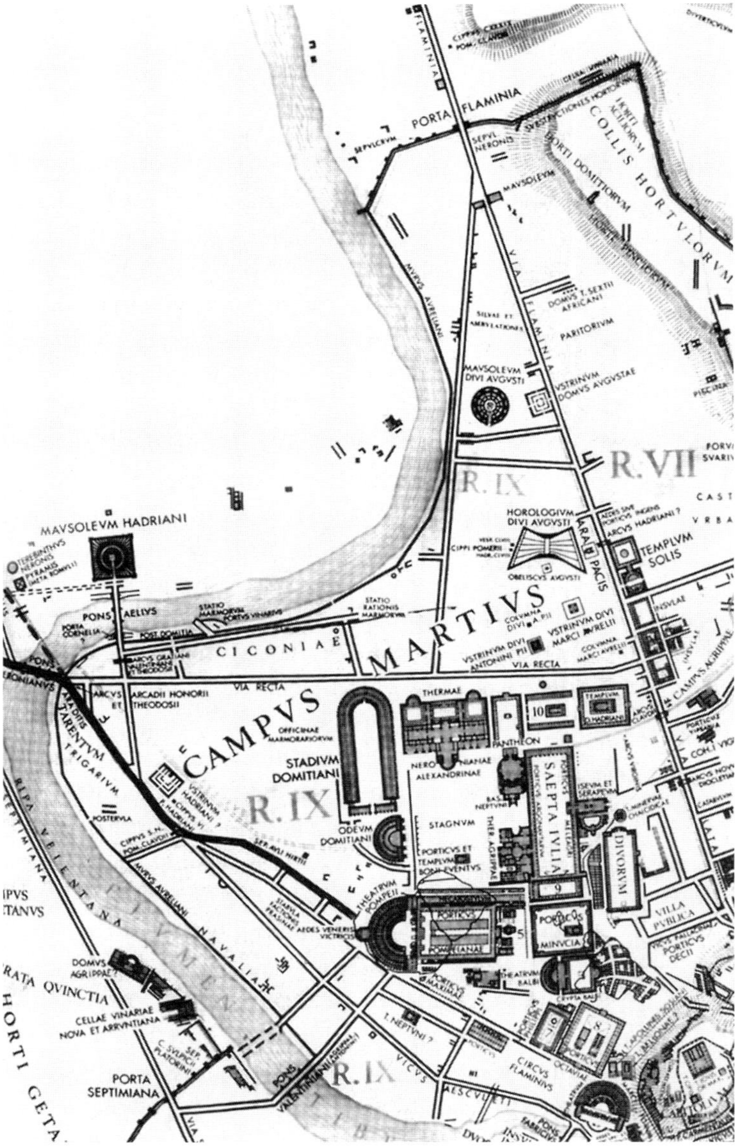

is unlikely that Bramante would have simply ignored the topographical prominence and symbolic significance of the *meta Romuli*.[24]

At a pragmatic level, the pyramid may have been construed simply as a convenient device for terminating an otherwise open passage. The precedent of via Alessandrina-Borgo Nuovo may well have influenced this relationship, considering that the earlier pilgrimage street terminated at its east and west ends at the monumental buildings of Castel Sant'-Angelo and St Peter's Basilica. In the specific case of via Giulia, the inclined walls and pointed apex of the pyramid would have provided an

12.7 Sebastiano Serlio, *Tragic Scene*, seventeenth-century engraving. Courtesy of Museo Teatrale alla Scale, Milan.

effective visual device for closing the perspective of the street, even taking into account its eccentric position. However, given the veneration of the *meta Romuli*, it is plausible that this visual apparatus was invested with a special symbolic function, invoking the meaning of pilgrimage as a redemptive passage from old Rome to the Petrine sanctuary across the river. More explicitly stated in the Cortile del Belvedere, the attempt to endow perspective space with redemptive meanings touches on what increasingly became a larger vision of the holy city during the Renaissance. At one level, this became a matter of internal coherence, as characteristic of the epistemological implications of perspective. Of course, this touches on the relation between real and ideal space and the manner in which perspective sought to bridge these two realms. Such a dialogue was implicit in the familiar theatrical street scenes of Serlio and Peruzzi.[25] In particular, one can identify in Serlio's famous *Tragic Scene* a disposition of monuments that could be construed as an idealization of the actual ceremonial passage of via Giulia (fig. 12.7). Located in the scene, just behind a triumphal arch, is what could be described as a ruined landscape with an obelisk and pyramid, both of which form important visual markers in the inscribed processional route of the passage. Set eccentrically in relation to the axis of the street, these monuments closely resemble, in their distinctive proportions, the famous obelisk of the Vatican and the *meta Romuli* in the Borgo.

The Vatican obelisk was originally sited on the south side of St Peter's Basilica prior to its relocation to the new piazza of St Peter's in the late sixteenth century, under Sixtus V. Moreover, the pyramid in Serlio's perspective is represented in what appears as exposed brick, or perhaps rough stone coursing, reminiscent of Renaissance descriptions of the *meta Romuli* following the removal of its marble relief in the Middle Ages, highlighted earlier.[26] Taken collectively, the sequence of elements that make up Serlio's *Tragic Scene* could be construed as an attempt to give formal and spatial coherence to the otherwise fragmented topography of the Borgo and Vatican. Consequently, perspective in this context may have functioned as a univocal construct, drawing together disparate monuments outside a common perspective frame and reordering them into an idealized landscape.

How far we take this comparison between Serlio's scene and via Giulia will depend in part on our understanding of them as paradigmatic of a common ideal model of Renaissance sensibilities of *renovatio urbis*. The theme of triumphalism was central to this model, as we see in the ritual and iconography of papal Rome.[27] In this context it is no coincidence that the noble setting of the *Tragic Scene* should be terminated by a monumental triumphal arch. Screening the ancient ruined landscape beyond, emblematic of the *ager Vaticanus*, the prominence of this monument may indicate a similar intention by Bramante to terminate via Giulia. It is certainly conceivable that, as part of the initiative to reconstruct the Neronian Bridge under Julius II, there were plans to incorporate triumphal arches at either end of the river crossing in the tradition of Roman triumphal bridges. While the original bridge does not align with via Giulia, it is plausible that the archway on the east bank was intended to be on axis with the street. The idea of a triumphal gateway mediating between two territories, one axial and formal and the other an open landscape punctuated by ancient monuments, could exemplify the project of *renovatio* as symbolic and metaphorical translations of classical paradigms. Accordingly, both pyramid and obelisk could have served as evocations of the *civitas sancta* of the Vatican, once the marshalling area for triumphant armies. This interpretation of the relation between real and illusory landscapes reinforces Erwin Panofsky's assertion that the coincidence of the "invention" of perspective with the emergence of historiography in the Renaissance contributed to a particular understanding of space as a "reflective medium."[28]

"INTER DUAS METAS"

Throughout the Middle Ages it was believed that a special relationship existed between the locations of St Peter's martyrdom, the *meta Romuli*, and Vatican obelisk:

> In Early Christian times, the memory of Peter's martyrdom was invariably connected to the grave of Romulus and the outlying ruins along the Via Triumphalis leading up to the Mole Hadriana. Whereas St. Jerome recalled the spot near the naumachia of Nero ("iuxta ad naumachiam"), already in Romanesque paintings of the late twelfth century artists began to represent the crucifixion enframed telescopically between two immense monoliths. Tactitus recounts how the apostle had been crucified in the Circus of Nero ... For whatever reason, the setting of this event was gradually transmuted in the collective memory of pilgrims as "inter duas metas," and the two conical goalposts of the circus metamorphosed appropriately into two pyramids.[29]

The conflation of pyramid and obelisk in these representations of Peter's martyrdom, in which a hybrid motif is used to define the "goal posts" of the *spina* of the Circus of Caligula, almost certainly influenced the so-called Stefaneschi altarpiece, attributed to Giotto (fig. 12.8). The subtext of this scene is that the site of Peter's martyrdom was somehow preordained in the location of these ancient structures in the *ager Vaticanus*. This reinforces the notion of a divine providential plan that is somehow embodied in the topography of Rome.

The assumption that such a providential plan could be disclosed through a historiographical and archaeological understanding of topography led to disputes among humanists, antiquarians, and theologians about the actual location of Peter's martyrdom. During the fifteenth century, there was increasing support for the idea that the Gianiculum, rather than Vatican hill, was the site of this solemn event.[30] A number of marble and bronze reliefs from the fifteenth century highlight a new interest in representing the drama by giving it topographical specificity, rather than relying on symbolic motifs alone to authenticate the setting, as we see in late medieval art.[31] A good example is the fifteenth-century bronze panel by Filarete, referred to earlier, located on the main entrance doors to St Peter's Basilica (fig. 12.9). The scene depicts Peter's martyrdom taking place on a hill, flanked by a number of monuments that include

12.8 Attributed to Giotto, *The Crucifixion of St. Peter* (Stefaneschi altarpiece), fourteenth century. Courtesy of Pinacoteca, Musei Vaticani.

the Castel Sant'Angelo and two pyramidal structures shown on the bottom corners of the relief. The earlier medieval tradition of representing the event *inter duas metas* is given greater clarity in this scene by how the monuments act as clear urban markers in the landscape, framing the site of the drama. It is generally recognized that the two pyramids represented in the scene, on the bottom left and right corners, are none other than the *meta Romuli* and *meta Remi.*

This change of identity of the "goal posts," from the earlier medieval construct of a hybrid between the obelisks of the Circus of Nero and the *meta Romuli*, is based on an observation made during the fifteenth century. Maffeo Vegio, a humanist canon in the papal curia, observed that the two pyramids are roughly equidistant from the supposed site of Peter's martyrdom (fig. 12.10). This "discovery" highlights a particular understanding of urban topography as largely measurable, undoubtedly reflecting developments in surveying and cartography during this period. The site of St Peter's martyrdom was later commemorated by the famous Tempietto of San Pietro in Montorio by Bramante.[32] The topographical relationship between the monuments is suggested in Filarete's bronze relief by how the upside-down cross of St Peter reads as a gnomon. When extended, the sloping sides represented in the relief frame the cross in the form of an equilateral triangle and relate to the locations of the two pyramids at the lower left and right corners.

12.9 Filarete, *Crucifixion of St. Peter*, bronze relief on door to St Peter's Basilica, fifteenth century, showing representations of the *meta Remi* (lower left) and *meta Romuli* (lower right). Photograph by author.

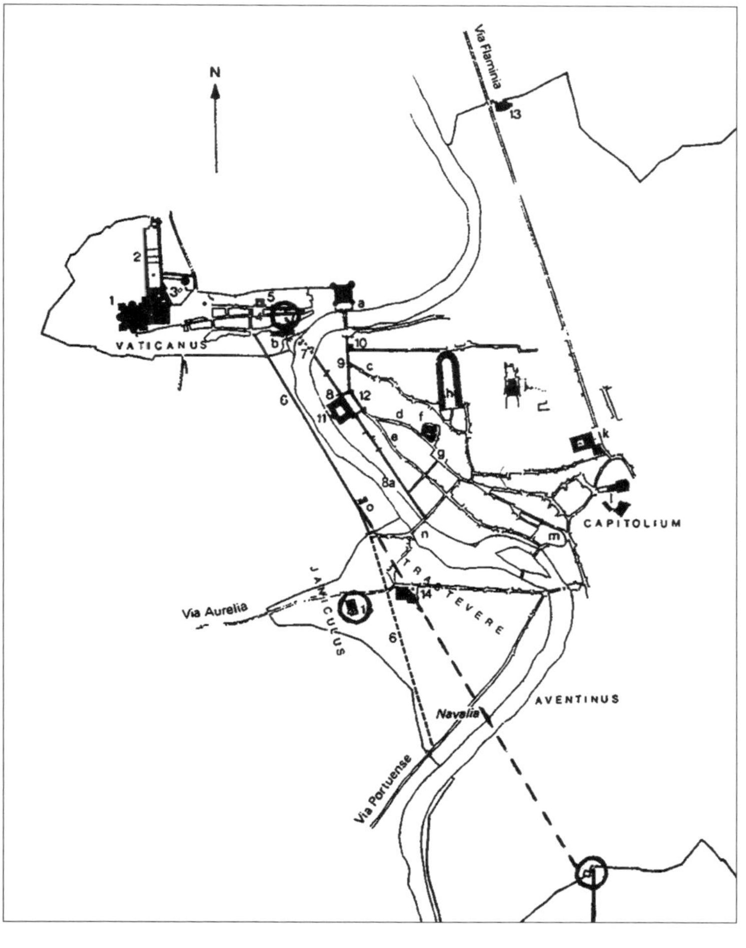

2.10 Plan of the western part of Rome during the Pontificate of Julius II, highlighting locations of the pyramids and the reputed site of St Peter's martyrdom (shown circled), as well as the hypothetical extension of via della Lungara (broken line) as far as the Pyramid of Gaio Cestio, or *meta Remi*, based on Arnaldo Bruschi, *Bramante Architetto* (Bari: Editore Laterza, 1973), 611.

In the context of the Tempietto, Bramante himself may have been aware of this topographical relationship between the pyramids and sought to convey it in his design. As highlighted in Serlio's reconstruction, Bramante probably planned a circular cloister around the *tholos* of the Tempietto that would have reinforced the centrality of the site in relation to the edges of the city. In doing so, the emanating effect of the plan, extended beyond the building itself (moving from centre to periphery) and signalled by the *meta Romuli* and *meta Remi* at the northwest and south edges of the city, resonates in the Stefaneschi altarpiece. Taking a slightly different metaphor, the compass-needle of the upside-down cross of Peter's martyrdom in the altarpiece appears to be "preset" by the flanking "pyramids."

The dispute over the location of Peter's martyrdom occurred at a time of important urban development, when symbolic objectives were influenced increasingly by a narrative understanding of topography. Of particular interest to this study is Bramante's design for via della Lungara on the west bank of the Tiber, which extends roughly north-south and runs almost parallel to via Giulia across the river. According to the sixteenth-century antiquarian Andrea Fulvio, Bramante had planned to extend this ancient road as far south as the Ripa Grande, the old river port of Trastevere.[33] This led one recent commentator, Marcello Fagiolo, to make the bold suggestion that this passage may have been intended to terminate beyond the bank itself – indeed, as far as the *meta Remi* across the river.[34] This theory is based on the observation that the existing passage of via della Lungara aligns almost directly with the *meta Remi*, thereby echoing the similar relationship between via Giulia and *meta Romuli* examined earlier (fig. 12.10). Whether this formed part of Bramante's intended scheme one can only guess. It is certainly plausible that the idea was at least considered by Bramante, given the importance of the *meta Remi* in the providential symbolism of Rome's topography. Moreover, extending the street this far would have forged a direct link between the sanctuaries of both princes of the Roman Church. In doing so, the connection would have provided a looped network of streets – consisting of via Giulia, via della Lungara, and the bridge crossings – for pilgrims moving between the basilicas of Peter and Paul. Furthermore, such a connection could be said to reinforce a late-fourth-century description, made by Prudentius, of the consecrated territory of the Tiber River: "Tiber separates the bones of the two [Peter and Paul] and both its banks are consecrated as it flows between the hallowed tombs. The quarter on the right [Vatican] bank took Peter into its charge and keeps him in a golden dwelling [St Peter's Basilica]."[35]

In suggesting that such a network of streets may have served as a precedent for the urban operations of Sixtus V, Marcello Fagiolo then asserts that Bramante's urban proposal constituted a complete and interconnected scheme, whose points of access were made visually legible by the preordained locations of the pyramids.[36] As both motif and referent, the pyramid served to render a place meaningful by virtue of what was effectively a euhemeristic understanding of inherited tradition since it was assumed that the *mythical* founders of pagan Rome were the legitimate predecessors to the *historical* founders of Christian Rome.[37]

THE ETRUSCAN REVIVAL

Bramante's project for via della Lungara developed at a time when there was much interest in the so-called Etrurian bank of Rome, the ripa Veientana, situated between the Janiculum and Vatican hills. This played an important role in the symbolic understanding of the pyramid during the Renaissance. Identified as one of the saved tribes of Noah's Ark, the Etruscans were seen as legitimate ancestors to the Roman Church. This is why Giles of Viterbo, Augustinian friar and chief spokesman to Julius II, declared in his *Historia XX saeculorum* that the ripa Veientana was the very "meeting place" of Etruscan, Hebrew, and Christian traditions. Furthermore, besides its association with Janus and St Peter's martyrdom, the nearby Gianiculum was also believed to be the location of the tomb of the archaic Roman king Numa, who, according to tradition, built the first temple to Janus in the Roman Forum. The typical form of the hero tomb (or *heroon*), the *tholos*, may have inspired Bramante's design for the Tempietto as one means of linking Peter, the founder of the Roman Church, with Numa, the founder of Roman pagan religion. In this respect, Numa may have been seen as a pagan "type" of pontifical authority.[38]

Giles of Viterbo believed that a parallel symbolism existed between the shrine of St Peter's and the territory of Etruria. Indeed, along with his compatriot, the Dominican Annio da Viterbo, Giles identified an etymological root of the word Tyrrenius (Etruscan for Etruria) from *turris* (tower).[39] The connection between Etruria, promoted by Giles as "the new Holy Land," and the tower inspired the Augustinian friar to urge Bramante to raise a "high tower" above St Peter's dome, thereby reinforcing the status of the *mons Vaticanus* as the fulcrum of the Christian empire.[40] In affirming the sanctity of Etruria, St Peter's Basilica was not just understood as the venerated site of martyrdom but more generally affirmed a genealogical relationship between the Apostolic Succession and Etruscan history.

It is worth speculating whether Giles's reading of this symbolism was influenced in some way by the legendary sepulchre of the Etruscan king Porsenna at Chiusi.[41] The mystery surrounding this monument inspired numerous interpretations and reconstructions during and after the Renaissance.[42] A fairly detailed description of the monument can be found in Alberti's *De re aedificatoria*:

> Some might commend our own Etruscans, whose magnificence in such works almost rivaled that of the Egyptians: and in particular Porsenna, who, close to the Town of Clusium [Chuisi], built for himself a sepulchre of squared stone, whose pedestal, fifty feet in height, contained a totally impenetrable labyrinth; on top sat five pyramids, one at each corner and one in the centre, each seventy-five feet broad at its base; a bronze globe rested on top of each of them, from which bells hung on chains; whenever they were agitated by the wind, their chimes were heard far away. Above this stood four further pyramids, one hundred feet high, and on top of these others still remarkable not only for their size but also for their lineaments.[43]

It is possible that this or other descriptions of the Etruscan sepulchre, such as Filarete's in his *Trattato di Architettura*, influenced Giles's call for a tall tower to be erected on the dome of St Peter's Basilica. As an aside, Filarete's interest in the Etruscan monument may have had a bearing on his design for the bronze relief of St Peter's martyrdom, discussed earlier. As highlighted, the way that the composition of the relief suggests a triangular relationship between the pyramids in the lower corners of the relief and the apex of the cross above could be said to echo the system of supporting pyramids in the Etruscan mausoleum.

The implication of a symbolic association of the Sepulchre of Lars Porsenna with the Petrine shrine in Giles's historiography reinforces the genealogical connection that the Augustinian friar sought to cultivate between pontifical rule and Etruscan kingship.[44] Moreover, the critical elements that constitute the massing of the sepulchre may have informed the topographical symbolism of the Roman pyramids, particularly how the *meta Romuli* and *meta Remi* "delimit" the supposed site of Peter's martyrdom.

Located geographically at the threshold between "the new Holy Land," as it is reconstituted in the territories of ancient Etruria (Vatican and the Holy See), and the old Rome across the Tiber River (*civitas terrenas*), the *meta Romuli* invokes a relationship of heavenly and earthly realms that underlies Giles's dialectical reading of tower and refuge.[45]

It is worth posing the question of whether the reconstructions of the Sepulchre of Lars Porsenna actually influenced the designs for the new St Peter's Basilica. This is suggested in the work of Antonio da Sangallo the Younger. His involvement in the design of the new basilica coincided roughly with his reconstructions of numerous ancient monuments, including the Sepulchre of Porsenna.[46] Probably relying on the description by Alberti, via the ancient Pliny, Sangallo's sketches of the sepulchre reveal obvious formal similarities to his scheme for St Peter's (figs 12.11 and 12.12). In particular, the details of the lantern of the basilica could be compared easily to his reconstruction of the pyramids of the Etruscan tomb. Whether these similarities resulted from a conscious attempt to emulate the ancient mausoleum in the new basilica is open to conjecture and clearly requires a more extensive investigation than can be undertaken here.

THE CHIGI CHAPEL

An interest in pyramids during the Renaissance is also evident in the interior of the Chigi Chapel in Santa Maria del Popolo.[47] Designed by Raphael with the assistance, interestingly enough, of Antonio da Sangallo the Younger, the chapel was to function as a mausoleum for the powerful Sienese banker Agostino Chigi and his family. John Shearman has observed that the proportions of the pyramid tombs that are located on adjacent walls of the chapel coincide roughly with those of the *meta Romuli*, albeit on a much smaller scale (fig. 12.13).[48] This relationship is supported by another similarity: the original design of the wall-tombs in the chapel incorporated marble relief-work on the inclined surfaces of the pyramids, much like the marble cladding for the *meta Romuli* discussed earlier.[49] Raphael's interest in the ancient pyramid is evident in a

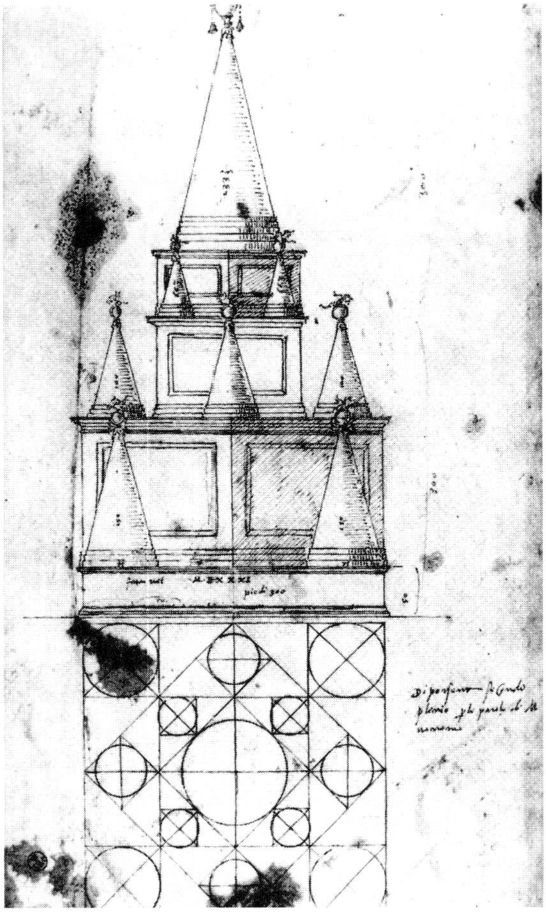

12.11 Antonio da Sangallo the Younger, reconstruction of the Mausoleum of Lars Porsenna, Florence, 1531. Courtesy of Gabinetto Disegni e Stampe, Galleria degli Uffizi, 1209A.

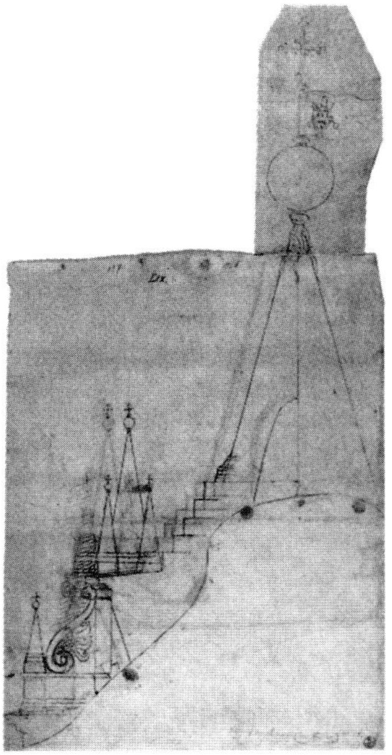

12.12 Antonio da Sangallo the Younger, sectional view of the lantern for St Peter's Basilica, Florence, 1540–45. Courtesy of Gabinetto Disegni e Stampe, Galleria degli Uffizi, 261A.

letter that he wrote to Leo X, in which he lamented its demolition in the second decade of the sixteenth century as a deplorable act of vandalism. Ironically, soon after the destruction of the pyramid under Leo X, a replica was constructed in 1515 to celebrate the entry of the Medici pope into Florence.[50] However, not all the influences on the design of the tombs of the Chigi Chapel were based on the *meta Romuli*. Another likely source was the Vatican obelisk. This is reflected in the globes that originally crowned the apex of the pyramid-tombs, which remind one of the famous orb of the Vatican obelisk, long thought to have contained the ashes of Julius Caesar.[51] The hybrid nature of the design of the wall-tombs is clearly reminiscent of the "goal posts" in the famous Stefaneschi altarpiece, referred to earlier.

Set within large triumphal arches that frame the adjacent walls of the Chigi Chapel, the pyramids clearly allude to the notion of triumph over mortality, as underlined by the projection of the apex of the pyramid beyond the cornice of the arch. This disruption of the frame is echoed in Serlio's later *Tragic Scene*, where the obelisk and pyramid loom above the triumphal arch that terminates the street. Like the "perspectival" effect of the *meta Romuli*, which partially closes off the passage of via Giulia, the projection of the pyramids in the Chigi Chapel similarly evokes the idea of ascent into a transcendent realm.

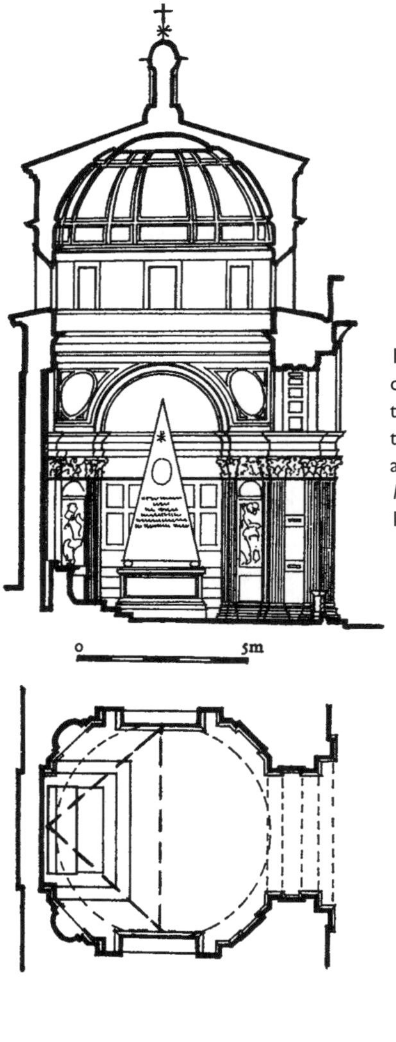

12.13 Raphael, Chigi Chapel (begun c.1513). Section and plan indicating the triadic relationship between altar and tombs, based on Ludwig Heydenreich and Wolfgang Lotz, *Architecture in Italy, 1400–1600* (Harmondsworth: Penguin, 1974), 168.

This outline interpretation of the Chigi Chapel raises the vexed question of whether the actual layout of the pyramids in the chapel was influenced by the larger topographical relationship between the *meta Romuli* and *meta Remi*. Both as "sign posts" to the burial sites of Peter and Paul and as beacons to the supposed place of Peter's martyrdom on the Janiculum, the urban pyramids delimit a sacred territory on the east and west banks of the Tiber River. The resulting triangular matrix of the *meta Romuli*, *meta Remi*, and Tempietto could have provided a spatial analogy to the triadic relationship between wall-tombs and altar in the Chigi Chapel (fig. 12.13). In such a connection, by demarcating a territory for ritual procession and sacrifice, the tombs define spatially what their urban counterparts achieve topographically.

There is one possible reason for such a direct relationship between the layout of the Chigi Chapel and the topography of the east and west banks of the Tiber River. This concerns the life of Agostino Chigi, Sienese merchant banker and friend of Julius II and Leo X. In Rome, Agostino Chigi owned property on both sides of the Tiber River. On the west side, the Sienese banker had built a lavish suburban villa, later called the Farnesina. Sited along via della Lungara, close to the river, the villa is near the Tempietto, which looms above on the summit of the Janiculum. On the east bank of the Tiber, Chigi had his bank headquarters in the so-called Quartiere dei Banchi at the northern end of via Giulia. In the course of his daily journeys between his residence, the Vatican Palace, and his offices, Agostino Chigi would have become very familiar with the topography of the east and west banks of the Tiber River. Therefore, it was perhaps fitting that upon Chigi's death in 1520 his funeral cortege ceremonially reenacted his life. Commencing at his residence, the Villa Farnesina, it passed across the Ponte Sisto and along via Giulia to his bank headquarters. From here, it probably continued along via dei Coronari (via Recta) and the Corso (via Lata), before finally arriving at the Chigi Chapel in Santa Maria del Popolo.

Agostino Chigi's life could be said to have mediated between the two faces of Rome, between the *otium* of his *villa suburbana* and the *negotium* of the banking district of Rome. These places of work and leisure were located within the very sacred territory delimited by the pyramids. Therefore, it is plausible that his mausoleum was designed to evoke this relationship. The principle of an underlying topographical reading of interior space was not unusual in Renaissance Rome, as noted in

Manfredo Tafuri's assertion that the iconography of the frescos of the Stanza della Segnatura, also by Raphael, formed a "manifesto" of the urban projects in Rome under Julius II.[52]

THE ENIGMA OF PYRAMIDS

As both motif and referent, the pyramid in Renaissance Rome operated as a metaphor of transformation, by which the eschatological event of martyrdom was reconstituted as a motif of salvation. In an age that sought to give order to urban space, it is instructive how the topographical and projective functions of the pyramids were informed by their accumulated symbolic meanings. As I have emphasized, this was based on a particular understanding of urban topography as a sacred text, whose careful disclosure through *renovatio* provided a "redemptive horizon" for individual salvation. This understanding of topography could be likened to Poliphilo's journey in Francesco Colonna's *Hypnerotomachia Poliphili*, where architectural fragments, including the monolithic pyramid, allude to a recondite past awaiting rediscovery and renewal.[53] These monuments, like the *meta Romuli* and *meta Remi*, possess sedimented meanings, and their disclosure and reconstitution have the potential to create a new teleological order.

In the context of this rich backdrop of symbolic and historical themes, it may seem paradoxical that Alexander VI partly demolished the *meta Romuli* to make way for his new street. As I have argued, the apparent contradiction between the reverence for these monuments as religious and antiquarian objects and the sometimes uncompromising nature of conscious urban planning indicates an irreconcilable relationship between a still embodied tradition and an emerging epistemological order. Indeed, this essentially residual problem in the Renaissance develops into a veritable bifurcation by the late eighteenth century, when questions of historical continuity are reduced to little more than a repository of available motifs.

NOTES

1 A notable example of this interpretation of ancient myth is Annio da Viterbo's reemphasis of the legendary founding of the Vatican and Etruria by the dual identity of Janus/Noah; see Walter Stephens, *Giants in Those*

Days: Folklore, Ancient History and Nationalism (Lincoln: University of Nebraska Press, 1989).

2 The proposed scheme of Nicholas V, whose intended layout is unclear, consisted essentially of three streets lying between the Vatican and Tiber River. They were to connect two piazzas, one at the eastern edge and the other at the western edge of the Borgo district, the former adjacent to the Mole Adriana (Castel Sant'Angelo) and the latter in front of St Peter's Basilica; see T. Magnuson, *Studies in Roman Quattrocento Architecture* (Stockholm: Almquist and Wiksell, 1958), 74–7; Carol William Westfall, *In This Most Perfect Paradise: Alberti, Nicholas V and the Invention of Conscious Urban Planning, 1447–55* (University Park: Penn State University Press, 1974).

3 The piazza adjacent to the Mole Adriana was mirrored across the river by an earlier medieval piazza, the Platea Pontis, the landing point to the Ponte Sant'Angelo. During the Middle Ages, this was one of the most important public spaces, serving as the bridgehead to the Vatican for pilgrims crossing the Tiber River to St Peter's Basilica. This was to form part of a larger urban scheme by Bramante during the pontificate of Julius II, which included via Giulia.

4 Lucio Fauno, *Delle antichita della citta di Roma* (Venezia, 1548), f26v: "Papa Alessandro IV ... drizzo a Riga la strada [via Alessandra] infino a la di palazzo [Papal Palace?], togliendo di mezzo la via una certa piramide che l'impediva."

5 This is indicated by the various names given to the monument during the Middle Ages: "memoria Romuli" (Bull of 21 March 1053 by Leo XI [*Patrologia Latina*, 143, 714]); "sepulchrum Romuli" (Ordo Romanus XI of Benedetto Canonico [c. 1140]); "pyramis Romuli" (Ranulphus Higden, Polychronicon [fourteenth century], bk 1, ch. 25); and finally "meta Romuli" as shown on plan of H. Schedel (Nuremburg, 1493). According to Francesco Albertini, *Opusculum de mirabilibus novae et veteris Urbis* (Rome, 1510), the monument had three names: "Scipionis sepulchrum," "sepulchrum Aepulonum," and more popularly "Romuli meta." The most authoritative bibliographical source on the history of the pyramid is S.B. Platner and T. Ashby, *A Topographical Dictionary of Ancient Rome* (Oxford: Oxford University Press, 1929), 340. For a comprehensive account of the history of the pyramid, see M.B. Peebles, "La 'Meta Romuli' e una lettera di Michele Ferno," in *Atti della Pontificia Accademia Romana di*

Archeologia Rendiconti, vol. 12, 21–36 (Citta del Vaticano: Biblioteca Apostolica Vaticana, 1936).

6 Peebles, "'Meta Romuli,'" 28–30.

7 In the early fifteenth century the pyramids were given titles taken directly from the princes of the Church: "meta Sancti Petri" (*meta Romuli*) and "meta Sancti Pauli" (Pyramid of Cestius); see Ludovico Antonio Muratori, *Rerum italicarum scriptores: Raccolta degli storici italiani dal Cinquecento al Millecinquecento*, vol. 24 (Citta di Castello: S. Lapi, 1900), 1014, 1038.

8 Platner and Ashby, *Topographical Dictionary*, 478.

9 This contrived concordance between Rome's origins and its "refoundation" as the sacred city of Christianity was further emphasized by the celebration of the martyrdoms of Peter and Paul on the same day, 29 July. This implied twinship has obvious associations with the traditional partnership between Romulus and Remus. In a sermon delivered on their feast day in 441, Leo I compared Peter and Paul to their pagan counterparts, asserting that the apostles "had refounded the city under more felicitous circumstances than those of whom one gave you the name Rome and defiled you through his brother's blood"; quoted in Philip Jacks, *The Antiquarian and the Myth of Antiquity: The Origins of Rome in Renaissance Thought* (Cambridge, UK: Cambridge University Press, 1993), 27.

10 For a study of the obelisks in Rome, see Cesare D'Onofrio, *Gli Obelischi di Roma* (Rome: Bulzoni, 1967).

11 Richard Sennett, *The Conscience of the Eye: Design and Social Life of Cities* (London: Faber and Faber, 1990), 153–4:

> Obelisks are tapering, three or four sided columns set upon a boxy plinth, with the tip of the obelisk either sharpened to a point or capped with a small round ball. The sliver of stone would, at a distance, serve as an effective means for creating perspectival vision. The reason lay in the tip of the obelisk: it creates a point in space … The obelisks hover in the terminal space, their very existence dramatized by the perception that above them things are just about to disappear … The system of such displaced sculptures meant that in making a pilgrimage, the eyes of the pilgrim led him or her from marker to marker rather than to the inside of a particular church.

Marcello Fagiolo asserts that the topographical role of the pyramids may have served as a precedent in Sixtus V's urban scheme for Rome; see his "La Roma di Sisto V: Le matrici del policentrismo," PSICON 8–9 (1977): 25–39.

12 For an account of the reasons for the demolition, see the letter of Michele Ferno in Codex 555 (Biblioteca Capitolare di Lucca, 3a), 452r–473r.

13 F. Saxl, *Lectures* (London: Warburg Institute, 1957), 2 and plate 122. For an examination of the Borgia Apartments and Pope Alexander VI, see Ingrid D. Rowland, "Alexandria on the Tiber (1492–1503)," in *The Culture of the High Renaissance: Ancients and Moderns in Sixteenth-Century Rome*, 42–67 (Cambridge, UK: Cambridge University Press, 1998).

14 See the sources in note 2.

15 "Letter to Pope Leo X by Raphael," in Vincenzo Golzio, *Raffaello: Nei documenti, nelle testimonianze, dei contemporanei e nelle letteratura del suo seculo* (London: Gregg, 1971), 83: "ne senza molta compassione posso io ricordami, che poi ch'io sono in Roma che anchora non sono dodici anni, son state ruinate molte cose belle, come la meta ch'era nella via Alessandrina ... Ma perche ci doleremo noi de Gotti de Vandelli."

16 See Christoph L. Frommel, "Il Palazzo dei Tribunali in via Giulia," *Studi Bramanteschi* (1974): 523–34.

17 Nicholas Temple, "*Renovatio urbis*: Architecture and Topography in Rome during the Pontificate of Julius II" (PhD thesis, Leeds Metropolitan University, England, 2000), 188–253. The northern termination of via Giulia is located in a district traditionally called the Quartiere dei Banchi, which lies at the confluence of three older streets, via Recta, via Papali, and via Peregrinorum, all of which lead to the piazza at the entrance to Ponte Sant'Angelo (Platea Pontis).

18 Arnaldo Bruschi, *Bramante Architetto* (Bari: Editore Laterza, 1973), 625–57.

19 For an assessment of the relationship between the pyramid and via Triumphalis, see Christian Huelsen, "Sul sito della 'Meta Romuli,'" *Diss. della P. Accademia Romana di Archeologia* 2nd ser. 8 (1903): 383–7 and plate 9.

20 See Flavio Biondo, *Roma Instaurata, tradotto in buona lingua volgare per Luzio Fauno* (Venice, 1542). Flavio's description of the route of via Triumphalis is quoted in Andrew Martindale, *The Triumphs of Caesar by Andrea Mantegna* (London: Harvey Miller, 1979), 61.

21 The idea of a direct relationship between the pyramid and via Giulia was first suggested by Gugliemo De Angelis D'Ossat during a conference on

Bramante held in 1970; see C.L. Frommel, S. Ray, and Manfredo Tafuri, *Raffaello Architetto* (Milan: Electa Editrice, 1984), 101n51.

22 M. Tafuri, "Roma Instaurata," in Frommel et al., *Raffaello Architetto*, 101n51.

23 The visual significance of the pyramid in the urbanscape of Rome is indicated by the numerous representations of the monument in paintings and plans. According to Peebles, there are thirty-eight such representations; see his "'Meta Romuli,'" 51–63.

24 According to Lucio Fauno, about half the pyramid was demolished during the building campaign of Alexander VI. However, this contradicts Platner and Ashby's assessment of the evidence, which suggests that only one-third of the structure was actually removed; see Platner and Ashby, *Topographical Dictionary*, 340. It also seems that the monument was tampered with in varying degrees since the time of Sixtus IV and that Julius II had altered parts of it for "practical reasons." This may have been in preparation for the construction of what Tafuri describes as "una casa da dare in usufrutto ai cantori, ai maestri della Cappella Giulia"; see his "Roma Instaurata," 101. Perhaps Julius II had planned in some way to incorporate this "casa" within the body of the pyramid.

25 For general descriptions, see Richard Krautheimer, "The Tragic and Comic Scenes of the Renaissance: The Baltimore and Urbino Panels," *Gazette des Beaux Arts* 33 (1948): 327–46.

26 According to the *Liber Pontificalis*, Pope Donus (676–78) paved the atrium of St Peter's Basilica with the marble reliefs from the pyramid. However, this contradicts Giovanni Rucellai's description dating from the 1450 Jubilee celebrations, which states that the pyramid was "tutta coperta di marmi"; see Giuseppe Marcotti, *Il Giubileo del' anno 1450 secondo una relazione di Giovanni Rucellai* (Rome: Forzani e C, 1881), 572. Also in John Shearman, 'The Chigi Chapel in S. Maria del Popolo,' *Journal of the Warburg & Courtauld Institutes* 24 (1961): 129–60 at 133n25. On balance, it is likely that some of the reliefs were removed during the seventh century. The fresco *The Vision of the True Cross before the Battle of Ponte Milvio* in the Sala di Costantino by Giulio Romano clearly shows the pyramid with reliefs, perhaps an imaginary reconstruction.

27 See Charles L. Stinger, "The Campidoglio as the Locus of *Renovatio Imperii*," in Charles M. Rosenberg, ed., *Art and Politics in Late Medieval and Early Renaissance Italy, 1250–1500*, 135–56 (Notre Dame: University of Notre Dame Press, 1990).

28 Erwin Panofsky, *Studies in Iconology: Humanistic Themes in the Art of the Renaissance* (New York: Harper and Row, 1972), 27–8.

29 Jacks, *Antiquarian and the Myth*, 27.

30 For an extensive, albeit biased, examination of this issue, see F. Pacifici, *Dissertazioni sul Martirio di San Pietro nel Gianicolo e sulla Venuta e Morte nello stesso Monte di Noe Simbolo del Santo Principe degli Apostoli ivi Crocifisso Umiliate alla Santita Din. SPP. PioVII* (Rome: Nella stamperia di Lino Contedini, 1841), ch. 2.

31 One interesting example is a tabernacle erected by Sixtus IV that has a relief showing Peter's upside-down martyrdom between two pyramids; see ibid., 17: "Sisto IV fu quello, che circa l'anno 1442 fece fare nel magnifico Ciborio di marmo della confessione Vaticano fra i bassi rilievi in marmo degli altri Apostoli quello di S. Pietro nell'atto di esser crocifisso fralle due grandi piramidi di Cajp Cestio [meta Remi], e l'altra vicina alla mole Adriana chiaramente indicanti il Gianicolo."

32 Ibid.

33 Andrea Fulvio, *De urbis antiquitates* (1527), i.45: "This road he [Bramante] had built from St. Peter's Square as far as the docks under the Aventine. This place is commonly called the 'River bank' (Ripa dicitur), and from here he moved the road forward, having demolished the buildings."

34 Fagiolo, "La Roma di Sisto V," 25–39.

35 Prudentius, *Prudentius*, trans. H.J. Thomson, Loeb Classical Library (Cambridge, MA: Harvard University Press, 1953), vol. 2, 325.

36 Ibid.

37 For a study of euhemerism in the Renaissance, see Jean Seznec, *The Survival of the Pagan Gods* (Princeton: Bollingen Press, 1972), 11–37.

38 Charles Stinger, *The Renaissance in Rome* (Bloomington: Indiana University Press, 1998), 188.

39 Andre Chastel, *Arte e umanisme a Firenze* (Turin: Giulio Einaudi editore, 1964), 75. For a discussion of the pyramidal symbolism of St Peter's Basilica, see Marcello Fagiolo, "La Basilica Vaticana come Tempio-Mausoleo 'Inter-Duas-Metas': Le idee e i progetti di Alberti, Filarete, Bramante, Peruzzi, Sangallo, Michelangelo," in *XXII Congresso di Storia dell'Architettura, Roma*, 566–74 (Rome: Centro di Studi per la Storia dell'Architettura, 1986).

40 Giles of Viterbo, *Historia XX saeculorum*, MS 504, Bib. Ang., fol. 21, Biblioteca Angelica, Sant Agostino, Rome; G. Signorelli, *Il Card: Egidio da*

Viterbo, agostiniano, umanista e riformatore, 1469–1532 (Florence: Libreria editrice fiorentina, 1929), 115, 214n24.

41 The best ancient description of the monument that Giles may have consulted can be found in Pliny's *Naturalis Historia*, 36.91–2.

42 Stefano Borsi, *Polifilo Architetto* (Rome: Officina Edizioni, 1995), 30–1, 79, 84, 139, 212.

43 Leon Battista Alberti, *On the Art of Building in Ten Books*, trans. Joseph Rykwert, Robert Tavernor, and Neil Leach (Cambridge, MA: MIT Press, 1996), bk 8, 3.

44 This is highlighted in the following extract from a sermon by Giles of Viterbo, "Fulfillment of the Christian Golden Age under Pope Julius II," quoted in Francis X. Martin, O.S.A., *Friar, Reformer, and Renaissance Scholar: Life and Work of Giles of Viterbo, 1469–1532* (Villanova, PA: Augustinian Press, 1992), 229. The sermon was delivered in St Peter's Basilica in 1507, in the company of Pope Julius II, to commemorate the Portuguese expedition to the Far East, as communicated to the pope by King Manuel I of Portugal:

> The historians tell us, however, that before the arrival of Saturn[,] Janus ruled with Golden laws over Etruria on the other side of the Tiber. I may be able to examine his government more fully on some other occasion; now, when a new world has been discovered by the effort and zeal of golden King Manuel, I will confine myself to what is relevant to the appointed sermon ... Why did divine providence arrange that a bronze model of a ship should be hidden in Janus' temple, if not because the Etruscan throne of Janus, which Your Holiness [Julius II] now occupies, already accustomed as it was to rule benevolently, was to be dedicated to the benevolent laws of the barque of Christ? Why was that bronze model of a ship hidden in Janus, if not because the Etruscan hill of the Vatican was to send the most holy laws of Christ to the end of the earth through the ships of a noble king.

45 Chastel, *Arte e umanisme*, 75: "il papa rifugiarsi in Toscana, come nello 'eterno rifugio e difesa della Chiesa.'"

46 Franco Borsi, *Fortuna degli etruschi* (Milan: Electa, 1985), 36–7.

47 John Shearman, "The Chigi Chapel in S. Maria del Popolo," *Journal of the Warburg and Courtauld Institutes* 24 (1961): 129–60.

48 Interestingly, according to Peebles, "'Meta Romuli,'" 45, the dimensions

of the base of the *meta Romuli* also closely match those of the Sepulchre of Lars Porsenna, as described by Alberti (see note 39).

49 See note 24.

50 Another replica was constructed in the same year in Rome in the Piazza delle SS. Trinita; see E. Müntz, *Les antiquités de la ville de Rome* (Paris: n.p., 1898), 455.

51 See Jacks, *Antiquarian and the Myth*, 241–2. This association inspired Bramante to propose reorienting the new Basilica of St Peter's so that it would face the obelisk. This was probably to emphasize concordance between Caesar and the "second Julius," Julius II; see Giles of Viterbo, *Historia XX Saeculorum*, fol. 194r.

52 Tafuri, "Roma instaurata," 63.

53 See Liane Lefaivre, *Leon Battista Alberti's Hypnerotomachia Poliphili* (Cambridge, MA: MIT Press, 1997), 1–45.

About the Authors

Manuela Antoniu

Manuela Antoniu obtained her professional and master's degrees in architecture from Carleton University and McGill University, respectively. Her undergraduate research thesis was published (*sans* poetry, alas) by Princeton Architectural Press, and her collaborative work on "condemned" buildings was exhibited at various places in the United States. At the Architectural Association in London, she has been engaged in the cross-millennial task of writing a doctoral dissertation on architectural *phagias*, as exemplified – she insists – by the now moribund category of sectional drawings. To feed her *idée fixe* about sections (and for more prosaic feedings as well), she has been working undercover in imaging departments of hospitals throughout London for a number of years. She still dreams of one day being able to play the cello.

Barry Bell

Barry Bell was educated at the University of Waterloo (BES 1981, BArch 1983), the University of Cambridge (MPhil 1988), and McGill University (PhD 2007). Barry died shortly after completing his doctoral studies, just as this volume of *Chora* was going to print. His doctoral research was focused on the narrative structure of the Thai temple. His previous work in Thailand investigated issues of architecture and urban design with respect to cultural sustainability in Chiang Mai and Mae Hong Son. More recently, his research had centred on Bangkok and its potential to reveal implicit cultural ideals in novel ways. The results of these investigations were published as *Bangkok: Angelic Allusions* (2003). Barry was an architect licensed in the Province of Ontario. He was also an adjunct professor at Dalhousie University in Halifax and a Visiting Research Fellow at Chulalongkorn University, Bangkok, in 2004–05. He was previously an associate professor at Carleton University in Ottawa and an adjunct associate professor at the University of Waterloo. This volume of *Chora* is dedicated to his memory.

Ramla Benaissa

Ramla Benaissa began her education in Tunisia, followed by a master's degree in architectural history and theory from McGill University and a doctorate from the University of Pennsylvania. She lives in Philadelphia, where she practises architecture, teaches architecture studio at the University of Pennsylvania, and teaches architectural theory and history at Drexel University.

Martin Bressani
Martin Bressani is associate professor of architecture at McGill University. He has published in journals such as *Revue de l'art*, *Assemblage*, *Journal of the Society of Architectural Historians*, *Rassegna*, *Architettura*, *Art History*, and *Architecture and Ideas*. He is currently preparing a monograph on the thought and work of French theoretician Eugène Viollet-le-Duc.

Jennifer Carter
Jennifer Carter is preparing a doctoral dissertation in the history and theory of architecture at McGill University. She holds an honours baccalaureate in art history from the same institution and a master's degree in art history, theory, and criticism from the School of the Art Institute of Chicago. Her dissertation, entitled "Re-creating the Poetic Imaginary: Alexandre Lenoir and the Musée des monumens français," examines the role of narrative and the influences of eighteenth-century theories of landscape, perception, and the imagination on the curatorial practices of Alexandre Lenoir. Jennifer has worked in several galleries and museum institutions in Canada and the United States, including the Betty Rymer Gallery (Chicago), the National Gallery of Canada (Ottawa), the Montreal Museum of Fine Arts, the Art Gallery of Ontario (Toronto), and the Canadian Centre for Architecture (Montreal).

Edward S. Casey
Edward S. Casey is Distinguished Professor of Philosophy at the State University of New York at Stony Brook. He is the author of a number of books in phenomenology and the philosophy of place, including *Imagining*, *Remembering*, *Getting Back into Place*, and *The Fate of Place*. More recently, he has taken his interest in place into the art world in two books: *Representing Place in Landscape Painting and Maps*; and *Earth-Mapping: Artists Reshaping Landscape*. A volume entitled *The World at a Glance* is forthcoming. He is currently at work on a sequel, to be called *The World on Edge*.

Ricardo L. Castro
Ricardo L. Castro is an associate professor at McGill University's School of Architecture, where he teaches architectural design, architectural history, and criticism. Grants from the Canada Council for the Arts and the Graham Foundation have supported his photographic work, the publication of his mono-

graph on Colombian architect Rogelio Salmona, *Salmona* (1998), and his book *Arthur Erickson: Critical Works* (2006), a collaborative project with Nicholas Olsberg. From 2001 to 2003 Castro was director of the Institut de recherche en histoire de l'architecture (IRHA), for which he organized the international colloquium "The Limits of Place in Architectural Discourse" (2002) in collaboration with the Canadian Centre for Architecture. The chapters by Edward Casey and Marco Frascari in this volume of *Chora* were presented at this colloquium.

Marco Frascari

Marco Frascari, who was born under the shadow of the dome of Leon Battista Alberti's Sant'Andrea in Mantua, received a *diploma di professore di disegno* from the Accademia di Belle Arti in Venice, then completed a *dottore* in *architettura* at the Istututo Universitario di Architettura di Venezia (IUAV) in 1969. Frascari began his professional career in Verona while teaching at the IUAV and has run a small architectural practice since then. His early professorial and professional experience began under the tutelage of Carlo Scarpa, Valriano Pastor, and Arrigo Rudi. In the late 1970s Frascari moved to the United States and earned a master's degree in science in architecture at the University of Cincinnati and a doctorate in architecture at the University of Pennsylvania. He taught at the University of Pennsylvania from 1981 until 1997, when he became the G. Truman Ward Professor of Architecture at the Washington-Alexandria Architectural Center of Virginia Tech. In 2005 he became director of the School of Architecture at Carleton University in Ottawa. Frascari has taught and lectured at many schools, including the Architectural Association, Georgia Tech, Columbia University, and Harvard University. Frascari's writings have been published in *AA Files*, *Assemblage*, *Daidalos*, *Journal of Architectural Education*, *Perspecta*, *Res*, *Terrazzo*, *Via*, and several other journals. "The Tell-Tale-Detail," a seminal essay published in 1981, has been translated into Spanish, Japanese, and Chinese. In 1991 he published *The Monsters of Architecture*, and in 1996 *Una Pillola per sognare ... una casa*.

Jose Jacob

Jose Jacob was born in Kerala, India, where he received a bachelor's degree in architecture in 1992. He received a master's degree in science in architecture from the University of Cincinnati in 1996 and a doctorate in architectural history and theory from McGill University in 2004. He worked at the Canadian

Centre for Architecture in Montreal as a researcher for the exhibition *Sense of the City* and is currently conducting research on recently built university chapels.

Panos Leventis

Panos Leventis was born in 1968 in Famagusta, Cyprus. He studied in Los Angeles, where he received a bachelor's degree in architecture from the University of Southern California and a master's degree in architecture with an emphasis on urban design from the University of California, Los Angeles. He worked and taught in Los Angeles, Milan, and Athens and carried out research in Montreal, where he received a doctorate in the history and theory of architecture from McGill University. He contributed to the establishment of a new Department of Architecture at the University of Cyprus in Nicosia, and since 2004 he has been teaching architectural and urban history and theory at the Drury University Centre in Volos, Greece. Along with being a registered dreamer, Panos is a practising architect, working on projects and competitions in Cyprus and Greece. His research and professional work have been published in Canada, Cyprus, Greece, Italy, and the United States.

Daniel M. Millette

Daniel M. Millette holds master's degrees in historical geography and architectural history and theory, as well as an interdisciplinary doctorate in architecture, classical archaeology, and historical geography. He maintains archaeological projects in France and Tunisia, which complement his research on Vitruvius and Roman architecture. Having completed terms as a postdoctoral fellow at the Institut de recherche sur l'architecture antique in Aix-en-Provence, with support from the Social Sciences and Humanities Research Council of Canada and the Université de Marseille, he now teaches at the University of British Columbia. Currently, he has two projects in production: one on the Vitruvius canon and the other on the archaeological excavations at the theatre of Lugdunum Convenarum (Saint-Bertrand-de-Comminges), France.

David Spurr

David Spurr is a professor and director of English Studies at the University of Geneva. He has also taught at the University of Illinois, Chicago, and the University of Neuchâtel, Switzerland. He has published widely on modern English and French literature and is the author of *Conflicts in Consciousness* (on T.S.

Eliot, 1984), *The Rhetoric of Empire* (1993), and *Joyce and the Scene of Modernity* (2002). More recently, he coedited a volume of essays entitled *The Space of English* (2005). His current book project, entitled *Architexture*, studies relations between literature and architectural space.

Nick Temple
Nick Temple is an architect, professor of architectural design, and head of the School of Architecture at the University of Lincoln. A graduate of Cambridge University, he was a Rome Scholar in architecture at the British School (1986–88) and has a doctorate in architecture and urbanism in early-sixteenth-century Rome. He has taught at universities in the United Kingdom and the United States, including the University of Pennsylvania and the University of Liverpool, and has been an invited lecturer at the Moscow Institute of Architecture and the Ion Mincu Institute of Architecture in Bucharest. Having published many academic papers on the history and theory of architecture, his most recent and forthcoming books include: *Disclosing Horizons: Architecture, Perspective and Redemptive Space* (2006); *Thinking Practice*, coedited with Soumyen Bandyopadhyay (2007); and *Renovatio urbis: Architecture, Urbanism and Ceremony in the Rome of Julius II* (2008).